Courier from Warsaw

The author, 1943 passport photo.

COURIER FROM WARSAW

by Jan Nowak

Wayne State University Press, Detroit   1982

Copyright © 1982 by Wayne State University Press,
Detroit, Michigan 48202. All rights are reserved.
No part of this book may be reproduced without formal permission.

Library of Congress Cataloging in Publication Data
Nowak, Jan, 1913-
  Courier from Warsaw.

  Includes index.
  1. World War, 1939-1945—Underground movements—Poland—Biography.
2. Nowak, Jan, 1913-   . 3. World War, 1939-1945—Personal narratives, Polish.
4. World War, 1939-1945—Diplomatic history. 5. Poland—History—Occupation,
1939-1945. 6. Diplomatic couriers—Poland—Biography. 7. Diplomatic
couriers—Great Britain—Biography. I. Title.
D802.P6N68 1982   940.53′438   82-8599
ISBN 0-8143-1725-1   AACR2

Publication of this book has been supported in part by a grant from the
Polish Studies Program of Wayne State University.

Contents

Abbreviations   9

Preface   11

Foreword by Zbigniew Brzezinski   13

Maps begin page 15; illustrations begin page 29

Chapter 1.   Father's forgotten ducat unfolds my future. A childhood
               among dramatic memories. First rumblings of the storm.
               Bright prospects, darkening horizon.   21

Chapter 2.   Nazis invade Poland. The nightmare of September. Battle of
               Uscilug. Taken prisoner with a future prime minister.
               Escape.   44

Chapter 3.   Warsaw after the surrender. Assassination attempt on Hitler.
               Life in the black market: butter, paraffin, and vodka. Exciting
               contacts: the underground and the Gestapo. ZWZ oath.   57

Chapter 4.   Topography of the underground. Black leaflets: menus from a
               Polish kitchen. Action "N" for "Niemcy." First border cross-
               ing. I meet "Wildcat." Disguised as a railwayman.   67

Chapter 5.   Lavatory leaflets. By the night trains. Life of a "German" rail-
               wayman. The art of smuggling.   81

Chapter 6.   Action N expands. A railwayman in the Reich. "Klimek" dis-
               appears. Learning the art of deception. A psychological urban
               bombardment. Popular pamphlets in the German trenches.
               Organizing a German underground.   90

Chapter 7.   A rent-collector's double life. Learning English from a Scots-
               man. A Jewish martyrdom. The prophetic curse.   102

5

170157

EMORY & HENRY LIBRARY

Chapter 8.   Prospects in the Baltic. A stowaway volunteer. Stockholm or London? Courier "Hilda." A cigarette from General "Grot." Where is Courier "Zych"?   108

Chapter 9.   Two nights in a coal bin. Forced landing at Gotland. The guest of a policeman. Delivering the statue, the key, and the pencil.   116

Chapter 10. Stockholm, a city of spies. Discovering the real British attitude toward Poland. Meeting a Polish double agent for the Japanese. Liberation of two Polish military standards.   129

Chapter 11. A coal mattress again. Diverted to Szczecin. Arrest of "Hilda" and "Thaddeus" on their rescue mission. Gestapo searches for Jan Kwiatkowski. Saved by the *Drabant*'s change of course. From Szczecin to Gdynia.   137

Chapter 12. Trouble on the Underground Railway. White nights in Luleo. Re-living Jack London in the beachcombers' camp. Taking leave of Klapp.   144

Chapter 13. "Robak" under death sentence, a major disaster in Poznan. Return to Warsaw. "Zbik" in Torun Prison. Passing on the Stockholm microfilms. Epilogue: Courier "Tadeusz" reappears in Bolton.   153

Chapter 14. "Black Week" 1943: General Sikorski killed in Gibraltar; "Grot" arrested by Gestapo. Conversation with "the Chairman" of the underground propaganda. Orders to London at last. Communist attacks on the Germans.   163

Chapter 15. Wishful thinking of the underground politician. Social life in the underground. An old university friend—now German agent?   172

Chapter 16. A note from "Zbik" in prison. Collecting "English hairs." A question of boots. "Zbik" entices warder Alphonse. Zbik and company escape the gallows.   179

Chapter 17. Briefing by the AK Big Three: "be like a sponge." Four-point message for London. Catastrophe in Gdynia. Can we trust agent "Redhead"?   186

Chapter 18. I become "Jan Nowak." A gift for Churchill from Action N. Gydnia without a safehouse. Sleeping in a water tank on the Baltic. In a Malmö prison. A plane seat with the help of *Admiral Hipper*. To Scotland in a bomb bay.   195

Chapter 19. At the "Patriotic School" in London. My report to the commander-in-chief. Explaining the Home Army.   208

Chapter 20. The political geography of Polish London. Christmas dinner with General Sosnkowski. The Polish prime minister and commander-in-chief: a confrontation of personalities and styles. Poland's future after Teheran.   215

Chapter 21.   Attitudes of the Allies toward Poland. The division of Europe into occupation zones dooms Poland. General "Bor" plans Operation TEMPEST. Polemics with General Sosnkowski. The British withhold arms drops. The prime minister gives assignments.   227

Chapter 22.   Conversations with the British. Poland's enemies and defenders. Warnings against anti-Soviet postures from Hugh Dalton and Ernest Bevin. Air Minister Sinclair resists Polish airlift. The Cardinal-Archbishop of Westminster promises prayers, the Archbishop of Canterbury tries to help. *Times* refuses Jeffery's account of the slaughter of the Polish Jews. Meeting with Anthony Eden.   235

Chapter 23.   An "editorial lunch" at the *Times*. My address in the House of Commons. Polish attempts to have a British mission sent to Poland. Mikolajczyk shifts the decision on accepting the Curzon Line to Warsaw.   249

Chapter 24.   The anti-Polish intrigues of Churchill's aide. Churchill gives half of Poland to Stalin.   260

Chapter 25.   Censorship at the BBC and Polish Radio. My "Postscript after the Nine O'clock News." Meeting with the Zionist Ignatius Szwarcbart. Why the West refused to believe in the extermination of the Jews. A painful meeting with Churchill.   270

Chapter 26.   Unsuccessful parachute jump spoils my plans. Agent-provocateur betrays communication network. First "air bridge." Appeal of two emissaries. AK-captured booty opens my way home.   282

Chapter 27.   General Tatar hinders my return. Sosnkowski to the rescue. Talks before the trip. Last meeting with Mikolajczyk. His idea of how to save Poland. Mysterious words of farewell.   291

Chapter 28.   In Gibraltar with the commander-in-chief. Last conversation with Sosnkowski in Algiers. Instructions for the AK commander. Abrupt separation at Caserta.   304

Chapter 29.   At Daybreak. Tempest heading for Warsaw. Operation WILDHORN. Dramatic night near Tarnow. Back on Polish soil.   311

Chapter 30.   Return to the capital. The story of a man from the portrait. Warsaw before the "tempest."   322

Chapter 31.   An emissary's late report. Meeting with the Government Delegate. "W" hour at five. A controversial uprising.   331

7

Chapter 32.   Hotel Victoria, "Monter"'s headquarters. Echo from London. Freedom on the streets of Warsaw. Execution of a Gestapo officer.   343

Chapter 33.   Struggle to start up Radio Lightning. Talking to the wall. John Ward, British war correspondent. Lightning's broadcasts finally reach London.   354

Chapter 34.   Death of "Jula." Giant missile hits "Adria." Warsaw salutes liberated Paris. With "Monter" in rescue operation. A tragic night.   363

Chapter 35.   Move to Ericsson. The man on a barricade. Dramatic night crossing through Warsaw. Marriage in a bombed chapel. Behind the front lines.   375

Chapter 36.   A third-time emissary. Briefing from "Teddy Bear." Shortcuts through sewers. Capitulation. Great and small tragedies. Trials of a dog named "Robak." Farewell to Warsaw.   383

Chapter 37.   A mistake and its victim. "We lost a daughter—we gained a son." With General Okulicki in Czestochowa.   389

Chapter 38.   On a circuit: Cracow—Czestochowa—Pruszkow. The Government Delegate takes responsibility for the Rising. Sketch drawn by "Teddy Bear." Okulicki speaks about the Battle of Warsaw.   395

Chapter 39.   Secret mail in the Jasna Gora chapel. A dramatic night. Fourth "air bridge" canceled. "Zo" tries out the route to Switzerland. En route to London once more.   400

Chapter 40.   Across the Third Reich. The longest tunnel in the world. "Grüsse für Brunhilde." Christmas Eve in the Black Forest mountains. Comsomols from Orel. "Your homeland's over there."   407

Chapter 41.   The long march. Abandoned by the guides. Adventure at the border. Arrest. Asylum in Basel. Escape from the internment camp. Hiding in Bern. Betrayal at La Vierzonne.   416

Chapter 42.   Swiss interrogation. In a cell with a Soviet spy. Lyon—Paris—London. The journey's end.   430

Chapter 43.   A report from Warsaw in the world press. Major Morton's second intrigue. A last meeting with Mikolajczyk.   437

Epilogue   447

Personalities   455

Appendix of Documents   459

Index   474

Abbreviations

Action N	Action *Niemcy*; black propaganda, aimed at German population and army
AK	Armia Krajowa, or Home Army; Polish underground army
AL	Armia Ludowa, or People's Army; communist military organization, previously called People's Guard
BIP	Bureau of Information and Propaganda
"Dairy"	*Mleczarnia*; cell supplying AK members with forged documents
Gestapo	Geheime Staats Polizei, or Nazi secret police
General Gouvernement	Generalna Gubernia; Polish territory occupied by Germany in World War II but not incorporated into the Third Reich
Home Army	Polish underground army, or AK
NKVD	Narodnyj Komisariat Wnutriennych Diel, or People's Commissariat of Internal Affairs; Soviet political police.
NSDAP	National Sozialistische Deutsche Arbeiter Partei, or National Socialist Workers Party of Germany
NSZ	Narodowe Sily Zbrojne, or National Armed Forces; extreme right-wing underground organization
People's Army	*see* AL
People's Guard	*see* AL
PWP	Polish Workers Party [Communist], or Polska Partia Robotnicza
SA	Sturm-Abteilungen; paramilitary organization of Nazi Party
SD	Sicherheitsdienst; German security police
SOE	Special Operation Executive; British liaison office with resistance organizations in Europe
SS	Schutzstaffel; Nazi military guard
Volksdeutsche	Polish citizens who adopted German nationality and signed a special loyalty declaration
Volksliste	special loyalty declaration
V-1, V-2	rocket-propelled weapons used by Hitler against London
Zaloga	liaison department in AK maintaining constant contact between Poland and London military headquarters
ZWZ	Union for Armed Struggle; became AK

Preface

I was the eyewitness to the Polish drama in World War II from the perspective of both London and Warsaw. My first secret trip, from Warsaw to neutral Sweden, was taken at the time when Stalin had broken off relations with the Polish government in London. It was the beginning of a game which would lead to the subjugation of Poland by the Soviet Union. My fifth and last journey as a courier ended in England ten days before the Yalta Conference. I was the first eyewitness to, and participant in, the Warsaw Uprising to reach the West. By that time most of Poland was occupied and the Lublin puppet government had been put in place by the Soviets. The events which I witnessed, and the politicians' reactions to them, led to the division of Europe and, later, to the Cold War.

I intended to write this book just after the war ended. However, I immediately became absorbed in such activities as broadcasting to Poland over the BBC and, later, Radio Free Europe. Only after retiring in 1976 did I dig out my old notes, reports, minutes of my conversations, and diaries. I could construct my courier routes across Europe from the coded radio messages between London and Warsaw, copies of which had been preserved in the Polish Archives in England. My correspondence with some of the persons who play a role in this story was also of enormous help in establishing the chronology of events. Her Majesty's Public Record Office gave me access to secret documents pertaining to my mission. The British archives were made available to the public in the early seventies. Many of these documents were included in a Polish edition of the story published in London in 1978 and later circulated in Poland by a dissident publishing house, NOWA. In 1948 the BBC Home Service broadcast a one-hour feature based on these war adventures. The author of the script, Marjorie Banks, gave it the title "Courier from Warsaw," which I adopted for both editions of this book.

I should like to extend my thanks to all those who have helped me in the research for this book, above all, to my wife, who helped in the search for documents, checked facts, and made corrections, all with boundless devotion. Mrs. Jean Owen deserves special appreciation for reconstructing in English with great skill and care my way of telling the story.

Memoirs written immediately after the events belong to political journalism, and the writer must exercise caution in dealing with secrets affecting others. But a testimony given after so many years belongs to history. I have therefore felt free to present a complete picture as I saw it then and now.

J. N.

Foreword

War memoirs can be fascinating, or revealing, or historically important. Rarely are they all three—but *Courier from Warsaw* is exactly that kind of book. It is a gripping account of personal heroism. As a young member of the Polish underground, Jan Nowak undertook numerous secret missions to keep the resistance in contact with the West. He served as an emissary, surreptitiously crossing enemy lines. Employing many disguises, Nowak traveled in secret to Scandinavia, Britain, North Africa, and even across Nazi Germany itself to Switzerland and France. He faced countless dangers, was usually only a step ahead of the Gestapo, but miraculously escaped arrest and certain death. He was involved in adventures which read like a film scenario.

The book is revealing in a historical sense as well, for it sheds new light on major events that have been little known or poorly understood. It is an eyewitness account of the political trends which led ultimately to the division of Europe and the coming of the Cold War. Jan Nowak was in a unique position to play the role of participant-observer in Warsaw and London. He encountered personally many of the great statesmen of that era, including Winston Churchill, Anthony Eden, and members of the British Cabinet, and had access to secret documents and policymakers during the critical period between the Teheran and Yalta conferences. He was also the last emissary to reach Warsaw before the Uprising and was the first survivor of the Rising to reach London, only ten days before Yalta.

13

This book is important because it provides acute insight into the psychology and organization of the Polish resistance. It is not only an autobiography. Rather, Jan Nowak writes about himself as one of many underground fighters who played their part in history. The book offers a panorama of the components of the resistance movement and a detailed account of many episodes previously untold. Nowak reveals information about the anti-Nazi propaganda campaign waged against the German people and among the Nazi troops on the Eastern Front. Sabotage, political intrigue, and even an attempt on Hitler's life are just some of the stories that Nowak tells. He also smuggled out to London the microfilmed report of those Jewish resisters who survived the Warsaw Ghetto uprising, but the reports of genocide had little impact on official London.

Although *Courier from Warsaw* deals with the Second World War, it is particularly timely because of current events in Poland. The roots of Solidarity spring from the unity of the Polish people forged during the uprising and from a history of struggle and resistance to foreign oppression. This will to resist asserted itself in 1944 and again in 1980. The continuous struggle preserved the Polish national identity despite overwhelming efforts to erase it. Political censorship could not prevent *Courier from Warsaw* from being a tremendous success in Poland. Although the leader of the underground publisher NOWA, Miroslaw Chojecki, was put on trial, his statement to the court starkly defined the importance of this book—it reveals the historical truth which was withheld from an entire generation of young Poles who have grown up under communist rule.

Written with verve and flair, *Courier from Warsaw* deserves a wide readership. An authentic account of a unique historical drama and of extraordinary personal courage, it will doubtless earn a lasting place in any select shelf of war memoirs. Its author has shared with us a small chapter from his own life, a life which has been dedicated for some forty years to the single task of defending the Polish nation from physical, as well as philosophical, destruction. Both as the courier from Warsaw and later as the head of the Polish Section of Radio Free Europe, Nowak demonstrated exemplary dedication, skill, and initiative. There is no doubt that he has earned a special place for himself in the pantheon of those who have made sacrifice a way of life since the first ugly shots fired on September 1, 1939. The writing of this book is but another milestone in his remarkable life.

ZBIGNIEW BRZEZINSKI

Map 1.

Legend:

General Gouvernement

Polish territories incorporated into the Reich

Polish territories occupied by the Soviets in 1939 and incorporated into the Soviet Union; occupied by the Germans after June 22, 1941. Ceded to the Soviet Union at Teheran and Yalta.

O cities visited by the author on his secret trips

Partition of Poland, 1939.

Map 2.

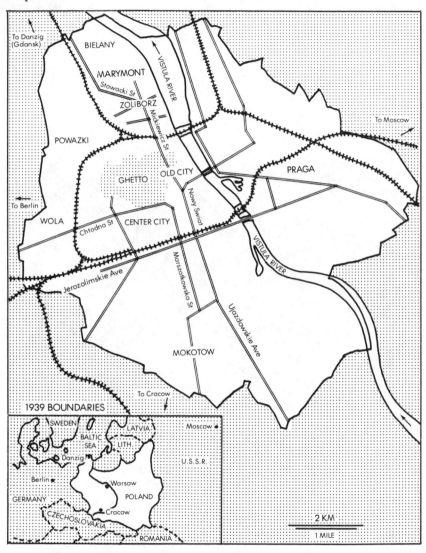

Warsaw, 1939. (After Julian Eugeniusz Kulski, *Dying, We Live: The Personal Chronicle of a Young Freedom Fighter in Warsaw* [*1939-1945*] [New York; Holt, Rinehart and Winston, 1979].

Map 3.

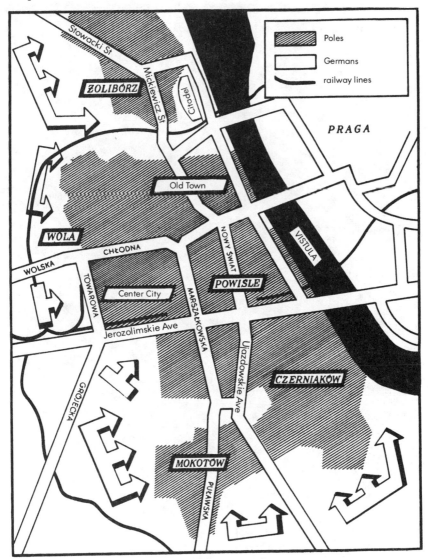

Warsaw, early August, 1944, at the beginning of the Rising.

Map 4.

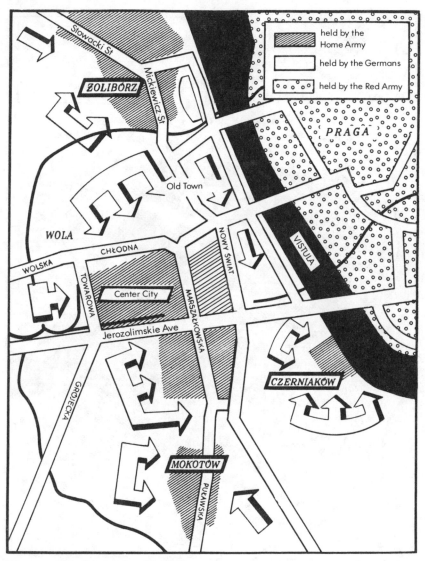

Warsaw, after September 15, 1944.

Map 5.

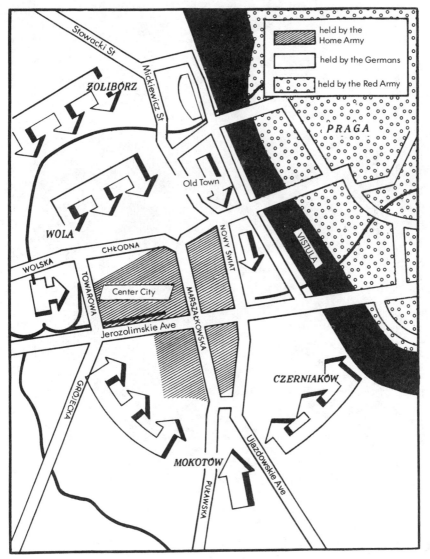

Warsaw at the end of the Rising, early October, 1944.

Map 6.

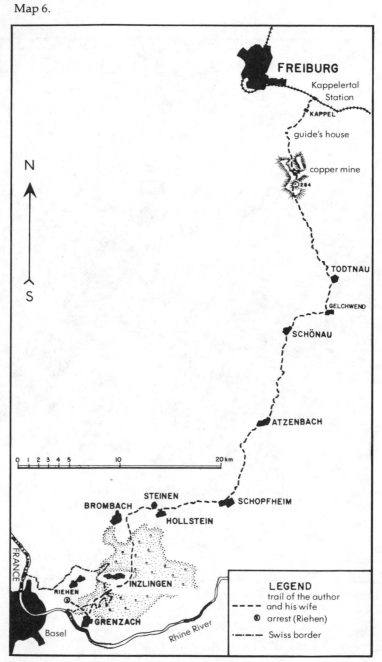

Author's escape route from Germany to Switzerland, December 24-25, 1944.

Chapter 1

There are crossroads in any man's life that decide his whole future. Sometimes one consciously chooses his direction; sometimes one is led by pure chance. The latter is true of me.

Having just graduated from my Warsaw secondary school, I had to decide what to do next. For various reasons which I shall explain later, I wanted at any price to study economics. Unfortunately, the only university that had a faculty of economic sciences was not in the capital but in the provincial city of Poznan. I did not know anybody there, I had no chance of getting a job, and I was penniless. I did not even have enough money to get to Poznan, spend the night there, enroll, and return to Warsaw. I thought that I could worry later about a job: what really mattered was to enroll before the deadline. There were only a few days left. I calculated that I would need exactly forty-eight zlotys for a return ticket, the enrollment fee, and a bed at a student hostel, but I had no way of getting even this paltry sum anywhere. Pride stopped me from asking strangers for a loan that would, in fact, be tantamount to a gift. At the last minute I decided to telephone my paternal uncle, the only man whom I felt I could ask for a loan in my situation. His maid answered the phone: "The master is away; he will be back next week." I put down the receiver, completely discouraged.

At the time my family was in the midst of moving to a smaller apartment. As usual with moving day, a jumble of miscellaneous objects that had been forgotten at the back of bureau drawers was lying around. My eyes lighted on a cigar box, its lid kept closed with metal pins. I tore off the lid. In it were mementos of my late father: his shaving brush, a straight razor, a penknife, eyeglasses, a fountain pen, and a few worthless trifles. What caught my attention was a small linen bag, sewn together at the top. I tore at the linen: inside I found a chunk of dried bread, a pinch of salt, and—by the grace of the Holy Virgin—a large gold ducat, a traditional present that the bride's parents give to each newlywed. Without a moment's hestitation I rushed down the stairs and ran to a bank, as I knew that the banks were buying gold. I got to the nearest free window; a phlegmatic bank clerk put my father's ducat on the scales and said, "forty-eight zlotys." I nearly fainted with emotion. I felt that my father's spirit must have been helping me in this emergency. The next day I had an interview with the dean and completed all the formalities for enrolling at the University of Poznan.

My father died when I was four years old. He was killed by the epidemic known as Spanish influenza, which became rampant in eastern Europe toward the end of the First World War. My childhood memories preserved his image, like a photograph in an old album. When I close my eyes, I can still picture him sitting at the table, with me on his knee playing with his long moustache. I can see him standing in the door of my nursery and, using a childish form of my Slav name, Zdzislaw, calling to me: "How are you, Sisio!" I can see him shaving in the bathroom, and I can recall him in a white tie and tails, returning with my mother from some reception. No one took me into his sickroom when he was dangerously ill, but I felt that something frightening was happening on the night he died. All the lamps were lit and there was a continuous bustle in the apartment. Later I heard my mother sobbing her heart out.

My childhood memories also include some historical events. Six months after my father's death Poland, divided for one hundred and twenty-three years between three powerful neighbors—Russia, Austria, and Germany—was united again and returned to world maps as an independent state. This was after the First World War, with Germany defeated, the Austrian Empire dismembered, and a revolution progressing in Russia. I remember the last moments of the German occupation: the fat German soldiers in their round caps without visors at the entrance to the main railway station, issuing permits to passengers wishing to leave Warsaw; I remember a platoon of German soldiers, in steel helmets with a spike on the top, marching down the street, and a balloon floating above the city, and later, when the country suddenly became free, the joyful marches and celebrations. Best of all, I remember the moment two years later in 1920, when the Bolshevik troops approached Warsaw. Having won the civil war in Russia, the Bolsheviks (this is how they were referred to at the time) were attacking Poland to carry the revolution into Germany.

I did not, of course, realize then the seriousness of the situation, nor could I imagine that Lord d'Abernon later, in a book published in London in 1931, would call the Battle of Warsaw "the eighteenth decisive battle of the world."* Yet I did feel that we were in danger of some sort. I remember the procession of people through the city singing hymns, and the crowded churches. And later that night, from beyond the Vistula, one could hear the sounds of battle. The distant roar of artillery was echoed in the slight chinking of the crystals in a chandelier in the drawing room and in the whispered prayers of my mother.

The events of that night of the Russian attack did decide my fate: I did not get my schooling in a Komsomol and did not become a product of Soviet education like my contemporaries in Russia. The swift advance of the Bolshevik troops, already approaching the suburbs of Warsaw, abruptly changed into a rout. In the few days that followed I saw Russians in Warsaw, not as conquerors but as prisoners-of-war, trudging through the streets under guard. The commander-in-chief of the Polish forces, Jozef Pilsudski, had been a civilian, a revolutionary fighter, all his life. He had gained his military experience as a commander of a small Polish brigade fighting the First World War on the Austrian side. Having found himself at the head of a military force of eight hundred thousand men, recruited only over two years, he brought his troops round behind the rapidly advancing Bolsheviks and, in a classic maneuver in Napoleonic style, routed them.

War had rolled over Poland from so many sides that the country emerged from it completely devastated. Hunger and epidemics

*Edgar Vincent d'Abernon, *The Eighteenth Decisive Battle of the World* (London: Hodder and Staughton, 1931).

raged, and children were their particular victims. We found potato peelings in the bread which my mother had waited in line for hours to obtain. There were shortages of meat, flour, sugar—practically everything. I was fed on tinned food and soups provided by the relief committee headed by Herbert Hoover. The name of the future president, who rescued hundreds of thousands of people from death by starvation, was connected in my childish imagination with an image of distant America, a great power which gave help and asked for nothing in return.

After my father's death, my older brother Andrzej and I were brought up by my mother and grandmother. When my mother was widowed, she was a well-to-do woman, completely without experience of practical life. She could not cope with her inheritance, a large block of city apartments and a plot of ground in the suburbs. The country was riddled with inflation. In 1918 a dollar was worth ninety Polish marks; five years later it was worth five million. At that point my mother decided to sell the block of apartments and the plot of ground, and, as the only way of protecting herself against the depreciation of the Polish currency (the purchase of gold or dollars was considered an unpatriotic action), she invested everything she had in Polish government bonds. A year later, one could use these shares as wallpaper, and we found ourselves destitute. My mother, my grandmother, and we boys lived by selling jewelry, antique furniture, paintings, and other valuables collected by the family over several generations. When my brother finished his university studies and I was to begin mine, we had nothing left. My mother had to pawn the wedding rings and the remains of her jewelry to pay for the move to a smaller apartment.

At home I listened endlessly to tales of the distant past. Poland's history in the last century was in some respects similar to that of Ireland. The once-powerful country had declined and finally disappeared from the map of Europe at the end of the eighteenth century. Some people maintained that it was the victim of rapacious neighbors, others, that it succumbed because of our weaknesses, national faults, and lack of the will to make sacrifices and fight for the values we held dear. The will to fight revived with great force just before the final partition of Poland, much too late. The state had ceased to exist, but the passionate desire for freedom remained so strong that time after time it took the form of desperate uprisings that usually ended in defeat, enormous losses, and a wave of persecution. The last rising, in 1863, was still vivid in the memory of older people when I was a child. My maternal grandmother remembered how, when she was seven years old, the Cossacks attacked the family estate and burned down their manor house before their eyes. My paternal grandmother when a young girl was sitting on the balcony of her parents' apartment one day and, by chance, took out a white handkerchief just at the moment when a bomb was thrown into the open carriage of the tsar's general, Berg, as he drove by. A Russian in the general's escort suspected that the showing of the white handkerchief was a signal to the conspirators, and the young girl was dragged out of the apartment to prison and kept there for a few days.

The person who told us these stories was my father's sister, Aunt Aniela. One day she showed me the cross on the slope of the ancient tsarist Citadel, erected to commemorate the public hanging, in 1864, of the leader of the 1863 Rising and four members of the "provisional" government. One of them was a distant relative of ours; I read with pride on the base of the cross the name of Jan Jezioranski.

In later years a small incident had an enormous influence on my plans for the future. During Boy Scout exercises in the Carpathian mountains I encountered for the first time the desperate poverty of the Polish hamlets. On a hot afternoon we called at a hut and asked to buy some milk. The peasant woman gave us the whole container, while her children—she must have had at least six little ones—began to scream to heaven and weep.

"What's the matter? Why are your children crying?"

"Now they won't have any milk for supper," the good woman said.

"So why do you sell us the milk, instead of keeping it for the children?"

"Because I have no money for matches. If I don't earn a few coppers, they will still go hungry."

The milk suddenly acquired a bitter taste. All the boys produced pocketbooks and collected what little small change they had. The woman thanked us, sobbing and wiping her eyes with a corner of her apron.

After my return to Warsaw, I began to think about that event. How many peasants were there in Poland who could not afford even milk or potatoes for their children? The utter poverty of the Polish countryside could only be compared with the misery of the Jewish inhabitants of small cities. It was a large section of the population about whose lot urban, educated people like my family knew little; actually we hardly knew that they existed. Under the influence of these thoughts I began to develop my first social and political ideas. The generations of my parents and grandparents, I reasoned, had survived a revolution and a war which now, in retrospect, seemed to them a romantic, beautiful slice of history. These were great adventures that would not happen again. The country needed qualified, progressive economists to improve the general standard of living and to strive to remove social inequalities. I decided to follow this path.

From the moment when my father's gold ducat paid for my journey to Poznan to study the discipline I had chosen, it seemed as though an invisible hand were opening all doors for me. It was 1932 and the country had reached the nadir of depression. The number of unemployed had never been so great. It seemed impossible for a nineteen-year-old student to find employment in a strange city, but an unexpected set of circumstances made it possible for me to get work at once as a bookkeeper in a lawyer's office. Professor Edward Taylor, a leading Polish economist of Scots extraction, was curious about a young man coming from Warsaw to read economics. He became my thesis supervisor, and when I had finished my courses he appointed me his senior researcher. While I was writing my doctoral thesis clouds began to gather on the political horizon. After the annexation of Austria by Hitler and his march into Czechoslovakia a year later, I realized that Poland's turn would come, and just when attractive prospects for my academic career were beginning to appear. After I had obtained my doctorate Professor Taylor was going to get me a fellowship for further studies abroad. After that, the next step would be a lectureship at the university.

I began to believe so strongly in the invisible hand which had led me toward these objectives that even the signs of war could not mar my optimistic outlook—not even toward the end of August 1939, when, with a mobilization order in my pocket, I locked up the first chapters of my doctor's thesis in my drawer and left the building of the Economics Institute at Poznan. I felt apprehensive about my immediate future, of course, but this military service, I thought, would only be a stormy episode, after which everything would revert

26

to normal and life would continue as planned. I took my leave of Professor Taylor as if I were going on military exercises, not suspecting that the road I was now taking would lead me in a completely different, totally unexpected, direction.

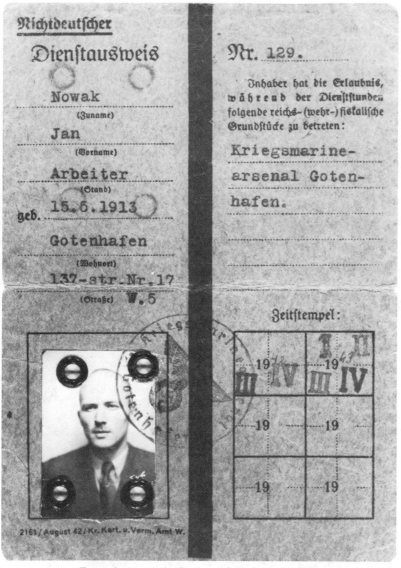

Forged pass to the harbor of Gydnia. ''I did not think that I was parting with my family name, Jezioranski, . . . and that, for the rest of my life, I would remain Jan Nowak.''

''Poland's Militant Underground Movement Fights On:
Scenes Enacted in the Very Shadow of the Gestapo,''
Illustrated London News, February 19, 1944, reproduced with
special permission.

A typical street scene in Warsaw. An S.S. patrol halts Polish
civilians at random, faces them to the nearest wall, and searches
them for weapons and documents. The tank in the background
carries German soldiers' pay, to protect it against Polish
underground troops.

Polish underground executioners leave the office of Hoffman,
Nazi labor exchange chief of Warsaw.

Polish underground judges sit in trial upon a German-
Polish police officer accused of excessive cruelty and other
crimes. The court, which lasted all night, was held in
the prisoner's flat, where he was found guilty and executed.

The execution of Bürckl, governor of the Pawiak prison, Warsaw,
on September 7, 1943. It was carried out by an underground
official, disguised as a street violinist, with a tommy gun concealed
in his violin case.

General Sosnkowski decorates the author with the highest
Polish military decoration, Virtuti Militari. The inscription
reads, ''To Lt. Nowak with brotherly handshake. London,
24 January 1944.''

Passport in the name of Jan Kwiatkowski.

SER.III. Nr 7075
Nr Kr 96.1 28/43

RZECZPOSPOLITA POLSKA
M. S. W.
REPUBLIQUE POLONAISE
M. I.

PASZPORT-PASSEPORT

Obywatel polski) KWIATKOWSKI,
Citoyen polonais)
Jan

zamieszkały w) Stockholmie
domicilié à)

w towarzystwie żony)
accompagné de sa femme)   dzieci
i   enfants
et de

Paszport ten zawiera 40 stronic
Ce passeport contient 40 pages

Anti-Nazi slogan along the Vistula, Warsaw, 1943. "Eden
looked at this photograph for a long time in silence.
At last he said softly, as if to himself, 'Poor Warsaw.'"

Author *(extreme left)* with Commander-in-Chief General
Kazimierz Sosnkowski *(third from left)*, in Algiers.

Jadwiga Wolska ("Greta"), the author's wife. "I was
waiting in a small sitting room . . . when a slim, very
shapely girl with snub nose and large, beautiful, slightly
slanted eyes appeared in the doorway. . . . 'My name is
Greta. I am a liaison girl for the Third Section.'"

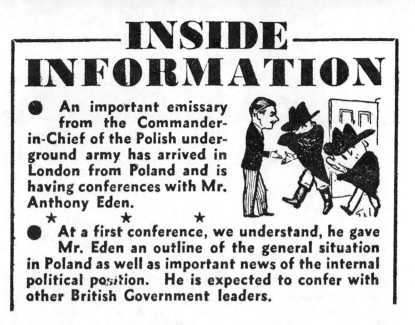

INSIDE INFORMATION

- An important emissary from the Commander-in-Chief of the Polish underground army has arrived in London from Poland and is having conferences with Mr. Anthony Eden.

  ★   ★   ★

- At a first conference, we understand, he gave Mr. Eden an outline of the general situation in Poland as well as important news of the internal political position. He is expected to confer with other British Government leaders.

Cartoon in the *Daily Sketch* (London). By permission of Associated Newspapers Group Ltd.

Seating plan for lunch in the editorial office of the London *Times*, February 17, 1944.

THE TIMES BOARD LUNCHEON

February 17, 1944

Colonel Astor

Lieut.-Gen. Bedell Smith (U.S. Army)	Air Marshal Sir Arthur Coningham (R.A.F.)
Mr. Barrington-Ward (Editor of Times)	Mr. Kent (Manager of The Times)
Captain Nowak	Major Lord Coke (Army)
Sir Irving Albery (Member of Parliament)	Mr. Kinnaird (Barclays Bank)
Sir Harold Hartley (Director of The Times)	Sir Campbell Stuart (Director of The Times)
Major Lord Denham (Army)	Rear-Admiral Wilson (United States Navy) (Naval Attaché & Chief of Staff)

Mr. John Walter

Honorable Winston Churchill, Prime Minister of the
United Kingdom of Great Britain and Northern Ireland.

Sir Prime Minister!

We have the nonour to send You one of our editions
wchich may be of some interest to You.

We endure now in Poland the hartest period of struggle
with our common foe. We stand against extraordinary
persecution and terrorism. We have'nt yet cannons.
aeroplanes and tanks as our lucky countrymen who
fight side by side with the glorious British Army,
but we fight as Polish „underground soldiers" with all
strength and all means we have. This pamphlet is one
link of the long chain of our diversive projectiles, with
which we try to weaken the nazi moral strength.

We ask Your pardon, we have placed on the pamphlet
Your caricature, though we assure that we have nothing
caricatured from the words of the real greatest lier
of the world.

Let Your words come true and let an early Victory release
us from the horrors of the nazi occupation and war!

With greatest respect and admiration

Yours Editors, Printers and Collaborators
of the Polish Diversion Action „N"

Warsaw, September 1943.

Dedication to Churchill in the Polish black propaganda
pamphlet.

Cover and page from the propaganda pamphlet showing Churchill, "the biggest liar in the world," and Hitler in a prayerful pose.

Zwei Gebete

WIR HABEN IN DIESEN LANGEN JAHREN KEIN ANDERES GEBET GEHABT, UND WIR WERDEN AUCH KEIN ANDERES HABEN, ALS DAS: HERR, GIB UNSEREM VOLK DEN INNEREN UND GIB UND ERHALTE IHM DEN ÄUSSEREN FRIEDEN!

Parteitag 1936, (Führerrede)

ALLMÄCHTIGER GOTT, SEGNE DEREINST UNSERE WAFFEN; SEI SO GERECHT, WIE DU ES IMMER WARST! HERR, SEGNE UNSEREN KAMPF!

„Mein Kampf", S.—715

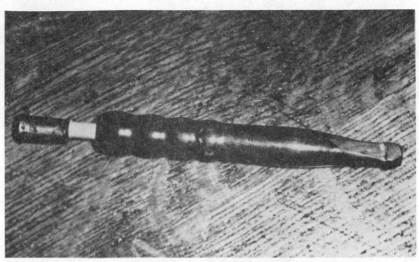

Objects used by the author to hide microfilm on his missions: a cigarette holder, a religious statue, and a door key.

Giant artillery shell which hit the Adria building where the
author was staying on August 18, 1944. It pierced through
six floors but did not explode.

After the surrender of Warsaw, the author and his wife
leave the city with other civilians, carrying microfilm
hidden under plaster casts.

Estimating the time necessary for passing through the sewers from the Old Town to the center of Warsaw.

Insurgents' wedding.

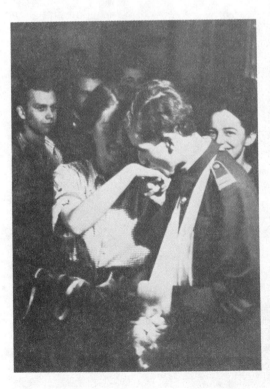

Warsaw in flames as seen from a U.S. bomber.

Jerozolimskie Avenue. "So this is how 'the other side' looks, this mortally dangerous sector of the street, soaked in the blood of messengers, liaison girls, and couriers. One must cross these few yards under the fire of snipers on the upper stories of the Polish Bank of National Economy."

BRITISH LEAGUE FOR EUROPEAN FREEDOM

A SURVIVOR

OF THE

WARSAW RISING

TELLS ITS STORY

LIEUTENANT NOVAK

CAXTON HALL

Caxton Street, Westminster, S.W.

FRIDAY, FEBRUARY 16th

6 p.m.

In the Chair: Duchess of Atholl, D.B.E.

Tickets 1/- to be obtained of the Hon. Secretary, British League for European Freedom, 79, Gloucester Road, S.W.7 (FRObisher 6109) ; and at the Caxton Hall! (February 16th only, from 5.15 p.m.)

St. Clements Press, Ltd., Portugal Street, Kingsway, W.C.2

London publicity for Lieutenant Nowak's story.

Insurgents pick up a parachute with weapons and ammunition dropped over Warsaw by an American bomber.

Chapter 2

*I*n the train from Poznan to Warsaw there was an air of almost joyful excitement. I had time to spend one day in Warsaw to say goodbye to my mother, my grandmother, my brother, and my dachshund Robak. All were in good spirits. We were not alone: Poland had two powerful allies, France and Great Britain. The enmity between Nazi Germany and Soviet Russia made it certain—or so it seemed—that our eastern neighbor would preserve at least a friendly neutrality; we believed in our army, which seemed well equipped; and wishful thinking accounted for the rest of our optimism. Posters on the walls showed Commander-in-Chief Marshal Rydz-Smigly against the background of a blue sky filled with Polish air squadrons. The legend read: "We won't give away what is ours—we shall repel the invader!" Only the news about Ribbentrop's flight to Moscow, as unexpected as a clap of thunder, made us all uneasy, although no one expected that its outcome would be a secret German-Russian pact to partition Poland, signed before the Nazi troops crossed the Polish border.

When I reported for duty in the small town of Dubno, on the Russian border, my Second Squadron of Horse Artillery had already left and was in its battle position on the opposite side of the country, facing the German frontier. The reserve soldiers were collected in the barracks. When I left early in the morning to have breakfast in the officers' mess on Friday, September 1, 1939, I saw another officer running toward me. Waving his hands he shouted excitedly: "The war has started—the fighting started at 5 A.M.!"

None of us realized that at that moment we had crossed a line that would cut our lives in half and forever prevent us from returning to what had been before. The excitement at the thought that history was knocking at our door did not last long. Our military convoy, bombed continuously by the Luftwaffe, took three days to reach the reserve center for horse artillery at Zamosc, 150 miles southeast of Warsaw. The old fortress and the barracks could accommodate only some seven hundred reservists from all over the country. The center had only two field guns, so there was no question of conducting military exercises or preparations for battle. Condemned to enforced idleness, we lived through the nightmare of the next few days as spectators. During air attacks panicky soldiers and civilians sought shelter in the old forts, where the ceilings were in danger of collapsing even had there been no bombing. There were some casualties in our small group. We looked at the endless procession of civilians and soldiers, at the government cars filled with dignitaries escaping from Warsaw, at the convoys of civil servants evacuating the capital. England and France had declared war on Germany but as yet had made no move. German troops attacked from the west, from Czechoslovakia in the south, and from East Prussia in the north. A glance at the map showed that the country's armies were surrounded on all fronts. The German ascendancy was shattering. News of the occupation of large towns like Katowice, Poznan, Cracow, and Lodz, one after the other, stunned us. As in a nightmare, we lost all conception of time and I cannot now remember the date on which we heard that the Germans had crossed the Vistula and were nearing Zamosc from the west and the south. Should we wait there, we wondered, for the Germans to slaughter us on the spot or drive us into captivity, like cattle? If only we had some arms and could organize some kind of resistance. At last came the decision to evacuate the reserve center to the east, on foot, of course, for there was no motor transport. All semblance of order disappeared as we marched along outside the city. The main road was filled with refugees in carts, on bicycles, or on foot. The organized units of the armed forces tried to cut through those unruly multitudes heading toward the east like the army, but it was obvious that in such chaos we would cease to exist as a unit.

Someone in the group of my closest friends, young G., put forward his own plan. His father's estate was a few miles distant. We could get a cart and some horses there, and move on the country lanes in the direction of the River Bug. If, as the command of the center maintained, there was an organized front line at the river, we could ask to be admitted to the first unit we encountered. And if this line proved to be only imaginary, we could turn toward the Hungarian or the Romanian border. Anything not to be taken captive without having fired a single shot. We did not devote much time to discussing this plan. The next morning, from the house of Mr. and Mrs. G., we started across the fields on a cart pulled by two of their best horses toward the nearest bridge on the River Bug. We crossed to the other side near a little village called Uscilug.

The stories of attempts to organize some resistance on the line of the River Bug, the last natural obstacle before the frontier between Poland and Russia, were not completely false. On both sides of the river one could see camouflaged nests of machine guns, and the houses along the river were manned by considerable numbers of soldiers. We reported to the first senior officer we met in Uscilug. As far as we could see, he was organizing an operational unit on his own account. His method was to stand on the bridge, stop all the armed units withdrawing to the east, and, as long as they had no precise destination or orders, to take them under his command and deploy them to various positions along the river.

"You will report to Captain Herdegen," he commanded after we reported to him. I took heart when I heard that name. Witold Herdegen, an old friend of mine, was an officer of the Horse Artillery. He explained the situation to us. He had six field guns and a full complement of gun crews at his disposal. The guns were placed along the river, with two in front of the church. The terrain was quite favorable for defense: the east bank of the river rose almost straight up, several yards above the plain west of the River Bug. From there one could see clearly a sizable tract of land spreading beyond the edge of the forest.

"We shan't be able to resist long," said Herdegen, "but firing straight ahead we might have some superiority. We can get as many soldiers and officers as we wish. We must post military police on the road and stop those who are retreating. What we lack are guns, equipment, and ammunition. I don't even have a decent pair of field glasses."

The waves of refugees and soldiers crossing the bridge over the Bug throughout the night ceased abruptly in the morning. The valley was completely empty. At last a Polish armored car appeared in the distance with two disarmed Germans in steel helmets on a motorcycle in front of it. For the first time we saw German prisoners of war. They had fallen into the hands of a Polish advance patrol and were subjected to detailed interrogation at once. They proved to be Austrians from a Viennese motorized division which was advancing toward the Bug with no expectation of any resistance there. Reconnaissance reported that the bridges were intact and the roads filled with refugees. Soon our patrols and reconnaissance units returned. They all reported that the enemy was advancing in several motorized columns toward Uscilug.

On September 15 at about 9 A.M. the German motorized columns appeared in the distance from several directions, as predicted. Herdegen was observing the perimeter through a pair of antediluvian field glasses, grabbed from a forester in the crowd of refugees. Through them one could see troop carriers covered with dark tarpaulins and tractors drawing field guns. For the time being Uscilug was silent. Only when the head of the column was about half a mile away did our guns begin to fire. At the same time, the field telephone rang: fire straight ahead. Direct fire at one mile is no great art: almost every shell meets its target. The German vehicles scattered and came to a halt. Their troops dismounted and dispersed into the fields. The caissons were driven off the road, the drivers tried to loop back in the fields, found that they could not move forward, and so moved back seeking cover. Two or three guns got stuck in the roadside ditches, and we immediately took aim at them. Exploding shells put them out of action one after the other.

After about ten minutes the German artillery began to fire. At this point they were firing air-burst shrapnel, highly dangerous to personnel, as the shells exploded right above our heads. My modest military knowledge, acquired in cadet school, was enough to tell me that this would not last long. Our guns were well camouflaged and our ammunition protected in dugouts, but the flash of our direct fire betrayed our positions. As soon as their heavy artillery showed up, it would finish us off in a few minutes. For the moment, though, we tried to ignore the shrapnel and were hitting the German vehicles one after the other, though most of them were empty by now. One of our loaders got hit in the back, but his place was at once taken by a cadet officer. After a while Herdegen came up and said: "Our gun on the other side of the Lug has been silent for three-quarters of an hour. They may have all been hit, or they may have run away. Take four men with you and go and find out what has happened. If they are all dead or wounded or have gone, get the gun back in action. There should be plenty of ammunition left."

The streets of Uscilug, still only under shrapnel fire, were completely deserted. Everyone was hiding in cellars or dugouts. Only a few horses, mad with fear, were galloping from one end of the street to the other. Blood was running down their cruppers and flanks from shrapnel wounds.

Uscilug took its name from the mouth (ujscie) of the River Lug, which, at the southern end of the village, ran along a fairly deep gully to the Bug. Not far off, on the opposite high bank of the Lug, there was a row of peasant huts, and it was there that we had to go. We skirted the deserted village in a wide circle, as Herdegen had ordered, and halted on the fringe of a small grove of trees. A sizeable field of stubble still separated us from the huts behind which our gun should have been. At that moment one of the men called out in a panic: "Sir—Germans!" He was pointing to the left. About four hundred yards away, the road crossed a field sloping gently down to the river. I could not see anything. "Are you dreaming or what?" I shouted. "There are no Germans here." But others then said that they had seen a few helmets showing, so there must be a detachment there. I decided to wait a few minutes. I was beginning to be puzzled by the absence of any sound from the huts, a hundred steps in front of us. There should have been a considerable number of our troops there.

After a few minutes I decided to abandon caution. I drew my pistol from its holster and said firmly: "There aren't any Germans here. We shall cross the field at the double: follow me!" I emerged from cover certain that the other four would follow, but halfway across the field I saw that none of the soldiers had budged. At the same moment I heard the whine of a bullet, then a second and a third. I looked to the left and, far beyond the road, saw Germans rising to their feet. I ran toward the nearest hut, still many yards away. Bullets were hitting the dried-out soil all round me, sending puffs of dust into the air, but I reached the fence unscathed and sprang over it (though I was no athlete). I found myself in the court-

48

yard of a farm. I did not have a second to lose. Without hesitation I threw myself into a large pile of straw in a corner where the farmyard wall joined the hut. Hardly had I done so when Germans appeared in the courtyard. They didn't see me and ran off in pursuit of a soldier who had crossed the field outside a moment earlier. One of them stepped on my pile of straw, and I could feel the weight of his boot on my chest.

For a while everything was silent, but after fifteen minutes or so I heard German voices again. They returned to the courtyard, but this time not in pursuit. I could not see anything, but from the feverish pitch of the commands being given I guessed that they were setting up a machine gun post only about a dozen steps away from where I lay. A few minutes later there was a long burst of fire. An immediate answer came from the other side of the Lug, so I knew that our men had not been taken by surprise.

I attempted to work out what had happened. While their artillery was bombarding Uscilug, the Germans must have built a pontoon bridge a few miles south of the village in order to outflank us. Our men at Uscilug must have realized that a considerable force was advancing on them and decided to withdraw beyond the Lug, where they could better defend themselves. I assumed that, after an exchange of fire, the Germans would push on through the gorge to drive us out of Uscilug and secure the crossing of the River Bug, but for the time being there were plenty of them still in the courtyard.

I began to consider the possibility of escape. If I waited until nightfall, I might manage to creep through the undergrowth and return to my position at Uscilug. I might also attempt to go further east. After a few hours the German voices became more distant, but, alas, toward dusk they were heard again. Apparently they intended to spend the night here, in the hut and in the barn. Escape would not be easy.

Dusk began to fall. Suddenly I heard heavy steps coming straight toward my hiding place. A German, almost touching me, pulled out an armful of straw and walked away. There was now not a second to lose: the Germans were collecting straw for bedding. If I tried to cross the courtyard, they would shoot me on sight. The only way out was over the farmyard wall. I recalled that in the morning a German who was pursuing me had jumped it and I was trying to remember how high it was. Suddenly that German was back reaching for more straw from the pile but his hands found me instead. He shouted with fright. Pushing him away with all my strength, I leaped out of the straw and tried to grab the top of the wall, but it was too high and I fell flat on my back. In a flash there were two Germans on top of me. Others rushed out of the hut and pinned my legs and arms to the ground, all shouting at once. I got a sharp kick in my side, which took my breath away. I was sure that in a moment they would either trample me to death or shoot me, but, having recovered from the shock of finding me, the Germans, or rather Austrians, as they turned out, dragged me to my feet and into the hut. They took away my revolver and emptied my pockets. To hell with the revolver, I thought, but I was sorry to lose my good old turnip-shaped Omega pocket watch, which had been my father's.

My captors looked at me with interest. My knowledge of German was very limited, but in the group there was a student from Vienna who spoke passable French. They fired questions at me. How did I get there? What was I up to? How long had I been there? In a short while, they brought me a canteen full of hot soup and a piece of rye bread. The Austrians are not like the Germans, I thought; they treat a prisoner like civilized people. To my delight, they returned to me not only my documents and my wallet, with the money still in it, but also my father's watch and my forage cap, which they had found in the straw.

An hour later, three armed soldiers escorted me to a lorry waiting on the road. The night was bright with the glare of fires: Uscilug was burning, but no sounds of battle could be heard. We crossed the river on the pontoon bridge. The vehicles that we had shelled the previous day were there; several which had been destroyed had been dragged into a ditch. I was told to sit on the ground and not to move. I was wearing fatigues, and after the warm day, the September night was cool. The ground was covered with dew, and my teeth were chattering from the cold. The soldier guarding me noticed this and without a word threw me a blanket from the lorry.

It was almost light when a group of German soldiers came by and saw me. One of them stopped, pointed to my spurs, and, with a rough gesture, indicated that I was to give them to him. Slowly and reluctantly I loosened the leather straps.

"Schnell!" ("Quickly!") he roared.

I felt as if somebody had slapped my face. Only then did I realize the full indignity of being a prisoner. I felt as if my life were over. The state of Poland, whose resurrection I had observed with my own eyes and which had seemed a mighty edifice, had collapsed like a house of cards in a few weeks. After only one day at the front I was a captive. I fell into a depressed and indifferent gloom, from which I was awakened by a strange commotion. The Germans, my guard included, started shouting to one another and running into the fields. I remained all alone, sitting above a ditch beside a German lorry. I looked up and saw a formation of bombers approaching from the south. This sight had become so common that it usually attracted no attention. But why were the Germans running away? I then recognized them as our good Polish planes, "Elks."

For so many days we scanned the cloudless September skies for at least one Polish bomber—and now here is one at last. Bombs will begin to drop now, I thought. Too late; I don't care whether I am hit or not. It doesn't matter now; I shan't bother to move. But suddenly a thought flashed through my mind: why should I be killed by a Polish bomb? I slowly raised myself from the ground and had run only a few feet into the field when I heard the characteristic whistle behind me. I did not have time to throw myself down before a powerful blast picked me up and flung me about five yards away. There was a long series of explosions, then silence. I got up and looked back at the place where I had been sitting. There was a crater two yards deep. Of my blanket only a few scattered scraps remained. A car was turned over on its side and crushed, as if someone had squashed it into the ground with a giant boot. I too would have been squashed into a bloody mess had instinct not saved me in that last second.

Around me I could hear moaning. Although the bombing had not been very accurate, some shrapnel had hit the lorries in which soldiers were sleeping. The survivors were pulling out the dead and wounded, and vehicles marked with a Red Cross began to arrive: also a jeep came and took me away.

On the journey a few other prisoners of war, officers and other ranks, were picked up. From them I heard that the Germans had withdrawn from Uscilug, which had been abandoned and burnt by our forces, to the opposite side of the Bug. Why didn't they push further east, I wondered, just as I had wondered the day before why we did not see a single German plane overhead.

On September 17 we were delivered to a large assembly point

in a churchyard for all the prisoners from the area. The Germans had surrounded and disarmed several Polish divisions, and new groups of Polish troops were arriving all the time. Now we were no longer in the hands of the Austrians but of the Germans, who treated us brutally. A few officers of the Wehrmacht (or perhaps it was already the Gestapo) began to select Jews "by sight." They avoided officers, but concentrated on privates and non-commissioned ranks, pulling out soldiers with "Semitic" features and leading them away, to the accompaniment of shouts and face-slapping. They tried to drag away an officer cadet, who answered them haughtily in German quoting the Geneva Convention. Deathly pale, he showed them an identity card on which his religion was shown as Roman Catholic, and also produced a religious medal from under his shirt. The Germans then let him go. We observed these scenes with clenched teeth and a feeling of helpless fury.

Late in the afternoon further groups of prisoners were brought in, bearing other news. That morning the Soviet troops had crossed the Polish frontier, advancing toward Lwow. At first this news was received with delight. Now we thought there would be a clash between Hitler and Soviet Russia. Everything might change. But the new arrivals soon dampened our joy. From communiqués issued in Moscow and Berlin, it appeared that the Red Army had entered Poland by agreement with Hitler and that it was going to occupy the eastern part of the country. This explained why the Germans had withdrawn from Uscilug. The River Bug was to be the new Russo-German boundary line. A gloomy silence fell, interrupted by a voice behind me. "I have always said that one could expect anything from those sodding bastards."

I turned around to see who had spoken and saw a slim, handsome lieutenant with an oval face and regular features who had until then been silent. A few hours later I learned that his name was Jozef Cyrankiewicz, a well-known Social Democrat in Cracow who had been especially active in politics among the students of Jagellonian University.*

*I became acquainted with Cyrankiewicz during the next few days while we were marching together in the same column. As a Social Democrat he hated the Soviet system, and I certainly did not foresee that he would become the prime minister of a postwar communist government in Poland, nor could he guess that he was sharing his fate with the future director of Polish broadcasting for Radio Free Europe, considered by the communist government as its greatest enemy. Later in the war, Cyrankiewicz and I joined

The number of prisoners collected by the Germans was too great for their transport and supply facilities, the more so as bridges and railway lines were mostly destroyed. An enormous column of perhaps several thousand prisoners was formed and sent off on foot to the railway station of Jaroslaw, some seventy miles away. The railway line from Przemysl to Cracow was practically the only one still functioning. Our column was so long that from its head one could not see the rear. It was guarded by soldiers on lorries with machine guns pointed at the marching men and by guards on foot spread along both sides of the road. There was no possibility of escape. The Germans repeatedly warned that they would open fire upon anybody who left the road.

Before nightfall we were locked up in churches or farm buildings that were easy to guard. There was so little room that in the churches we slept mostly sitting up where we could: on the benches, on the stone floors, on the altar steps. Most comfortable were the confessionals. Food was scarce. On the first day the Germans halted the column and allowed us to spread out within a radius of a hundred yards or so to dig potatoes. In the evening they brought cauldrons of soup. The next morning, before the march was resumed, they brought us coffee and loaves of bread. There was not enough food for everybody, and there were ugly scenes when it was distributed. One could then learn to what degradation one can sink when one feels hungry or even fears that one might become hungry. People fought to be allowed to hold the soup kettles and the stacks of bread, and later fought again over the distribution of the food. Those who did not wish to engage in an undignified scramble after the day-long march went hungry.

The officers and officer-cadets whom the Germans put at the heads of columns to guard them better and to separate them from the other ranks were in a slightly better situation because in the villages

---

the ranks of the same resistance movement. Arrested by the Gestapo, he spent several years in the concentration camp at Auschwitz. He lived to be freed, but he emerged from prison a changed man. He sided with the communists, and in 1947, after they came to power, he became the head of the government. He held that post from 1947 to 1970, surviving all purges; when there were intrigues within the party he always managed to find himself on the winning side. Cyrankiewicz the politician, an opportunist and self-promoter, was so diametrically the opposite of the man I got to know during captivity that in postwar years I often wondered whether he was not hiding his true self and waiting, unsuspected by anyone, for the right moment to play some constructive role.

peasants pushed into our hands whatever they had to give: an apple, some broad beans, a slice of bread, a single cigarette, glasses of water, a few baked potatoes. A little woman who had nothing else to give pushed a few nasturtiums into my hand. The peasants had nothing left by the time the rear of the column reached them. The Germans did not interfere, on the whole. Lack of supplies also presented a problem for them.

There were ever more frequent cases of fainting from hunger and exhaustion, but the worst thing was to hear the constant complaints not only against those responsible for our defeat but against the whole nation. There was some kind of compulsion to heap abuse on one's own people. High-ranking officers behaved in many different ways. One colonel ordered that the regimental cash carried by his adjutant should be distributed equally among everybody, notwithstanding rank. He did not keep a single zloty for himself. Another commander always carried a heavy metal box containing his regiment's cash. He did not put it down for even a moment, even if he had to relieve himself. At night he used it as a pillow, probably none too comfortable. He must have had weighty dreams. He must have carried that money right to his POW camp.

On Cyrankiewicz's initiative the first "conspiracy" was concocted. We decided to use our influence to restore some morale, discipline, and dignity to our ranks and to react strongly against any slur on our nation, government, or army. We stood guard in turn during the distribution of food, each guard taking the last smallest portion. The food obtained from the peasants in the villages went into a common pool and was fairly shared. The results of these endeavors were quickly evident. As soon as the "conspirators" gained confidence, a modicum of order was restored, at least within the group nearest us. After two days' march we were loaded onto lorries and driven toward Jaroslaw.

There we were loaded into cattle trucks forming a train about a mile long. We noticed that our German escort was well armed, but numerically weak. When we stopped at a station, POW's under guard had to carry round buckets of water and bread. As the opening and shutting of wagon doors each time took a lot of time, they took to leaving the doors open. On the fifteenth wagon machine guns were mounted on each side. We were warned many times that the guards were under orders to open fire if there were any attempt to escape.

During the night a thick fog descended and the train had to slow down to about twenty-five miles per hour. Someone suggested that we should try to escape then, because by first light we would be inside the borders of the Reich, and it would be too late. We were excited by the idea, but opinions were divided. Someone pointed out that we were in uniform and that we didn't know whether there were any German detachments in the area. Besides, the guards had enough machine guns to finish us all off even if they couldn't see well to aim in the dark.

"We must wait until we are nearer Cracow," said Cyrankie-wicz. "I know a workers' settlement there not far from the railway lines. They will certainly hide us and give us civilian clothes."

A group was immediately formed of those who wanted to jump from the train. Cracow drew nearer. In the fog and darkness it was difficult to recognize our precise location.

"I think it's here," said Cyrankiewicz. "Let's go!"

We had already drawn lots to decide on the order in which we would jump. I was third. We had to jump one after the other, very quickly, to reduce the danger for those following. I jumped sideways and fell hard against the sloping embankment, rolled down it, got to my feet and started running blindly forward, sometimes tripping over bushes or tree roots. I must have run about a hundred yards when the machine guns began to fire. I looked quickly behind me. The train not only did not stop; it seemed to have speeded up, so there would be no pursuit. I started running again and heard the pounding feet and heavy breathing of my friends.

We reached some buildings. The inhabitants, awakened by the firing, were looking through the windowpanes. I rushed into the first house, breathless, capable only of saying single words: "Germans . . . escaped . . . from train." I pointed back in the direction from which long bursts of machine gun fire were still audible. A very large old woman in a shift and bodice without a word pushed me into the bedroom, threw me into a still warm bed, and covered me with an enormous feather quilt. I felt suffocated and tried to move, but she weighed about one hundred eighty pounds. For several minutes I attempted to get my breath. I was covered by the quilt, the pillow, and the owner of the bed. Some interminable minutes later, she must have decided that the danger was over and the terrible weight shifted. I extricated myself and sat on the edge of the bed. In front of me, staring, was the whole family.

"Thank you," I gagged, taking a deep breath with great relief. I was free.

Chapter 3

My transformation into a civilian did not present any difficulties. Some boys cycled to Cracow nearby to fetch clothes from somebody I knew. The jacket they brought proved to be too small, the shoes too tight, the trousers too short. I went to Cracow wearing my army boots, the civilian trousers hardly reaching my calves. In the streetcar people smiled when they saw me, but I got to my friend's apartment without incident.

The same day I heard the BBC Polish program for the first time. The British had begun to broadcast this program a week after the outbreak of the war, although neither they nor the French had taken the slightest action when the Germans attacked Poland on September 1. However, to hear a Polish voice from distant London was enormously cheering. The war was going on; one must be patient to survive the worst. The country was overrun by German troops from the west and Soviet troops from the east. Warsaw was still fighting, beleaguered and ruthlessly bombarded by day and night from ground and air. I was worried about my family and resolved to get closer to the capital. The fall of the city seemed to me to be only a matter of days.

Deciding to go to Warsaw was one thing; getting there was quite another. Most railway lines were at least partially destroyed, bridges had been blown up, and millions of people were wandering on the roads. The occupation authorities decided that to maintain some sort of order everyone should return home. By a roundabout route, constantly changing trains that no longer ran on schedules, I set off, with a few companions, in the direction of Warsaw. En route we learned that the city had surrendered. Standing in a railway station we saw one of the first trains carrying prisoners from the city. This time the train was heavily guarded and the coaches were locked. We could see faces at the small windows, but the guards did not allow any conversations.

At Pruszkow, some ten miles from Warsaw, everyone was ordered out: no train could go any further. A curfew began at 7 P.M., and we could not start for Warsaw until after 5 the following morning. I spent a terrible night in a crowd of refugees who completely filled the small station building. They were the ones who had suffered most. Escaping from the Germans, they found themselves in a strange, besieged city under bombardment, without shelter and mostly without money or food. They were now returning to their own towns and villages. Many were seriously ill and there were a lot of elderly people among them. During the night at least two babies died, while people looked on with dull indifference. The dead babies were buried wrapped in their nappies in a small square not far from the station. I kept asking about the degree of devastation in the capital and eventually found out that the area where my family lived was apparently more or less intact. Shortly after 5 A.M. we started toward Warsaw, walking against the continuous stream of refugees.

The last detachment of Polish troops had left Warsaw as prisoners the previous day. In the western suburbs of the city we saw abandoned guns and immense street barricades, sometimes reaching to the second stories of the houses. The city resembled an overturned ant heap. The streets were full of rubble, already with pathways trodden through and over it by people hurrying in all directions. Everybody seemed to be engrossed in his own affairs, and all carried something: a rucksack, a basket with provisions, a suitcase.

I headed for my aunt Aniela's apartment in the center of the city. From a distance I saw with horror that the building was in ruins. An enormous heap of rubble formed a hill filling the entire courtyard and overflowing onto part of the pavement. I looked up: my aunt's apartment had been on the highest floor, overlooking the courtyard. Only the gable end was left. Where the bathroom should have been, only the bathtub was left hanging from its pipes: of the sitting room,

58

only a familiar portrait remained on the wall. An old man was trying to pull something out from under the heap of rubble. I asked him if he knew what had happened to one of the inhabitants of the building, Mrs. Aniela Jezioranska.

"Ah, yes," he answered. "I know; she was killed on September 25. She was not the only one," he added: "I was lucky. I was in church at the time." As I turned away, he called after me: "Everybody who died here was buried in the small garden in front of St. Alexander's Church."

At that moment I was thinking only about reaching my home as soon as possible. I started to run toward our apartment house, but the nearer I came to it, the slower I went, as if to postpone the moment of truth. When I finally reached the corner of the street, I saw that all the houses were still standing.

Our apartment was on the ground floor. The windows were without glass, the shutters closed. The house looked empty. I entered the building, my heart pounding, rushed into the vestibule, and pressed the bell. All was silence, and then I remembered that all electricity had been cut off so the bell could not be working. I began to bang on the door and at that moment heard the barking of our dachshund, Robak. In a few seconds I was in the arms of my mother and grandmother, both crying with happiness.

"Where is Andrzej?" I asked anxiously. (My elder brother had been exempted from military service because of the effects of a childhood case of tuberculosis.)

"There were appeals on the radio for all men capable of carrying arms to leave the city. He went east with the others."

The next few days were spent trying to find food and searching for relatives and friends. Like everyone else, I instinctively pushed my thoughts about the general situation to the back of my mind and busied myself in the daily search for bread, potatoes, cooking oil, candles, and matches.

Several days after my return I set off towards the center of the city and met patrols of German and Polish police. All streets leading from the quarter overlooking the Vistula toward the main crossroads were closed. A Polish policeman whispered to me that it would be safer to go home and not wander about. Something was about to happen in the center of town, although he himself did not know exactly what. There were masses of soldiers around, also SS and Gestapo.

Only five years later did I learn from General Michal Toka-rzewski, the first commander of the Polish underground military organization, that on this day an event might have changed the course of the war, though it would inevitably have led to mass slaughter in the city. Hitler was coming to Warsaw to hold a victory parade, like those he had held when the Germans had entered Vienna and Prague. In the last hours before the city fell, when Toka-rzewski and a few senior officers and politicians were trying to create the nucleus of the future underground organization, a scheme was hatched for an attempt on Hitler's life during his triumphant entry into the city. The task was entrusted to the commander of a company of sappers in the Citadel.

It had been foreseen (rightly, as it turned out) that whichever route he took, Hitler and his entourage would have to cross the important intersection of Jerozolimskie Avenue and Nowy Swiat. While the sappers, in accordance with the capitulation agreement, were removing a barricade at that spot, they had planted two enor-mous charges of explosives under the pavement. The detonator was guarded in relays, day and night, in a nearby building by two groups of sappers under the command of an officer—all, of course, out of uniform. On October 4, everything was ready. The next morning Hitler was to have his parade, and a long procession of motorcars started to drive toward the point where the charges of dynamite were waiting.

Why did no explosion occur? Tokarzewski explained to me that he had no intelligence information of any kind and that the holding of a military review took the conspirators by surprise. The commander of the sappers could not get through to the firing point because the Germans had closed off access to all streets along which Hitler was to drive. The officer on the spot had been told to act on his own initia-tive, but only if he were absolutely sure that Hitler himself was there. The stakes were too high to allow for a mistake. Not knowing who would lead the cavalcade past, Hitler, Blaskowitz, or Brauchitch, he hesitated and did not give the signal to detonate the charges in the few seconds when the column of motorcars passed with great speed in front of him.

It is difficult to know what the course of the war would have been if the sapper officer had not hesitated. What is certain is that had Hitler and his party perished on that date, the Germans would have unleashed their fury on the helpless population of Warsaw and the rest of Poland. One cannot know the extent of the massacre that might have been unleashed but for that single small movement of a hand which did not occur.

A week after this incident my elder brother returned home with a piece of German shrapnel in his back, and my grandmother left us forever. During the siege of Warsaw she had preserved a stoical calm, hiding her deep fear for those dear to her, but she understood the extent of the debacle when it was all over. "Why have I lived to see it all?" she repeated over and over again, with tears in her eyes. She died of worry.

The morale of the younger generation recovered surprisingly fast. From the radio broadcasts from London and Paris, to which everybody in Warsaw was listening, they all knew that the new commander-in-chief, General Wladyslaw Sikorski, had formed a government in Paris and that a Polish army was being raised abroad. In a matter of weeks the terror—first atrocities, then detention of hostages, news of mass killing in western Poland, and deportations from the western lands—created a common front among the people and increased their bitterness against the prewar government, which was held responsible for the defeat.

One of the biggest mistakes made by the German occupation forces was to confiscate all radio receivers and introduce the death penalty for their possession. They did not go this far in any other country they occupied except Russia. This action was to a large extent responsible for the organization of clandestine groups. The hunger for news, on which the personal fortunes of almost every family in the country depended, was so strong that even the death penalty could not deter anyone. Secret listening centers for the London broadcasts were set up and news bulletins distributed. These became the nucleus of the underground organizations that began to proliferate. As early as October 1939 the first underground paper, *Poland Alive*, began to circulate in Warsaw.

I myself came into contact with these conspiratorial centers quite early on. I began by writing an article for the underground publication *Znak* ("The Sign"). While taking the typescript to the address I had been given, I had the impression that somebody was following me. I stopped in front of a shop window and noticed that a man had stopped at the next one and was apparently watching me.

Before I entered the front door of the house, I looked back once more, but the fellow had disappeared. Laughing inwardly at my fears, I knocked at the door of the apartment indicated and, after exchanging passwords, left the article and returned home.

The same night we were awakened by hammering on the front door. When I switched on the light, I saw two Gestapo men standing in the doorway. I at once assumed that they were there because of my article and the fact that I had been followed. In the linen cupboard, among the sheets, the monitoring bulletin of BBC news was hidden. The Gestapo men searched the apartment quite cursorily. One of them opened the linen cupboard and started searching among the shelves. This is the end, I thought, but luckily he did not find the hidden paper. He then turned and asked to see my identity card. He carefully noted my date of birth, threw the document on the floor, and left the room. The same procedure was repeated with my brother. It seemed that our danger was over, but we saw the Gestapo men drag away the son of the owner of the apartment next door.

The reasons for the nocturnal visit became apparent the next day. From several apartment houses in our street—no one knew why—the Germans were taking away men between nineteen and twenty-five years of age. The order was executed with Germanic precision. The landlord's son whom they arrested was just nineteen, while my twenty-fifth birthday had passed. There was no connection between my work for the underground press and the Gestapo visit. Pure chance decided between life and death.

In the first year of occupation, especially during the critical days of the invasion of Norway and the French debacle, my source of news from the front was the nearby State Institute of Hygiene, where I had a few friends among the doctors. I was a welcome visitor there because I usually brought some underground news bulletins with me when I came. The medical laboratory in the Institute of Hygiene worked on two levels: it took orders from the Germans and under this cover cooperated with our underground organization, the Union for Armed Resistance (ZWZ), later renamed AK, the Home Army. Some of the Weigl anti-typhoid serum produced for the Wehrmacht in the Institute found its way to our organization.

From the beginning of the occupation anonymous letters sent to the Gestapo accusing personal enemies of various "crimes" became a veritable curse. In every community there are people who have no scruples about ridding themselves of trouble or annoyance—an unwanted husband, wife, or mistress—if this can be achieved quietly, without risk. The methods of the Gestapo provided an excellent opportunity to do so. When Gestapo headquarters received such an anonymous letter accusing Mr. X of reading or circulating an underground paper or speaking disparagingly of the Führer, a so-called dogcart was at once sent to the home of the perpetrator of the "crime," and the victim, usually totally innocent, was taken to the Gestapo prison in Warsaw. From that place few returned.

The doctors in the Institute of Hygiene who specialized in growing all sorts of bacteria were asked by the underground to breed anthrax. Anonymous letters were then written containing imaginary names and addresses of "criminals," were infected with anthrax, and were sent to Gestapo headquarters. Shortly thereafter the Gestapo functionaries who dealt with anonymous letters began to suffer from an unpleasant itch, the first symptom of anthrax. Thereafter all anonymous letters were thrown out unread.

Until the spring of 1941 the worry which consumed most of our time was how to earn one's living. The Germans wanted to drain Poland of whatever they could for their war effort. The population was left with what could be stolen or diverted to the black market.

My brother Andrzej, who at the outbreak of the war was head of one of the departments in the Chamber of Commerce, returned to work in his office. Those like myself, who were unable to find employment in government offices or industry, maintained themselves with greater success by "trading." During the first weeks after our return to Warsaw I began to repair broken windows in partnership with my cousin. I had never before been a glazier, but it appeared to be a relatively easy job. The most difficult thing was to get the glass, the putty, and a diamond glass-cutter. During the air raids every window had been broken, and there was more work for us than time and strength to do it, but the job did come to an end after a couple of months.

I then learned there was a shortage of lamp oil in the countryside and that the peasants had to spend their evenings in darkness. By chance I met a man who was the owner of a typical black-market enterprise and found that he had acquired a whole tank of paraffin. I bought two cans of it and tried this method of earning my living. Every day at daybreak an Agril milk truck left a suburb of Warsaw for the north. Forming a partnership with the driver of the truck was not too difficult, and, since he had to set off at 5 A.M., as soon as the curfew ended, I spent the nights at his place.

At first the enterprise promised to go well. When the news spread in the villages that the man from Agril had paraffin, the van was surrounded by peasant women with containers for the valuable liquid. I did not accept cash but payment in kind—butter, a commodity as much in demand in Warsaw as was paraffin in the country. Unfortunately the van went to the same villages every day, so after a week I started to take a train to the market at Zyrardow or some other small suburban town. The exchange of paraffin for butter went fairly well until my Warsaw customers began to complain that the butter I supplied smelled of paraffin. I tried trading in soap instead of paraffin, without success. Nothing helped. My Warsaw customers still smelled paraffin in every pound of butter, a perfect example of the power of suggestion.

The production of condensed milk was even more of a disaster. It was not difficult to make, though sugar had to be obtained. The problem was to find suitable containers. With the help of a friend I managed to obtain a large supply of prewar waxed cartons. In Warsaw at the time people were obsessed with stockpiling provisions. The demand for condensed milk from the outset surpassed our production ability. Everything went capitally. Nobody could have foreseen that the cartons would not prove suitable and would begin to get moldy, along with their contents. In less than a month our customers, who up to then had been demanding at least several cartons of the milk, began to greet us with abuse. The telephone rang from morning to night. We had to refund money with great dispatch. Less pleasant people who were not satisfied with the refund themselves returned the spoiled milk.

Meanwhile, during the same period in 1941, for the first time there were rumors about the activities of the underground army or, rather, the Union for Armed Resistance (ZWZ). Although the country was ruled by the Germans, almost everyone recognized the authority of the Polish government formed in France after the defeat of Poland and moved to London after the fall of France. General Sikorski, who headed it, was both commander-in-chief and prime minister. He commanded not only the Polish army, formed in the West mostly from refugees from Poland, but also the military underground groups within the country. The group known as ZWZ was later renamed the Home Army (Armia Krajowa). At its head was a mysterious general who used the code name "Grot" and was under General Sikorski's orders. Only much later did I learn that "Grot" was Colonel Stefan Rowecki, an officer not widely known before the war, who had been promoted to general in the military underground.

Access to the ZWZ was extremely difficult, but I began to look among my trustworthy friends for a possibility of establishing contact with it. One such was a former professor of mine from Poznan, Czeslaw Znamierowski. I confided to him that I would like to be actively involved in the fight against the Germans but in military action, not in politics. After a while he invited me to tea. Also present was a man of about forty, who seemed to know all about me. The conversation centered on events at the front and the quite evident German preparations for a strike against Russia. It was March 1941. Before leaving, the man told me his name, Eugeniusz Czarnowski, and asked me to call on him at his home.

When I did visit him he told me openly that he was a member of the ZWZ, working in the political and propaganda section of its high command. The task of his cell was to gather political intelligence for the use of the ZWZ and its staff about the general mood of the community and the activities of the various political groups and conspiratorial factions. This was of great importance for the commander, who was trying to bring all military organizations under the control of ZWZ. "Adam" (this was Czarnowski's code name) suggested that I should be one of his "scouts." I felt that this was not quite the right role for me but nevertheless accepted his suggestion, as the important thing was contact with "the army."

Adam then began to question me about my personal situation, how I managed to live, and what Ausweis (German identity card) I had. He frowned when I told him that I maintained myself, like many of the Warsaw intelligentsia, by trading on the black market.

"Without a German work permit* you will be endangered at the first street roundup. Before you were connected with us, you endangered only yourself. Now, when you may be carrying various compromising bits of paper, a chance arrest in the street can put

---

*A German certificate of employment which protected the bearer against arrest and deportation to forced labor in Germany.

many others in jeopardy."

He himself had an Ausweis of the Technical Group, a type of business established before the war that was known to supply some merchandise to the Germans. He asked if I had already tried to obtain a more or less fictional job which would protect me if I were apprehended in the street, in a train, or during a house-to-house search.

"I tried to obtain a job as a manager of apartment houses through the Chamber of Commerce," I replied, "but I did not get it."

"Fine. You will go now with a letter from me to Jozef Glowacki in the Kommisarische Verwaltung der Sichergestellte Grundstücke [Housing Administration]. He is our man, a prewar deputy to the Diet. He will fix you up. There is one condition," he added, smiling: "If Glowacki agrees to the plan, I must have a place to use in one of your houses."

Glowacki worked as chief bookkeeper in the central office of the Housing Administration. He worked through the secretary of the director, who was a German and a member of the Nazi Party. Glowacki could, at a suitable moment, recommend his own candidates. In this way many activists of the underground movement obtained a cover which protected them against forcible deportation for labor in the Reich.

Two days later I took over the administration of two sizeable apartment buildings in the center of Warsaw and received a work permit. In one of the houses, 6 Krolewska Street, I found a room on the top floor with direct access to the staircase. After investigating my neighbors, I selected it for my "office." It was in this room that in the late spring of 1941 I took my oath of loyalty in Adam's presence and acquired the code name "Janek."

Chapter 4

*I*n the first half of 1941, the underground in Poland was a mosaic of large and small political and military organizations. Nobody knows exactly how many there were. Almost every prewar political party continuing its activity in the underground began by setting up its own private "army." In addition to units based on the larger prewar organizations, which had in fact some real strength at their disposal, there were ephemeral groups consisting of only a few persons whose weakness in numbers was often disguised by an imposing name. Under conspiratorial conditions, discovering which were serious groups was often impossible. Genuine ideological motives were quite frequently mixed with the ambitions of individuals planning for their personal and political postwar futures.

While the initiative came from below, so to speak, the multiplication of underground organizations threatened in the long run to waste our efforts in personal intrigues instead of concentrating them on fighting the common enemy. Therefore the creation of a single organization for the military underground became the first task of the ZWZ and its leader, General Stefan Rowecki. All plans and actions of a military nature were to be under one command, although each unit would have full freedom to devise its own political and social programs and to recruit members for them. The Bureau of Political Information (BIP for short) which Adam invited me to join, was to provide background information for the command of the ZWZ so that it could survey the complicated topography of the political underground and so facilitate the discussions and establish the contacts that would make an amalgamation possible.

Although Adam spent some time persuading me of the importance of this work, I quickly decided that I had no wish to play the part of a political informer. In fact, I did not quite know how to go about it. I lacked political experience, contacts, and access to the various underground political groups. I was anxious to remain in ZWZ but hoped to find another assignment which would suit me better. An opportunity did come, by sheer luck.

Two months after the Nazi attack on Russia, while on a train trip outside Warsaw, I made a discovery which seemed to me at the time to be crucial. I learned from another passenger that, in an army hospital in a small provincial town, a leaflet from a German military underground organization had been circulated. I made furious attempts to lay hands on a copy of it. Throughout the country people had been comforting themselves with false stories like this, but in this case the story did appear to be true. Several reliable people stated categorically that they had read the leaflet, one adding that he was shown it in great secrecy by a German non-commissioned officer billeted in his house. The leaflet, I was told, was distributed by an organization within the Wehrmacht and had been brought back from the Eastern Front. I guessed that it was probably published by a cell of German communists after the outbreak of war with Russia.

The leaflet foretold a speedy defeat for Germany, I heard. For the time being, though, nothing pointed to that, as the Germans were waging yet another Blitzkrieg in Russia. Nonetheless, the news about the German leaflet at once raised the morale of the Poles. "Among the Germans," people said to each other, "there is unrest, and where? In the army. The Krauts have had enough of their victories— they've had a craw full of them—they want to go home."

When, greatly excited, I told Adam about my discovery, he burst out laughing, to my amazement. "I know that you can keep your mouth shut," he said, "so I won't play games with you but will share one of the best-guarded secrets of the underground: it is *we* who produce these leaflets. One of my closest friends, a very energetic and inventive fellow, is in charge."

"But the leaflet I heard about was printed in Gothic type and was full of typical army slang. And besides how could it pass from

Polish to German hands without causing suspicion?"

"We have plenty of people who speak German better than Polish and who picked up the slang in the German army during World War I."

"But how are these leaflets distributed?"

"Never from hand to hand. Only by being dropped in barracks, hospitals, railway coaches, marked *Nur Für Deutsche* ['Germans Only'], or being sent through the post. The Germans do not even suspect that these menus come from a Polish kitchen. They believe only their own; they reject everything that the enemy says."

"Is it done on a large scale?" I asked.

"It is now only starting, but, knowing the man in charge, I'm sure that it will develop and that he will always come up with new ideas. The cell is known as 'Action N'—'N' for 'Niemcy'" ("Niemcy" being the Polish word for Germany or the Germans).

What a brilliant idea, I thought: in one fell swoop one both demoralizes the enemy and improves the morale of one's own people.

I at once asked Adam to transfer me to Action N, and he agreed. Very soon a blond man of about thirty in a light gray suit appeared at our flat. At first sight he looked like a government clerk. He introduced himself as a seller of fountain pens.

"Have you got Pelican pens?" I asked.

After this exchange of passwords, the stranger introduced himself as "Leszek" (Antoni Szadkowski) and started to talk business. He knew everything about me, including the fact that I did not know much German, that I had lived in Poznan before the war, and that I had a work permit as a housing manager.

Leszek informed me that Action N was in the development stage. For the moment there was quite an efficient distribution network in Warsaw and in the *General Gouvernement*. The Germans, having occupied Poland, had incorporated all the western provinces into the Reich. In the center they created a state that they called the *General Gouvernement*, which was like a vast cage for about 12 million Polish people, completely surrounded by closed and well-guarded frontiers. Poles had no right to cross the frontiers, and crossing permits were issued only those special cases in which the journey of a Pole was in the German interest. Although the leaflets were dropped in trains going to Germany and back or were sent by mail, the lack of distribution outside the *General Gouvernement* area would sooner or later lead to the exposure of the scheme. Action N foresaw an extension of its activities both to the west (the lands which had been incorporated into the Reich and the Reich itself) and to the east, the area which included the Eastern Front.

"You have lived in Poznan," said Leszek; "you know people there. Perhaps you could undertake to organize regular drops of N pamphlets in the western territories and in time build up a network for distribution in the Reich itself."

I accepted this suggestion without hesitation, not stopping to consider how the job could be done. Leszek told me once more that, to be effective, Action N must remain unknown not only to the Germans but also to the Polish community and even the other parts of ZWZ, not excepting its intelligence service.

The next meeting was held in my room on the top floor of 6 Krolewska Street, the house that I also administered. That time Leszek brought with him a girl known as "Black Janka," a short, shapely brunette, who was to maintain contact between him and me. From then on each day Janka would appear and produce the secret mail from a capacious bag. She was highly intelligent and consistently cheerful but, alas, hopelessly unpunctual—always late and on each occasion shamelessly blaming someone else for it. She was Jewish, so being on the Warsaw streets from morning till night with compromising documents required special courage.

I started work with great enthusiasm. What was required was not the dropping of Action N literature at random or through friends: a troop of couriers had to be found and conditions created for safe and frequent crossing of the frontier in both directions. It was also necessary to build up, in the western territories, a network of safe people who could handle distribution in their areas or pass material into the Reich. This effort necessitated frequent journeys.

I began by meeting a representative of "The Dairy," a cell that supplied people with false documents. I needed a certain number of frontier permits called Durchlassscheine empowering the bearer to cross the frontier between the *General Gouvernement* and the Reich. At the outset I suffered a disappointment. The real documents, produced in Germany, had watermarks which could not be counterfeited. The false papers produced by The Dairy were such bad forgeries that they had gained the nickname "passes to a better world." As for military documents, they obviously could only be used by people who spoke fluent German.

"What documents are used by the intelligence?" I asked.

"That you will never learn. Everybody guards his own secrets. Otherwise one piece of bad luck could start a chain reaction."

I knew that hundreds of smugglers were crossing the frontier daily in both directions, and I decided to find out for myself how they did it. It was not too difficult to establish contact with the smugglers. To mask my real intentions I provided myself with several cartons of cigarettes. If I were caught, the Germans would think that they had a smuggler.

My guide across the frontier was a young girl. In order to make a crossing to the nearest village beyond the frontier one had to wait until the German patrols changed at lunchtime. Our expedition took place in a group quite widely spread out but maintaining visual contact. At a given signal my companion rose from the ground and, although burdened by a rucksack full of goods, started running through a wood with the speed of an Olympic champion. Following her, and completely winded, I reached the appointed hut on the other side. Hardly had I caught my breath than the owner of the hut rushed in shouting "Raid in the village—get out into the potatoes!"

In one jump I was outside. From the threshold he added a warning: "Crawl, don't run! The bastards have field glasses!" Luckily the potato field came right up to the walls of the hut. I crawled slowly on my belly as far into it as I could. I had been told not to move until I heard that the raid was over.

I stayed there until darkness fell. During the night, again with the smuggler's help, I returned in the same way safely to the other side of the frontier. There was no question of penetrating deeper into the Reich. The "game" for which the Germans were hunting was myself. It was quite simple. Through their field glasses the Germans had noticed somebody in city clothes, while most smugglers were peasants or workers from the suburbs of Warsaw and wore quite different things.

Almost exactly the same story was repeated a week later. Not disheartened by my first failure, I renewed my attempt at another spot, nearer the city of Lodz. This time I realized that although I might eventually find a gap in the "green frontier," this was not enough. One must be able to travel inside the country, and for a Pole to travel inside Germany without documents was a suicidal undertaking, in view of the numerous controls on the trains, at the railway stations, and on the roads.

Even before the start of my activities, a certain number of Action N leaflets had entered the Reich through the so-called drop point at Czestochowa. Leszek had a man there, called "Sobieslaw." With him I at once found a common language. He was a shortish man of about forty, with a bony face, rather silent. He was involved in a number of clandestine activities, Action N being only one of them. He transported the leaflets across the border through the intermediary of a friendly locomotive engineer. The method was good and safe, but limited. The locomotive engineer would take any amount of printed matter without hesitation, but he was not so keen when Sobieslaw asked him to carry a passenger over the border hidden in his coal bin.

After much thought Sobieslaw had an idea that seemed to me a stroke of genius. The railway line from Czestochowa to Cracow passed through Reich territory for several miles. What would be simpler than to push bundles of leaflets down the lavatory toilet while the train was passing through the Reich? All we would need was a lineman prepared to pick up the bundle on the tracks where it fell and send it on to a certain address. Sobieslaw agreed to find the lineman on that run through his railwaymen friends. When I met Sobieslaw to make final arrangements a week later, however, he had disappointing news: the lineman was a Volksdeutscher and was not to be trusted.

I also tried, at a distance, to find somebody in Poznan who would act as key man in a distribution network. The majority of my colleagues and acquaintances, apart from those who had died or been imprisoned, had been deported to the *General Gouvernement*. However, I was given the address of a young instructor of the Boy Scouts, Adam Plucinski. I established contact with him through a colleague from Poznan University, Kazimier Wandelt, who ran a company which supplied the Germans and therefore had various privileges: for example, he was permitted to travel to Poznan as often as he wished.

Plucinski immediately agreed to cooperate with me. The recognition sign of my courier was to be one half of a five-mark note. The problem was how to get in touch with Plucinski. The organization of regular drops across the frontier to the Reich was not so easy, as there was a severe shortage of crossing permits.

Frequent meetings with other departments of the organization which had similar problems with smuggling liaison officers and intelligence agents produced no results. The outlook for getting Action N propaganda into the heart of Germany was not favorable. At the beginning of June, 1942, I decided to report to Leszek that the attempts begun the last September had not produced the desired results. I went to the meeting in a subdued mood. My rather gloomy report was given in the presence of another man, who said suddenly: "I know a young railwayman who might help you."

We exchanged code names. The stranger introduced himself as "Mazur." Two days later I met him at the streetcar stop on the corner of Nowy Swiat and Jerozolimskie Avenue and we went together to the suburb of Praga. We rode in the crowd on the platform, without talking. It was a hot, humid day. The railwayman, described by Mazur as a man of infinite resource, was to meet us at 5 P.M. We were there punctually. After ten minutes I looked at my watch. Another five and then ten minutes passed. Streetcars were coming and going. More minutes passed. Mazur began to look at his watch with embarrassment, while I became increasingly angry. I was wearing my heaviest shoes, which were most uncomfortable on this hot afternoon.

"Your colleague," I eventually said to Mazur, "is a rotten conspirator. He keeps us waiting in the street, in plain sight, for more than half an hour. Anybody watching us from a window will know that we are not waiting for a streetcar."

At that moment, without waiting for the car to come to a stop, a young boy jumped off, ran toward us, greeted Mazur with a friendly slap on the back, and, seeing my furious face, called out, "Hey, you— why are you wearing such heavy boots on such a hot afternoon? Look at me!"

He was wearing a checked shirt, light trousers, and a pair of wooden clogs on his bare feet. To better show off the latter, he leaped into the air a few times and gave a rather clumsy but spirited tap-dancing demonstration. A severe reprimand had been on my lips, but I could not help laughing instead.

A few minutes later we arrived at his small, two-room flat. "This is my Zofia," he said, introducing his young wife, not pretty but pleasant-looking, who looked, with her two braids, like a schoolgirl. Newly married, I thought, and felt uneasy. In this peaceful, clean, sparkling, sunny nest the atmosphere radiated the warmth and happiness of these two young people. Am I not bringing some tragedy here to ruin their lives? I wondered. But I told myself that we were at war—that there was no room for such sentimentalizing.

I explained what I had in mind to my host: "Could you go to Poznan, deliver a message to a certain address, return, and later fix it for me to travel there?"

"It shall be done," he answered, as if I had asked him to arrange a Sunday outing to the countryside outside Warsaw. "I'll go there this coming Sunday, and you can go the week after."

"How will you get documents for me?"

"Just give me a photograph and a name. The rest will be my concern. You will be given the uniform of a railwayman on the Ostbahn, the identity card of an official of the railway workshop, and a permit to visit your family in Poznan."

He is boasting, I thought. He has promised too much too quickly. But I got out a passport photo and wrote on the back the name of my friend Jan Kwiatkowski, who died during the war. Then I began to observe my new acquaintance more closely. He looked about twenty years old, but it later turned out that he was slightly older. His body and face were boyish, almost childlike, but what attracted one's attention were his exceptionally blue eyes, shining with some inner fire. His whole slight form expressed enthusiasm and a fanatical faith. His name, he told me, was Stanislaw Witkowski, and he used the code name "Wildcat" (zbik in Polish). He had been seriously wounded at the beginning of the war. After being released from hospital, he became a distributor of underground papers. Before the war he had completed a training course for railway auxiliary staff and had worked on the railways, so he managed to get a job in the personnel division of the Warsaw-East railway headquarters, with the help of one of his prewar pals, Roman Makiela, a man much older than himself. The pass forms and leave permits he and Makiela stole from the desk of the German personnel chief. He then returned the completed forms to the official folder for signature. He was sent from time to time to the German stationmaster of Warsaw-East, one Amtmann Fetzer, with a batch of such documents. An accurate copy of the official stamp had been cut out in linoleum and the mark affixed to the stolen forms with great skill. Fetzer never imagined that he was signing various *Passierscheine, Durchlassscheine, Urlaubsscheine,* and *Dienstausweise** for members of the Polish underground.

I handed "Zbik" my half of the torn five-mark note, the recognition sign for Plucinski, and explained how he could find him. I promised to come back the next Monday for news.

But on Monday Zbik was not at home. He was to have come back the night before, but did not. His wife was not particularly alarmed: "I know him too well by now," she declared.

"And what will they say at work?"

"He will manage somehow—don't you worry."

Zbik did not appear until the following Tuesday. As proof that he had arranged everything, he handed me the other half of the five-mark note, the one that Wandelt had left with Plucinski. He had arranged with "Robak" (Plucinski's code name in Action N) that I would meet him the following Saturday in St. Martin's Church, and minutely identified the pew in which we would find each other. A rosary brought by Zbik was to serve as our recognition sign.

Next Friday afternoon, dressed for the first time in my life in the uniform of a railwayman of the Ostbahn, with the identity card of an official of the railway workshops (my dead friend Jan Kwiatkowski), and a pass stating that I was traveling on furlough to my family at Kutno and Poznan, all supplied by Zbik, I found myself in the station. Zbik was waiting for me on the platform, as jolly and carefree as ever. At the bottom of my railwayman's bag I hid the copies of the N leaflets which I wanted to show Robak.

Zbik put me on the train to Kutno, the first station on the other side of the border. I was to stop for the night at the flat of Regina Celmer, the daughter of a local railwayman, and leave for Poznan the next day. Kutno, a frontier station, would have particular importance for us. It was vital to establish a rendezvous point at Celmer's.

The train was badly chosen. The passengers consisted mostly of professional smugglers of foodstuffs, most of them Warsaw peddlers famous for both obesity and foul language. The overcrowding in the

---

*General passes, transit permits, furlough passes, and work permits, respectively.

compartment was indescribable. I was sitting in the middle of the long seat, squashed on both sides so that I could hardly breathe and could not move my hands at all. A large and very sweaty harridan was half-lying on me. She had tried to stand up at first but was thrown off balance when the train started, and came to rest on top of me. On my head I had a basket and on my feet my railwayman's bag. In spite of the open window there was a horrible smell in the compartment. It was stifling. Every few minutes somebody would step on my foot or some object would fall off the luggage rack onto a passenger's head, provoking a stream of curses. I suffered in silence rather than risk irritating any of the female passengers. I consoled myself with the thought that Kutno was not far away.

At Jackowice, the last station in the *General Gouvernement* area, all the passengers with smugglers' bags, suitcases, and rucksacks left the train. I found myself alone in the compartment, and when we started toward Kutno and the frontier I realized that I was the only passenger on the whole train. In a few minutes, I would face a German frontier guard for the first time with false documents in my hand and at my feet a bag in which was hidden the most compromising material. I suddenly found myself missing the noisy Warsaw crowd.

I looked through the window. Dusk was falling. I was in the carriage next to the engine, and it suddenly looked to me as though large formless lumps were rolling down the embankment from under the train wheels. I strained my eyes in the fading light and suddenly realized that they were lumps of coal, thrown down by the driver or his mate for somebody to collect. Well, everyone had to live, and the Germans allotted the Polish population only a meager ration of coal on the principle "Alles für Deutsche!"

When the train stopped at the station, it was completely dark. I got out, the only passenger. At the other end of the platform was a wooden shed and the exit from the station, brightly lit. Next to it stood a Gestapo man and an officer of the border guard. The Gestapo man beckoned to me. My steps resounded loudly on the empty platform. My heart began to pound. Had it been wise to bring the secret literature with me before the documents Zbik prepared had been tested?

The Gestapo man looked in silence at my identity card, then the travel permit. He compared me with my photograph, handed back the documents without a word, and with an imperious gesture waved me on. A few moments later I was knocking at the door of the Celmers.

The old man was out on duty. After exchanging passwords I felt as though Regina Celmer and I had known each other for years. I realized that on this side of the frontier I was in a completely different atmosphere, as if I were on another planet. In Warsaw and the *General Gouvernement* area we were lost in a crowd; we lived in our own world, impenetrable to the invaders. Here everybody met Germans all the time and lived in a state of constant danger. In the little house of the railwayman one could feel the atmosphere of terror. Regina Celmer could not stop talking. She told me of arrests and executions. In a small town where everybody knew everybody else, these affected people much more directly than they did us in Warsaw. For instance, a few days earlier two young railwaymen were caught stealing food from a goods train. She used their nicknames; she probably had been to school with them. "What if they did steal?" she said. "Everybody must live. And yet the Krauts at once put up notices that they would be publicly executed on Wednesday. I went out into the street. I saw how they were driving them along, their hands tied behind their backs. They looked as though they did not know what was happening. I ran to the square—it was all over—they had already been hanged."

Half the night passed while I listened to these grim stories. In the morning I gave Regina detailed instructions, we discussed future passwords, and I set off for Poznan.

It was an eerie feeling to find myself again in the city in which I had lived for six years. The same buildings, trams, and streets; nothing was changed, except that everywhere were German shop signs and German was spoken. The Poles were still in the majority, but they crept along the streets in silence as if hoping that they were invisible. In the former student dormitory where I had lived there was now a labor office. I walked along Matejko Street, where the former porter of the university, Jan Olejniczak, lived with his wife and two daughters in an attic. A week earlier Zbik had spent the night there.

The next day, when I arrived at St. Martin's Church at the appointed time, a young blond man corresponding to the description of "Robak" was sitting next to the aisle. I knelt next to him and produced a rosary from my pocket. The man was so engrossed in pray-

77

ing that I did not want to interrupt him. At last he lifted his head and, without turning it, whispered, as if still praying to the Holy Virgin, "I shall wait for you in front of the church. Walk twenty steps behind me."

Our conversation took place in a former university laboratory. It was a Sunday, and there was no one there except us. I realized at once that before me was an idealist who was ready for any project. I talked to him about Action N and put the sample literature on the table. The mini-newspaper *Der Hammer* purported to represent an underground organization of German social democrats; *Der Front-kämpfer*, ostensibly put out by front-line troops, agitated against *party bosses, Goldfasanen* ("golden pheasants," army slang for party big-wigs), and *Etappenschweine* ("pigs with gold braid"). These papers carried sensational news about a split in the Wehrmacht High Com-mand and about discord between Hitler and his party and the old-line generals, many of whom, like Marshal Reichenau, had fallen from grace or been liquidated. *Der Frontkämpfer* represented Marshal Rei-chenau as a hero, the leader of the army opposition against Hitler and the ablest general, whose moral courage cost him his life. It claimed that the war had already been lost by Hitler, who had no idea of military strategy, and that meanwhile the army was suffering unnec-essary casualties in order to protect the party and the Gestapo. In the literature I brought for Robak there was also a leaflet carrying the name of Rudolf Hess, which appeared to be put out by the myste-rious NSDAP-Erneuerungsbewegung, Hess's underground opposi-tion group within the Nazi Party.* This leaflet began with the greeting "Heil Hess" and, being destined for party members, used a series of arguments completely different from those in a similar leaflet aimed at the army and the anti-Nazi social democratic opposition. In those days Rudolf Hess's flight from Germany still remained a mys-tery to most of the German people. The N pamphlet presented Hess as chief of those forces inside the party who, realizing the hopeless-ness of the military situation, wanted to plead with Great Britain for a separate peace. From the leaflets of the Erneuerungsbewegung, or "renewal movement," in NSDAP the members of the Nazi Party would learn that Hess had succeeded in negotiating very favorable

*NSDAP, National Sozialistische Deutsche Arbeiter Partei.

terms with the British for a cease-fire arrangement that would allow Germany to keep most of its war booty. Only Hitler, some of the party bosses, and the Gestapo, in defense of their own skins and stomachs, opposed the ending of the war and the conclusion of a non-punitive peace.

With great satisfaction I observed that Robak was becoming more and more engrossed as he read, and more and more enthusiastic. "This is superb!" he exclaimed again and again. "What magnificent ideas! What translators you must have!" He laughed out loud at the thought of the impression the leaflets would make on the Germans.

Robak was up to his ears in underground work, conducted mostly through the local boy scout organization. He told me proudly that his young people from the very beginning of the occupation had prevented the Germans from moving about easily by planting homemade but absolutely effective tire-puncturing devices on the roads. He also told how on March 2, 1942, he, with the help of two other boy scouts, hung an enormous Polish flag on the tower of the headquarters of the German security service. As a result, several Germans from the Hilfspolizei (auxiliary police) were sent to the Eastern Front in disgrace for lack of vigilance.

I listened to these stories with some anxiety: security required that Action N not join forces with those engaged in any other underground work. A piece of bad luck while they were sabotaging Poznan's roads might jeopardize the Action N network. But Robak did not share my objections. "Only in Warsaw can you talk like this because there are so many more of you, so the work can be divided. Here we are a small group; we must combine with one another." I explained to Robak that we did not care so much about distributing the pamphlets to the local Germans as we did getting them into the Reich and distributing them from there. Could his men undertake that task?

"That is out of the question," he answered. "Everybody here who has not joined the Volksliste is suspect, is observed, has limited movement—indeed, cannot travel. To be absent from work can mean deportation to a camp. But don't worry; we will deal with the matter differently. What about the special boxes in front of hospitals, in the railroad stations, and in public squares into which the Germans are asked to throw books and illustrated papers for the soldiers at the front? We shall stick the N pamphlets into German magazines and they will get to the front lines by courtesy of the German field post. Not a single copy will be wasted. Send me this dynamite, as much of it as you can.''

Robak then introduced me to his assistant, just in case something unexpected should happen to him. His name was Tadeusz Kolodziejczyk, and he also was a boy scout.

On my return journey to Warsaw I passed the frontier control without incident. Zbik's documents were completely reliable. No one had searched me.

Chapter 5

My successful journey to Poznan marked the beginning of a much wider distribution of underground N literature in the incorporated territories and eventually its mass circulation. After Poznan came Torun, Bydgoszcz, then Lodz, Gdansk, and, in East Prussia, Deutsche Eylau (Ilawa) and Marienberg (Malbork). Last came Upper Silesia, which was to become the gateway to the Reich itself.

As soon as the problem of getting men and material across the frontier had been solved satisfactorily, thanks to Zbik, we had to find local distributors and couriers to supply the subversive literature regularly to the addresses indicated. At first the couriers were recruited by Zbik from among the railwaymen. Through his various acquaintances he found suitable candidates and went ahead to screen them. If they seemed suitable, I followed to finalize things, administering the oaths, explaining the details of the job, and establishing passwords and contacts.

We made some journeys together, Zbik and I, and a real friendship developed between us. I worried about his safety as if he were my brother. In underground work he was a near-genius, although he had a great contempt for the simplest rules. He did not know what fear was; he went into the most dangerous situations without batting an eyelid; he had an unbelievable gift for deceiving the Germans and for charming all others. He was risking not only his own life, but the life of a young wife who was expecting a baby at that time and those of his two sisters, who had come to live with him. Adding to the risk of his expeditions into the Reich was his lack of knowledge of German. My vocabulary was limited to something like a hundred words, which I could use if I had to, but Zbik was totally incapable of learning even the simplest German sentences. Through Zbik I came to know the railwaymen's community. They were the salt of the earth. They undertook the most dangerous tasks without expecting any reward. Unlike many educated people, they had no personal ambitions and did not expect to benefit from their wartime exploits in the future. Not only the distribution of underground literature from Warsaw but also the whole program of sabotage and military intelligence relied to a large extent on them.

From the railwaymen I quickly learned many useful things that made my increasingly frequent expeditions to the Reich safer. I became acquainted not only with signaling and the technical terms and duties of railwaymen but also with the construction of passenger coaches. During my expeditions to the west I always carried a railway staff key for opening doors and secret compartments. I never dreamed that there were so many of these in each passenger coach. Not all of them were safe, I was warned. For instance, placing pamphlets in a cache at the bottom of a door was risky because then one could not lower the window completely. I had also been taught that when it is necessary to escape in a hurry while in motion, one can momentarily slow down the train without touching the emergency brake. A steampipe runs under all the carriages, and one only has to turn off the stopcock, found between each pair of carriages, in order to apply the brakes; then, just before one jumps, one moves the stopcock handle back to its former position. It was really quite simple.

There were some misadventures all the same. One day I went to Poznan to meet Robak. I took the Berlin express, as it stopped there. While I was still in Warsaw-East Station I locked the parcel with the underground papers in the hiding place in the lavatory. Once I had distanced myself from my dangerous luggage I calmly went to sleep. Document control at Kutno usually passed off without trouble, so, as the train was approaching Poznan, I decided to remove my parcel from its hiding place but found that in front of the lavatory there was a queue of impatient passengers, stamping their feet in agony. I had to leave the train at Poznan without my N literature, furious but still remembering to note the number of the coach. On my return to Warsaw, I passed on the number to the people at the sidings in Warsaw, where there were many of "our" women among the cleaners. A few days later the parcel was delivered to Zbik's flat. It had traveled safety to Berlin and back to Warsaw.

The second adventure was much less funny. It also occurred at Poznan. On arrival I realized that I had lost my ticket. I was traveling on an Urlaubsschein, a furlough pass, and with such a document one received a free ticket in the booking office at the station in Warsaw. During the checks, the ticket was an additional proof of the authenticity of the pass. A feverish search in all my pockets produced nothing: it was certain that the ticket had disappeared. Standing at the exit, along with the ticket collector, there was usually a German policeman or the Gestapo. A declaration that a ticket was lost led invariably to an investigation. I would have to tell who I was visiting and where I was to stay the night. In my situation neither a false nor a true declaration was possible. In addition, what could I do with the underground literature?

On the platform there was a wooden shed that served as a waiting room for workmen going to their jobs in the vicinity of Poznan. I went in, and began to scan the faces. On instinct I selected a young man with a pleasant look. I asked him to come out to the platform with me and, without any introduction, said to him, "Look, I've just arrived from Warsaw and I've lost my ticket. My situation is such that I cannot risk any kind of interrogation. Do you understand me? I appeal to you as one Pole to another. As a workman you have a season ticket; you can pass through the checkpoint at will. Here is some money. Could you please buy me a platform ticket or better still a return ticket to Wrzesnia?"

The young man gave me a long and penetrating look. After some hesitation, he took the money and without a word went toward the booking office. After a while he returned with a ticket in his hand. He did not return to the shed, however, but followed me out. In the square in front of the station, when I thanked him warmly, he breathed a sigh of relief and spoke at last.

"I was afraid the whole time that it was a German trap. What if they had sent you? I nearly told you to go to the devil. Well, you were lucky. Good luck! And don't ever lose your ticket again."

Half an hour later, when I took off my railwayman's jacket, I saw that under it I was wearing a vest. I reached into the pocket and there I found my ticket.

In time Zbik and I perfected our methods. We realized that the safest way to travel was by the night military trains, the so-called *Sonderzuge* (specials) carrying soldiers on leave from the Eastern Front or from Germany to the front. Not even German civilians had access to these trains, but railwaymen on duty did. No tickets were necessary. One traveled singly or in twos, pretending that one had to take over a train or a locomotive at, say, Lodz or Torun. Zbik stole the necessary passes. On these there was space for the signature of the stationmaster who was sending out a conductor or an engine driver and the name of the station from which the train was to be collected. In another space there was room for a small rubber stamp with the name of the home station. Each station had its own stamp, and we were armed with a supply of these quite small stamps and an ink pad. The stamps were beautifully counterfeited. On departure from Warsaw-East one stamped the chit and signed and dated it; on arrival, say, at Katowice, one stamped it with that name and entered an illegible signature in the space for the stationmaster there.

In these ''specials'' we felt safer than in the streets of Warsaw. Not only the compartments but the corridors were full of rucksacks and sleeping, dead-tired soldiers, so that passing from one coach to another became impossible. Interrogation posed no threat. The mood of the soldiers was sullen, and no Gestapo would dare set up any kind of control. Anyone bold enough to awaken these people would be shot out of the train as from a gun and would end with a broken rib or two for his trouble.

We also discovered that traveling in the uniform of a Polish railwayman of the Ostbahn (i.e., the railway of the *General Gouvernement*) was safe within the prewar borders of Poland, but in Gdansk, Berlin, and Szczecin, or in Prussia or Silesia, the Polish uniform of an employee of the Ostbahn was too noticeable. Therefore, when undertaking those longer expeditions we decided to appear in the uniforms and with the documents of the Reichsbahn. Getting the uniforms was not difficult: the problem seemed to be a lack of knowledge of German, but Zbik and his mates explained to me that this did not matter. The railways in the Reich employed many so-called Volksdeutsche from Poland and the other occupied countries who had only recently joined the Volksliste and who spoke very little German. For greater safety, I was given a new identity card that was an accurate copy of that of a Volksdeutscher railwayman attached to the central depot, Warsaw-East, Adalbert Kozlowski. My identity card was an exact copy of his card. That identity card was later to save my life. Poor Kozlowski did not suspect that he had a double.

The first journey in German railway uniforms that Zbik and I made was to Torun and Bydgoszcz. Even after all the intervening years, I remember the atmosphere in those hours as though it were today. It was night when the *Sonderzug* left Warsaw-East. In the crowded railway car the loud snoring of sleeping soldiers resounded. As a precaution in the event of some mishap, we placed our literary cargo in the soldiers' knapsacks, which were lying on the floor.

The sleeping Germans did not suspect that in their knapsacks were several hundred thousand pamphlets and leaflets, every one of which would reach its target like a bullet, causing bloodless but painful damage. We laughed inwardly at the thought of these poisonous missives being sent along strange routes. Soldiers in barracks in Torun or Bydgoszcz would find in their lavatories issues of the satirical periodical *Der Klabautermann* ("the bogeyman"), an imitation of *Simplicissimus* or the military underground newspaper *Der Frontkämpfer*. It would be read with great interest because it was not an insignificant experience to have tangible evidence that in the Fatherland—yes, even in the Wehrmacht—people were beginning to rebel against war, against the Führer, against party bosses, and against the Gestapo with their comfortable lives. Every one of these publications, brilliantly conceived and written in a style suited to the taste of their intended readers, would plant a seed of doubt, rebellion, and agitation in the soul of the enemy which would grow when the fortunes of war began to turn against him. A soldier would show it to a trusted friend and then to a second and to a third friend. From then on, they would look in the same places to see whether there was something new there.

Most of that literature would go further, carried by self-sacrificing people; on their days off they would go to Berlin, Dresden, Hamburg, Munich. From there, by way of the German mail, our publications would go to selected addresses in the Reich. A German postal clerk would put on the stamps, a German letter carrier would distribute these underground publications without suspecting anything because the envelopes prepared and addressed in Warsaw were usually marked *Drucksache* ("printed matter"), *Buchhandlung* ("bookshop''), or something like that. An official opening a menu in a restaurant would be surprised to find inside a manifesto of the Rudolf Hess opposition within the Nazi Party. In the books, magazines, and newspapers to be sent to soldiers our pamphlets would be hidden. Those would travel in this way to Smolensk and Stalingrad, to Tobruk and Bengasi, or finally to the far north, to the garrisons in Norway. It is easy to imagine a soldier opening an *Illustrierte Zeitung*, sent from somewhere in Cologne, and finding inside of it *Der Durchbruch*, a pamphlet published by the German Socialist intelligentsia. He would find there ''the real truth'' about the scandals and abuses among officials in the central administration, the Party, and the military; about the intrigues, the ghastly supply situation, the arms production breakdown, and the true results of the Allied bombardments; he would find a whole mass of facts from which it would be apparent that the war had been lost, and that the longer it lasted the larger the losses and sufferings of Germany.

This unknown soldier to whom we now sent his ''primer'' would not believe a single word of this if he heard it from the mouth of the enemy, even from the BBC broadcasts. But how not to believe what his own people wrote, people who, at the risk of their own lives, were publishing these pamphlets somewhere in Cologne or Frankfurt? Suppose such a pamphlet fell into the hands of a fanatical Nazi. It is easy to imagine his reaction: here I am roasting in an overheated tank in this Libyan desert (or shivering with frostbitten hands and feet somewhere near Stalingrad), and there at home treachery is spreading and they're getting ready to put a knife into our backs.

Of course some would run to the authorities to give them such newspapers. So much the better. Such obliging citizens would be subjected to painful interrogation because the Gestapo would want to know where this abomination came from. They would not believe that it was found on a bench in a waiting room, in a park, in a canteen, in a restroom, or inside an ordinary newspaper. Then statements would be taken from the citizen; circulars would be sent out; menacing orders would be issued; letters would be censored; and searches made at the train stations. Civilians would be suspected. Thus one of our pamphlets in the hands of the Gestapo would create more confusion than one hundred dispersed among soldiers or ordinary civilians.

The tremendous source of satisfaction for us was the enthusiasm and support which our black propaganda evoked among people in our sphere of activity. We transported as many copies as we were able to carry without attracting attention, and they always complained that they did not get enough. This time they would be satisfied, we vowed. We had rubber stamps bearing slogans like "Hitler nieder—Frieden wieder!" ("Down with Hitler—Up with Freedom"), "Hitler Sturz—Deutschlands Freiheit!" ("Hitler's Fall—Germany's Freedom"), and "Gestapo an die Front" ("Gestapo to the Front"). A huge stamp reading "Wir scheissen auf Preussen!" ("We shit on the Prussians") was intended for our people in Vienna, as it was well known that Austrians could not stand Prussians. Those slogans would be stamped everywhere—on posts, on houses, inside books and newspapers sent to the front, and everywhere else possible. Posters reading "Nur für Deutsche" ("Germans Only") served a special purpose. They were stuck on lampposts in occupied cities to remind the Germans that, on the defeat of the Reich, these useful installations to illuminate streets were handy and could serve an entirely different purpose.

We spoke of these affairs throughout the entire journey. We found most fascinating an experience which we made into a big game, in which the stakes—as with the soldiers at the front—were one's own life and in which one ingeniously cheated his opponent and skillfully avoided danger. Now for an example. At the station in Torun we railway employees in German uniforms, surrounded as at all other stations in the Reich by Gestapo and SD (Sicherheitsdienst), pushed our way through fearlessly, probably not even reaching for our documents because who would detain a German railwayman on duty?

We left the station separately, Zbik walking on one side of the street and I, following him, on the other. I was highly amused to see Zbik straighten up at the sight of a German in uniform and stiffly raise his arm in a Nazi salute. A few minutes later, for the first time in my life, I had to do the same, replying "Heil Hitler" to the greeting of a railwayman walking toward me. Shortly afterward we met at our rendezvous point in Torun, the flat of a former non-commissioned officer called Leszczynski, and were given breakfast. Leszcz, as we nicknamed him, was the assistant to the local leader of Action N, another prewar artillery officer, Kazimierz Orientel.

Orientel was a clever and enterprising man. He was married to a German and with her help distributed our literature inside the Reich. Her family was somewhere in the Reich, and she could travel to and fro at will. Orientel's people planted leaflets in the local barracks, in military hospitals, on German military lorries, and in German offices—everywhere the reactions of readers could be observed. I made mental notes of the effectiveness of Action N, as I needed the information for periodic reports prepared by Leszcz for his chief, who in turn incorporated them into his reports for the commander-in-chief, from whose office they were passed on by courier or shortwave radio to headquarters in London. We realized that these reports were very important because they documented to the British the contribution the Poles were making to the war against Hitler.

Orientel was not an uncritical enthusiast of Action N. He assessed each pamphlet from the point of view of the Germans, whose way of thinking was familiar to him. He most valued our various "official" pronouncements. In the barracks at Torun young recruits who were sent to the Eastern Front were given short basic training. Orientel particularly liked the leaflet about frostbite, ostensibly signed by a Berlin physician, but in reality devised by Polish medical specialists in such a way that while it instructed recruits on how to avoid frostbite, it at the same time terrified them with its warning of the horrors and dangers of a Russian winter; it even recommended as essential various ointments that (we knew) were not available to the Wehrmacht. A desperate appeal to those at home by the soldiers in one of the infantry regiments on the Eastern Front served the same purpose. The authors of the appeal described the horrors of the winter and complained about the lack of warm clothing, while furs found their way exclusively to SS men and their mistresses. These two publications were the subject of discussion among the recruits, who did not hide their bitterness and their fears of what awaited them in Russia. Another "hit," Orientel said, was "The Ten Commandments for the National Socialist Front Soldier." The pamphlet urged soldiers who were party members to identify and denounce their non-party comrades.

I can't remember whether it was Orientel or another of our men who had the daring idea to check what the authorities, and especially the Gestapo, thought about our N publications and what they were saying about them. A trustworthy Volksdeutscher, who was a party member, went to the Gestapo with a proclamation of Action N sent to his address by post. To avert all suspicion, he took to the Gestapo not only the printed sheet itself but the envelope it came in. He asked innocently what the meaning of this was. In reply, he heard that this must be the work of these "red scoundrels" from Munich. He was reassured that the police were on their track and that they would be hanged any day now.

From Torun a lengthy journey led to Bydgoszcz, where Action N was run by two eighteen-year-old boys who worked at the local bakery. The hatred of the local Germans for Poles who remained in town was particularly violent, so our stay in that town was unusually short, a couple of hours or so. At night we would arrive at Deutsche Eylau in East Prussia, where a cousin of Zbik's, Ignacy Tucholski, the manager of a local butchershop, ran Action N. Tucholski found us accommodation in a former workers' club now occupied by some Polish girls imported as forced labor from the Poznan region. They craved the company of young Poles. A gramophone and some prewar records were found in the club, and, in spite of our fatigue from lack of sleep, we performed one more patriotic duty and danced until late that night.

Moving around in East Prussia was particularly dangerous, and Germans were frequently stopped and required to produce their documents. Our man at Marienburg warned us to walk about as little as possible and to leave the area as soon as our business was concluded. I thought that those unusual precautions were concocted by the local Gauleiter, Koch. Only after the war did I learn that Marienburg was not far from Hitler's headquarters.

Chapter 6

The quick expansion of Action N earned a mention in the quarterly report by "Kalina" (General Rowecki), sent to headquarters in London in October, 1942. The commander-in-chief of the Home Army reported: "Among the more important achievements of the past period has been the creation of new N outposts at Torun and in Silesia; these open up possibilities for sending pamphlets to the Reich itself, especially to Berlin, Heidelberg, etc. . . . . The problem of getting the material across the frontier of the *General Gouvernement* and providing regular supplies of suitable material has now been solved."

When the next distribution network had been established, I was promoted to the rank of second lieutenant. The promotion order was handed to me by Leszek and was written on a scrap of tissue paper signed by "Grot" (General Rowecki).* At the same time I met the chief of Action N, "Kowalik," who until then had been a slightly mysterious figure for me. At the appointed time he came to my room at Krolewska Street. A very tall man, almost seven feet, he seemed to me to look very much like the Romanian King Carol, whom I had seen at Sinaya before the war when I had a summer vacation job in Romania. "Kowalik" was his code name. I think this was in Septem-

---

*In order to confuse the Germans, General Rowecki used two code names, Grot and Kalina. All his radiograms to London were signed "Kalina"; his orders, proclamations, and the like within Poland were issued by "Grot."

ber 1942. He listened with visible satisfaction to my report about the progress of Action N in the western territories. To encourage me, I think, he gave me some information to show that our work was effective. From various points in the heart of the Reich, outposts of our intelligence service were sending secret enthusiastic reports about the appearance of a German underground press and about the appearance of symptoms of disintegration and resistance among civilians and soldiers. Rowecki passed on these intelligence reports to our superiors, sometimes with jocular remarks in the margin. Other evidence of their effectiveness came from letters between German soldiers in the East and their families. We had our men in the post office, and letters in transit to and from Germany were a valuable source of information about the morale of the armed forces and civilians in the Reich. N pamphlets were frequently mentioned.

At that time I must have been the only "railwayman" traveling under a false name and with documents that were partly counterfeit and partly stolen. Apart from Zbik, who was the most mobile and who went off to the west on every day off, our material was distributed by several real railwaymen: Klemens Szewczyk (code name "Korwin"), known by us simply as Klimek (a diminutive of his Christian name), a man called Sztajerowski and his son Miroslaw, and Tadeusz Rek.

The first victim in our team was poor Klimek. He was caught in unknown circumstances at the frontier station of Poraj near Czestochowa, although it was said that he was shot when trying to escape. Fortunately, Klimek's loss did not have any dire repercussions for the rest of us, although N pamphlets were found on him, but we felt his loss very deeply.

The small group of people who met in Zbik's flat were like members of a family. The return of one was awaited by the others with deep anxiety, especially when he was overdue. The object of the greatest concern was usually Zbik, who tended to arrive one, two, or even three days late, dealing on his way with matters not included in our strict program. Against orders he often undertook jobs for other underground units. I am still amazed that he was not given the sack by the railway authorities for his constant absences or latenesses. But Zbik knew how to charm his German supervisors, and the brave old railwayman Roman Makiela used to cover for him. However, I was most impressed by the behavior of Zbik's wife, Zofia. This young girl, barely twenty years old, spent many sleepless nights and dreary hours waiting for Zbik. When he left on a trip she parted from him without tears, with a smile, a fierce kiss, and a sign of the cross on his brow. Frequently it seemed that this time Zbik would not return. Days of unnerving waiting passed, and he was not back. I took the streetcar out to his apartment every day to ask his wife for news from him, and each time I returned more dejected and anxious. He would finally appear—care-free as usual, smiling, and completely unmoved by our anxiety and reproaches.

Our use of professional railway workers involved some difficulties. First of all, most Polish railwaymen from the Warsaw Regional Headquarters worked their trains only to a station near the frontier: Kutno, Nowy Dwor, Lodz, Poznan, Sosnowiec, or Katowice. There they handed over their trains to Reichsbahn teams. The Poles were not always alloted trains that were going to our destinations, and not everybody wanted to, or could, depart on his day off with a leave permit. Then too, if we used that method of border crossing too often, it might attract the attention of the authorities and end badly. I did not wish to expand our small team of people too much. They all knew one another, and the exposure of one could result in the arrest of all, but we needed more people who would be entirely at our disposal. I therefore decided to recruit volunteers from outside, people whose expenses would be covered by the organization and who would be available night and day, not from Warsaw or the *General Gouvernement* area but from the territories incorporated into the Reich. They would know conditions there and could move about freely in those territories.

Zbik immediately suggested that we start by approaching one of his pals, Wos Sobieszczyk, who lived in Naklo. He was sure the man would agree, so we took a spare railwayman's uniform and a blank identity card with us so that there would be no trouble in getting him to Warsaw. We left all these accessories with Leszczynski at Torun and took the train to Naklo. It was nightfall when we reached Wos's parents' house somewhere in a Naklo suburb. Wos was not at home. The Sobieszczyks had refused to sign the Volksliste, so Wos had had to take a manual job some distance away from the small town. He had to take a workers' train, and, in order not to be late (for being late for work one could have been sent to a concentration camp), he had to get up at 4 A.M. and did not get home until late at night.

While waiting for him, we talked to his parents. I learned that Wos was their only son, and sole wage-earner in the family, and the apple of their eye. He was twenty. The couple looked more like his grandparents than his parents, and his father was obviously too old to work. I again felt as uneasy as I had when visiting Zbik's flat for the first time, shortly after his marriage. What will these people say when they realize that we have come to take their only son away?

Wos returned late, so tired and sleepy that he was unable to talk to us. We would have to get up the next morning at four to talk to him. It was bitterly cold in the room, so we both slept on Wos's bed in our uniforms, while the old people slept in the kitchen. At three I was awakened by a whispered conversation between Zbik and Wos. Zbik was speaking in an almost imperative tone.

"We are from the Polish forces. That man is my commander. We came to take you to Warsaw to join us. You will be given a uniform and documents, and you will smuggle various things into the Reich. My boss will tell you the rest. Will you come with us?"

"I will."

I interrupted the conversation. "Don't worry about your parents. Our organization will take care of them. They will get enough money to live on. We will also take care of them if, God forbid, anything should happen to you. But you must think carefully about this proposal. Once you have disappeared from here, there will be no return."

"I know," said Wos. "I'll come with you." His mind seemed quite made up. "But what will I do if I am caught by those bastards? You don't know what you might do when they start pulling your nails out."

"You will be given a little thing like this." Zbik produced from his pocket a pill covered with some stuff like rubber. "If they catch you and you feel that you won't be able to stand the things they might do to you, you put it in your mouth, bite through it, and that will be it; you won't feel anything anymore."

"What will your parents say," I asked, "when you tell them that you are going to Warsaw with us?"

"They won't say anything," said Wos after a moment's thought, "because I won't say anything. They will think that I've gone to work as usual. I'll write a few words, and they will find the letter when we are on our way. It is better like that."

We had some hot corn coffee, and then the three of us set off for the station. Before leaving the house, Wos kissed his mother's hand and his father's cheek. He must have done this every day because the old couple did not suspect anything. We walked to the station in silence. Wos did not look back. In the train he kept silent. He smiled for the first time only when, a few hours later, he looked at himself in the uniform of a German railwayman in a long mirror in the Leszczynskis' flat in Torun.

Wos proved to be a most valuable recruit. He seemed not to know what fear was. This lean, phlegmatic individual had no nerves. For carrying the leaflets, most couriers had suitcases with false bottoms or other often primitive hiding places, but Wos would tie them up in a parcel with the string so tightly knotted that one could not untie it. Once he was carrying papers not on a "special" but on an ordinary passenger train, as he wanted to get out at a small station where the "special" did not stop. Some Bahnschutz men (special railway police) rushed into the compartment looking for smuggled goods and ordered the passengers to open their suitcases. One of them noticed the parcel tied with a string.

"What is inside it?" he asked.

"Papers," answered Wos very quietly, not budging from his seat.

The man reached for the parcel and tried to untie it. Soon he reached for his bayonet to cut the string. At that moment Wos rose to his feet.

"How dare you ruin my parcel!" he roared in German. "You don't believe that there are papers inside, so I'll show you." He tore the wrapping so that one could see that the parcel contained sheafs of pamphlets, newspapers, or leaflets. He shoved it under the German's nose. "I told you there are papers inside and not pork fat," he shouted angrily. Not giving the German a chance to look at the papers, he threw the parcel onto the rack and resumed his seat. The Bahnschutz man hesitated for a second, then put his bayonet back into its sheath and moved on to the next compartment.

One area where the work of Action N was being developed most satisfactorily was in the region of Lodz, and we had "Gertruda" to thank for that. Gertruda was the code name for Major Zygmunt Janke, who, when I first met him, was AK chief of military intelligence for the Lodz district. The Lodz district had a bad name at headquarters in Warsaw as the most dangerous area for underground work in Poland and in incorporated territories. One disaster followed another, and no commander lasted for long. The first of them had to leave Lodz in September, 1940. His successor for security reasons spent most of his time in Warsaw. Officers who stayed in the city were betrayed one after the other. In the end, the only one who survived was Gertruda.

Janke from the start impressed me as a strong personality, a man well above the average for a prewar staff officer. He had an oval face, with hair cut short in the German style. He spoke quite rapidly, in short sentences and almost in a whisper. It is possible that this had become his conspiratorial style. He expressed himself clearly, concisely, and logically. I sensed in him a leader who knew exactly what he wanted and how to come to a decision quickly, an impression which was fully confirmed in our later work and contacts.

I arrived in Lodz working a goods train. I got off at Lodz-Chojny, where there was no control, and met Gertruda at an appointed place in the street. We talked while walking through narrow alleys, and I quickly understood why Lodz was so dangerous to all underground organizations. In cities like Warsaw, denunciations to the Gestapo were rare, and one could always count on strangers for help. In Lodz things were difficult. For centuries it had been inhabited by ethnic Polish-speaking Germans hostile to the local Poles. There was no separate German quarter, and this made it easy for the Germans to spy on the Poles, who frequently found themselves victims of informers. An added difficulty was that the city had no proper sewer system, so that our apartment block had to share one communal privy in the courtyard. It was always best to stay indoors so as not to attract attention, but in Lodz a stranger had to walk to the lavatory in full view of the German tenants.

Gertruda arranged that my only contact would be with him and with his chief of operations, who was not only a Volksdeutscher but a party member. On the instructions of the organization, he had declared himself to be an ethnic German at the beginning of the occupation and had subsequently joined the NSDAP. His name was Jan Lipsz ("Anatol"). Staying in his house involved no risk. He worked as a foreman in a textile factory and even appeared in Nazi uniform on occasion.

After assuming the role of a German, Anatol formed his own

small organization at the beginning of the occupation, called the "National Legion." Action N members in Lodz were recruited largely from Anatol's group. Until then I had been dealing with Poles who became Volksdeutsche under duress and who were treated with mistrust by ethnic Germans. Now for the first time I had direct contact with a man who not only was thought to be German but also was a member of the Nazi Party. He had useful contacts among genuine local Germans, and he was, as I would soon discover, a man of considerable intelligence.

Gertruda established several rigorous conditions dictated by the requirements of secrecy and by the specific situation in Lodz. Above all, I had to promise that I would myself bring the publications intended for them, and not rely on others. In the eventuality that I did have to send a courier, however, he was to leave the packet at the designated safe house. My own contacts were to be confined exclusively to Anatol and Gertruda. We agreed upon a warning system in the event of a raid in Warsaw, Lodz, or the surrounding area.

I was returning to Warsaw that day, thoroughly convinced that Lodz would play a key role in our psychological offensive. Action N men in Lodz did not limit themselves to the distribution of materials from Warsaw. They had their own printing facilities and began to produce their own literature as well as reprinting what I brought. Anatol, exploiting his knowledge of the German community, developed another activity, "S," which consisted of writing anonymous letters to Germans in senior positions, containing at least a grain of truth, about various commercial frauds, love affairs, etc., in order to cause trouble. Quarrels and sometimes fights soon broke out among the Germans. For his silence, the writer of the anonymous letter asked for money. "S" also sent out hundreds of fake demands for payment of taxes and fictitious notices of parcels waiting for collection at post offices, the latter usually addressed to police and Gestapo officers. As a result, rows broke out about "lost" parcels, all the more violent the higher the rank of the addressee.

As we pretended that Action N literature emanated from German organizations, it seemed to me that the greatest coup would be to find a real German center of discontent and establish contact with it. I rejected the view that there were no good Germans and that all of them without exception were criminals. The N leaflets were received not only with interest but frequently with enthusiasm, and the reaction indicated that their readers welcomed them. It seemed logical that somewhere some German resistance cells existed. I persuaded Anatol that his next task should be to find out whether there were such cells. Whenever I came to Lodz to meet him, I would ask whether he had found any traces of such opposition. Anatol did not like to be unable to deliver the goods, so one day he declared: "Since we cannot find a German underground cell, we will organize one ourselves."

I laughed, thinking this was a joke, but it was not. A month later he declared triumphantly that he had succeeded in creating an authentic German underground organization. He selected the Kraftfahrtheimatpark (motor vehicles depot) in Lodz for his experiment. Anatol knew the soldiers who served as guards there, sent them N literature, and observed their reactions. When it was clear that none of the recipients had informed the Gestapo, he set to work.

Each of five selected men received a letter signed by an organization called "Der deutsche Demokratenbund" (German Democratic Union) or something similar. This letter said that the recipient had been observed for a long time, that his character and views were such that an underground movement considered him to be trustworthy, and that it wished him to perform an important task. He was asked to come to an appointed place carrying a newspaper in his left hand. There he would be met by an emissary, who was minutely described. No "emissary" turned up at the appointed place, but Anatol was there in hiding. He of course suggested to each soldier a different day and hour. Only one did not respond to this invitation. Those who, after a long and futile wait, seemed disappointed as they went away received a second letter a few days later thanking them for coming and saying that that time it had been only a test.

The next time Anatol arranged a meeting between two "oppositionists," then gradually put each in contact with a whole group. From his hiding place he controlled them like marionettes pulled by strings and played with them like frolicsome "Dyzio,"* but he did so in a way so diabolically clever that the "conspirators," whom he supplied with slogans, paper, and instructions, obediently followed his orders for placing pamphlets in an assigned hollow tree or in a hiding

*A mischievous, trouble-making child from a well-known Polish story.

place in one of the public boat docks, and even supplied some small arms and ammunition.

After six months this game ended in disaster and the arrest of some of the soldiers. At least twice as many were sent to the Eastern Front. We never found out whether discovery was by chance or was the work of an informer.

The experiment seemed to show that the establishment of a resistance movement in Germany was theoretically possible. Probably many people would have been willing to join, but conditions were different than in Poland. A mass underground movement can develop only where the police have difficulty in infiltrating the community. The Nazis had created such a gulf between the occupation forces and the population in Poland that they had virtually no access to Poles. The number of their agents, informers, and traitors was too small for the Gestapo to suppress the conspiracy effectively. It involved a substantial segment of society, and the great majority of the people constituted a close and solid block.

It was different in Germany, where the Nazis relied on party members and those who were sympathizers either from conviction or opportunism. The Gestapo had millions of volunteers who would inform on their neighbors, colleagues, superiors and inferiors on their own initiative. During the war in the Reich a neighbor could be the greatest plague. In the then-popular *Illustrierte Zeitung* I once found a cartoon typifying this state of affairs. It showed Our Lord ushering Adam and Eve into Paradise and encouraging the young pair with the words, ''nicely furnished — no neighbors.'' In such conditions there was no question of organizing a massive underground movement. The only possibility was a conspiracy among generals or politicians, limited to a few people who completely trusted one another.

For quite some time I had longed to obtain German telephone books and the latest edition of the German *Who's Who* or, better, the list of members of the NSDAP, an enormous volume. The latter seemed beyond reach. The Party register contained names, registration numbers, biographies, addresses, and positions of Party members. It was, of course, a publication reserved for selected party offices and dignitaries. Anatol realized the vital importance of such booty for our work. He started by bringing me volume after volume of telephone books from localities all over Germany, which I duly carted to Warsaw. One day I was speechless with joy and admiration when he proudly placed before me a huge volume, the register of the members of the NSDAP. Up to this time our publications had been mailed at random. Now we could introduce some order and a rational plan for the dispatch of our literature.

In the National Library of Warsaw, closed to the public in the war years, I was able to study detailed statistics of elections to the Reichstag in the years 1932 and 1933 (in the latter year there were two elections). I roped in a few colleagues, and we began to study these statistics and compare the numbers. Eventually, we produced a schematic map showing the political configuration in the Reich by area. In the first place, it was important to determine where the number of votes for the Nazi Party had been the smallest, where the opposition seemed strongest, and what political coloration that opposition had had in a given district.

In spite of the shifting of votes in Hitler's favor, comparisons showed some stability in traditions and political sympathies in the various regions. We thought that these political sympathies might have survived, even after ten years, so using our political map of the Reich in the early thirties we now directed our literature to places that were probably the most sensitive and vulnerable. Even more important, we could tailor the political opinions expressed in our papers to traditional local sympathies. Thus the leaflets passed off as publications from a Social Democratic organization were directed to that part of Germany where the SD had had most adherents before 1933, while the Hess opposition material was sent where the largest number of votes had been cast for the NSDAP. I presented Leszek with a plan of action thought through in detail. From this moment on, we were to concentrate systematically on selected objectives. The addresses of individuals were taken from local directories. Leaflets were to be directed to towns of 20,000 to 100,000 inhabitants. Large cities with populations of more than 100,000 were entirely ignored, on the basis that in a small town every item of news travels quickly, while in a large metropolitan area news is readily lost. The "postal" bombardment of the towns selected was to be carried out simultaneously from numerous points in Germany, the number depending upon the number of pamphlet distributors it was possible to send out. All actions were to be carried out at the same time and very quickly — in a period of no more than three days.

We assumed that the checks in the post offices and the searches

EMORY & HENRY LIBRARY

would begin three days after the first discovery. The concentrated bombardment of the same town from various points in Germany over a short period of time was intended to create a sensation and at the same time to establish the conviction that the underground movement was powerful and widespread. We calculated that the number of pamphlets to be sent to one place should correspond to 1 percent of its population; e.g., 200 copies for a town with a population of 20,000.

We knew that the German security forces used special equipment to prevent the use of the post for distribution of subversive literature. Suspected letters were weighed on precision scales, and a bell was set off automatically whenever the weight corresponded exactly to that of any previously discovered control letter or package. In order to defeat that system, we merely used a large assortment of envelopes of various sizes and weights. The envelopes and the enclosures were sent to our points of distribution in the incorporated territories and the Reich, from Vienna to Gdansk, with detailed instructions and a precise date for mailing.

What mattered now was to see and assess the results of this strategy. Through the intercession of Leszek, we asked our intelligence from which city in the industrial part of Germany we could obtain an analysis of results. In reply, intelligence gave Leszek the names of several towns, from which we selected Munich-Gladbach. The next three-day assault was therefore directed there. We had to wait a long time for a detailed report, but the initial reports were encouraging. The bombardment of Munich-Gladbach had created the expected sensation, and for three days N literature was the subject of many conversations, conjectures, and inquiries.

A certain number of addressees had loyally taken the letters to the police. The Gestapo, security services, and military counterintelligence were alerted. The police were troubled about those who did not turn in the pamphlets. People were stopped in the streets and searched, and house searches were conducted. Many people were arrested, though the majority were later released. The post office ordered all letters opened, but as we had hoped, these controls were introduced too late to stop our mail getting to their destinations.

The party *Who's Who* proved to have a special use. Shortly before we got it, I was put in contact with a man in Cracow who was working in a printing establishment. After the bombing of a large factory of bond paper in the Reich, the production of certain station-

ery used by the NSDAP in internal correspondence had been transferred to the area of the *General Gouvernement*. This stationery, for the
the most part, was meticulously accounted for. The volunteer who
approached me maintained that he and his partners could steal a certain number of blanks, each with an official heading, a watermark,
and an embossed stamp. This stationery we used to post false notifi-
cations of briefings for Party officials. In selecting the names we were
guided not by rank but by function. We usually selected directors of
large factories, whose time was particularly valuable from the point of
view of the German war effort. For example, Herr Director "X" at
Essen, Party and SA member, would receive a message that he had to
present himself in uniform at a briefing in Vienna. The date of the
alleged meeting was close enough to exclude the possibility of a letter
of acknowledgment. And, on the other hand, some important per-
sonage in Vienna received instructions, on an official party form the
authenticity of which could not raise any doubt, the order to present
himself in Hamburg.

In this way it was possible to set in motion at least fifty Hitler
officials. It is easy to imagine their faces after they had traveled several hundred miles, registered at their destination, and then found
out that nobody knew anything about any briefing.

These were to be my last activities for Action N. Before long a
new chapter was to begin.

Chapter 7

The situation of people wanted by the Gestapo was not easy. They had to use false identity cards and work cards, and in case of arrest these represented a serious danger. The greatest difficulty was to find somewhere to live because a constant change of residence increased the danger. In this respect I was much luckier than many members of the underground. I could lead a double life, legal and illegal. My cover job in the Housing Administration proved to be most valuable. I was not tied to specific office hours and did not have to spend my time behind a desk or visit the tenants daily. Once every fortnight I went to the central office of the National Economy Bank to deposit the rent money received, to hand in my ledger of credits and debits, and to obtain permission for large repairs or investments. An absence of a few days did not cause any comment, and if need be, a school friend, who was also a housing administrator, could deputize for me. I did not tell him anything about my expeditions, but he must have guessed that I was involved in some underground activity.

I changed my identity in Zbik's apartment. The identity card and work card in my real name were left behind. After carefully discarding everything that might connect a certain young intellectual with a certain railwayman, I started for Praga, on the other side of the Vistula. When I exchanged my civilian clothing for an Ostbahn or a Reichsbahn uniform, I ceased to be Zdzislaw Jezioranski, and I changed, according to necessity, into Jan Kwiatkowski or Adalbert Kozlowski.

Zbik's wife would pull out from the hiding place under the floor identity papers, stamps, and various other articles needed by a railwayman on duty. If I were going to Silesia or deep into the Reich I took the identity card made out on authentic stationery with all the data for Adalbert Kozlowski, who was a real train conductor, as I have said. (I knew nothing about poor Kozlowski except that he was a recently registered Volksdeutscher one year older than I, born at Zgierz, and knowing hardly any German. This last detail was most important in my case.)

As I mentioned earlier, ability to speak German was not necessary as long as one sat in the train compartment. I usually pretended to be asleep. In the night "specials" everybody slept anyway. None of the dead-tired soldiers showed any desire for conversation. Complications began only during the wait for trains on platforms. I had not realized how many people ask railwaymen questions—what time does such and such a train depart, what platform, is it running late, etc., etc. One day in the Reich a passenger became suspicious because this railwayman in German uniform did not know any German. He must have reported the matter because a short while later a policeman asked to see my identity card. I showed him the service Ausweis of Adalbert Kozlowski. For this eventuality, I had ready the explanation that I had only recently received the Volksliste and had not yet had time to learn my "native tongue." There were many such bakery-fresh Germans about. The policeman took my documents and me to the office of the stationmaster. From there an official telephoned to the personnel department of the head office of the railways. All Kozlowski's papers were in order, and I was released with apologies.

Although my mother and brother realized that my sudden disappearances and returns were connected with underground work, I tried not to tell them any more than I needed to. In the case of a bad break it was safer for them not to know too much. I knew that my brother was also engaged in secret work, but I did not ask for details.

One of the most unusual visitors to my apartment at 6 Krolewska at that time was my English teacher. At the beginning of 1942 I met in the street a friend from Poznan University, who had begun to give me English lessons just before the war. "Listen," he whispered.

"I have something for you. Would you like to learn English from a real Englishman?"

"How do you come to have such a person in Warsaw?" I asked.

"He was taken prisoner in France and escaped from a POW camp in Poland. We placed him with a Polish family, and he has been given Lithuanian papers, but he must earn some money."

I agreed at once. Thomas Muir was not an Englishman but a Scotsman, something he stressed very strongly when we met. Tom could not speak Polish, and my English was practically nonexistent; perhaps this is why the classes went so well. He was an electrical engineer and did not have any teaching experience, but necessity overcame these handicaps. Lessons began with Tom pointing to an object, giving me its name in English, and then writing the word on a piece of paper. The next day I had to repeat to him the words I had learned. The daily dose was thirty English words. After a few months we could exchange simple sentences. I would never have guessed that those lessons would be needed so soon. Two years later, when Anthony Eden asked, at the beginning of his conversation with an emissary from Warsaw, where and when I learned English, I answered: "In Warsaw, not long ago, from a Scotsman from Airdrie by Glasgow who escaped from captivity." Eden laughed and said, "I cannot detect any Scots accent in your English." True, Tom could not impose any Scots pronunciation on me: I spoke English with a pure Polish accent. The important thing was that, thanks to Tom, Eden and other important people to whom I had to talk later were able to understand what I was trying to say to them.

In spite of the occupation, life in the Polish community continued as normally as possible. Politicians held meetings and indulged in complicated intrigues; underground tribunals passed sentence and meted out punishment; the AK was busy with its underground actions and was preparing for an uprising against the Germans; underground universities and schools awarded degrees. In that world, separated from the occupier and his organs of oppression by an invisible wall, an unfettered freedom of speech and democracy reigned. The country lived by faith in the Allies, in Churchill, Roosevelt, and Sikorski; it rejoiced in Hitler's first defeats in the east and in Africa, and—trying to forget the daily reality of arrests and executions, of death camps at Auschwitz and Majdanek—it lived with a vision of a sunny future.

Hatred of the Germans, a desire to fight them, and most of all nostalgia for the loss of the independent Polish state did not leave much room in the souls of ordinary people for anything else. Prewar political and social antagonisms were suspended temporarily. The Germans personified all evil. The Allies, by contrast, represented the ideals of justice, truth, and freedom. The fact that radio news from London was usually the only source of information played a considerable part in this attitude. The Polish government and the commander-in-chief were symbols of independent Poland, and as such not subject to criticism. As with the English sovereign, the government in London reigned but did not rule. Sikorski's orders were sacrosanct. Without his authority many political organizations with some military arms would not have surrendered themselves so easily to the control of the ZWZ.

The Germans tried to force the hostile population to submit through the use of total terror, disregarding all political methods. Terror exercised on the principle of the collective responsibility of both the active and passive segments of the community increased social cohesion and the feeling of mutual solidarity by its very nature. Thus the Germans themselves created ideal conditions for underground organization on a scale unparalleled in any other occupied country. The German intelligence service knew, of course, that in the occupied territories several radio stations maintained daily contact with the Allies; they knew about the movement of couriers in both directions, about the drops of arms, ammunition, and men, about the extent of sabotage and diversion, and about the preparations for a rising behind the front. They caught individuals, including some leaders, but until the end of the war the Gestapo, the German army, and the police were in fact largely helpless in the face of the underground movement.

The invaders proved to be rotten psychologists. Because of the constant escalation of repression, terror lost its power to terrorize. People simply stopped being afraid because they had nothing much to lose. The mass extermination of the Jews and the liquidation of the ghettos seemed to be the turning point. The rest of the population began to realize that their turn would come next.

During the occupation I witnessed only a few atrocity scenes with my own eyes. I remember vividly the corpses covered with newspapers lying on the ghetto sidewalks, as one saw them when it was still possible to ride through the Jewish district in a "transit" streetcar to the suburb of Powazki.* These were mostly people who had died of starvation or typhus. The bodies were collected twice a day, like garbage, by the street-cleaning department. Nor could I forget the sight of men and women arrested by the Gestapo and bundled into prison vans with blood-stained sacks over their heads.

The scene that made the strongest impression on me, however, occurred one day early in 1943 at the district court of Leszno, where I was summoned as a witness in some housing dispute; the magistrates were Polish. The building had an entrance from Ogrodowa Street on the "Aryan" side, but the windows overlooked the Jewish quarter of Leszno.

After the first deportation, the ghetto population was reduced to about 70,000. On that particular day the deportations to the death camp at Treblinka were being resumed after a long interval. From the third-floor courtroom we could hear frightful shrieks from the street below—the voices of men, women, and children mingled in an outcry of bitter lamentation. The loudest shouts were the hoarse outcries of the SS men: "Los! Los! Aber schnell!"

I pushed forward to the window and saw a crowd of Jews being herded along the middle of the street, probably toward the branch railroad line at Stawki. They were half-running, jostling one another, harried from both sides by SS men with long whips. Their tormentors had rolled up their long sleeves and wore their caps pushed well back. They seemed like drunken men, with an expression of animal excitement on their sweating faces. Along the pavement two old Jews with much toil were pushing a handcart full of sick people. No sound was heard from these; their bodies dangled limply, like dolls. Suddenly a well-dressed woman with a baby in her arms detached herself from the throng and tried to reach a Gestapo man on the sidewalk, making signs to him and waving a roll of banknotes—a last, desperate attempt to save herself and the child. I heard the swish of the whip; the woman staggered and dropped the child, who rolled along the

*The ghetto was already surrounded by a wall, and the Jews were forbidden to leave it without a permit under penalty of death.

106

pavement. At that moment an old Jewish woman raised her hands and eyes to heaven and screamed at the top of her voice like one possessed: "Hitler, may grass grow on the walls of your house!" I turned my head away and stepped back from the window, not wishing to see what would happen.

In the middle of the courtroom was a table covered with green baize, and on it a crucifix. The judge behind the table—an old, distinguished-looking man with a dry, wrinkled face—was rummaging through a pile of papers. The room was full of people waiting for various cases to be heard.

Continuing his examination, the judge addressed a witness: "Did you see the accused pick up the sack?"

"Yes, your honor. I was just going by on my bicycle."

"Did he pick it up on the street or in the courtyard?"

This was evidently an important legal point. It was a sack of wheat, sugar, or something of the kind, and the question was whether it had been found or stolen. Meanwhile, just outside the window. . . .

Suddenly, there was a burst from a tommygun, followed shortly by another. There was a crash of broken glass, and more shouting. The judge stopped looking at his papers, and the courtroom fell silent. The old man behind the table, facing the crucifix, closed his eyes and sighed heavily. Here he was dispensing justice and deciding a case about a sack of wheat, while outside the window people were being murdered.

The old woman's curious curse, "may grass grow on the walls of your house," came back to my mind years later, in the summer of 1952, when I visited the ruins of Hitler's villa at Berchtesgaden, blown up by the Americans. The bathroom walls had been faced with expensive tiles, and the grass was now growing luxuriantly between them.

Chapter 8

*B*y the early spring of 1943 the existing machinery of Action N
was running of its own momentum, and I felt that it was time to look
for new ideas. In a conversation with Leszek I put forth the idea of
setting up special distribution centers in the Baltic ports of Gdynia
and Gdansk whose task would be, apart from distributing our stuff in
German warships and U-boats, supplying pamphlets to Swedish
sailors. There were many Swedish ships in these ports bringing in
iron ore and returning with coal. Sweden was a neutral country living
in fear of sharing the fate of her neighbors Norway and Denmark.
Suppose copies of the "German underground pamphlets" reached
Sweden? They would create a journalistic sensation and a considerable public stir. I could see the headlines: "Opposition in the Reich
Raises Its Head" or "German Social Democracy Establishes Its Own
Underground Press." The more Swedish faith in the Reich's victory
weakened, the better for the Allies.

Leszek accepted my idea. Two days later I went with Zbik to
Gdynia. It seemed that he had friends everywhere; in Gdynia he
sought out the family of Jan Zgoda, where we could spend the night
and establish our base. The family consisted of parents and their two
daughters. As a boy during World War I, old Zgoda had been con-
scripted for the German navy. Between the wars he specialized in the
repair of ships' boilers. This saved him from deportation from the
Baltic coast when the Germans invaded. He had refused to sign the

Volksliste, and that usually meant deportation to the *General Gouvernement*. I decided not to distribute through him but to keep him in reserve as a possible future asset.

In Gdynia and Gdansk we found people to undertake the tossing of the pamphlets onto German and Swedish ships. Zbik reached Szczecin and Kolobrzeg and even there got ordinary people working on the waterfront involved in the action. The following brief reference is found in an Action N report radioed to London at the end of 1942: "Among the most important achievements during the reported period belongs the organization of N cells in Gdansk, Gdynia, and Szczecin. These cells direct the distributions to German warships and cargo ships and to others [Swedish and Finnish]. Recently, pamphlets have been planted on the ship *Servegebel*, on its way to Sweden, as well as on a munitions ship going to Finland."

While working in the Baltic area we made a discovery which was to change the course of my war career. We learned from Zgoda that a number of Polish workmen employed to load boats used to stow away to Sweden. The Gestapo knew about this, and before putting to sea every vessel was searched with the help of police dogs. Those refugees who were lucky escaped across the Baltic.

Immediately after my return to Warsaw, I told Leszek that I was ready to go to Sweden and then to London in order to establish contact and cooperation with the British, who were conducting "black propaganda," mostly through the radio stations "Pas-de-Calais" and "Atlantic." I had been interested in the monitoring of these stations for some time. The British had infinitely greater technical capabilities than we, and also had acquired an enormous amount of information from German prisoners. We, for our part, had a considerable organizational network in enemy territory. The establishment of direct cooperation might open up new horizons for Action N. Of course, after completing my mission, I was ready to return to Poland either by the sea-and-land route or, if this proved impossible, by parachute.

Leszek passed my proposal higher up. A few days later I received a message from "Zaloga," a cell whose function at the headquarters in Warsaw was to maintain liaison by courier with, and to transmit mail to, our military authorities in London. On the day and hour arranged through intermediaries, I rang the bell of a flat on Widok Street, where I was to meet a Zaloga representative called

Seweryn. A small man with dark hair combed straight back opened the door for me.

"Did you place an ad in the paper that you have women's astrakhan fur coats to sell?" I asked.

"Yes, but I advertised sealskins, not astrakhans."

After the exchange of these passwords we came to the point. Seweryn was interested in my proposal. Our headquarters in London had a base in Stockholm that passed on the intelligence mail from Warsaw to London. Until the autumn of 1942 this had been done by Swedish businessmen, who could travel from Stockholm to Warsaw. Unfortunately, that quick route to headquarters had been blocked. The southern route through France was cumbersome and communication took several months. Seweryn suggested that I should try to re-establish a route to Sweden in both directions via Gdynia or Gdansk and organize a regular "mail" and courier service to "Anna," the base in Stockholm.

"Of course," I said. "I'll willingly undertake that task on condition that I be allowed to go to London from Stockholm in order to set up a liaison with the British for Action N, through our General Staff, naturally."

"That decision cannot be made by us," said Seweryn. "Our task is to organize couriers' routes and mail drops. For us your task ends in Stockholm."

"The chance of visiting the London headquarters is a condition of my trip."

"I repeat, that is outside my control. Sending a courier to London requires Grot's agreement. We would prefer you to return by the same route, exploring it in both directions."

I left Seweryn in a somewhat irritated state of mind. The journey from Warsaw across the Baltic to Stockholm was an enterprise bristling with danger. On the other hand, I imagined a leap from Stockholm to London as an ordinary business trip. Since the fall of France the eyes of all Poland were fixed on London. To get to London was like getting to heaven. Why turn back when I was so near this goal?

I wrote a report supporting my request to continue my expedition from Stockholm to London and handed it to Leszek, asking him to pass it higher up. No answer came, and it seemed that the project would have to be abandoned. But eventually Seweryn organized a meeting with a man whose code name he did not disclose. He was about fifty and seemed to be a regular officer. In the course of our conversation I decided that he worked in intelligence. He appealed to me not to create difficulties and not to delay preparations for my trip to Stockholm. "Don't disparage the task given you by Zaloga. You have a good chance of getting to your destination quickly and of passing on mail containing military information of great importance. We are sending microfilms by several routes,* but your route should be the fastest. We could have sent somebody else, but you are experienced, you should have your own methods of crossing the frontier, and you have contacts on the coast."

He illustrated his argument with an example. Though important army information sent by short-wave could reach its destination in a matter of a few days, including coding and decoding time, not everything could be sent by radio. A few months earlier the AK got important intelligence regarding the location of anti-aircraft artillery around some kind of unusually important target. I could imagine, he said, how much difficulty, effort, and risk that required. Unfortunately, it took three months for these important plans and sketches to reach London. In that length of time the Germans had changed the position of the batteries.

Again I explained that this had nothing to do with my reaching London. In the end it was decided that I should not delay preparation for my journey until a decision was taken. I was waiting for an opportunity to get on a Swedish boat in the port of Gdynia. I might have to wait in Gdynia for several weeks, and every day spent waiting would be dangerous for a stranger from Warsaw. Seweryn therefore decided to reduce the risk by sending in a woman courier from Zaloga known as "Hilda." She had lived in Gdansk before the war, had worked in the Polish-British bank, spoke German like a native, could move easily in the coastal region, and had experience as a courier between Warsaw and the coast. I entrusted her with details of my contacts, with the exception of the name and address of Zgoda, which I held in reserve in case of trouble. Hilda had her own backup in the person of Maria Pyttel. Maria's home had for a long time been a hideout for

*The overseas communication system included Polish bases and outposts in, among others, Stockholm, Budapest, Bucharest, Constantinople, Cairo, Swiss Bern, Marseille, Paris, and Lisbon.

Zaloga. Hilda was to notify us in a predetermined way, by postcard mailed to a post office box, when our people succeeded in locating an appropriate ship, gained the cooperation of a Swedish crew member, and had everything ready for hiding and protecting the stowaway.

From Seweryn I obtained an identity card as a workman at the port of Gdynia (renamed Gotenhafen by the Germans) in the name of Jan Kwiatkowski, which entitled me to enter the dock area. At my briefing by Kowalik I received a mass of instructions. I was asked to obtain photographs of the activities of Polish forces in the West and other suitable material for the underground press, and to pass on various requests to headquarters.

I wanted to laugh when I met Hilda for the first time: the name suited her so admirably. I saw before me a typical stout German woman, dressed in a manner characteristic of the *Herrenvolk*. She did not need a German identity card—her appearance was quite enough.

After Hilda's departure I anxiously awaited the arrival of the postcard and the final decision of General Rowecki as to whether I could travel to London from Stockholm. Coded messages concealed in a doorkey were handed to me: the others, hidden in a small statue of St. Anthony or inside a cigarette holder, had been taken away by Hilda. The mail of the Information Bureau contained several photographs of N literature, copies of underground newspapers, and even the words and music of a few songs composed in the underground, which were destined to be recorded by the Choir of the Polish Forces for frequent broadcasting by the Polish Radio and the BBC. I did not know the contents of the microfilmed intelligence reports which I was to carry. I had to memorize the address of the Polish legation in Stockholm and the names, addresses, and passwords of my contacts in Malmö, Göteborg, and the port of Karlskrona. Inside the sole of my shoe I carried one thousand Swedish kroner and one thousand German marks. I took a month's leave from the Housing Administration and made an arrangement with one of my colleagues that he would report me as sick if I should not return within the month. Everything seemed to be ready, but the promised postcard did not arrive.

Meanwhile, in the apartment next to my hideout at Krolewska Street a boisterous farewell party was given in my honor by Leszek, in defiance of every possible rule of clandestine life. Almost all my colleagues and liaison girls of our group appeared at the same time.

Bimber (home-made alcohol), generously supplemented with herring and other hors d'oeuvres, flowed freely, and a war-like and patriotic spirit soon developed. Leszek, who had not been denying himself *bimber*, sat down at the piano and began to bang out the national anthem, "Poland Still Lives." We sang so loudly that in spite of closed windows and doors, our song must have been heard not only by the residents of our apartment building but by people passing by on our street and in the nearby square. Luck was with us because those uninvited and rowdy guests the Gestapo did not show up, and the merrymakers walked shakily but safely home.

The next day, April 10, a liaison girl handed me the long-awaited postcard. After decoding the message I could guess that I was to be stowed away on a Swedish ship. I was to leave Warsaw at once. The postcard indicated that the ship was scheduled to sail on April 14. Leszek asked headquarters for instructions: was "Zych" (my new code name) to return to Warsaw, or could he proceed to London? No answer would be taken to mean that he could make his own decision. He told headquarters that I was leaving on the night of April 11 and gave the precise time of departure.

Late in the afternoon of the 11th, I took leave of my mother and brother. This time I could not tell them even approximately when I would be back, but I did not conceal my destination. Andrzej said, "See you after the war."

It took me a quarter of an hour by streetcar to reach Zbik's flat. I arrived without notice and faced an unexpected problem. Zbik always kept a few railwaymen's uniforms there for use of couriers. By bad luck they were all out that day. I was furious that I had not foreseen such a possibility. If Zbik had been available, he might have found a solution, but he was away on a trip somewhere. In the kitchen a few of his railwaymen friends were chatting as usual. One of them now got up and prepared to go. "Don't worry," he said from the doorway. "Wait here and I'll be back." Within twenty minutes he returned with the uniform, cap, and coat of a German railwayman.

"How did you get it so quickly?" I asked, overjoyed.

"I stole it from the warehouse. I have a pal there."

But my joy did not last long. The uniform and the coat had no buttons; they must have come from a new shipment, buttons for which were to be sewn on in Warsaw. I could not travel in a uniform with no buttons on it. The same man got up again. "Have you got a razor blade or a small pair of scissors?" he asked Zofia. I was getting worried, as my departure time was imminent. Finally he returned, with two handfuls of uniform buttons.

"And how did you manage that?" I asked, feeling that nothing could surprise me any more.

"Simple. I went to the German canteen. There are lots of coats and jackets in the cloakroom. I cut off all the buttons from two German coats. Won't they be surprised! To be on the safe side, I stripped the next two coats so that I wouldn't have to come back for more."

Zofia sewed on the buttons quickly, and I ran to Warsaw-East Station. To be on the safe side I avoided taking a civilian train going straight to Gdansk. I wanted to start on a military train (there were no military trains direct to Gdansk) and change to a passenger one at Poznan. I had not received any instructions to the contrary from Grot, so I was all set for London.

Waiting on the platform at Warsaw-East was "Ela," a liaison girl, smiling sweetly. She was the wife of "the Chairman" (Colonel Jan Rzepecki). I can still remember how elegantly dressed she was, in a broad-brimmed hat.

"Have you a message for me from Grot?"

She opened her bag and produced a cigarette case. "Third cigarette from the left," she said.

I feverishly removed the shred of tissue. On it were two short commands: "Zych not to go to Central, but to return from Anna after completing his mission: Grot."

I was mad with frustration. I still did not understand the reason for the refusal, but I guessed that the decision not to proceed was deliberately given to me at the last moment.

"I won't go," I said through clenched teeth.

"Calm down," said Ela. "You are a soldier, not a civilian who can do as he pleases. You can choose not to go, but in that way you would cancel out your whole record so far. Besides this, what you are carrying *must* be important."

I had to hurry; the train was about to leave. Ela gave me a warm, lovely smile: "May you return safely. We shall all keep our fingers crossed. *Au revoir.*"

Five days later the underground radio station "Wanda," not far from Warsaw, sent a radio message to London: "Zych left Danuta

April 14 on S.S. *Szwenger*. Landing at Stanislawa.* Will report your contacts. Independently observe arriving ships. [signed] Kalina."

Unfortunately, the news proved to be false: Courier Zych was not on board the *Szwenger*.

*Danuta was the code name for Gdansk, Stanislawa the code name for Stockholm.

Chapter 9

Without complications I reached Gdynia on the afternoon of April 12. At Poznan, between trains, I managed to see Robak, the boy scout instructor; I could not know that this was to be our last meeting. In Gdynia I reported to the address given me in Warsaw by Hilda. It was the home of Maria. Hilda and Maria discharged their task very successfully.

The next day the dock workers cooperating in the plot were to hide me under the deck of the *Szwenger*, which had a cargo of coal. For two thousand Swedish kroner, one of the Swedish officers of the boat was willing to be drawn into the plot. He was to do nothing until the *Szwenger* was outside German territorial waters but was to help me to get off the ship on its arrival at its distination, which he confirmed as Stockholm. Since everything seemed to be going according to plan, I asked Hilda to return to Warsaw as fast as she could. I was anxious that "Anna" be informed of my impending arrival, as it would take at least four days for even an urgent message via London to get through to the radio operator in Stockholm. During that period the *Szwenger* would certainly have docked there.

After saying goodbye to Hilda, I went to a hiding place. It proved to be a modest room occupied by a young couple named Szwarc. The wife worked as a janitor of the building; her husband, an official of the Polish customs at Gdynia before the war, was now working on the docks. Mrs. Szwarc was expecting a baby. I learned from Szwarc that I would not be alone below deck. Two Polish stowaways were already hidden in the coal. I decided that that was probably good news. I was to tell the Swedes that I was a student caught in a street roundup in Warsaw and deported for forced labor to the port of Gdynia. Seweryn warned me that, should they learn that I was a courier for the Polish underground, I might be interned until the end of the war and that, should they discover the messages I was carrying, I might be arrested and charged with infringing Swedish neutrality. Landing with two other escapees seemed to me a favorable circumstance, averting any suspicions on the part of the Swedish authorities.

I went to sleep firmly believing that this was my last night in Poland before the voyage across the Baltic. The morning of April 13 brought disaster. A crane operator called Franek[*] who was loading the *Szwenger* learned from our Swedish officer that the ship was to be diverted to Copenhagen!

"What will happen to the stowaways who are already on board?" I asked.

Franek shook his head sadly.

"They are in a closed hold with the coal," he said. "And no one can now get to them. The dock workers will find them when they unload in Copenhagen."

"And then what?"

"The captain will notify the port authorities, and they will tell the German security police. He would be risking his neck if he did not do so."

So the two Poles on the *Szwenger* would have no inkling of what awaited them at the end of their voyage. At the same time I learned that there were risks connected with traveling on a Swedish vessel of which I had not heard before. The Swedish merchant navy was carrying cargo between German ports and ports in occupied countries such as Copenhagen, Oslo, and Rotterdam. Swedish cargo boats plying between Swedish and German ports were liable to be torpedoed by Russian submarines on blockade duty. A neutral flag gave no protection. In order to reduce that risk, a captain would be given his course and destination at the last moment in harbor or by radio when

[*]Franciszek Trepczynski.

117

he was already at sea. The journey across the Baltic was thus an expedition into the unknown. The odds in favor of our landing unexpectedly in the port of a German-occupied country were two to one—a real lottery. In one other respect too the situation was far from good. Those who knew the plot, apart from the Szwarcs, were the crane operator Franek and a man from his team called Jan Sledz. To enlarge this circle might have been risky, so I would have to wait until Franek's crane began to load some Swedish boat which in all probability would sail direct to Sweden.

"How long could this take?" I asked.

A shrug and "God knows—perhaps two days, perhaps a month" was his answer.

There was nothing for it but to wait patiently, two days or perhaps even a month. By good luck, I had with me quite a sizeable supply of forged ration cards brought from Warsaw. Without these in the Reich one could not even obtain a plate of soup in the station buffet.

In my temporary quarters I got my new collaborators Szwarc and Sledz to take a soldier's oath together; later, in Szwarc's small room, I administered the oath to Franek. (Maria had already been sworn in by a ZWZ emissary from Warsaw toward the end of 1940). Standing at attention, all three solemnly repeated the oath. Franek, an old workman with a thin, somewhat wrinkled face, was so overcome that he uttered the oath in a half-whisper, nervously crumpling in his hands a cap smudged with coal dust. That must have been an emotionally powerful experience for him.

For reasons of security I forbade them to have any contact with other underground groups. From now on, they were to limit themselves to helping couriers and emissaries on their way. The leader of that unit was to be Maria, as she was the most experienced. From the beginning of 1941 she had served as a "mailbox" for Zaloga. She worked in a German naval supply depot and quietly removed drugs and medicines from it for the use of the local organization whenever she could. Her greatest feat, however, was stealing entry permits to the docks and other useful documents from checkrooms. These found their way to our experts in Warsaw and, after some professional alterations, returned to Gdynia and Gdansk, removing the roadblocks for people like myself.

The days of waiting were dreary, as I could not leave my hiding place. Whenever there was a knock at the door, I had to hide in a small kitchen. My only diversion was listening to the radio. Here on the coast, Poles who had signed the Volksliste could keep their radios. Although the penalty for listening to broadcasts from London was a concentration camp or even death, everybody listened to the news in Polish and in English. I listened assiduously to Polish and English broadcasts from London and also listened to some German broadcasts, though I could understand little of those.

Early in the period of my enforced wait, the German radio broadcast the news of the discovery, in the forest of Katyn near Smolensk, of mass graves of Polish officers captured by the Russians in September 1939. "One more German crime," I thought at the time. The source of this tragic story undermined its credibility. We were used to all sorts of German propaganda lies, and mass murders perpetrated by the Nazis were familiar enough. In this case, however, the crime had no precedent: the German announcement gave the number of prisoners of war killed as ten thousand. Most of them were people from the educated class, the flower of the Polish intelligentsia. I thought of Captain Herdegen and all my other friends who were taken prisoner by the Russians in 1939, a few days after the battle of Uscilug. Apparently—I thought—the Polish prisoners fell into German hands after Hitler invaded Russia. I did not believe for one moment the German radio's allegations that the Soviets were responsible for this mass murder. Suddenly, a radio communiqué from the Polish government in London came like a thunderbolt. After hearing the first sentence or two, I had no doubt that the crime really *had* been perpetrated by the Russians. The two-year-long fruitless endeavor to extract information from the Russians about the whereabouts of those Polish officers captured by the Red Army in 1939 was described, and the broadcast ended with a request that an investigation by the International Red Cross be undertaken immediately. I now remembered the anxiety of families in the spring of 1940, when letters from the Polish prisoners of war in Soviet hands suddenly ceased; letters sent them from Poland were returned stamped "Addressee Unknown." In 1940, a year before the German attack on Russia, prisoner-of-war camps were still controlled by the NKVD. I imagined how this murder of defenseless prisoners would affect public opinion in the

West. Indeed, London radio exercised some restraint, but that was understandable. The British would wait for the results of an investigation by the International Red Cross.

I did not learn of further developments in this case because, after a week of tiresome waiting, an excited Franek rushed into the Szwarcs' flat.

"Get ready," he called. "Quickly."

He produced from his bag a dirty pair of overalls and an equally dirty cap. He poured some soot or coal dust from a paper bag on his hands and rubbed it on my face and hands, after which he wiped them with a none-too-clean wet towel. Within two minutes I was ready and had taken on the necessary appearance. Franek looked at me critically and seemed to feel that everything was in order. I stuffed into an enormous pocket the objects containing microfilms, a large turnip watch, and a pass for the docks with which I had been supplied in Warsaw. Franek put into his bag a flashlight, a candle, matches, lumps of sugar, two tablets of chocolate, some dry sausage, and two bottles, one with water, the other with vodka. Hurriedly, but wholeheartedly, I took leave of my hosts, wishing Mrs. Szwarc a son.

As we were walking towards the docks I asked softly: "Where is the boat going?"

"To Stockholm," Franek replied. "Don't worry. It really is sailing to Stockholm. You will be at sea for eighty or ninety hours. You will have to look at your watch to keep track of the time!"

We entered the dock gates: the watchman glanced indifferently at my identity card. My appearance did not arouse suspicion. For the first time in my life I found myself in the port of Gdynia. On the pier at which the Swedish boat was moored, two German customs officials were walking up and down. We passed them without looking in their direction. The dockers were returning from their midday break. I was given a shovel and, along with two workers in on the plan, went on deck. The hatches were open and cranes were positioned over the ship. Walking forward, I noticed a Swedish sailor leaning on the rail, smoking a pipe. He looked at me, took the pipe from his mouth, and then seemed to be staring at me. I followed one of the dockers and jumped down into the hold. The narrow space under the deck was filled with coal. We began to push it aside. Franek remained on the dock; he must have been keeping watch. After a while he jumped down into the hold and handed me the bag with my supplies.

"Now keep away from the hatch so that you won't get buried under the coal. We shall now fill the hold with coal so that not even the devil could find you. God be with you on the voyage, good luck with your mission, return safe and sound!"

He made a sign of the cross on my forehead and jumped back up on deck. Obediently I moved away from the opening of the hatch. After a few minutes I heard the noise of the crane overhead. From above came an avalanche of coal, completely obscuring the entrance: then another. There was impenetrable darkness in the hold. Where I lay on the coal I could touch the metal plates of the deck. Above me resounded the steps of workmen and sailors, shouts, and the noise of the cranes. Later everything quieted down, and other voices were heard. Again steps along the deck, German being spoken, and the barking of dogs. The customs officials were checking the ship. Let them! They would have had to empty the hold to find me. For a moment I thought of the Swedish sailor observing me closely. Well, if he had suspected anything and reported it, I would not be here.

The German voices receded and again everything became quiet. After about an hour or so the boat began to vibrate, at first slightly, then more and more: the engines had been started. I felt at that moment incredibly blissful, and completely safe. Behind me were the Germans, the Gestapo, the occupation: before me an unknown adventure, another country, other people, and an important mission. My heart surged with hope, as if all dangers were past.

Only when the engines changed rhythm and the ship began to roll as we reached the open sea did I switch on my flashlight for a moment. My father's watch showed eleven o'clock in the morning. The date was April 20. According to Franek the voyage was to last eighty hours: three days plus eight hours.

My mood of euphoria passed when it became bitterly cold toward evening. I was wearing warm underwear, thin overalls, and a knitted woollen sweater, but this was not enough: I was shivering violently. I reached for the bottle of vodka, took a sip, and poured some on my hands. Rubbing myself with alcohol helped a little, but then a new torture began.

The coal was damp and steamy. On the metal plates above my

head great drops of water mixed with coal dust appeared, and drip, drip . . . every few seconds drops of frigid carbonic rain fell on me. There was no question of falling asleep. Lying on my side, my face covered with a handkerchief, I awaited the fall of each large cold drop of water. After several hours my overalls were drenched and my face and hands were covered with greasy mud filled with coal dust. The thought that I would have to endure this torture for three whole days made me feel faint.

I had never before been suspended between heaven and hell, nor had I ever had so many hours for reflection and prayer. I looked at my watch quite often, so as not to lose track of time. After twenty-four hours the incessant rain of muddy water no longer prevented me from sleeping. On waking I had a terrible headache and realized I must have inhaled a considerable amount of the damp coal dust.

Unexpectedly, after forty hours or so, at five in the morning on April 22, the ship's engines stopped. The trip to Stockholm should take twice as long: could this be Copenhagen? Was I to end up in the hands of the Gestapo after this nightmarish voyage? The boat was probably in the roads. After four hours the engines started again, but ran for only a short while. From the voices I heard I guessed that the boat had been made fast at the dock. Steps on deck. I strained my ears to catch the words. What language were the people moving above my head speaking?

It was nine when the hatch cover was removed and the great scoop of a crane began to extract coal, once, twice, four times, and then daylight broke into the hold. I had nothing to lose. There was no question of my remaining unnoticed. Between one lowering of the scoop and the next, I crawled under the opening of the hatch and began to shout. Above my head I saw a square of blue sky and later a few fair-haired people looking down. In a short while strong arms pulled me out on deck like a trout from a stream. I had to shut my eyes, unused to daylight and sunlight.

"Wo bin ich?" I whispered in German.

"Gotland, Gotland, Slite," several voices answered.

"The island of Gotland," I said to myself. Sweden!

A wave of fresh air filled my lungs; then I felt a ringing in my ears and fell unconscious.

When I opened my eyes I saw the friendly but worried faces of a group of dockers leaning over me. A gulp of hot coffee made me feel better, and some minutes later I found myself facing the irate ship's captain. I could make out that he was asking whether I had an accomplice among the crew. I denied it with a shake of my head, and there followed a sharp altercation between the dockers and crew and the captain. I could not understand any of it, but the hostile attitude of the captain was a bad sign. I mobilized my small stock of German words and asked to be put ashore so that I could be granted political asylum. I repeated the same much more fluently in English, which made a visible impression. As I learned afterward, the captain quite simply was afraid for his own skin. The boat plied regularly between Sweden and the German ports, and there were frequent arrests of ship's captains by the Gestapo.

For the time being, the captain ordered me to sit down and wait. After an hour I became quite anxious. At last an elegantly dressed civilian appeared and after a short talk with the captain approached me and courteously extended a hand. In quite good English he introduced himself as the local policeman.

"Did you know that Gotland is a protected military zone," he asked, "prohibited to foreigners?" I explained that when I had hid on board I did not have the faintest idea that I would end up in Gotland.

As I was leaving the deck with the courteous policeman, a young workman approached me and handed me a bundle of banknotes and silver which he and the others had collected. In the sole of my boot I still had my thousand kroner and did not need the money, but was deeply touched by this gesture of sympathy.

Sweden greeted me with marvelous sunny weather, without a cloud in the sky. We passed lovely clean houses and villas. Everything was orderly, prosperous, and wonderfully peaceful. This little town was called Slite, the policeman told me, and was on the eastern shore of the island. Were it not for the radio, the newspapers, and the rationing of some imported articles, the inhabitants of Slite would not have known that a world war was raging. They had come directly in contact with it only twice. In September of 1939 the Polish submarine *Orzel* ("Eagle") had escaped from Tallin, a port in Estonia, where an effort had been made to detain her. Two Estonian security guards were overpowered by the Polish crew. One day later *Orzel* surfaced near Slite and left both men on the shore. That sensational incident was still recalled. "For the second time," smiled the policeman, "the war has brought a shipwrecked person to this quiet shore. Today it is

123

you!'' It appeared that I was the first refugee to reach Slite. The sight of a man covered head to toe in greasy coal dust caused a sensation. Passers-by stopped to stare, and I saw curious faces at the windows of the houses we passed.

I thought I was being taken to the police station. I was astonished when we entered a shop which sold clothing, and still more when the policeman urged me to choose everything I needed, starting with shoes and ending with shirts and ties. After half an hour I left the shop with a very large parcel, but even then I was taken not to the police station but to an elegant hotel and given a room with a view of the sea. The policeman suggested a bath and said he would return in two hours.

A glance in the mirror proved his point: even my mother would not have recognized me under the thick layer of grime. After a bath, and dressed in my new clothes, feeling like a human being again, I remembered that for three days I had not had a proper meal. After two days nothing had been left of the provisions I had taken with me from Warsaw, but nervous tension had prevented me from feeling hungry. The thoughtful policeman must have thought of this too. There was a knock at the door, and the woman who owned the hotel invited me to come down to the restaurant. Here I felt the shock most clearly. After almost four years of life under the occupation, I found myself suddenly on a different planet. In the center of the dining room stood a table loaded with Swedish smorgasbord. Instead of pathetic bread with beet marmalade, splendid pastry, butter, milk, sugar—all your heart desired—nicely set tables, elegant waiters! Sweden truly had not experienced war.

After about two hours the policeman reappeared. Instead of a very dirty fugitive dragged out of a coalbin, he saw a clean, well-dressed young man. I discovered that there was no police station at Slite. The sole representative of the police took me to his own one-story villa with garden. Our conversation did not resemble an interrogation. I was warned once again that Gotland was a restricted area. I was not being interned or arrested, he said, but if I wanted to leave the hotel I must each time tell the porter, who would explain how far I was allowed to walk. He clearly believed my story that I was a student captured in a street roundup and deported for forced labor in Gdansk. He could not understand, however, how people who were not criminals could be rounded up in the street. He asked me all about life in Poland and, every so often, shook his head in disbelief. How were the Germans managing? How did they react to the bombing? Have they got enough food? He wanted to know all.

This conversation went well as long as I spoke about Warsaw and everything that I had seen with my own eyes. The policeman now began to show interest in the situation in Gdynia. It was a military port and a submarine base, was it not? What units of the German navy had I noticed in port? I wanted to answer that the captain of the boat on which I had hidden might have given a more exhaustive answer to this question, but at the last moment I bit my tongue. An evasive answer could make the man suspicious and suggest further questions as a test of whether my story was consistent with the truth. Not wanting to take any risks, I decided to forge ahead and named without hesitation several torpedo boats, one cruiser, and some seven submarines.

The reaction was unexpected. My interlocutor decided that he had stumbled on a source of information of great importance that deserved to be passed on to his superiors. He put in front of me a pencil and a clean sheet of paper, and asked me to make a drawing of the port and to mark on it all the units of the German navy which I had been able to memorize.

The situation was becoming dangerous. I had spent, literally, only a few minutes in the port of Gdynia on my way to the ship. Making a drawing from my imagination might show that I had no idea what the port looked like. The sketch would probably be sent on and get into the hands of experts. What was I to do? Luckily my host was so excited by everything he had learned that he went off to tell his wife. On his shelves I saw a big Swedish encyclopedia in many volumes. I quickly took out the volume for G. What a relief! Gdynia was there, and next to the text there was a small plan showing the outline of the town and the port. I quickly copied the layout of the pier and the drydocks. The placement of the ships and submarines presented no difficulty or risks, as in wartime all names are obliterated and I could not be expected to remember the signs and numbers.

I laughed to myself when my host looked at my drawing with some excitement and carefully placed it in an envelope. I asked him what my fate was to be. "For the time being, return to your hotel and get some rest and sleep. We will expect you for supper. Meanwhile, I'll get in touch with the police at Visby."

The next day I did something which may have caused my sojourn in remote little Slite to be unnecessarily prolonged. I remembered what the mysterious Polish intelligence officer had said about the importance of getting the military reports quickly to our headquarters in London. A fortnight had passed since I left Warsaw, and each day was important. I knew that the chief of Section Six of the legation staff in Sweden had been informed that he was to expect the arrival of a courier called Zych, and he could not know that I was stuck en route on an island in the middle of the Baltic Sea. I decided to write a letter to the legation in Stockholm to see if they could get me out of here. I had memorized the address of the legation but did not want to admit that, so I asked the porter to help me find it in the telephone directory. In my letter I repeated all that I had told the Swede, adding that as a Polish citizen I asked for protection and help. I did not put the letter in a box but gave it to the porter to avoid any suspicion that I was trying to contact the legation surreptitiously.

As I found out later, my letter never reached the legation. The next day, having returned from a walk, I noticed, or rather felt, that someone had been in my room. I always carried with me the key, the statue of St. Anthony, and the cigarette holder. From then on I was afraid to put them on my bedside table at night and kept them in a linen bag hanging around my neck. My fears increased when the owner of the hotel asked me whether I would be interested in having a pretty young Swedish girl visit me in my room. The suggestion was unexpected but quite enticing, but, concerned about the safety of the mail that might be within the girl's reach during such a visit, I said that as a refugee I did not have enough money to reward such a visitor. Luckily, disinterested services were not offered.

I remembered Seweryn's warning that I might be interned if the Swedes learned who I was. I felt that I was being discreetly spied upon and came to the conclusion that pretending to be a student was a mistake. I should have pretended to be an ordinary workman who could not speak any other language. Then I might have been sent straight to a refugee center, from which it would have been easier to establish contact with the Polish legation.

The hospitable policeman suggested that to pass the time I might help him in his garden, and he allowed me to listen to the radio. From London programs I learned of new and alarming events. Moscow had severed diplomatic relations with the Polish government in London because of the Katyn Affair, an ominous development for the future should Poland's liberation come from the east. Surely—I thought—England and the United States are aware of the danger which would threaten all of eastern Europe if it found itself in the lap of the Soviets. The Anglo-Americans, I consoled myself, would surely stall the weakened Russians by an invasion from the Balkans.

Meanwhile, my stay at Slite continued, and I decided to ask the policeman casually whether I would remain on the island for the duration. He replied that unfortunately he must disappoint me. Foreigners were not allowed on Gotland; I would soon be taken to Visby, the capital, and from there to Stockholm. The difficulty was that he was the only policeman for the whole district and could not escort me himself. We had to wait until a policeman was sent from Visby. A lucky country, I thought, where one policeman is sufficient for a whole district.

My escort turned up at last at the beginning of May. I parted cordially from my guardian and, accompanied by a very tall and pleasant uniformed policeman, went by bus to the other side of the island. At Visby we got out in the center of the town in front of an imposing building. As I was led along the corridors, I thought anxiously that I might be about to be subjected to a search, but I discovered to my astonishment that instead I was to face the governor of the island. An elderly, gray-haired gentleman in pince-nez greeted me with exquisite politeness in impeccable French. He explained that for a time before the war he had been the director of a bank that had some business with Poland. For that reason he had spent a lot of time in Warsaw and had much sympathy for the Poles. He would like to learn the details of the situation there from an eye-witness. He listened to my report attentively and finally produced a paper from his drawer and spread it on the desk. With horror I recognized my masterpiece: the drawing of the port of Gdynia with the fictitious locations of the German navy units.

I hastened to explain to the gentleman that he should not attach too much importance to my drawing. What can a dock worker learn when he is daily conducted under escort to and from the docks? I drew it all because I did not want to disappoint my friend the policeman at Slite, but I really could not guarantee the accuracy of the sketch. The gentleman nodded, smiled, and the bit of paper ended up in a wastebasket.

The next day I was escorted to the passenger boat for Stockholm and entrusted to the captain's care. The waiter in the dining room showed me a menu but asked for ration coupons when I had chosen what I wanted to eat. So there was food rationing in Sweden, but in Slite no one had asked me for coupons. As I had none, the waiter bowed and left, but he returned after a short while. "You will be the captain's guest," he said. "You can choose what you wish. No ration coupons will be necessary."

We docked somewhere south of Stockholm. A new escort was waiting for me there, and the remainder of the journey was by train. We took a taxi to the Polish legation, where I was handed in like a parcel to the porter. My escort politely took leave of me and vanished. In a few moments the counselor of the legation, Dr. Tadeusz Pilch, greeted me like a long-lost brother.

"We know everything about you and have been awaiting your arrival. The police in Gotland informed us ten days ago that they were holding a refugee from Poland, a student by the name of Jan Kwiatkowski. We guessed who that was, but could not let the Swedes know that we were more interested in you than in others who had escaped."

On the wall of the counselor's desk hung photographs of the Polish president, W. Raczkiewicz, and the commander-in-chief, General Sikorski, and the emblem of Poland, the white eagle. For the first time since the war started I was on sovereign Polish territory.

Dr. Pilch took me to the commander of "Anna," Colonel Edmund Piotrowski. With a feeling of immense relief I handed him the figure of St. Anthony, the key, and the cigarette holder. It was May 5, 1943. My expedition from Warsaw to Stockholm had taken exactly twenty-four days.

Chapter 10

*D*uring my first long conversation with Colonel Piotrowski, which took place just after my arrival, I explained my assignment. First, I was to discuss and prepare with him a detailed route for regular courier service from Warsaw to Stockholm via Gdynia or Gdansk and back. Second, from Stockholm I was instructed to establish contact with the leaders of the British "black propaganda" service through our General Staff in London. I was to present our requirements to them and establish a basis for long-term Polish-British cooperation in a subversive propaganda campaign against the Nazis. I also had a shopping list of materials from the British requested by Action N and the Polish underground press. These I would take back with me to Warsaw on microfilm.

Piotrowski estimated that it would take from four to six weeks to clear away these tasks and to prepare for my return trip to Poland under conditions of maximum safety. This meant that I would be in Stockholm at least one month. I was warned that if I wanted my mission to be successful and my return to Poland uneventful, I would have to use even more stringent precautionary measures than in the underground.

During World War II neutral Stockholm had become what Bern and Geneva were during World War I: a great spy center for both sides. Embassies, legations, and consulates served as bases for espionage and counterespionage. Most reports from the German spy network in the Allied countries went to Stockholm and thence by diplomatic couriers or German embassy short-wave radio to Berlin. Allied traffic in the reverse direction, from the Reich and occupied Europe, was still more intensive. The Swedish capital became the battleground for the hidden struggle of two enemy intelligence services which relied mainly on observing the enemy's maneuvers, discovering and compromising each other's agents, and stealing documents and information. Everything was permitted in this game, which had no limits: intrigue, provocation, tricks, forgeries, bribery, denunciation to Swedish authorities—even assassinations.

Sweden's situation was not easy. The community, completely democratic, secretly sympathized with the Allies, but the authorities did not wish to suffer the fate of Norway and Denmark. Hitler threatened Sweden not only with violation of its neutrality but also with the closing of the Danish straits, the only outlet from the Baltic for its shipping. The only reason he had not done this already was probably because neutral Stockholm was an important center for the activities of his own spy system. Attempts to infiltrate the other side's intelligence apparatus, surrounded by the deepest secrecy on both sides, went on constantly, as discussions of the possibility of concluding peace and the exchange of prisoners of war, convicts, etc., were taking place in Stockholm.

The Swedes, though trapped within their own neutrality, showed much courage in their invariably humanitarian attitude toward refugees. Children evacuated *en masse* from Finland found shelter among Swedish families. Hardly a day passed without hundreds of people crossing the long frontier with Norway to the Swedish side. They were helped and taken care of at once. The same applied to the many refugees from Denmark and the whole German-occupied Baltic coast.

Nevertheless, the Swedish police waged an energetic war against foreigners whose activities might jeopardize Swedish neutrality. Piotrowski thought them unusually vigilant and efficient. To avoid arrest and internment, I must observe rigorously the rules he laid down. First of all, I was forbidden to make friends and contacts within the Polish colony in Stockholm, except for a small circle in the know, and I was not allowed to use the telephone. I did not mind, as I wanted to spend my time in Stockholm assessing the general military and political situation. Sweden presented a most suitable observation post because English newspapers were readily available through the helpful Tadeusz Pilch.

The whole question of Katyn—the Polish demand for its investigation by the International Red Cross and the severing by Moscow of diplomatic relations with the government in London as a result of the Polish allegations of mass murder—preoccupied me most. To a newcomer from Warsaw, who, along with all Poles at home, had maintained an uncritical admiration for England, British reaction to these events was the greatest blow since the beginning of the war. With a few exceptions, the British newspapers directed their indignation not against Russia, as the party suspected of having perpetrated a mass murder of prisoners of war, but against those who had disclosed the circumstantial evidence and demanded that the truth be established. The comments of the British press were so selective that its readers would not doubt that Katyn was the work of the Germans and that the Polish government had slandered an ally and had acted with blatant political stupidity. However, this concentrated attack was not reflected in the Polish programs of the BBC or the Polish Radio, so the Poles within Poland continued to live in a world of make-believe, getting only information that had passed through British filters.

The most disquieting aspect of the British reaction to Katyn and the whole chain of subsequent events was the possible effect it might have in Moscow: would its attack on our government not be considered as clear encouragement of the Russian expansion into Poland? Moscow had already set up a "Union of Polish Patriots," formed in Russia, a group of Polish communists and non-communists prepared to follow its orders. When he severed relations with the Polish government in London, Stalin also organized a unit of Polish forces under the command of Colonel Zygmunt Berling, who was at once promoted to general. Berling was one of the few captured Polish officers who was not transported to the forest of Katyn: he survived because he had already offered his services to the Soviet Union before Hitler's attack on Russia. Inside Poland, Stalin had at his disposal a small but obedient group of communists who were concealed under the name of the underground Polish Workers Party. This party was supported from Moscow by a radio station bearing the name of Tadeusz Kosciuszko, which broadcast propaganda in Polish. Stalin's purpose was transparent. One could clearly see the nucleus of a puppet government. What were the views of our Western allies on all this?

131

I sought the answers from Pilch, politically the best-informed member of the Polish legation. He was level-headed, sober, and pragmatic. "You are greatly mistaken," Pilch said, "to think that the British are guided in politics by moral considerations and by the search for objective truth. Even if the Polish side could present not only circumstantial evidence but witnesses and the most convincing proof of Soviet guilt [in the Katyn affair], the government and the press either would not believe it or would pretend not to believe it. The British want to win the war and know that they cannot do so without Russia. Moreover, as long as there is no Second Front in the West, they feel guilty about the Russians, on whom the whole burden of war and casualties now rests. It would be a dangerous illusion to imagine that the western Allies will support us against Moscow. That would be suicide from their point of view."

Pilch's reasoning seemed simple and convincing, but I wondered why those same thoughts did not occur to the Polish government at the time when it was deciding to publish its suspicions about the Soviet part in the Katyn affair.

My second great disappointment in these conversations was to hear Pilch say that there was no question of an Allied forces landing in Europe in 1943. His opinion was shared by two colonels on the staff of the legation, who had close contacts with the British in Stockholm and particularly with the military attaché. Time was working against Poland. If the Second Front were not opened until 1944 at the earliest, Poland would probably be occupied first by Soviet troops, not by Allied forces. Russian documentary films of the Battle of Stalingrad were being shown in all the movie houses in Stockholm. Even in Poland everyone was happy about this first resounding defeat of Hitler; however, I left the cinema in a depressed mood. The documentary was selective and created the greatest possible effect. An impression of ominous might came from the screen: "Today they are far above the Volga, but where will they be next year?"

Not everything that I learned in Stockholm was so depressing, however. Pilch entrusted me with a great secret. The Hungarian government, through its traditional friends the Poles, was secretly seeking contact with the Allies. In the event of a landing in the Balkans, the Hungarians were prepared, if conditions permitted, to go over to the Allied side when the Allied armies approached their frontiers. These overtures might convince the Allies that the Balkans were

132

the soft underbelly of German-occupied Europe and the logical direction for the strike of the Anglo-American armies, which might cut the path of the Red Army into the center of Europe.

While I was on my way to Sweden, the BBC and the Polish Radio from London brought news of a rising in the Warsaw ghetto and of the massacre of the insurgents and the remnants of the Jewish population and the razing of the Jewish quarter to the ground. The Poles could do little to protect the doomed people except to alert the Allies and request that they issue a warning of some sort of retaliation if the genocide continued.[*] The Jewish tragedy also raised the question of what would happen to the rest of the population in the event of Germany's collapse, in case it did not come suddenly but as a gradual retreat. One could not exclude the possibility that there would be a similar extermination of non-Jewish citizens. The murder of three million Polish Jews showed that the Germans were capable of anything. To undermine the physical survival of the Poles, Ukrainians, and other "inferior races" living in Poland, several million people need not be liquidated: the extermination of certain age groups would suffice.

Under the impact of the news of a genocide without precedent in history, I wrote two reports to General Sikorski. The first contained a detailed description of the liquidation of the Jews, the economic oppression of the population, the street roundups and atrocities. The second outlined the dangers threatening the populations of the occupied countries in the event of Germany's defeat. A declaration by the Allies threatening retaliation against the German population after the conquest of the Reich might be a precautionary measure. Such a dec-

---

[*]After my return to Poland I learned that contact was established between the Polish Home Army and Jewish militants several months before the final onslaught on the Warsaw ghetto. The AK shared some of its meager stocks of ammunition, guns, and hand grenades with two Jewish organizations and helped them to buy weapons on the black market. After the outbreak of the Rising in the ghetto, one company of sappers under the command of Captain Jozef Pszenny tried to blow a hole in the wall surrounding the ghetto to let civilians escape. The SS units were well prepared for this possibility, and Pszenny's group had to withdraw after two AK people were killed and four wounded in the first few minutes. Killed were Eugeniusz Morawski and Jozef Wilk; the wounded were Jerzy Postek, Zygmunt Puchalski, Eugeniusz Domanski, and Henryk Cepek.

Since the beginning of the Nazi occupation, the underground authorities in Warsaw had been sending regular reports to London about the progressive extermination of the Jewish population, but these Polish sources were not believed either in London or in Washington, as I was to discover myself a few months later.

133

laration might arouse the German population to oppose an extermination policy within the conquered countries and might even save the lives of those Jews who still survived.

While I waited for "mail" from London and Piotrowski organized my return expedition, I filled my time by writing other reports destined for London. The most exhaustive was a detailed description of Action N, its methods, aims, and effectiveness. It was illustrated with the news sheets and pamphlets I had brought from Warsaw, taken from microfilms developed in the legation. This report was intended for the British and was to provide an example of the AK contribution to the Allied war offensive.

For the British Department of Psychological Warfare, I prepared a list of requirements for Action N and for the propaganda of AK's Bureau of Political Information. I asked for cooperation with the "black propaganda" from England and especially with the radio stations "Freiheitssender" and "Siegfried." I suggested that they should quote from the Action N press as the voice of the German opposition. My list of requirements included information concerning the activities of German political exiles in the West, photographs of the activists of that emigration, and copies of its newspapers and books; also photographs of wounded German POWs and of any British war equipment which captured the imagination—for example, huge aircraft bombs, German prisoners on the battlefield and in prison—clearly contrasting conditions here and there. All four reports went to London by British diplomatic bag.

I realized that no materials and letters would replace conversations on the spot, but I decided to obey Grot's orders and made no plans to go to London. The AK commander must have had some motive unknown to me, since a week after my arrival at Anna I received a message via London confirming the orders which Ela had given me at the train station in Warsaw: "After fulfilling his liaison tasks with you, Zych is to return directly to Poland. I do not authorize him to go to London. [Signed] 'Kalina.'"

My endless discussions with Piotrowski were devoted to the problems of liaison. From my own experience I knew that organizing speedy communication with London via Stockholm did not present great difficulties. The Swedish route promised to be the fastest one for couriers and mail and one which might considerably increase the effectiveness of Polish intelligence. We decided that on my way back to Poland I would stop for a couple of days in Gdynia to make final preparations.

My work in Stockholm was completed, and now I waited only for the arrival of the mail from London. Colonel Piotrowski and others tried to relieve the boredom, but it was not safe for a refugee to appear in the street or in a restaurant with Piotrowski, as the Swedes had been keeping an eye on him for a long time. One day he came up with an interesting proposal. "There is someone," he began, "who must live in complete isolation from our countrymen and who cannot speak Polish to anyone. He would like to have first-hand information about the developments in Poland. As you are in the same situation, perhaps you two could meet." Piotrowski explained in vague terms that this person was a Polish officer and referred to him by his Christian name, Michal.

I was delighted to accept the invitation. The meeting with Michal (Major Michal Rybikowski) came about late one evening in his apartment. We were alone. Michal knew from Piotrowski that I was to go back to Poland soon, and spoke freely. Before the war he had worked in a department of the Polish Second Bureau (Military Intelligence), which had its spy network in Germany. There he gained the reputation of an outstanding operator. In Sweden he had not only changed his surname and nationality but had taken care to hide every single thing connected with his past. Before the war he had contacts with agents of the Japanese intelligence, and now, with the knowledge of the British, he had established contact with the head of Japanese intelligence in Europe, who had his headquarters in Stockholm, and became his closest collaborator, while of course continuing to work secretly for Polish intelligence. The British fed him information, which he duly passed on to his Japanese colleague, and Tokyo became very pleased with the work of its agent in Stockholm. This gave Michal excellent cover for his own activities and was of enormous benefit to Polish intelligence and, indirectly, to the British.

He showed me photographs of especially dangerous functionaries of the German embassy whose business was espionage and also photographs of documents stolen from the embassy safes or photographed on the spot. For the first time I saw with my own eyes how deeply and invisibly a modern intelligence service peers into the opposition's pocket.

In the company of his Japanese superior, Michal traveled to

Berlin during the first years of the war, a proof of his extreme bravery. Had he been recognized by the Germans he would certainly have been executed. During one of those risky journeys, he as usual deposited at the Japanese attaché's office in Berlin the "mail" he had brought and was asked to take back a sizeable parcel which the Japanese consul had brought from Kowno in Lithuania before the outbreak of the war between Germany and Russia. That parcel contained two standards: one of the Polish infantry regiment and another, embroidered by Polish women from Wilno with the legend "Love Demands Sacrifice," which was intended for the Polish air force in Great Britain. The parcel was so big because along with the flags it contained the flukes with their metal eagles. The Japanese insisted that the "hot" luggage be taken away. At first Michal refused; he had no place to hide anything safely in Berlin, and his work was too important to take risks for sentimental reasons. But still he did not like to think that the standards might be destroyed or, at best, kept until the end of the war in a Japanese safe. Finally he took away the dangerous cargo and began to think how best to smuggle it through the customs at Tempelhof airfield. He discovered what suitcase his Japanese chief always used and scoured the Berlin shops for a similar one. Luckily, he found it. He transferred the seal securing the diplomatic pouch from the Japanese gentleman's case to his own before the customs inspection. Both standards left Berlin for freedom as luggage of the Japanese general, after which the diplomatic seal was returned to its proper place. (These standards can now be seen in the Sikorski Museum in London.)

When telling me about all this, Michal did not give any details. I was at a loss to understand, for example, how he could travel to the Reich on a Japanese passport. Everything became clear when we met again after the war in London. I then learned that Major Michal Rybikowski had been promoted to lieutenant colonel and decorated for bravery with the Polish order Virtuti Militari and high British honors, that before the war he had been nominated to be chief of Polish intelligence in Germany, and that in the Japanese service he was known as "Peter Ivanov," a Russian émigré who had lived in Manchuria before the war, which gave him Japanese citizenship. His cover was as translator in the Japanese embassy at Stockholm. His chief was Colonel Makoto Onodera, promoted to the rank of general thanks to Michal's information-gathering.

Chapter 11

At the beginning of June, Colonel Piotrowski invited me to his room to meet someone who would organize my return journey. I saw a large man of athletic build with a square head on very broad shoulders. He had a deep, slightly hoarse voice that betrayed a love of alcohol.

"This is Mr. Franek Klapp," Piotrowski introduced him, "a sailor in our Merchant Marine who has been here in Sweden since the beginning of the war and has excellent contacts with Swedish sailors. Mr. Klapp had undertaken to get you onto a Swedish boat sailing to Gdansk."

Klapp looked me up and down as if he were assessing the value of a calf in the market. I thought there was a slight contempt in his gaze.

"We must dress him differently, for a start," he addressed Piotrowski over my head. "Such a smartiboots in a suit and low shoes cannot be taken to the docks."

The rest of the conversation was entirely between Piotrowski and my future guardian, to whom I was handed like a parcel to be smuggled through customs.

Klapp's plan was as follows: through his buddy, a Swedish sailor named Karl Olandson, he would contact the bosun of a ship that sailed regularly with a cargo of iron ore from the port of Luleo, in the extreme north of Sweden. When the ship was at Luleo they would take me there and, with the help of the bosun, hide me on board, after which Karl would join the ship's crew or, if there was no vacancy on her, join another one bound for the same destination. If need be, he was also to help me at Gdansk and bring back news about the course of the voyage, which would take six or seven days from Luleo to Gdansk, depending on the weather and cargo.

When Klapp had left, I said to Piotrowski: "The plan is fine, but Klapp does not inspire me with confidence. He looks like a cold fish and a drunkard who would sell his own mother for a bottle of spirits. I don't care to think what might happen to me in his company."

Piotrowski was clearly offended. "You may lack confidence in Klapp, but you should trust me. I know this man and have been using him for quite a time. And it is I who am responsible for your safe return."

There was nothing more to be said, so I had to conquer my instinctive distrust of Klapp and hope for the best. Anyway I was tired of beautiful Stockholm, the true Venice of the North, with its famous Skansen, its theaters showing the newest films from the West, its elegant cafes and restaurants. The Swedish capital was a real oasis of peace, plenty, and safety when compared with suffering, impoverished, occupied Europe.

Around June 10, I was pleased when the long-awaited "mail" arrived from London by British diplomatic bag. At almost the same moment, Klapp sent word that the ship with the friendly bosun had reached Luleo and would be there for a week unloading coal and being reloaded with iron ore for the return trip.

Luleo, the most northerly port of Sweden, like Gotland and the naval port of Landskrona, was out of bounds for foreigners and refugees. Klapp insisted that my departure from Stockholm should be at the last possible moment because I could not stay in a hotel at Luleo without registering with the police. I would have to go straight onto the ship from the train. I assumed that, instead of waiting in a hotel, I would have to spend some time in my hiding place on board before the ship sailed.

More than two months had elapsed since I left Warsaw, and much might have happened during that time. The railwayman's documents and uniform were waiting for me at Gdynia, but I would need a pass with the right date, or a blank space for the date, to travel between Gdansk and Warsaw as a railwayman on duty. The Germans quite often changed the format and color of service passes, so to be on the safe side I asked that on June 10 a radio message be sent from Stockholm to Warsaw informing people that I would arrive at Gdynia approximately June 20-25 and asking that someone from N deliver the frontier pass to me at the appointed place.

The message took a long time to reach its destination. It was decoded in London on June 12 but was sent to Kalina only on June 16. It crossed the radiograms about me sent at the same time from Warsaw. Meanwhile Piotrowski began to have premonitions of impending disaster. At my farewell dinner with him and Mrs. Leonhard, he tried to persuade me to delay my departure and wait for the next opportunity, but he could not explain his sudden anxiety, and I could not see any valid reason to do so. The next morning something occurred that made me decide to leave as soon as possible. The postman delivered to Mrs. Leonhard's apartment a summons for me to appear at a police station. Probably the contacts of a refugee from Poland, discreetly observed by the Swedish security service, had awakened suspicions. Whatever the reason, it was better not to wait to find out what was going on.

Therefore, on June 14, having taken leave of Mrs. Leonhard and a somewhat concerned Piotrowski, I went to the railway station. Olandson and Klapp, accompanied by his girl friend, were already waiting on the platform. The presence of an unknown Swedish woman upset me: I thought it was quite unnecessary that a strange person should know of my departure. God knows who she might talk to about it.

The three of us traveled in a very comfortable first-class compartment on the Stockholm-Luleo Express, a journey of some seven-hundred miles that was to last eighteen hours. We were due to reach our destination on June 15 at 5 A.M. From the windows of the train we saw a typical, slightly melancholy northern landscape: rocky hills covered with conifers and birch trees, picturesque lakes and fjords with small wooden houses here and there, spotlessly clean and mostly whitewashed. At that time of the year the nights were white, and darkness did not obscure the views. There was no twilight; the sun sank on the horizon and seemed to emerge immediately at another point and begin to rise again. Klapp and his companion talked constantly about their maritime adventures which vividly reminded me of Joseph Conrad's novels. Olandson spoke very good

English, and we were all in excellent spirits. I did not realize what dark clouds were gathering over my head.

At the beginning of May, two disastrous arrests were made in the group of my closest collaborators, and these, it seemed, had compromised forever the false railwayman's documents and the whole method of crossing the frontier of the *General Gouvernement.* The identity card and the railwayman's uniform which I had left at Gdynia would have led me straight into the hands of the Gestapo. Around June 10 Zaloga warned of my impending return, sent Hilda to Gdynia with a frontier pass for one Jan Kwiatkowski, but she was arrested on the frontier of Nowy Dwor. The Gestapo got hold of her railway ticket to Gdynia and my frontier pass with its photograph.

On June 12, two days before I left Stockholm, a radio message was sent to London from Kalina that the safe houses at Gdynia were in danger and asking that Zych's departure be stopped. The underground short wave radios did not work, however, with the efficiency of the post office. The delivery of a message to a place somewhere in the forests near Warsaw, from which it could be sent on, was often complicated because it had to be sent by underground channels. After that, it might still be some time before the message was sent, as the operators had to wait until there was no immediate risk of discovery. Thus the radiogram to stop Zych's departure, sent from Poland on the evening of June 15, was received by Piotrowski only on June 18, three days after I had left.

Meanwhile Kalina kept up his barrage of ever more excited messages. On June 16, Warsaw radioed: "If Zych had not left, his departure was to be absolutely forbidden. Danger on the "Danuta" sector.* Peril serious; awaiting further news."†

This message was received in London on June 17 at 3:30 P.M. The next day, the Polish station "Wanda I" was heard for the third time. On this occasion the telegram was an SOS: "Do all you can to stop Zych from leaving Stockholm." London replied that the SOS had come too late: I had gone.

When we arrived at Luleo station very early in the morning of June 15, I had no premonition of danger. A colleague of Karl Oland-

---

*Code word for Gdynia.

†All radio messages concerning these secret journeys are in the archives of the Polish Underground Movement in London.

son was waiting on the platform with bad news: the ship on which I was to be hidden was already in the roads. As the customs officers had already visited her, there was no chance of going on board without attracting the attention of the harbor police. My companions were very worried, since waiting at Luleo for the next opportunity would be too dangerous. They suggested an immediate return to Stockholm. I was strongly against this. There must be other boats sailing to Gdynia or Gdansk. On the spot it might be easier to find an opportunity and seize it. I had absolutely no wish to repeat the whole procedure yet again.

"But there is no place where you can stay here," Klapp objected. "Any hotel will notify the police immediately that there is a foreigner there."

"In that case," I suggested, "let's go to a sports shop, buy a tent, and camp outside the town. The nights are warm."

"Nonsense," said Olandson. "Even if I, a Swede, should go to the shop, within the hour the police would learn from the shop assistant that a stranger bought a tent and they would start looking to see where the tent was pitched." It was not easy to hide in a country where the whole population cooperated with the police. A policeman in Sweden was not an enemy but a keeper of the public peace and someone to be assisted.

Franek and Karl decided to go to the bar down at the harbor and assess the situation. It was crowded with sailors of various nationalities, and my two friends soon found people they knew. They began to whisper with them; an hour later we left the bar in the company of another man.

"Swell," said Klapp. "We are going to the beachcombers. They will give us shelter and help us."

The beachcombers were sailors who had signed off from one ship and were waiting to join another when the opportunity arose. In order to save their money for drink and women, they did not stay in the small waterfront hotels in the summer but slept under canvas in their own camp outside the town.

The camp was an odd collection of types from every country and every continent. It seemed to me that I was living in a Jack London story. Looking at the faces of some of the men, I had a first impression that I was surrounded by criminals escaped from long prison sentences. Nonetheless, their reception of an outsider like

141

myself was on the whole friendly, even warm. My two guardians spread the story that I was a Polish workman who had escaped from Gdynia a year before, leaving behind a wife and child, was longing to see them again, and had decided to go back and try to smuggle them out to Sweden. This story evoked general sympathy and a clear feeling of solidarity, which was strong in the sailor's fraternity.

The camp consisted of several smallish tents, each sleeping at least three men. Several beachcombers agreed to help Klapp and Karl to find a ship and a friend among the crew for me. It was striking that both my companions showed absolute trust in the odd community, and it was contagious. A tent was found for us on the edge of the camp, near an enormous pile of planks, among which a hidingplace was made. If the police or unknown civilians appeared in this part of the camp, somebody would whistle. I would then dive into the hidingplace and await the all clear. Policemen visited the camp quite frequently during the day, but at night they preferred to stay away. The white nights were no different from the days, but it was easier to sleep during the day. At night a host of harbor prostitutes would arrive and parties would start in the tents, interrupted at more enjoyable moments by the women's screams.

The beachcombers did not return to work on board until their last penny had been spent. Their time was filled by women, drink, cards, chat, and other attractive occupations such as being tattooed. Two specialists in this art were at hand. Some inhabitants of the camp were tattooed all over, not excluding their most intimate parts, where as a rule an anchor would be displayed.

Most interesting were two particular beachcombers, one tall, one short, who were inseparable. One was called Sing-Sing; he was a fair-haired man with gentle blue eyes, distinguished by his enormous height and incredibly powerful biceps. His friend Kim, on the other hand, was very slim and short. He coughed incessantly, and one had the impression that he was about to expire. The slim, slightly stooped Kim ordered his athletic friend about all the time, although Sing-Sing could have disposed of him with one swipe of his hand.

"Sing," one would hear again and again, "fetch the water." "Sing, fetch the vodka." "Sing, where are my cigarettes?" "Sing, peel the potatoes!" Sing obeyed these orders without protest, with the mildness of a lamb.

The days of waiting passed quickly and I was not bored in the camp, although I could not leave it. Meanwhile, Klapp and Karl sat from morning to night in the harbor bars, looking for transport for me. After five unforgettable days in the camp, Klapp brought news that everything was arranged.

"Prepare yourself. Tonight we will get you onto the *Drabant*, which leaves tomorrow afternoon for Gdansk. A stoker on board will get one thousand kroner and a bottle of vodka. The boat is already loaded and standing in the roads, but the customs have not visited her yet. We can row out to her because the crew is ashore and a dinghy won't attract any attention. Tomorrow Karl will try to join the same ship, but if he can't get on, he can try the *Jonasson*, which is also bound for Gdansk."

Before leaving the camp, I scribbled a few words to Piotrowski to thank him for providing Klapp as my guardian: it would have been difficult to find a better escort. I did not want Klapp to get into trouble because the original plan had not worked. I handed the letter to Klapp for delivery.

When we set off for the harbor, Klapp seemed increasingly anxious. At two in the morning, in the light of a cloudless white night, we walked through the sleeping town in the direction of the shore, where a small boat was tied. One of the beachcombers undertook to take me aboard. Karl went with us. Walking next to me, Klapp kept repeating in his deep, hoarse bass, "May it all succeed, may nothing go wrong! It will be at least two weeks before we know that you have reached Warsaw safely."

We took leave from one another on the shore with a firm handshake. I jumped into the boat and looked up: there loomed the enormous bulk of Klapp. It was unbelievable — his eyes were full of tears. The motorboat set off in the direction of the *Drabant*, visible some distance from the pier. Klapp stood motionless looking toward the receding boat. He was standing there when his diminishing figure disappeared from my sight.

Chapter 12

---

*I*t was light as day, but all was as quiet in the port as it was in the town. The cranes were idle; nothing moved except the motorboat of the port police, which cut across our bows at a distance of several hundred feet. The guard on deck lifted his binoculars lazily and turned them on us. Apart from a stranger at the wheel, I was accompanied by Karl and the beachcomber who had arranged my journey. A small boat with four sailors going toward a ship anchored in the roads did not arouse suspicion, and the police motorboat passed on without changing course. Our merchantman was near: I could see the name *Drabant* and that of her home port, Malmö. The man who was awaiting us let down a rope ladder, and we hastened on deck. The boat seemed to be empty, the crew members asleep or celebrating ashore. I shook hands with the man to whose care I was being transferred. He told me that his name was Johanson and looked at me with sympathy when Karl said something in Swedish. I guessed that this must have been the touching story about my being a workman returning to Poland for his wife and child. Finally Karl handed Johanson a bundle of notes and a liter of vodka: the transaction was completed, and Johanson looked at me more sympathetically than ever. I took leave of Karl convinced that I would see him the next day, after he had signed on the *Drabant*. I then went to Johanson's cabin to change into overalls.

The hiding place where I was to spend seven days and nights

144

was, as before, in a pile of coal, but this time the coal was destined for the boilers. As I crawled along on all fours, I grumbled to myself that it was just big enough to make a cozy coffin for a cardinal. I would have to lie flat throughout the trip; this time my bed consisted of large lumps of coal, not small pieces and coal dust as on the previous trip. The discomfort was compensated for by the proximity of Johanson, who was to supply me with food and hot drinks. We could communicate in a mixture of English and German.

Johanson expected the ship to sail the following morning. I thought that a week in this dark and narrow hole would seem an eternity, but reckoned that I would be safe. I would have two guardians, Johanson and Karl. In my pocket, apart from the old work permit for the Gdynia docks, I had a second permit for Gdansk supplied by Piotrowski. At Gdansk, getting from the docks to the apartment of the Szwarc family would be neither difficult nor dangerous. They had my identity card and the uniform, and Zbik would have left some new documents if they were needed. At least two days would be necessary for organizing and preparing everything on the coast for the journey of the next courier.

The *Drabant* engines came to life only at six the next morning, June 21, two months and ten days from the start of my journey at Warsaw East. I thought of my blissful feeling of excitement at leaving Gdynia. The return was in a different mood. The pleasure I felt from a mission accomplished was marred by the uncertainty about what I would find on arrival in Warsaw. A lot might have happened in the underground in this length of time. Were my mother and brother safe in their apartment? And Zbik, Zofia, and their friends in theirs? And had my whole "underground family" survived these two and a half months?

About 8 P.M. Johanson crawled into my hole, bringing me not only supper and a mess tin full of coffee but also the first item of bad news: Karl had not got onto the *Drabant* but would try to join another ship. His presence was important for my morale but, I consoled myself, not really important for my safety.

In spite of my coal mattress, conditions were better than during the trip to Gotland. I was not cold, nor were freezing drops of black water dripping onto me. Nevertheless, the time passed slowly, and the only relief was provided by Johanson's visits in the morning and in the evening. Although I had been told that the voyage would take at least six days, when he brought me my supper on the second day I asked Johanson exactly when we would reach Gdansk.*

"Gdansk?" he said! "But we are not going to Gdansk, only to Szczecin!†

"Oh my God" I exclaimed. My world seemed to fall about my ears. "To Szczecin? Are you sure? Is it quite definite?"

"Absolutely certain."

"When did you learn about it?"

"The captain got his orders to set course for Szczecin immediately after we left port."

This is the end, I thought. The game is up.

"You can go from Szczecin to Gdansk by train," Johanson tried to comfort me. Oh, that stupid Swede, I thought. He does not understand anything. I had never been to Szczecin, I had no contacts there, no hiding place, knew no one. Zbik had told me that the port was full of people deported for forced labor, mostly Russians and Ukrainians. How could I get out of the port area without documents? How could I get into the station, which would be particularly well guarded to prevent the escape of foreign workers? And most of all, how could I avoid the Gestapo control on the train? Identity cards would certainly be checked several times between Szczecin and Gdynia, and I would have no documents, only a thousand German marks in my pocket. I would not have a dog's chance of reaching Gdynia. On Johanson's next visit I explained the dangers of the situation to him.

"Nothing doing," he said. "You must return to Sweden on this ship."

"How long would it stay at Szczecin?"

"Nobody knows. At least three days, perhaps a week."

"And do you know where it will sail from Szczecin?"

Johanson shrugged his shoulders. Then he added: "Sooner or later we shall return to Sweden, anyway."

This "sooner or later" might mean a week or a month. I could not bear it physically. Anyhow I might fall into the Gestapo's hands if they searched the boat with police dogs. And what about the Swedish customs officers and police, and once in Sweden how could I get back to Stockholm unobserved?

*Danzig was the German name.
†Stettin was the German name.

Having concentrated my thoughts on the problem, I rejected the idea of returning to Stockholm, and devoted my time to thinking how to get from Szczecin to Gdynia. Every time Johanson came to see me, I bombarded him with questions. How strict was the control of sailors leaving ship at Szczecin? Were the passports checked individually or collectively? Could the Swedes go into town from the harbor? What means of transport were there between the docks and the railway station? He could answer all these questions. After the boat docked, the captain would give the Germans a list of the crew and their passports. No one would be allowed ashore until the customs officials had finished searching the ship and the Gestapo had returned the passports to the captain. As a rule the sailors went to town in a group, with the bosun or one of the officers at the head. On leaving ship, each sailor would have his passport in his hand, but the passport control was minimal; the customs officials only counted the men. A more careful examination of documents was made on return to the ship.

Johanson told me that he would release me from my hiding place shortly before the ship tied up. I would be able to wash, shave, and change in a cabin. He would lend me his own passport. At the last minute he would disclose my presence to his mates, who would take me ashore, while he stayed on board. If there were trouble, he would explain that his passport had been stolen; in this unpleasant eventuality I would have to admit to being the culprit.

Johanson's plan, and particularly the sharing of the secret with the other members of the crew, was very risky indeed. The captain would have to hand me over to the Germans if he were told that there was a stowaway on board his ship. Yet the small chance of getting off the *Drabant* and into the town of Szczecin was now a better one, and this was something. On the other hand, the crossing of the next Rubicon, in the light of my own experience of travel inside Germany, would require a miracle.

All my life I have been deeply religious, but I cannot remember ever having prayed as fervently before or since. In moments when I was in the depth of despondency and salvation seemed completely impossible, my hope and trust were restored by the simple words of St. Bernard's prayer: "Remember, O most merciful Virgin Mary, never was it known that anyone who implored your help and called for your protection was left unaided." I even made a vow that if

147

my prayers were heard, I would tell the story of my miraculous escape and dedicate it to the Holy Virgin.

The time passed quickly now. In my imagination I was going from Szczecin to Gdynia. I planned every step: at the station, gaining access to the platform; in the train, during the checking of documents. I had to reach Gdynia. There I knew how to get from the platform into town. I was most uneasy about my Swedish outfit—an anorak bought in Stockholm, a round navy blue cap with a visor like those used by the Swedish sailors, a new suit, and superb Swedish short boots. Everything was selected by Klapp so that I would look like a typical Swedish seaman. When leaving the ship and during any control in port, these clothes would be helpful; on a German train, on the contrary, they would attract attention.

Engrossed in these thoughts, I sailed on, completely unaware of other, even greater, dangers awaiting me. Meanwhile, radio messages were feverishly exchanged between Warsaw, London, and Stockholm, in which the code word Zych appeared over and over. On June 22, the day on which I learned that the *Drabant* was not going to Gdansk but to Szczecin, Klapp returned to Stockholm and reported to Piotrowski, whereupon a radio message was sent to London saying that Zych had sailed for Gdansk on board the *Drabant* and that the voyage would take about a week.

From the notes made at the time by an officer of Section Six in London, it appears that after the radiogram was decoded, read, and encoded again at Upper Belgrave Street, the message was received in Poland on June 24, when the *Drabant* was halfway to Szczecin. After receiving the message, Seweryn of the Zaloga group decided that the luckless courier proceeding straight into the clutches of the Gestapo could not be left to his fate. He sent a man to Gdynia with a new set of documents for Zych to replace the "blown" railwayman's. The choice of messenger fell on one of the most experienced men in Zaloga, "Tadeusz," who had excelled in frequent crossings of the borders with Slovakia and Hungary. He was a native of western Poland, had graduated from school there before the war, under German rule, and, like Hilda, spoke German like a native. The following day he went to Gdynia with false papers in the name of a Reichsdeutscher. Hilda had been caught at Nowy Dwor, so he was ordered to take the roundabout way via Kutno. Kutno proved to be no better than Nowy Dwor, and Tadeusz was arrested. A thorough search must have revealed documents destined for a mysterious person in Gdynia. Within a fairly short space of time the Gestapo had now collected two sets of photographs and false documents for the same man, whom a Polish underground organization was trying to get out of Gdynia. If the connection between the arrests at Nowy Dwor and Kutno were made, the Gestapo would come to the conclusion that a big fish was being awaited at Gdynia or was already there, and that it should be caught at any price. The life of courier Zych now depended solely on two people: Hilda, arrested at Nowy Dwor, and Tadeusz, and on their ability to withstand interrogation. In Warsaw it was decided that my fate had been finally sealed, and London thought the same.

I, of course, had no idea of these dramatic developments when Johanson woke me up at dawn on June 29. "Prepare yourself, mate," he whispered. "We are in the roads at Szczecin. In two or three hours we'll be at anchor."

I washed in Johanson's cabin and put on my suit. Then the Swede led me to the mess, where a few sailors were having breakfast. My appearance was no surprise to any of them. My guardian must have had time to tell them the story of the Polish workman who was returning for his wife and child. By patting me on the back they tried to show that I need not fear anything, that they sympathized with me and wished to help. For the first time in a week I was sitting at a table. The boat had been tied up for two hours; the customs visit was over, and the cranes were to start unloading any time now.

I went ashore surrounded by seven Swedes, clutching Johanson's passport. The German official merely counted the sailors leaving the boat. I passed him without a glance. The Swedes did not abandon me even after we had left the docks. Three of them boarded the trolley to the station with me. On the way I looked with interest at the town, not yet touched by air raids. There were many foreign workers in the streets.

My three Swedish companions waited in front of the station while I looked around. I did not want to cut off my line of retreat to the boat until I made sure that there was a possibility of reaching the platform. I mingled with the crowd in the ticket hall and watched the ticket offices. Within the Reich, luckily, one did not have to show an identity card in order to buy a ticket, but I had to see what kind of control there was at that entrance to the platform. A policeman in uniform stood next to the ticket collector looking indifferently at the people hurrying for the train. At one point he stopped a man who looked like a workman and asked for his documents. While busy with these, he paid no attention to any other traveler.

"Not bad," I thought, and went to say farewell to the Swedes. I wanted to tell them that until I died, whether my life was short or long, I would be a friend of Sweden and the Swedes and, most particularly, of Swedish sailors.

Returning to the station, I saw that the express to Königsberg via Gdynia and Gdansk was leaving in two hours. The checks were most frequent and most thorough on long-distance trains. For a moment I thought of hiding on a goods train, but rejected that idea. A civilian on a siding would be noticeable, and also one never knew precisely where a goods train was going or whether it might not be shunted into a siding for days on end.

I knew from experience that at stations police patrols, and the gendarmerie, controlled passengers in waiting rooms or restaurants more carefully than they did on platforms, from which, in case of danger, it was easier to escape, so I decided to try to get through to the platform as soon as possible. Positioning myself not far from the ticket collector, I waited until the policeman started checking somebody's documents. After ten minutes an opportune moment arrived, and I stepped safely onto the platform. But how to avoiding attracting attention in my Swedish sailor's clothes, and most of all what was I to do if a document check started on the train? I selected a coach in the middle of the train, as plainclothes Gestapo usually got into the first and last cars. I did not sit down, but stood at a window next to the lavatory and the door. I tried to recall what Zbik and his friends had told me. There were two methods of avoid the controls. One was to get out on the steps while the train was moving, shutting the door and hanging onto the handle and the handrail until the Gestapo men had passed on. Unfortunately, there were too many people in the corridors and at the windows for this maneuver to pass unnoticed. The other method was a simple psychological device: hide in the lavatory, leaving the door wide open and swaying along with the train. The searchers insisted on locked lavatory doors being opened, but when they were left open they went by without investigating.

At Stolp, as I had expected, two civilians in long leather coats boarded the first coach behind the engine, but no one dressed like this boarded the last coach at the same time. I therefore decided to push myself slowly toward the end of the train. Before the Gestapo men could get through several tightly packed coaches, I calculated, we might be at the Gdynia station.

And so it came to pass. Saying a prayer of thanks, I made my way through the blacked-out station toward the Szwarcs' apartment. I thought the worst was over.

"Is it a boy or a girl?" I cried gaily from the Szwarcs' door, remembering that they had been expecting a baby. They did not answer, but stared at me as if I were a ghost.

"What's the matter?" I asked.

"How did you get here from the docks?" Szwarc asked at last.

"I have not been in the harbor at all. I landed at Szczecin and came here by train."

Szwarc was still staring at me in disbelief. "You were very lucky. For a week now the docks at Gdansk and Gdynia have been so tightly guarded that a fly could not get through. They search everybody three times. This morning they put up posters with your photograph. They are looking for Jan Kwiatkowski."

I was surprised and startled: how did they get hold of my photograph?

"Has anyone from Warsaw been here with documents for me?" I asked with great anxiety.

"No one at all has been here."

I then realized that Zbik or someone else must have been arrested while carrying the documents with my photograph on them.

"Do the posters say that they are looking for railwayman Kwiatkowski?"

"No," said Szwarc. "There is only the name, Jan Kwiatkowski, and the date of birth." This meant that it could not have been Zbik who had been caught. If it had been he, they would be looking for a railway worker.

The situation was grim, even more so for the people who had sheltered me. I would be gone the next day, but they must stay put. But Szwarc and his wife were still free, and the Gestapo had not followed me to their flat, so perhaps things were not too bad. I would learn what had happened when I got to Warsaw. One thing was certain. I must leave the flat without wasting another minute. It was too risky to go back to the station right away, as I did not know when the next train to Poznan would leave. I had to limit my public appearances on the coast to a minimum. My hosts insisted that I spend the next day with them and go out only after nightfall, timing it so that I could jump onto a train immediately.

Should I go to Warsaw without any documents in my Swedish-made clothes, I wondered, or risk returning with railwayman's documents that might be compromising? I decided that the second alternative would be less dangerous. I asked Maria to bring me the railwayman's uniform that had been in her cellar when I left for Sweden, and I removed the travel passes from their hiding place behind a mirror on the wall.

The day of respite at the Szwarcs' was spent in conversation with Maria, Szwarc, and Sledz. I gave them the passwords for couriers from Warsaw and Stockholm. I told them about Karl's visit and explained the enormous importance of their task. They listened intently, and Sledz discussed plans and methods for the safe smuggling of emissaries from Warsaw to Stockholm.

Later in the evening I sneaked out from the janitor's quarters in my railwayman's uniform, after Mrs. Szwarc made sure that no suspicious person was loitering nearby. I was again carrying my service case, lantern, and signal lamp. Szwarc walked some distance behind me. I got on the platform by the staff entrance two minutes before the departure of the train. Somehow no one recognized in this railwayman the Jan Kwiatkowski for whom there was such a general hue and cry.

Chapter 13

There was no direct train to Poznan. I reached the city by taking local trains and changing several times on the way. I did not want to go on to Warsaw before contacting Robak (Adam Plucinski). By a well-established route, via a Polish woman employed in a pharmacy, I handed her a message on a scrap of paper saying that I would wait for Robak in St. Martin's Church, where we usually met. In the pharmacy many people were bustling about. The woman, without a word, hid my note in her apron. I realized that she did not want to speak, so I left the shop.

At the appointed time it was not Robak who turned up in the church but his nearest collaborator from N, Tadeusz Kolodziejczyk. I saw from his expression that something had happened. "Robak has been arrested," he whispered in my ear. "A major disaster. Since Easter he and others have been held at Fort VII. He's waiting in line for the guillotine."

My heart stood still. Adam Plucinski, a boy scout leader in his twenties, was one of the bravest and most dedicated soldiers of the underground. In my mind's eye I saw the dark scene so often described: Adam, in shirtsleeves with hands tied behind his back, standing in a corridor before the iron door leading to the place of execution waiting his turn in a long line of the condemned.

"Mightn't they just send him to a concentration camp?"

Kolodziejczyk thought not. "There is only one way out from the Fort: the guillotine. He knows it."

I asked what had happened. He told me that it had nothing to do with the distribution of N literature and that Adam, although tortured, had not said a word about our work. Plucinski, alas, had in hand several interests; he was heavily involved in the underground scout movement and in education. That was where the catastrophe had occurred. I gathered that Kolodziejczyk was also in danger, so I suggested that I could provide documents for him to move to Warsaw. He refused: "I have my family here. If I don't report to work, they will come to my home the next day. If they don't find me, they will arrest my family. I must stay." He was arrested a few months later and was guillotined at Fort VII.

The next morning, when I went to the station at Poznan, I could not find a timetable anywhere. Massive Allied bombing had disorganized a large part of the railway system. Most transports loaded with civilians from Berlin and other cities of the Reich were traveling toward Lodz and the towns of western Poland, considered safe zones beyond the reach of enemy bombers. On the platform were about a hundred soldiers returning to the Eastern Front from leave. They had been waiting for several hours without being able to get onto either a civilian or a military train, which were all equally overcrowded.

Another train appeared. It was so full that I did not see any chance of getting on it. The soldiers stormed forward desperately, but it appeared that all the coach doors except one were locked from the inside. In that one door a conductress barred the way. "The train is full!" she screamed, "completely full! No more in! Nobody!"

The soldiers started cursing her in no uncertain manner, but she was adamant. I was standing almost opposite her with my railwayman's bag and lantern, quite resigned. In my situation it was better not to push. Suddenly, I felt her looking at me. "On duty?" she cried in my direction. "Yes, on duty!" I shouted back.

With an imperious gesture she allowed me into the coach. Out of that whole furious throng, I was the only one to get on the train. I thought with satisfaction that there was such a crush that one could hardly stand on one's own feet, so that no document control would be possible. I was mistaken. Two hours later, when the train stopped at the frontier station of Kutno, I discovered that there would indeed be a control, and more stringent than usual.

I knew that station better than any other frontier point, but the guards at the exit were reinforced. The place was full of Gestapo both in uniform and in plainclothes, with long leather coats reaching to the ground. Several of them boarded the train with uniformed customs officials. At the same time, from both ends of the platform, they started checking the documents of those passengers who, as the stop was a long one, had gotten off to catch a breath of air. In my uncertain situation I had to avoid the control at any price. Perhaps the Gestapo at Kutno did not have the photograph that was on the posters on the coast, but it was better not to take the risk.

I extricated myself from the crowd with difficulty and stood close to the conductress, in a pose which I hoped would indicate that I belonged to the railway crew. On my belt I wore the type of lantern carried by train conductors. From the direction of the locomotive three men were approaching, one in uniform and two civilians, comparing the face of every passenger with the photograph on his documents. My heart beat faster. They were looking for somebody in that crowd. In the end the three Gestapo men went up to an elderly civilian standing a few steps from me. I was to be next. With bored indifference I stood one step from the conductress, still pretending to be a member of the train crew, while my heart pounded and my nerves were ready to snap. At last the three passed by the conductress, then me, and approached the next passenger. "Ausweis, bitte" ("Identity card, please"), I heard behind me.

As the train approached Warsaw, I felt a growing anxiety. The search for Jan Kwiatkowski at Gdynia and Gdansk proved that the Germans were on my heels. The wording on the poster, on the other hand, indicated that the Gestapo did not know much about this Kwiatkowski: both date and place of birth were fictitious, and they did not even know whether he lived in Warsaw.

From the East Railway Station I telephoned my brother at his office, and heard his voice on the line with immense relief. When we parted at the beginning of April, he was certain that I would stay in the West, and now he seemed shaken. He warned me: "Don't go to Zbik's under any circumstances." So it *was* Zbik, I thought, and felt sorrow and depression wash over me as if I had lost a brother.

Not far from the East Railway Station we had a safe house in the apartment of Celina Karpik, where I could change my clothes. I asked my brother to get me some underwear and a suit, and arranged to meet him on the street. It was obvious that I was not compromised and could return to my family, since the Gestapo had not visited them yet in their apartment, where I was registered under my own name.

From Celina Karpik I heard about Zbik. He was arrested in Torun on May 1 in the apartment of the Leszczynskis. He might well have had compromising documents on him. He and the whole Leszczynski family had been taken to Torun, one of the worst and best-guarded prisons. "However well guarded he is," I thought, "we must achieve the impossible and save him. As long as a man is alive one must not give up hope."

Alas, the series of misfortunes did not end with Zbik's arrest. When the news of his arrest reached Warsaw through the railway workers, the brave Wos decided that he must at once warn the Witkowskis, Zbik's family. His colleagues begged him not to do anything rash, as their apartment was undoubtedly being watched by the Gestapo, but Wos would not listen. He thought that it was worth taking any risk to save his friend's family. What was feared happened. The Gestapo had left Zbik's family as decoys, and when Wos arrived the police followed on his heels. He was beaten up on the spot, but succeeded in swallowing his poison pill before they could handcuff him. It did not work: he lost consciousness but did not die. In the ambulance called by the Gestapo his stomach was pumped out, after which he was taken to the hospital at Pawiak Prison. Wos's fate was all the more horrible for being an unnecessary sacrifice: a few days later, in spite of the watch on the house, Zbik's friends succeeded in getting his family away through a neighboring apartment block and hiding them in a safe place.

I spent the next few hours re-establishing my contacts—first of all, with Seweryn, to hand him the microfilms that I had hidden in my bag among small personal articles. We met in the center of the city. On seeing me Seweryn began to shake his head in disbelief: "I cannot believe that I am seeing you alive and well. We had already buried you," he said.

He told me briefly about the arrest of Hilda at Nowy Dwor, then about that of Tadeusz at Kutno. Now I understood the reason for the search for Jan Kwiatkowski at Gdynia and Gdansk and the posters with "Jan K'''s photograph. But the Germans lacked one vital fact, for neither Hilda nor Tadeusz had betrayed Maria's address in Gdynia. Had either of them talked, the Gestapo would have been waiting for me at the Szwarcs'. And if, instead of Szczecin, the *Dra-*

bant had gone to Gdansk, I would have been caught and identified right at the port—the change of course which had seemed fatal had proved to be my salvation.

But most of all I owed my life to Hilda and Tadeusz. After a year, in which Zaloga had no word of them, they were both declared killed in action. At the suggestion of Emilia Malessa, the head of Zaloga, they were posthumously awarded the Virtuti Militari, Poland's highest military decoration.

The story of courier Tadeusz does not end here, however. Its last chapter was written five years later, on a Sunday in England, February 22, 1948: a typical Sunday evening, when the average Englishman preferred his easy chair to the cold and fog outside. That day the BBC Home Service was broadcasting an hour-long program in the dramatic series "The Undefeated." The title of the program was "Courier from Warsaw." The writer of the script was the well-known broadcaster Marjorie Banks. Against the background of the wartime experiences and adventures of a courier of the Polish resistance movement, the Home Army and the tragedy of the Warsaw Rising were discussed. My role was played by an actor, but at the end of the program I said some closing words, which I dedicated to my dead colleagues. I mentioned, among others, Tadeusz the courier.

While the program was on the air, a Pole in the town of Bolton, in the north of England near Manchester, who earned his living as a sweeper in a textile factory, sat in his modest rented room, lonely and thinking of his past life. A knock on his door brought him back to the present. His elderly English landlady came to tell him that something about the Polish underground was being broadcast; perhaps it would be of interest to him. Instead of sitting alone in the dark, he might prefer to join her in her sitting room and listen to it.

He entered the room just as Tadeusz at Kutno was being mentioned. There was no doubt about it. His name and the name of the railway station were given. A minute earlier Tadeusz had thought that he was forgotten by everybody, but now millions of English people were listening to his story. And at the end somebody called "Jan Nowak" mentioned his name and dedicated the program to him and people like him—the forgotten ones. A few days later, among the pile of letters sent to the BBC, I found one signed by a one-time fellow-student at the University of Poznan. It read: "I listened last Sunday to the radio drama on the Home Service of the BBC, in which a sizeable part of the story must refer to me, or rather to my arrest by the Gestapo at Kutno. At that time I was carrying documents destined, as it later appeared, for my prewar colleague from Poznan. His name was Zdzislaw Jezioranski, however, not Jan Nowak, who took part in the program. This I find rather puzzling. Could you please explain?'' Life is more fantastic and full of surprises, I thought after reading this letter, than the most elaborately concocted thriller.

My meeting with Tadeusz, whom I had not seen since we both lived in the students' hostel, remains one of the most extraordinary events in my life. After five years I had found not only the unknown courier to whom I owed my life and had believed to be dead but an old colleague and friend. Expelled by the Germans from Poznan in 1939, he went to the mountains and here was recruited for underground work in a foreign liaison cell, "The South." His chief was Adam Smulikowski. Tadeusz proved to be extremely brave and crossed the Slovak and Hungarian frontiers many times on the courier route Nowy Targ-Budapest. Trouble at Nowy Targ compelled him to leave the south of Poland for Warsaw, but he continued his activities as courier in spite of the fact that the Gestapo were looking for him under his real name. He acquired false papers and with those usually traveled on the route Warsaw-Mulhouse. Adam Smulikowski, who was in even more danger, also moved to Warsaw. At the beginning of 1943, Smulikowski reached Bern in Switzerland and was ordered to stay there. His place in Zaloga was taken by Seweryn.

In June, 1943, just back from a successful trip to Mulhouse, Tadeusz was summoned by Seweryn, who asked him to leave immediately for Gdynia with documents for a courier returning from Sweden. Seweryn warned him that the trip was dangerous because the safe house at Gdynia was threatened with discovery: two weeks earlier a woman courier had been arrested while on the same assignment. There was a serious obstacle right at the start: Tadeusz was using a German Durchlassschein in the name of a Reichsdeutscher.* As luck would have it, the document had just expired. An extension was possible but would take a few days. Seweryn could not bring himself to postpone the departure of another courier, as the man from Sweden was already at sea and might reach Gdynia at any

*Citizen of the Reich.

moment. That man and the "mail" he had with him must be saved at any price.

Tadeusz obediently left that same day. For his journey he was given a false frontier pass and a copy of *Mein Kampf*, in the cover of which the documents destined for me were hidden. False passes, as mentioned above, had a bad reputation among couriers. He knew that the Gestapo could recognize them by the different shade of paper used; by the badly falsified watermarks, which could be removed by rubbing with a finger; and by the fact that the color easily disappeared when a corner of the document was creased. In spite of this, he accepted the mission without hesitation, not knowing for whom he was taking so great a risk—not even his code name. He bought a ticket to Gdynia. Because Hilda had been arrested at the Nowy Dwor station, he went via Kutno and Poznan. The purchase of the ticket to Gdynia was a gross error which would later backfire on him. In the railway compartment he put the dangerous book on the shelf opposite his seat. At Kutno the frontier police took away the documents of all passengers for checking. In about ten minutes the policemen were back. They handcuffed Tadeusz at gunpoint. All passengers in the compartment were then ordered to identify their luggage. As no one claimed the book, it was taken away along with Tadeusz' suitcase.

In the station, before any questioning, he was subjected to a meticulous personal search. They stripped him naked and took all his clothes for examination. His suitcase was unpacked in his presence and was torn into little pieces. The cover of *Mein Kampf* was removed and the compromising documents found: a frontier pass with a photograph, German and Swedish banknotes, and a piece of paper covered with small writing, probably some instructions. At the end of the search he was taken to the prison at Inowroclaw. Bad luck dogged him at each step. At the prison a Volksdeutscher from the prison service who knew his real name from before the war immediately recognized him and spoke to him in Polish. His first session with the Gestapo involved no questioning; he was again stripped, tied to a table, and beaten by two thugs. That was his punishment for cheating the Germans and a prologue to the next session a few hours later, when he had recovered.

The next time he was presented with the incriminating evidence: the ticket to Gdynia, a pass with the photograph in Jan

Kwiatkowski's name, and other papers. He looked at the photograph and was at once struck by its resemblance to his prewar colleague at Poznan University, Zdzislaw Jezioranski. Perhaps it was he? A second look at the photograph dispelled all doubt.

> *First Question:* "Who is the man in the photograph, what is his real name, and where is he?"
> *Answer:* "I don't know. I agreed to take the book, and had no idea what was in the cover."
> *Second Question:* "To whom and to what address in Gdynia were you to deliver the book?"
> *Answer:* "I was to hand it to an unknown man who was to wait at an arranged place at an agreed time."
> "Lüge! Lüge!" Lies!

They began to beat him. Heavy whips with pieces of lead at the end of the thongs were used on fresh wounds from the previous session. The beating was interrupted from time to time by the same question: "Are you now ready to tell the truth?" And each time he answered: "I have already told you the truth." They beat him again. Moaning, Tadeusz began to repeat to himself the words of the litany to Our Lady of Loretto. When he reached the words "Refuge of Sinners, pray for us," he lost consciousness. He awoke later in a cell, limp and bloody.

On the same day some dignitary arrived to make an inspection of the prison at Inowroclaw. Tadeusz was ordered to stand upright among the other prisoners. He was unable to stand on his own feet, so he hung onto the arms of the prisoners on either side of him until the dignitary arrived in front of the row, and the command *Achtung* resounded. Without his supporters, he crashed to the ground at the feet of the important German. Perhaps some human feeling was touched in the man, or perhaps it was for the sake of further interrogation: for whatever reason, he ordered the removal of the prisoner to the prison hospital.

At this moment Tadeusz at last had some good luck. The hospital doctor, also a prisoner, was a Pole, arrested two days previously, who took particular care of him. To avoid gangrene the doctor cauterized his wounds, an operation more painful than the beating itself, but one that saved his life. When he was taken back to his cell, some time later, he was unable to walk or even stand. Day and night he remained in a kneeling position, propped up against the bed by his arms and the upper part of his body. He had a high temperature, could not talk coherently, and was only rarely fully conscious.

The German conducting the investigation probably decided that one more interrogation "session" would deprive him of the possibility of learning anything more from this prisoner. So Tadeusz was left alone for the time being, but when he had fully regained consciousness, he was brought some paper and a pencil and told: "Write down the truth about what happened at Nowy Targ and about what happened here. If you don't, you will go back to the table and we will make jelly of you."

Beatings were replaced by psychological torture. Tadeusz was put in a cell with a man condemned to death, but he had long ago come to the conclusion that there was no hope for him and was not concerned about living but only about dying with dignity and without destroying the lives of the others. Twice the Gestapo demanded that he continue to his destination, to Gdynia. He did not refuse outright but asked for time to think about it. He guessed that the Germans were more interested in "Kotwicz" (Adam Smulikowski) than in the unknown man in Gdynia. Knowing that Kotwicz had been safe in Switzerland for a long time, he decided to divert the Gestapo's attention to him. In a written deposition he denied that he was a member of an underground organization. Yes, at Nowy Targ he had helped an acquaintance, Adam Smulikowski, under the influence of a woman who was his mistress. He gave the full name of a woman courier from Nowy Targ who he knew was no longer alive. After the raid, he said, the other man told him that he would denounce him to the Gestapo if he didn't go to Gdynia. The proof that he was not trusted was the fact that the instructions and documents were not given to him but hidden in the cover of a book.

The Gestapo took the bait. All their questions were now centered on Smulikowski. Tadeusz had to repeat his description and everything he knew about him twenty times over. The Germans interrupted their interrogation in the middle of November, when a major assault on the underground was mounted and about two hundred people were arrested. The prison in Inowroclaw was short of space, so many prisoners were taken to the woods and shot. However, they kept Tadeusz in case they needed him to identify Adam Smulikowski or Jan Kwiatkowski. As happened occasionally, he was sent for safekeeping to the Mauthausen concentration camp and from there, after a few weeks, to an even more dreadful camp at Ebensee. Prisoners died there like flies while drilling galleries in the rock for an underground factory. Thanks to his excellent command of German, he became a foreman and survived until the Americans liberated the camp.

After the war in England he never asked for recognition for his wartime exploits and never spoke about what he had been through. Although he had a Master of Laws degree and was an experienced civil servant, he seemed unable to carry on the struggle to re-establish himself. He earned his living by hard physical work among strangers, alone and forgotten until that winter night in 1948 when he heard the story of his war experiences on the radio. He agreed to tell me his whole story on the condition that, while he was alive, his full name not be divulged. I can do so now, as Tadeusz Wesolowski died suddenly two weeks before the Polish edition of this book was published in London.

Chapter 14

The arrest of Robak in Poznan, the jailing of Zbik, of whom I
had become so fond, the arrest of brave Wos, whom, together with
Zbik, we took away from his elderly parents, the imprisonment of
Hilda and Tadeusz—this tragic news greeted my return to Warsaw.
We could expect all of them to be executed after torture and interroga-
tion.

The bad news was not limited to my circle of colleagues. The
last day of June and first days of July, 1943, have become known in
Polish history as "Black Week." On June 30, when I was leaving
Gdynia for Poznan and Warsaw, a posse of Gestapo men under the
command of SS Untersturmführer Erich Merten arrested Grot, the
commander of the Home Army. News of his imprisonment and
almost immediate transfer to Berlin was kept secret by his entourage
until it became certain that he had been recognized and identified by
the Germans.

The news of this terrible blow for the Polish underground coin-
cided with another loss which shook the whole country. I was in the
street when loudspeakers were heard in Plac Trzech Krzyży (Three
Crosses Square). The Germans used them mostly for propaganda
communiqués of the Wehrmacht high command. The groups of
people standing around the loudspeakers looked depressed; some
women had tears in their eyes.

"What's happened?" I asked one woman.

"Sikorski is dead," she answered, between sobs.

The prime minister and commander-in-chief of the Polish Armed Forces perished in an air crash at Gibraltar, a stopover on his return flight from an inspection of Polish troops in the Middle East. Within one week, Poland had lost two of its most valuable leaders. While the name Rowecki was known only to a relatively small number of conspirators, everyone knew of the legendary and mysterious "General Grot," who signed communiqués and orders that appeared in the underground press. On the other hand, to the people Sikorski was the symbol of the continued existence of the Polish state. At the moment when German announcers, with jubilant *Schadenfreude*, were noisily proclaiming the news of the Gibraltar catastrophe, the pavements and walls of houses in the city were covered with such slogans, chalked or painted by youngsters from the Small Sabotage,* as "the country with Sikorski." The reputations of Sikorski, a name known even to small children, and of Grot-Rowecki were so great that, apart from the communist organizations under Moscow's orders and the fascist groups on the extreme right, all the Polish underground parties were their partisans. This unusual national unanimity of opinion under current conditions was really Rowecki's doing, although it was achieved under the name of Sikorski as premier and commander-in-chief.

The two officers from Grot's immediate entourage considered to be most important were the chief of staff, "Grzegorz" (General Tadeusz Pelczynski), and "the Chairman" (Colonel Jan Rzepecki), men of completely different political and military backgrounds, but the underground information bulletin in the middle of July contained an appeal signed by a commander-in-chief with a new and unknown code name, "Bor."

One week after my return to Warsaw, I was summoned to a meeting with the Chairman, the chief of BIP. I knew that I would be speaking to a very important man in the Polish underground, perhaps even more influential than the Delegate of the government in London. As chief of the Bureau of Information and Propaganda, he was in a sense minister of AK internal propaganda and policy. He

---

*An organization of youngsters from the boy scout movement who carried on such "small sabotage" as painting anti-German slogans on walls, slashing the tires of military and police vehicles, etc.

controlled not only the military underground press, but also a widespread information network. A panel of highly qualified civilians continually assessed the political situation, and its periodic reports had great influence on the thinking and decisions of the military command. Also, as chief of propaganda, the Chairman was in charge of setting up a clearing-house for information in the event of a general uprising.

The Chairman was not an impressive man to look at. Of average height, with black, thinning hair and a slightly hoarse voice, he did not look like a career officer. His first question was: "Have you heard about the misfortune that we have suffered?" He went on: "We have sustained an irreparable loss, but the AK is not just one leader, however outstanding. The continuity of our fight and preparations for an uprising will not be interrupted. The duties of General Rowecki were at once taken over by his deputy."

After this introduction he showed me a message from headquarters in London. Addressed to "Kalina," another of Rowecki's code names, it congratulated me on my work and confirmed the receipt of my memoranda. "You have been very lucky and have done well," the Chairman said, "and you will be rewarded for it. But first tell me about your journey."

I concentrated mainly on one subject, the reaction of the British press to Katyn and the severing by Russia of diplomatic relations with our government. I told him what a shock it was for me, an average Warsaw-educated man, fed exclusively on radio reports from London, to face reality. The BBC bulletins cannot be faulted where information from the front is concerned, I said, but they are selective when it comes to matters such as Polish-Russian relations. I expressed the view that the Polish people did not appreciate the true situation, idealized the Allies, and overrated the importance that they attached to Poland. The Chairman listened attentively but with a shade of reserve and apparent incredulity. "I am not doing well." I thought. "He thinks I am exaggerating. I should have kept my conclusions to myself."

The Chairman, however, understood that I was addressing him in his capacity as chief of propaganda. "The task of wartime propaganda," he said, "is to sustain the population's morale and will to fight. Pessimism, which is premature anyway, would be grist for the enemy's mill because it tries to spread defeatism and to denigrate the

Allies. It would also lend support to diversionary communist groups if we talked too much about the Soviet danger, as opportunists would flock to the various formations under Moscow control. I understand the shock you had when you read the English newspapers, but the press in a democratic country does not always present the views of the government. What counts is not what the papers write but what people like Churchill and Roosevelt are thinking and doing."

He asked me to write a detailed report as soon as possible and then changed the subject. "I heard that you wanted to go from Stockholm to London and could not understand why you weren't allowed to do so. It is to your credit that you loyally obeyed the order to return to Warsaw. The reason for the refusal was simple. We knew too little about you, and you knew too little about the general situation. You knew only what you yourself had seen and lived through, which was too little. Now we know more about you, we know your past, we know that you have certain views and political interests, but that you are free from any party loyalties and, as envoy of the armed forces, won't be drawn into any intrigues. We have decided, as a reward for your obedience, to send you back on the same route—because you already know it well—this time as emissary of the new AK commander to the new commander-in-chief in London."

"I know the route," I interrupted him, "and getting to Sweden is not difficult at all. I can start in a few days' time."

"Oh no, my friend," the Chairman replied. "In London you will have to answer thousands of questions without making a mistake. Before you undertake another journey, you must memorize a lot of things and must be well informed about many others. You will have a series of long conversations with the chiefs of various departments of BIP, who will pump you full of information. Finally you will get a briefing from General Bor. All this will take a month."

I received from Zaloga an enormous number of developed and blown-up microfilms which I had brought from Sweden for Action N, the BIP press, and "Roj," the department responsible for propaganda during the Rising. I had to write captions on the back of each one and hand them over personally to Kowalik, who told me that there would be a meeting in Mokotow, a suburb of Warsaw, on July 13.

I was waiting in a small sitting room of a flat in Mokotow when a slim, very shapely girl with snub nose and large, beautiful, slightly slanted eyes appeared in the doorway. She had a Greta Garbo hairdo and indeed looked slightly like her. She greeted me with a pleasant smile and introduced herself:

"My name is 'Greta.' I am a liaison girl for the Third Section of Action N.* Kowalik asked me to apologize because he was unable to come himself. He wants you to give me everything you have brought for him."

In a few moments the sizeable load of photographs went into a cache at the bottom of an enormous black bag filled with various feminine trifles. Somehow I did not feel inclined to leave, as Greta was very attractive. I felt an interest on her part that pleasantly tickled my vanity. I tried to make some conversation.

"What's wrong with your hand?" I asked, looking at her bandaged palm.

"Actually it was all *your* fault. I did not want to be late, and in hurrying I spilled some hot water on it."

We left the flat separately but got on the same streetcar going toward the central station. "May I invite you for a coffee in that cafe?" I asked when the streetcar was near it.

"I can't, thank you. I must hurry." She jumped out of the streetcar before it stopped, waved her hand, and disappeared in the crowd. A pity, I sighed. I did not even have time to suggest another meeting. I would probably never see her again. But I was to meet her again only two days later, under most dramatic circumstances.

On July 15, 1943, at 1:30 P.M., I was to be at an apartment on Pius XI Street for a meeting of the chiefs of Action N, presided over by Kowalik. It was a fine warm July day. I found myself at the address half an hour early. I did not want to go up for fear of interrupting a discussion about matters that did not concern me, so I strolled up and down near Ujazdowskie Avenue. Suddenly the faint sound of an explosion came from that direction. Everyone stopped and looked toward the noise. After a moment a few young men appeared in the middle of the street, running fast, obviously escaping. They were quite near Marszalkowska Street (the main throughfare in Warsaw)

---

*Action N was divided into four sections: the first, my section, distributed and organized our network of agents; the second was in charge of research and intelligence; the third was the editorial office; the fourth carried on sabotage through forgeries of official German documents, letters, orders, instructions, etc. Kowalik was the head of the entire department, Leszek of the First Section.

where they could easily fade into the crowd or jump onto a moving streetcar, when a large military truck full of SA men drove up at terrific speed. Several Germans with revolvers drawn hung on the runningboards, shouting excitedly. Following behind were trucks with more armed SA men, in uniform.

Evidently the escaping men had thrown a bomb or a hand grenade at a German column. If they had had time to hide in one of the houses, the street would be cordoned off at any minute and a house-to-house search begun. I thought of the people upstairs at the meeting. They must get out at once—there was not a minute to lose. The house where they were meeting was between the German embassy and Marszalkowska Street. I rushed upstairs to warn Kowalik and his colleagues, and as I did, two liaison girls, Ela and Greta, appeared in the doorway with the news that the street was closed at both ends. They had got through at the last moment.

There were now nine of us gathered in the two-room apartment. Our very number was suspicious. Somebody suggested that we should find a deck of cards and start a game of bridge, but it was an odd time of day to play cards and an odd number of card-players, and, apart from myself, all those present had false identity documents.

This apartment house at Pius XI Street, No. 21, had once been owned by my parents, and I had spent the first years of my childhood in an apartment on the third floor. It was also there that my father had died. I knew not only every corner of that apartment block but also a considerable number of the tenants, who were mostly relatives or old friends of my father and mother. On the upper floor lived the Malinowskis, friends of my father. I therefore suggested that we should split up. Two people moved to the apartment opposite and two more into another one on the same floor. In the meeting place we left a bridge party of two men and two women. I myself went to the Malinowskis' apartment at the front of the house so that I could watch the street. The gateway to the house was shut; the street had emptied. The blockade was not over, however, and any moment one could expect a search party. But the ''guilty'' parties must have been caught because the minutes passed and nothing happened. After less than an hour normal traffic was restored in the street.

I decided to walk downstairs, assess the situation, and then let the other people know if the danger were over. The gateway was again open. I wanted to ask the porter whether it was safe to go out in the street, but there was no one in his lodge. The minute I stepped outside, I felt a heavy hand on my shoulder.

"Ausweis bitte!" The German in civilian clothes studied my German identity card and work permit carefully. After a moment he suddenly asked in German, "Who were you visiting in this house?"

Apparently those about to drown think and react with lightning speed. Looking over the German's arm, I could see a small brass plate on the door with the name of a woman dentist. Without hesitation I gave her name and the number of her apartment. I again felt the heavy hand on my shoulder. Without a word he pushed me toward the pharmacy on the corner, my identity card in his other hand.

Inside the pharmacy he asked for a telephone directory, found the name of the dentist, and dialed her number. "I am done for," I thought. "Why didn't I say the Malinowskis' flat?" Quite resigned, I heard the question in German: "Has a patient by the name of Jezioranski just left you?"

I could not hear the answer, but the Gestapo man gave me back my documents. "Sie können jetzt gehen"—"you can go now."

I thought I had misunderstood him.

"Sie können gehen!" he repeated, louder now.

Another miraculous escape. The unknown woman, whom I had never seen and never would see, had not hesitated for a second. She understood in an instant that someone's life was at stake.

The remaining members of the meeting did not leave the house too soon, as I had done, and the adventure at 21 Pius XI Street ended well for our little group. It later appeared that grenades thrown by activists from the communist People's Guard had exploded among an SA troop that was marching along Ujazdowskie Avenue. Some Germans were wounded. One of the perpetrators was caught near Marszalkowska Street and betrayed the others. On the same day the People's Guard threw a grenade into a streetcar compartment reserved for Germans. The following day more than one hundred people in Pawiak Prison were dragged at random from their cells and shot in the area where the burned-down ghetto once stood.

As these events show, a new problem had to be faced by the underground authorities and the country as a whole. Such actions by

the communist People's Guard, which were more and more frequent, had a completely different character from the actions of the
Home Army. Most of our attacks were directed against selected
Gestapo men, SS officers, or German civilians, especially those
engaged in the persecution and often murder of civilians. Our aim
was to have a restraining influence. One counted on a certain number
of prisoners being shot in retaliation for the killing of a high-ranking
SS officer or official, but one could also expect others to be reluctant
to step into his shoes. In contrast, the attacks of the communist People's Guard were directed blindly against all Germans. For example,
grenades had been thrown into an SA column, at German passengers
in a streetcar, and at guests at the German Café Club. They had also
thrown grenades through the windows of a military hospital, killing
several wounded soldiers. Such occurrences, which killed a few Germans almost by accident, were followed by mass retaliation against
the Poles.

The Home Army followed an entirely different strategy. In the
countryside, it attacked military objectives—fuel dumps, military
transports, railway junctions, etc. It burned down offices containing
lists of names of local inhabitants and all other information useful in
the commandeering of foodstuffs, the deportation of people, etc. But
the partisans of the communist People's Guard, and the even more
numerous detachments of Soviet partisans, acted in a way which provoked the most severe repressions, disorganized normal life, and
created the greatest anarchy. The People's Guard would come to a
village and order all inhabitants to gather for a propaganda meeting.
After it was over, they withdrew into the forest. A German punitive
expedition would then arrive, decimate the population, and burn
down the village. After a time nobody waited for the Germans to
appear and retaliate: the entire population escaped into the forest
before they showed up.

On the whole, the actions of the Polish Workers Party and of
the Soviet partisans were calculated to provoke the Germans to even
greater repression and to uproot the greatest number of people from
their normal way of life. A policy of provoking German retaliation
was not without sense from the point of view of Moscow and the
communists. The Polish Workers Party and its military arm, the People's Guard, was formed in January, 1942, but was not able to start its
propaganda and fighting activities until the autumn of that year. In

comparison with the giant which the Home Army would become, the PWP was too small and unimportant for the communists to dream of gaining the leadership of the masses. However, in the conditions of general chaos and the breakdown of communications in the underground, in an atmosphere of despair and a fierce desire for retaliation, a small organized minority had a chance to take the lead.

The communist underground press, profiting from the general hatred for the Germans and the will to fight, but without proper planning, made frequent patriotic appeals, calling for immediate mass armed insurrection against the Germans. At the same time they accused the Home Army of doing nothing. Quite often the PWP press went so far as to imply a silent understanding between the leadership of the Polish underground and the Nazis. This agitation was supported by broadcasts of the Soviet-sponsored radio station Kosciuszko in Moscow, the radio programs of the Union of Polish Patriots, and the broadcasts in Polish by Radio Moscow.

Thus the situation that I found in Warsaw after nearly three months' absence was different from the one I had left. The German terror was growing but at the same time was becoming less effective. By the end of May, 1943, prisoners in the Pawiak were being shot not in tens or fifties but several hundred at a time. The result of this policy was not general intimidation but a determination to retaliate, fed by news of the German reverses in Africa and on the Eastern Front. A visible escalation of violent activity by the Home Army followed. It was not difficult to foresee that with more German reverses at the front the mood of the population would become more militant. The underground leaders planning a well-timed general rising were in control of the situation for the time being, but even in the summer of 1943 it was becoming obvious that they would have to consider the mood of the population as a whole and of their own rank-and-file militants, who were inflamed by the war news and by German atrocities in Poland. It was possible that the now swelling wave of exasperated people might burst into disorganized, leaderless, and chaotic revolt.

171

Chapter 15

My conversations with the BIP people helped me to widen my horizons and deepen my knowledge of the internal situation of Poland. Some forty years later I cannot remember the details, but the general picture remains in my memory. These briefings consisted of several conversations with the chief of each department. Of course the BIP was also vitally interested in the Communist underground. The Chairman's assistant, "Thomas" (Makowiecki), advanced the view that the Polish community had undergone considerable radicalization during the war and that the AK must fight the communist Polish Workers Party with its own weapons, by adopting a program of far-reaching social and constitutional reforms.

I took no part in any discussion with the BIP chiefs, having decided that I was there to listen and learn. To me, however, social reforms, and especially radical agricultural reform, seemed most necessary, but to introduce them or even to promise to introduce them now would arouse opposition from more conservative elements and could lead to the breakup of national unity in the underground. The moment was not right for reforms as far-reaching as Makowiecki wanted. I also thought that the masses in Poland were undergoing a process of democratization rather than radicalization. The German persecutions and the wish to fight for a victorious end to the war pushed social antagonisms far into the background. The danger of native-born communism springing up inside Poland did not exist.

The threat from the Polish Workers Party was only as strong as its external arm, that is, Russia and Russian power to impose solutions by force. The communists were not attempting to outbid other parties in the underground and the Home Army, as well as the government in London, by promises of changes in the social structure but by false patriotic appeals for an immediate armed uprising against the Germans.

During one conversation I was introduced to an emissary of the Polish government in London, a young man in his twenties who had been dropped into Poland by parachute a few months before. His name was Jerzy Lerski, and he used the code name "Jur." Lerski gave me a detailed lesson in the political geography of the London Poles. The picture of conflicts, divisions into camps and coteries, open or secret, and personal and political enmities was glaringly different from that of the political life inside underground Poland. Battles cannot be avoided when political forces are allowed free play, of course, but in a country under the pressure of an invader, a united front was presented in matters of principle. This was lacking in London. Lerski's information and assessment made an even deeper impression because he himself had no firm commitment to any one faction. He struck me as deeply idealistic, and what he said seemed worthy of attention.

My conversations were longest and most exhaustive with "Waclaw" (Henryk Wolinski), the chief of the Jewish section in BIP.[*] In the West, even in Jewish circles, the "liquidation" of three million Jews did not arouse the response that this greatest human tragedy of our times deserved. I was to be the first man to reach London after the rising in the Warsaw ghetto and the total extermination of its inhabitants. (Before the rising the vital role in alerting world opinion was played by my predecessor, Jan Karski, who reached London in November, 1942.) The reports, sent from Warsaw by radio, were beamed back to Poland in the broadcasts of "Swit," the BBC, and the Polish Radio, but in the editorial offices of the world press they were received with incredulity. The collection and memorization of the greatest number of facts, figures, and specific examples therefore seemed to me one of my most important tasks. Waclaw, a short, dark-

---

[*]After the war, Wolinski was decorated by Yad Vashem in Israel with an award, "The Righteous among the Nations."

haired man with heavy horn-rimmed glasses, knew most of the organizers and leaders of the Jewish Fighting Organization who had perished during the ghetto rising. He had had direct contact with the enormity of human misery and death. He was totally devoted to the task of saving the Jews and impressed me as a man defeated by his helplessness. He gave me all the facts and reports, which were horrible in their eloquence. Moreover, my "mailbag" was to contain photographs, documentary evidence, and comprehensive reports from the ghetto. One of them was a pamphlet, entitled "The Liquidation of the Warsaw Ghetto," written and published by the underground press before the final destruction of the Jewish quarter and the extermination of the remnant of its population.

In my conversations with Ludwik Widerszal, who dealt with the international situation and foreign policy, I tried to discover what sources of information, unavailable to the man in the street, the Home Army had at its disposal. Apart from listening to Polish broadcasts from London, Widerszal relied on the excellent news service of Reuter's transmitted from London by Morse code. The communiqués were transcribed as they were received by a man who did not understand a word of English but was an expert at the Morse alphabet and a skillful typist. Moreover, Widerszal received the special transcripts of the English-language service of the BBC. In addition, the commander-in-chief of the Home Army, the Government Delegate, and the leaders of the parties received assessments and information in radiograms which must have been by the nature of things laconic. Some of this secret information was provided Widerszal by the Chairman.

In spite of this daily information diet, lavish compared with what one could get, for instance, from neutral Stockholm, the BIP, although very well informed on the internal situation of Poland, did not have much insight into the realities of the international situation as it was in the middle of 1943. Here also the influence and position of the Polish government in London was seriously overrated; exaggerated trust was put in the western Allies. On the other hand, the extent of the Soviet threat was realistically assessed by the BIP.

Beside the military organization (the Home Army), a second wing of the Polish underground state formed a kind of shadow cabinet (the Government Delegacy), divided into a number of civilian departments that were in charge of the preparations for taking over power when Germany collapsed. The entire administrative apparatus, organized and prepared for its future responsibilities, waited in hiding to begin functioning. The third part of the underground state consisted of its political parties, which together formed something like an underground parliament. It later adopted the name "Council of National Unity."

The Government Delegate and the parties with their own contacts in London were even more out of touch with reality than the AK general staff. I was taken to a lonely villa near Warsaw, surrounded by forests, the residence of Roman Knoll, a director of the Department of Foreign Affairs of the Government Delegacy. Like many others, he imagined that Poland was a power supported by the United States and Britain, which would be able to dictate terms at the peace table not only to the Germans but to the Russians as well. Some circles in the various parties, like Knoll, still indulged in the dream that Poland's eastern neighbor would emerge from the war so exhausted and ruined that Poland would have a free hand in determining her eastern frontier.

From my visit to this villa I remember one small incident. Some time about noon, a few ragged and emaciated figures emerged from the forest which came up almost to the front of the house. They were young Jews, saved from the ghetto by a miracle and now in hiding. The mistress of the house took them a large kettle of soup and an enormous loaf of bread. She had been feeding them daily since May.

By the end of all these conversations and meetings my head was bursting from the facts, assessments, and proposals that I had to commit to memory, as no notes could be made, of course. However, I was to have on microfilm the most important points.

During this period, when preparing for my mission and "learning" all about underground Poland, I was able to establish a closer acquaintance with Greta, although this was against our conspiratorial rules. Social life in the underground, meetings with friends in private apartments, always posed a risk of exposure; larger social gatherings or weddings between members of the underground sometimes ended in tragedy—in Gestapo prisons. But human nature prevailed, and no one could hermetically seal off one's contacts in the organization from one's ordinary personal life.

175

My first visit to the small one-room apartment at 11 Grottger Street was an official one: I was to meet Kowalik there. The head of Action N, after the imprisonment of his wife, was being looked after by two sisters, Barbara and Jadwiga or Wisia ("Julia" and "Greta"). Barbara was one of his closest collaborators; Wisia, the younger of the two, had come from Cracow in June 1941 to work in Action N. She was later appointed liaison girl with the editorial offices of the Third Section.

This tidy little apartment was a focal point for the exclusive circle of young underground activists. On Sundays and holy days, if there was free time, the whole group went swimming in the Vistula or played volley ball. Weekdays were for hard work from morning into the night, for the job of a liaison girl, going from one safe house to another with a false identity card and a bag stuffed full of compromising papers, did not stop at nightfall. One of the sisters banged away at a typewriter in the kitchen, while the other filed documents. Under the windows one could sometimes hear the heavy steps of German patrols; there was a police station just around the corner.

After Zbik and Wos had been arrested, I could not use the uniform and identity card of a railwayman any more. At any price, I had to obtain a different kind of frontier pass. I refused to travel on a false Passierschein because such documents had caused Hilda's and Tadeusz' arrest. It was not only my courier's "mail" that was at risk: I knew too much, and no one who has never undergone police interrogation and torture can be sure how he will behave when water is being poured through his nostrils, or when he is hung by his hands from a beam with his feet off the floor, or when his genitals are being pounded with a metal bar.

Each section of the underground which sent people over the border of the *General Gouvernement* jealously guarded its methods and documents, and rightly so. It was thus up to me to obtain an authentic permit.

I looked into the possibility of getting a pass by bribing someone. Various businesses working for German enterprises or for the German armed forces could obtain passes for their workers if the journeys could be justified. Greta was helping me, and one day she had a piece of good news. Antoni Kawczynski, the principal translator of N literature, had a boyhood friend in Poznan who moved in German circles and who now offered to get me a legal pass. Very gratified, I went to see this helpful friend, accompanied by Greta, Kawczynski, and Kawczynski's wife, Ewa. When our host opened the door, my legs almost gave way under me. I was standing at the back of the group, hidden by Greta and the Kawczynskis, and my first instinct was to turn and run, but it was too late for that. Our host was politely inviting us to come in. I only had time to grasp Greta's hand and to whisper in her ear: "Careful, a Gestapo agent!"

The man who faced us was one of my older university friends from Poznan. I had met him when I was living in the students' hostel there. Even in the early years of the occupation, acquaintances had warned me that "X" was running a hotel in the city called the Savoy, classified as "Nur für Deutsche," which was a meeting place for the SS and Gestapo, and that he himself was on the German payroll. Kawczynski's friend gave not the slightest indication that he had recognized me, but he and his red-haired wife must have noticed my shock. Antoni and his wife probably realized that something was wrong but could not make out what it was. Our hosts asked us to sit down, and a long, unpleasant silence followed.

"Mrs. X" then began to talk about the horrible times in which we now lived. For some time around their apartment house and even on the stairs, she said, suspicious-looking people had been seen, always in twos and threes. The janitor admitted that they had asked him about "X"—when he left the house and when he got back, whether he came alone or with friends.

Now everything became clear. In all probability, a death sentence had passed on "X" and he knew it. It wouldn't be long before our men got him.

Meanwhile, the condemned man was taking official application forms for a frontier pass from a drawer. "Fill this in," he said, "and add a photograph, and I'll bring you a pass within a week." What was I to do? If I filled in the form with a false name, he would have in his hand damning evidence that I was in hiding. He must have recognized me and remembered my real name. No hesitation was possible: I had to give my real name and address, and then my fate and that of my family would be in the hands of a Gestapo agent. I started to say that I had forgotten to bring a photograph, but stopped myself at the last minute, realizing that I had not much to lose. He must remember me. If he wished to do so, he could pick up the telephone as soon as the door shut behind us, and the Gestapo would be waiting for me when I got home. The man was clearly in fear of his life, though, and perhaps he thought that he might save himself by doing me a service.

I determined to make use of him. "And what if this permit leads me straight to prison?" I asked, looking him straight in the eye.

"X" seemed disconcerted. "But that's impossible," he said. "It will be obtained completely legally. I take full responsibility for that."

Without further hesitation I filled in the questionnaire and signed it with my real name and address, adding a photograph. This man knows, I thought, that if I am betrayed, it will confirm our people's suspicions. For him, that will be the end. I can take the risk.

"X" asked me to telephone him a week later during his lunch hour, by which time the permit would be ready for me, and we left the apartment. When we were outside, I told Kawczynski everything I knew about the man, but he was indignant and seemed offended. "That's impossible," he declared. "If he is what you imply he is, I would have been imprisoned a long time ago. He knows everything about me."

On the day when I was to telephone "X" to arrange for the permit, I went out in the morning on other business. I found the nearby street closed off by a cordon of Polish police. In front of the Savoy were a number of uniformed Germans, two police vans, and an ambulance. It was safer not to stop and stare, so I turned back. At lunchtime, I telephoned "X"'s flat as arranged, and a tearful woman's voice answered: "My husband is not here. He has been severely wounded and taken to hospital."

"What happened? When?" I asked her.

"This morning at the Savoy some people entered the hotel, fired at my husband, and immediately ran off."

"Germans?"

"Not Germans!" she screamed. "Poles! Bandits!"

I put down the receiver. That was the end of that attempt to get my frontier permit. What bad luck!

Antoni Kawczynski even then would not believe that "X" was a Gestapo agent. "There must have been a tragic mistake," he declared when he heard the story. Perhaps he was right; I don't know.

Chapter 16

Since my return from Sweden, I had not stopped worrying about the fate of Wos and Zbik. From our sources of information in the prisons, we learned very soon what had happened to Wos after his arrest. When he was well enough to get off his bed, his interrogation started again, with the usual torture and beatings. Wos took poison at the time of his arrest because he was afraid he might confess under torture, but he underestimated himself. He bore everything bravely and betrayed nothing and nobody. To protect his old parents at Naklo, he would not even give his real name and address. At Szucha Avenue (the Gestapo headquarters in Warsaw) the Germans realized that their methods would not work with this man, and he was sent to the concentration camp at Mauthausen. At that point I lost sight of him.[*]

To get in touch with Zbik, in the prison at Torun, seemed an impossibility. Mikolaj got a message to me that the two Leszczynskis, with whom we stayed on our expeditions to Torun, had been arrested with him. Mikolaj himself was also in danger, and we could not use him any more although he was now our only contact left at Torun. I tried the usual methods, through railwaymen, but without success.

In spite of all this we did not give up hope. I believed in the

---

[*]Only after the war did I learn that Wojciech Sobieszczyk was executed there.

incredible cunning of young Zbik, his remarkable courage, and the strange power he had to charm people. It seemed to me that he would manage to extricate himself from any corner, however tight. And indeed, what we failed to do—to establish contact with Zbik, and to smuggle in some kind of sign from Warsaw to Torun and then from the town to the prison—Zbik managed to do on his own.

One day my liaison man, George, brought me a message from Torun. It was not in Witkowski's handwriting, but it contained news of him which was not good. He told us that he had been condemned to death, that he was expecting to be executed very soon, and that he wanted an "English hair" immediately. For the life of me, I couldn't imagine what this thing was. I made inquiries and finally learned that an English hair is a very fine saw, similar to a fretsaw, made from special English steel, which burglars use for cutting through iron grillwork. As I did not have any contacts in the criminal under-ground, I managed an introduction to a Warsaw lawyer who special-ized in defending professional burglars and was trusted by them.

"I doubt very much if I can obtain an 'English hair' for you because for a professional burglar it is his tool of the trade, a treasure with which he won't part because he knows he won't be able to replace it during the war," the lawyer told me.

"Couldn't you at least try?" I asked him. "We must save an extremely brave and valuable man." I told him Zbik's story and saw that he was truly impressed. "I will do what I can," he said.

A few days later I again went to his office and he put in front of me, without a word, four little fine saws. "You have got four?" I exclaimed. "As you can see—four, I underestimated these people. When I told them what I had heard from you and my clients realized that he was an important man from the underground, they started bringing me 'English hairs.'"

Immediately I began to look for a way of getting the precious "tool" to Zbik in time, as every day counted, but a couple of days later my aide Jerzy rushed into my room in Krolewska Street, all out of breath. "It's Zbik!" he gasped. "Is he dead?" I cried. "No! He is in Praga, at Celina Karpik's place. He has escaped! He took two others with him!"

Overwhelmed with joy, I rushed with Jerzy to Praga, on the other bank of the Vistula. Zbik was changed beyond recognition. His small, boyish face was now swollen and deathly pale. Only the bright blue eyes remained the same. Both his hands were bandaged, he had no jacket, and his shirt was dirty and torn. We embraced one another without a word. Two young men, wearing soiled and wrinkled shirts without jackets like Zbik, stood looking at us in surprise. These were the pals the rascal had helped escape the noose with him.

The most incredible adventures and feats of courage happened in this war so frequently that in the end they all seemed commonplace. Zbik's flight, however, was something so extraordinary, that I would not have believed his tale if he had not given me the details himself in the presence of his two fellow prisoners.

On May 1, 1943, he had arrived in Torun with a weighty parcel of N leaflets, which he handed over to Mikolaj. Late in the evening he was calmly returning, "clean," to the Leszczynskis' to spend the night. It was a beautiful moonlit night. As he approached the garden surrounding the Leszczynskis' house, he sensed danger. The gate leading to the house, usually shut, was now wide open. The moment he entered the little garden, he felt a terrible blow on the head and fell unconscious. When he came to, he was lying on the floor. Leszczynski, his wife, and his father-in-law were standing facing the wall, with their hands raised. Some Gestapo men were leaning over him, one holding his documents: "Where have you come from? What were you doing there? What are you doing here?"

Zbik felt quite secure. His papers were authentic. He gave his name, address, and place of work. He mentioned his German superior, Amtmann Fetzer. On the spot he invented a story to explain his trip to Torun. He had nothing with him that could compromise him. If the Leszczynskis had not talked, he would be safe. Unfortunately, the Gestapo must have had a tip. They seemed to know somehow that they had caught a valuable fish in their net. He was meticulously searched. The Gestapo men tore out the lining of his jacket, emptied the pockets, even ripped open the seams of his underwear. They found nothing. Repetition of the same questions and answers lasted until four in the morning. At last the Germans were tired and took all four to Gestapo headquarters. Zbik was handcuffed and put in a cellar alone, without bread or water. The next day the interrogation started again, now combined with beatings. He held out, not expecting that things would get worse.

Three days later, he was taken by prison van in chains to his native village, Skepe, near Lipno. Here he had to live through a tragic confrontation with his parents. The old couple had been so cruelly beaten that they could neither sit nor stand. They were kneeling, leaning on chairs. He tore himself away from the Gestapo men and rushed to his mother, but he was dragged back and again struck on the head. Further interrogation, interspersed with beatings, lasted five hours. The Gestapo then dragged in the local commander of the Home Army, Captain Roman Teodorczyk, with whom Zbik had maintained contact since 1941. Asked whether he recognized Zbik, Teodorczyk could not speak, and it was clear that he was dying. Next it was the turn of Czeslaw Lulinski, the distributor of N literature in Lipno and Kujawy (a western province of Poland). They failed to get him to make a deposition, so they brought in his father and beat him to death in Lulinski's presence. Lulinski kept silent to the end, but the list of names found on him, on which Zbik's parents were mentioned, caused further arrests.

Although the confrontation with Zbik in the village did not produce results, the Germans did not stop at that. Zbik was taken back to Torun, this time not to Gestapo headquarters but to prison. His shirt was by then a bloody rag stuck to his wounds. A fellow prisoner in the cell, an elderly Pole, probably a prewar army officer, washed his wounds and tried to raise his spirits. The next session followed only a few days later when he had somewhat recovered. This time a higher ranking Gestapo officer from Bydgoszcz was also present. He began by slapping the chained prisoner. Despite the assurances of the local Gestapo that the prisoner had already been carefully searched and that nothing had been found on him, the newcomer personally began to search Zbik's torn-up uniform. To Zbik's horror and fright, the man found a forgotten bit of tissue paper in the watchpocket of his jacket. It was a message from Warsaw that Zbik was to hand to somebody in Torun. It had nothing to do with Action N. As mentioned before, Zbik had a habit of carrying various messages and requests for his friends and could not be convinced that such "favors" might someday lead to disaster.

That day Zbik could not walk back to his cell but was taken there on a stretcher. He knew that nothing would save him now. What remained was the struggle against pain and suffering in order to reveal nothing. He thought of smashing a bulb in his cell and swallowing glass, but like many others he was stopped by the deep religious conviction that it is a sin to take one's own life.

After a time, he was left in peace. But he learned from the prison warder that he and five others had been condemned to death. The executions in the Torun jail took place in the courtyard by hanging. He had only a few days left. This warder was a certain Alphonse W. His Christian name was actually Alphonse but, Zbik maintained, he was also by civilian profession an "Alphonse," or pimp. He liked Zbik's new boots. "Listen," he said, "give me these new boots. It can make no difference to you whether you hang in boots or without them, and I could use them."

Zbik did not give him the boots. The next day the warder tried again. "I shall need these boots because I am going to make myself scarce. In September '39 we were rounding up some Kraut civilians at a collecting point, and I hit one of the buggers. The Gestapo does not know that yet, but sooner or later somebody will recognize me and squeal."

"We shall escape together then," Zbik at once decided. "Alfie, I shall get you to Warsaw, and there you can go to an underground cadet officers' school. I have influence and know people. You will become an officer."

Alphonse went away without a word. When he came back that evening, Zbik lent him his boots; it was Alphonse's evening off. He returned early in the morning to give Zbik back his boots and asked casually: "How do you figure we could do it?"

Zbik had a precise plan and took command. On his next evening off, Alphonse was to buy a bottle of wine and some sleeping tablets. They would wait until the guard on night duty was a fellow who lusted after one of the woman prisoners and used to go to her cell during his shift. Toward evening they would get him to drink the wine with the pills dissolved in it to make him both tight and sleepy. Alphonse had keys with which he locked the cells before nightfall in the presence of the guard. Instead of turning the key twice to the right as usual, he would turn it once to the right and once to the left, so that the door would be left unlocked. When the guard joined his girl friend and the love games began in earnest, Alphonse would lock them in. Then, Zbik continued, we shall both go out—but he had not worked out what would happen next.

Alphonse told him. Downstairs they would first get to the

183

garage and slash the tires of all the cars so that the Gestapo could not pursue them. There was a long ladder there. Over the wall lay the military stores in the compound of the Teutonic knights' castle; beyond was the River Vistula and the reeds along its banks.

At that point Zbik said: "Remember, Alfie, there are six of us condemned men here awaiting death. If one goes, we must all go." "If there are only two, it might succeed," Alphonse retorted, "but seven men won't make it." "Either all or none," said Zbik firmly.

All seven made it. The escape was successful, although not everything went according to plan. Though the guard drank the wine, that evening he was in no hurry for love. The prisoners were in an agony of suspense as the minutes passed. Then the garage ladder proved to be too short, and Zbik had to pull himself up on the top of the wall topped with broken glass, wounding himself badly in the hands. As the last prisoner was scaling the wall, the alarm sounded. The fugitives were still among the castle buildings when the search-lights came on, but they got out into the street through the anti-air-craft shelter, succeeded in reaching the Vistula, and hid themselves in the rushes until the first wave of pursuit was over. They could hear the throbbing engines of the patrol boats on the river.

Several hours later, moving cautiously forward through the rushes on the bank, they found a boat tied up, and under cover of darkness rowed to the opposite bank. Avoiding peasant farms, they reached a remote village and here, completely exhausted, took the risk of asking a peasant for help. He gave them something to eat and drink and took them to the nearest town on his cart.

At the town they broke up. Four of them decided to stay there and try to find help and shelter in a familiar region. Zbik, Alfie, and a third man Jan Filipski, were smuggled by a railwayman (Zbik had friends everywhere) onto a goods train going to Warsaw East. Thus they got to the apartment of Celina Karpik in Praga.

I ignored all the rules of conspiracy and took Zbik straight from Praga to our apartment in Nowy Swiat, where I left him in my mother's care. Jerzy took care of Alphonse and Jan Filipski. After a few days Zbik could be secretly placed in a hospital known to the underground. His wife and sisters shed tears of happiness: his tiny daughter Jaga would not be fatherless.

This story must end with a mention of Alphonse's future. We never told anybody what his first profession had been. His heart's desire was to study at the cadet officers' secret school, and he did. During the Warsaw Rising he showed such fierce courage that he was awarded the Virtuti Militari. He survived the Rising and the war.

Chapter 17

*I*n the middle of August, I sent a message to the Chairman that I was fully prepared to leave. There were people at Gdynia who were to find me a place on a boat, but I still needed a frontier pass. As soon as I had that, I could be off. In a week I was told to go to a rendezvous at a boathouse on the Vistula. Ela, a liaison girl, was to meet me there. The note from the Chairman ended with the instruction to tell no one else about the meeting. That led me to think that this would be the promised briefing by the new commander-in-chief of the Home Army, General Bor.

I went to the appointed place very excited and somewhat jittery, checking frequently to see that no one was tailing me and changing streetcars twice. I was early and Ela was not yet at the boathouse, but some twenty steps away from me stood a sailor of the Vistula fleet in a round peaked cap and a striped blue-and-white jersey. Normally I would not have paid any attention to him, but at this moment I smelled danger everywhere. For example, it was well known that Rowecki had been identified by a chance recognition in the street by a Gestapo informer who knew him from before the war.

When Ela arrived, very punctually, I pointed out the sailor, who must have seen our meeting. She listened without interest and did not even look in his direction. Perhaps it is a guard, I thought, but did not want to ask. When we set off to the Old City, I looked back; the sailor had not moved. When we entered the apartment house, we passed a fellow sitting at a window in the hallway who looked at us closely. I turned to Ela, who again seemed unconcerned.

The door was opened by a liaison girl. Ela then left, and I was put in a room to the left of the entrance. "Please wait. You will be called very soon," the girl said.

When I was shown into a small drawing room, I saw three men in shirtsleeves sitting at a table. The one on the right was the Chairman. The one on the left asked me to take off my jacket. "It is very hot," he said, "no need for us to be uncomfortable." I guessed that this was "Bor," the code name, I knew, of General Tadeusz Komorowski. He was short, slim, balding, with a small head, a little moustache, and rather feminine eyes. The third man, sitting in the middle with his arms folded, seemed to dominate the meeting. He was tall, with a squarish face and wise, very serious eyes. This was undoubtedly "Grzegorz," General Tadeusz Pelczynski, the chief of staff of the Home Army, who had been chief of intelligence before the war.

The meeting was friendly, informal, and most unmilitary. We addressed one another without titles or rank, as was the rule in the underground. I was very moved. In the fourth year of war, in the center of the occupied capital, under the noses of the Gestapo, here was the commander of the underground army holding a meeting with his staff officers. Without uniform or the trappings of his position, he knew that his orders would be obeyed throughout the country, as they would be in normal times. The Germans knew General Bor's name, and a whole Gestapo section in Warsaw had only one task: to track him down and arrest him.

"To begin with," Bor said, "I want to inform you that for your work in Action N you have been awarded the Cross of Valor." My surprise was so great that I had to force myself to listen to the rest of his words.

"When do you intend to start your journey?"

I told him the provisional date was September 5.

"In this case I must have your word of honor that you will not breathe a word of what you are told here to anybody—neither here nor in London. If, after leaving this room, you wish to ask any questions, you may ask them of the Chairman. I have four points to make. You may repeat them only to the commander-in-chief in the presence of persons accompanying him. We have full confidence in you, and I

187

know that you will not disappoint us." While enumerating these four points, Bor looked from time to time at the two other men as if to assure himself that he was repeating what had been previously agreed. Grzegorz occasionally made some remark at which the two others nodded.

"*Point One*," Bor began. "You will be the first emissary to arrive in London since General Sikorski's death and Grot's arrest. Rowecki was a very prominent commander. God knows what they might imagine the situation in the Home Army to be since his arrest. You will tell the commander-in-chief what you have seen for yourself. The Home Army is fighting on, the present resistance and the preparations for the general rising are continuing, and everything is proceeding according to plan. "In complete harmony" (he stressed these last two words, turning first to Grzegorz and then to the Chairman), "we are pursuing our usual activities. There is no dissent within our ranks nor any weakening. We cooperate very well with the Government Delegate. This is the first and most important point.

"*Point Two.* We must count on a continuing German retreat on the Eastern Front and on the possibility that Soviet troops will be in our eastern provinces before the invasion of the Allies and the collapse of Germany. The breaking of diplomatic relations with the Polish government by Russia will complicate the situation of our partisan units at the moment when the front is moving to the territories of the Polish Republic. You will report to General Sosnkowski that we expect from him, as soon as possible, a general set of instructions that will allow us to choose between various options according to our own on-the-spot assessment of any given situation. You will tell him that we ourselves are beginning to study various alternatives. It now seems probable that the arrival of the Russians on Polish territory will precede the fall of Germany, in short, that we shall be faced not with a defeated German army but with a slow enemy retreat through Polish territories. We are awaiting instructions from the commander-in-chief and the government to cover that eventuality. The matter is urgent and most important.

"*Point Three.* In the countryside a new danger has arisen: independent bands composed of various groups of social outcasts have appeared, people hiding in the forest from German reprisals and punitive expeditions. I am referring to those who have not been absorbed into the ranks of our partisan units. The existence of these gangs increases the suffering and losses of the rural population. The bands are a secondary product of German methods and the provocative behavior of Soviet and communist partisans. People in the countryside often cannot distinguish among our Home Army detachments, the Communist People's Guard, and ordinary criminals. You will report to General Sosnkowski that I am preparing an order for our units to combat these bands, and especially their leaders, in order to protect the population. The people in the countryside must see in the Home Army their true defenders and distinguish them from those who steal and rob them. I would like the commander-in-chief to understand the motives behind my order.

"And last, *Point Four.* You will tell the commander-in-chief that all our efforts to subordinate the military detachments of the National Armed Forces* to the commander of the Home Army in the ways which have been acceptable to other groups have come to nothing until now. My predecessor had informed General Sikorski in detail about this shortly before his arrest. We are determined to put an end to internal dissension. If we do not soon succeed in integrating the NSZ with the Home Army on the usual basis, we shall be forced to order the disbandment of the NSZ formations and to take disciplinary action against their officers should they not obey the order."

Bor ordered me to repeat these four points. I had been listening to him with such strained attention that I could repeat almost word for word everything he had said, sometimes using his own phrases. All three men seemed pleased with the result of this "exam."

Now Pelczynski spoke. "We expect that you will return to Poland after three months, by parachute. You must be like a sponge which absorbs the greatest amount of facts and figures here and which there, in London, is squeezed dry, only to repeat the same process before returning to Poland. You must keep your eyes and ears open, gather information and opinions, and obtain access to documents, so that on your return you can inform us precisely about the military and political situation. We shall listen to your personal views, but we will most appreciate your report of the facts. Your mission is very important. You must get to know those British who influence decisions and persuade them that support for our military effort is in

---

*The NSZ was an extreme right-wing group.

their best interests. They must realize what the potential of the Home Army is, so that they will increase, up to the limits of our requirements, the parachute drops of arms, ammunition, and other equipment. The help given us to date is not sufficient."

At this point I asked a question. One of the British POWs on the run in Warsaw, Ronald Jeffery, stood out above all the others in intelligence and political sense. Could I take him with me? The British would pay more attention to one of their own countrymen than to a Pole, and Ronny understood our situation very well.

Grzegorz thought for a while. "The journey," he said, "will be much more risky for two than for one, and we want you to get to your destination as quickly as possible. Ask this Englishman to write to the British press or make a report for his authorities. You can take a letter with you, but not a man." I noted that Grzegorz made that decision without asking the other two what they thought. Bor agreed with him. The conversation ended with a question: did I have many relatives and acquaintances in London? I answered that before the war I held no public post and that my circle of acquaintances and relatives there was quite small.

He continued: "You must treat your plans for returning to this country as top secret. Your propaganda and political mission may involve some appearances in public. A risk is attached to that, especially for the family you are leaving behind. You must try to ensure that German counterintelligence does not get to know who you are."

This was the end of the briefing; it had lasted for more than an hour, and I left encouraged by the thought that this triumvirate knew exactly what it wanted and had worked out future possibilities well in advance. At this critical time I was being sent on an important and very urgent mission.

The following week brought the news of a catastrophe that in one blow upset all the plans for my expedition: I received word from Seweryn that, on August 6, all the people to whom I owed the success of my earlier journey to Sweden, and who were to help get me there a second time, had been arrested, among them Franciszek Szwarc, who had sheltered me before I boarded the ship, Maria Pyttel, the principal organizer, and the two dock workers who had hidden me under the coal. The Warsaw-Stockholm route that we had organized with such effort and had already caused the loss of two people was blocked. One could only try to reestablish it.

After my return to Warsaw, Seweryn's greatest concern had been to warn Maria that she was in danger because of the arrest of Hilda and Tadeusz. They both had her address and were to give her the documents intended for me and made out in the name of Jan Kwiatkowski. Unfortunately, the entire group, encouraged by their initial success, did not wait for couriers and emissaries from Warsaw but began to smuggle refugees away from the coast for practice. With their assistance, some five or six people got to Sweden during the month of July. The last one was to have been Maria herself, whom Seweryn's warning reached at the end of July. Alas, the news that a group was helping people escape across the Baltic spread too widely. A certain Witold S. applied to go, and he turned out to be a Gestapo informer. He was to accompany Maria on her flight to Sweden. She was changing into overalls before being loaded aboard ship when the whole crew was arrested in the Szwarc flat. She survived interrogation and life in a Nazi concentration camp. Franciszek Trepczynski was executed just before the liberation. Franciszek Szwarc died after the war.

Luckily, the raid did not reach Jan Zgoda's house in Gdynia. Being cautious, I had not put Jan Zgoda in contact with anyone, and thus I still had a place where I could take shelter. New contacts on the coast had to be found. Now another danger appeared. Because of General Sikorski's idea of working for a Polish Czechoslovak Confederation, both the BIP and the Government Delegate showed great interest in Poland's southern neighbor. It was said that Grot even had a plan for cooperation between the military underground organizations in both countries in the event of a rising. In BIP there was a special cell collecting information from the territory of the Protectorate. Action N also made some attempts to smuggle its literature into Czechoslovakia. I myself once or twice had crossed the frontier into the Czech part of Silesia, but did not go farther than Bogumin. The inspector of Action N for Czechoslovakia was a man known as "Redhead," recruited into the organization by Leszek. I believe that Redhead was a Czech. His name was Rudolf Zazdel, or Zazdek, and before the war he had been a teacher at an agricultural college in Czech Silesia. In any case, his Czech was as good as his Polish, and he had extensive contacts on the other side of the frontier. In 1943, he was suggested as a suitable emissary to send to Prague to establish contacts with prewar Czech politicians. He went there several times and on his return made some sensational reports. At some point the authenticity of these reports came under suspicion, and it was decided to send to Prague an officer of the prewar diplomatic service who had spent many years in that capital and knew the Czech political world intimately.

I had felt an instinctive antipathy toward and distrust of Redhead from our first encounter. He was very tall, with bushy eyebrows that attracted one's attention on first meeting. He never shook hands firmly, and his hand was soft and wet.

Some time at the beginning of September I was ordered to meet our diplomat, who had just returned from Prague and wanted to transmit some important information to London through me. He used the code name "Goral." He was around fifty, and seemed a highly educated and very cultured man. In Prague he had seen various leaders and party activists and a few high-ranking officers whom he knew well from before the war. He obtained confirmation that Redhead's reports to General Rowecki and the Home Army command were fictitious. The individuals with whom Redhead said he had spoken denied having any contact with him.

The results of Goral's other mission were entirely negative. Whenever he raised the question of eventual cooperation between underground Poland and Czechoslovakia he met with rejection. "We are too small a nation," they told him, "to be able to do what you are doing. Our fate will not be settled within the country but on the battlefields of the war. We leave the fight for independence to Beneš's government. We have our airmen in Great Britain; they are our standardbearers with the Allies. When Germany starts falling apart, we shall organize ourselves very quickly."

We had a long talk. Goral told me about an adventure he had on his return journey. At the frontier station he was dragged from his compartment by the Gestapo, who obviously had been waiting for him. He was interrogated but not ill-treated, and was held for two days and nights. Luckily, he was going to Prague completely legally, under his own name, as the representative of a large enterprise under German control for which he worked. Nothing could be proved against him, and, under pressure from the German firm in Warsaw, he was released.

"Who informed on you?" I asked, "the Czechs?" Goral denied it. "I shall share my suspicions with you," he said, "if you give me your word of honor that you will never make use of what I tell you." Having obtained my promise, he continued: "I have studied all the circumstances and have concluded that the only man who could have told the Germans the day and the exact time that my train was due to cross the frontier was Redhead. Moreover, I believe that I owe to him not only the fact that I had been stopped at the frontier, but also my release."

"How is that?" I asked.

"Simply because the Gestapo did not want their informant's cover blown prematurely."

"It can't be true," I replied. "If Redhead were working for the Gestapo, Leszek and the people from Action N with whom he is in contact, including myself, would have been arrested long ago."

"I have a different theory," said Goral. "There are indications that Redhead was himself arrested on his last return trip from Czechoslovakia and that, in prison, to save his life, he agreed to become an informer. In any case he was, you must understand, the only person who knew my real name and knew about my journey."

"Why did you tell him in the first place?"

"I received a discreet request to check his contacts. I had to meet him to get the actual addresses and all the relevant information. We agreed to meet again immediately after my return."

"Did you report your suspicions?"

"I did not and shall not report because I am not certain. All I have is circumstantial evidence."

I tried hard to persuade Goral that it was his solemn duty to write a report. His suspicions seemed to be alarmingly plausible. But he refused: what if an underground jury should order the execution of an innocent man? I knew that Leszek had begun to be suspicious of Redhead and had stopped cooperating with him on Action N. From Seweryn, I heard that Redhead had turned up a short time before as Zaloga's collaborator and had adopted a new code name, "Jarach." He established contact with Zaloga in 1942 to get assistance in crossing the Czech frontier. The change of code name and the strict separation of different activities in the various cells of the Home Army resulted in Zaloga's ignorance of the fact that Redhead's reports had been completely discredited by Goral.

"If you don't warn the right people," I continued, "you might unwittingly bring about the arrest, and perhaps death, of not just one but many people. In such a case I feel I cannot be bound to silence: I must warn you that I shall inform my superiors of what I have heard from you.''

Immediately after that meeting I asked to see the Chairman and repeated Goral's suspicions to him. Colonel Rzepecki reacted to my report with skepticism. ''Mutual suspicion is a professional disease of all conspirators,'' he said. ''Hardly a day passes without my receiving similar reports.'' I left him still uneasy but convinced that, having done my duty, I did not have to take any further action. Unfortunately, I did not mention Jarach to anybody else. I considered any further disclosure of Goral's suspicions, told to me in confidence, inappropriate, but I could not help worrying that they might prove to have been justified.

Chapter 18

*A*fter the arrests at Gdynia, the number of people imprisoned by the Gestapo, whose activities revolved around a mysterious individual named Jan Kwiatkowski, was increased to six. It was time to change the name on my passport. The Germans had my photograph in their files, of course, but this did not worry me too much. They were looking for too many people; they had thousands of photographs, with assumed and real names attached to them. While a person was out of their clutches and there was no official identification, he was protected by the very mass of "offenses" and "offenders."

At about this time Seweryn's liaison girl, "Irena," brought the news that Stockholm had asked that I travel under another name. Jan Kwiatkowski was wanted by the Swedish police because two months after his arrival in Sweden as a refugee he had disappeared without a trace. I was immediately to supply Irena with a new Christian name and surname, in which the access card to Gdynia should be issued. "Kowalski," I suggested. Irena was opposed. "Sparks" (a code name for short-wave stations) "want short names, with as few letters as possible. One- or two-syllable names are best, since every second of transmission time counts." I made one or two other suggestions that Irena rejected. "Well," I said at last, "if you want one- or two-syllable names, let's have 'Nowak'—'Jan Nowak.'"

I did not think that I was parting with my family name, Jezioranski, and my Christian name, Zdzislaw, for good, and that, for the rest of my life, I would remain Jan Nowak. Not only the frontier pass but the consular passport in Stockholm was prepared in that name. Years later I realized that I had made a serious mistake: a conspirator must not assume a common name. Passport controls on various frontiers after the war finally taught me how many Polish and Czech "Jan Nowak"s there are in the world, at least one of whom appears on every country's "black list." Over and over I have had to produce documentary proof that I was not the Jan Nowak wanted by the police. The name has proved very troublesome.

After the liquidation by the Gestapo of our entire organization on the coast, I thought that the best chance to get to Stockholm would be for Piotrowski to send Klapp and Olandson to Gdynia, to an address indicated by us, and have them take me back on board the boat on which they had arrived. Zaloga transmitted these suggestions to Stockholm through London, and some time later news came that Klapp and Karl were ready to meet me at Gdynia or Gdansk, if we sent addresses and passwords. I knew that they would have to wait for the right opportunity and that coordination of dates would not be easy. The operation would take two weeks at least. I would have to spend time waiting at some safe houses on the coast, but one could not be limited to only one address because, at the last moment, any one of them might become unsafe.

The next few weeks were therefore spent looking in Gdynia or Gdansk for likely addresses. One came to us from the liaison girl Magdalena, who knew somebody called Filarska who lived in Warsaw but had a sister named Maria in Gdynia, who was a secretary in the local slaughterhouse. In the middle of September Zaloga radioed Stockholm three addresses for Klapp and Olandson: Jan Zgoda, in Oksywie; Karol Wojcik, manager of a German shop, in Gdansk; and Maria Filarska, in Gdynia. My escorts were given the passwords "I have a letter for Jan Nowak" and the response, "I'll give it to a friend." I was to leave Warsaw as soon as I received the radio message from Stockholm that Klapp was on his way. At my request Zaloga sent instructions that for security reasons Klapp should not contact any member of his family or prewar friends while in Gdynia.

My frontier pass was obtained at last by a bribe, together with an identity card belonging to a civilian working for a German firm supplying the Luftwaffe. The work permit was issued on paper whose color was reserved exclusively for the military, had the stamp of the Luftwaffe, and seemed to be foolproof. I now had only to wait for a signal from Stockholm, but there was still the question of collecting "mail." On my own initiative and responsibility, I resolved to take to London the Action N pamphlet *Der grösste Lügner der Welt* ("The Greatest Liar in the World"), one of its wittiest publications. I wanted to take it not on microfilm but in the original, to give to Churchill, inscribed to him from all the workers in Action N. If I succeeded in handing it to the British prime minister, it would be excellent propaganda for the Home Army, a tangible proof of the offensive spirit of his Polish ally. The pamphlet was relatively small and easily hidden in a rectangular shaving mirror. The inscription was written in India ink; the English used was not the most correct, but this only added flavor to it.

I was not well pleased when my liaison girl told me that the mail was already hidden away and that my final instructions from Zaloga were to be handed over by Jarach (formerly Redhead), who had taken over Seweryn's work at Zaloga. The meeting was arranged not indoors but at the bus stop in the center of the town. Jarach handed me the mail, hidden as usual in everyday objects, and reminded me that Zaloga wanted me, on arrival in Stockholm, to send back by radio the verified names and addresses of our new contacts on the coast and the new password arranged, so that other emissaries could follow immediately. He asked to be informed about the day of my departure from Warsaw so that "Anna" could know when to expect me. I told him that this would be in no less than a week.

Toward the end of the conversation he adopted a more personal tone. "If you are leaving family here," he said, "I will willingly do what I can for them. Give me their names and addresses." I thanked him effusively, assuring him that the care of my nearest and dearest had already been organized. I don't know whether it was my imagination, but I thought that at that moment a sudden flash of suspicion appeared in Jarach's eyes. If he is really a Gestapo informer, I thought, and has guessed from my behavior that I suspect him or know something, that is very bad. He will try to have me eliminated fast. I walked away, and after several steps looked back. Jarach continued to stand at the bus stop, apparently deep in thought. What luck, I said to myself, that my new documents did not pass through his hands and that he does not know either my real name or my new false one. I did not go straight to our flat in Nowy Swiat, but walked about for a good half hour. Jarach might not have been alone.

The next day I received news that Klapp and Olandson had already left Stockholm and were to collect me from Gdynia between October 12 and 22. I sent by return a message that I would leave Warsaw on the 13th and from the 16th on would be in Gdynia waiting for them.

But at the moment when everything seemed to be arranged, a new radio message arrived from Stockholm. Klapp's first choice of ship had been rerouted to Rotterdam, his second to Kiel. I now began to doubt whether my escorts from Sweden would ever arrive but nevertheless decided not to postpone my departure. It would be better to wait on the spot on the chance of getting a ship than to hang about in Warsaw. I realized that the chances of a ship were small and that I could not stay on the coast for more than two weeks, so prepared myself to return to Warsaw in that case.

I started for Gdansk on October 15: only my mother, brother, and Greta knew. I agreed with my brother that if I did not return within two weeks, he would announce my sudden disappearance to the Polish police and the Housing Administration. There would then be no question of my returning to my old job. I carefully cleaned out all my hiding places.

As I was walking to the railway station with Greta, the loudspeakers in the streets were blaring an announcement about a public execution of dozens of hostages in retaliation for the killing of a German. In the city the situation was growing more tense. People were picked off trams and in streets and marketplaces almost daily. From the other side the counterattacks of the Home Army were more frequent. During the early weeks of October I heard constantly of new successful attacks on the Gestapo and their informers.

My documents were accepted without question at the border and during a random check on the train in the morning. At Gdansk I changed to a local train for Gdynia and went straight from the station to the house of Jan Zgoda, where I was greeted like a long-lost son.

When I arrived here from Warsaw in April, everything had been ready for me. Now I had to mount the mission alone in a strange city where, apart from Zgoda and his wife and daughters, I did not know a soul.

The success of the venture was in the hands of this Maria Filarska, who had been recommended in Warsaw. The next day I went to see her at her office. My impression at the first meeting was slightly disappointing. I had expected an older person, experienced, and with a knowledge of the local people. I found a young girl of perhaps twenty, very shy, tongue-tied and rather embarrassed by the stranger from Warsaw. I explained the situation to her without much conviction. What could one expect from such a girl? Filarska did not promise anything, but did not refuse to help. She asked me to meet her in a few days' time.

Walking about the town was not advisable, so I spent all my time with the Zgoda family. I remembered my last trip, when the Swedish policeman at Slite wanted to know which German warships were in port. Intelligence work was not my specialty, but this time I would try to gather as much information as I could. Gdynia was now perhaps the most important port in the Baltic, especially for German submarines. I asked Zgoda, who repaired boilers in a dock assigned to warships, to give me some information about the movements of German warships and submarines. I memorized all that he told me. One night he returned from work and remarked casually: "Today they towed in the pocket battleship *Admiral Hipper.* She's in a bad way. She got hit several times at Riga. The Krauts won't have much fun with her now." "How do you know that she was *Admiral Hipper*?" I asked. "Surely her name must have been painted over." "I have known that ship for a long time," he answered. "I have repaired her boilers more than once. It is *Hipper* for sure!" I committed this news to my memory as well, not suspecting how useful it would be later.

Meanwhile, Filarska had not been idle. It turned out that she had acquaintances among shipbrokers who met the crews of Swedish ships every day. She put me in touch with two of them, one with the papers of a Volksdeutscher, the second having kept his Polish nationality.[*] Both were very ready to help but recommended patience. I must wait until a Swede came along whom they knew and trusted.

Days passed. I waited patiently, bored to distraction. Luckily, in late October it gets dark early in Gdynia, and I could walk about in

[*]I remember the Christian name of the first one, Adam. The other's family name was Stodolski.

the blackout and have supper in a restaurant where one of the waiters was a trusted friend of the Zgodas: with the counterfeit German food cards that I had brought from Warsaw I could always get something to eat.

In Gdynia, as everywhere else on the coast, the majority of Poles had been forced to sign the Volksliste. The Germans called them "Angedeutsche" (a short form of Angehörige) and tolerated them if they were useful as qualified tradesmen. A certain number of Poles, among them the Zgoda family, whom nothing would induce to sign the Volksliste, were under constant threat of expulsion or, if they were too useful, of loss of their apartment and relegation to life in barracks otherwise inhabited mainly by workmen brought to the town for forced labor.

One day I was returning from the center to Oksywie (a suburb) quite late in the evening. It was raining hard, and I reached the Zgodas' apartment soaked to the skin and half-frozen. The family was in despair. On the other side of Gdynia the Germans had begun to expel Poles en masse. They might turn their attention to Oksywie at any time. Zgoda asked me to pack my things and leave his house immediately. I tried to argue with him: "Jan, try to calm yourself. It is ten o'clock, dark, and pouring rain. Where can I find shelter at this hour? Let me hide in a cellar."

But Zgoda was adamant. "I am prepared to risk my own neck but I won't risk the lives of my wife and daughters. If the Germans come and find you, not registered as living here, we shall all hang, yourself included. Please leave and don't come back to us."

Even in so desperate a situation I could not blame Zgoda for not wanting to risk his daughters and wife on my account. I found myself in the street, like a stray dog thrown out the door, without a roof over my head. It was pitch black and still pouring rain. I remembered that Adam, one of the two shipbrokers recommended by Filarska, lived less than a mile from Oksywie. He was an Angedeutsche, so he was not under the expulsion order. Stumbling along the unpaved streets through the mud, I made my way to his home.

It was well after eleven when I knocked at his ground-floor window. It was dark inside. Everybody was asleep. After a long wait and a still longer dialogue through the closed door, I was let in and could explain what had happened. Adam's family, his wife and seven children, lived in two small and incredibly crowded rooms, but they did not show me the door. The host put two chairs together facing each other: I was to sit on one with my feet resting on the other. In this position I was soon asleep.

The second of the brokers, Stodolski, at last struck a bargain with the second engineer on the *Ludwig*. The Swede agreed to smuggle me through if well paid for it, and I met him in Stodolski's office. My new guardian was very cautious. To prevent any suspicion falling on him in case I was found, he would not take me on board himself. The boat was being loaded by day and night. The night shift came to work quite late, after the evening meal, when it was already dark. Stodolski was to take me to the pier and hide me behind a pile of goods ready for loading, very near the place where the boat was moored. When the night shift workers came aboard, I was to join them unobtrusively and walk aboard with the group. Then I was to go along the other side of the ship and down to a hold near the engine room, where a water storage tank was enclosed in a wooden partition. Two planks would be loosened. I was to remove them and, after getting inside, replace the planks. He would see that some food and water were placed inside my cubbyhole. He promised that, before the customs search, he would nail up the loose planks. He tore a page from a notebook and made a sketch. The plan seemed simple, but experience made me cautious. I asked him to be sure to tell me if the ship's destination changed and to give me the all-clear sign to come out of hiding when the ship was in Swedish territorial waters.

I could not leave Gdynia without thanking Filarska. Without the help of that young tongue-tied girl, I would have been preparing for a journey not to Sweden but back to Warsaw. As a farewell gift she wanted to give me some sausage, but I had to refuse, as the smell would attract the customs dogs. Anyway, I was hoping that the Swedish sailor would keep me supplied with food and water once we reached the open sea.

Everything went according to plan. Stodolski came to the dock with me. The night was dark and it was raining, ideal conditions. When I joined the group of workmen and walked past the foreman at the entrance, I thought that he turned his head after I passed him, and wondered if he noticed a stranger even in the darkness. I found the hiding place without difficulty, moved the planks, and found myself in a narrow space at most a foot and a half wide. Across the space was a piece of wood on which I could sit, but it was difficult to know where to put my feet, as there was water from the tank below me. In the end I braced my feet against the wooden wall.

Hardly had I time to put the planks back in place when I heard footsteps. Somebody shone a flashlight and, I imagined, was looking around. I held my breath. For a second a narrow beam of light shone into my hiding place through a crack between the boards. It must have been that foreman who looked at me so suspiciously. Having satisfied himself that the hold behind the engine room was empty, he left, but there was still the danger of discovery by police dogs during the customs search. According to his promise, the Swede came down later. In a whispered conversation he made sure that his passenger was in place, and nailed back the planks. He told me not to use my flashlight. Through the narrow cracks I could just see what was happening outside. During the search the Germans did not go into the hold with the dogs but only looked inside from the deck. Once again I had been lucky, for this time a search would have revealed my courier's "mail." In my razor I had some microfilm; in a mirror hidden in the voluminous pocket of my coveralls I had the pamphlet for Churchill, packed for me by Greta in Warsaw. Had the customs officers found these they would surely have wondered why a worker loading freight aboard a ship was carrying a mirror and shaving gear.

The boat left during the night. Again I spent long uncomfortable hours. Fearing that I would fall into the water, I fought sleep, but failed. I nodded off, propped against the wall. The Swede did not come back, so the *Ludwig* must be heading for Sweden. He did not appear until early morning on the fourth day. He removed the planks and told me to come out, that we were in Swedish territorial waters. I was to wait five minutes until he had got clear. Then I should ask the first sailor I met to take me to the captain. I thought that this man might be useful in the future and that, at any rate, in his own interests he would hold his tongue, so before we parted I pushed a few hundred kroner into his hands and suggested that in a week he call on the Polish consul in Göteborg. The consul was on the list of contacts I had memorized and had collaborated closely with Piotrowski.

It was very pleasant to come out of my narrow hiding place, go up on deck and breathe some fresh air. My third voyage across the Baltic was becoming much more comfortable than the two earlier ones. I could see the coast of Sweden and in a distance the cranes at the Malmö docks. Soon I was facing the captain. He treated me with complete indifference. Without speaking a word to me, he ordered one of his officers to summon the port police by radio. In ten minutes a police sloop arrived. I was uneasy lest "Jan Nowak" be identified as Jan Kwiatkowski, though this should be a worry in Stockholm rather than in Malmö.

For the first time in my life I found myself behind bars, in a police lockup. However, this was hardly a typical jail cell. I was incarcerated in a large, bright room with a scrupulously clean and comfortable bed, a rug in front of it, even an armchair and a radio. The thick, opaque windowpanes were the only sign that I was in a cell and not a hotel room. The door to the corridor was left open in daytime, and excellent Swedish food was brought to me from a nearby restaurant.

There were other prisoners with me, five young people from the Danish resistance movement. They had dynamited a German merchant ship in Copenhagen harbor the previous day, after which feat they had escaped across the straits to Sweden. Pleased with the success of their mission, they chattered incessantly. They all knew some English. I had heard about the increasing incidents of sabotage in Denmark from London broadcasts, but now I was able to learn much more at first hand. The blowing up of German ships, the destruction of military storehouses, the derailment of trains, and arson of military equipment at the airport were almost daily occurrences in Denmark. The Danes were well organized, and compared with our underground movement they were in a favorable situation, for after an action they could escape to Sweden, where they were never refused asylum and could await the end of the war in comfort.

The Danes' presence in the cell had other advantages for me as well. The police at Malmö and Göteborg were used to the mass influx of refugees. I was not a single prisoner, as at Slite on Gotland, so no one paid any attention to me. The prison warden, a jovial, fat man, came into the room to talk to the Danes. My interrogation was limited to a request for personal data. I identified myself as a worker who had escaped from Gdynia, and my false permit to enter the port of Gdynia served as a passport. On the third day of my detention, the Polish consul from Göteborg came to fetch me. He had been in touch with our legation at Stockholm and learned everything about me.

The next day, November 7, I found myself in Stockholm in the arms of Piotrowski and Mrs. Leonhard. With tears in their eyes, they greeted me like a dead man who had returned to the living. In June they had lost hope that I would be saved. In my first conversation with Piotrowski I asked when I would be able to fly to London. Over two months had passed since my briefing with General Bor and I did not wish to waste time in Stockholm.

"Not too soon," said Piotrowski. "Communication between Stockholm and London is through a Mosquito, a light bomber which can carry only one passenger. It flies over Norway, which is enemy territory, making a circle as far north as the supply of fuel allows. The flights are irregular and not daily, to avoid interception by German fighters. They depend on weather conditions and information about enemy fighters patroling the North Sea and the Norwegian coast. There is a long line of people waiting for this single seat: diplomats, diplomatic couriers, important agents of Allied intelligence, and journalists. The list of precedence is made out by the chief of 'Atlas' (British intelligence) in Stockholm. If you are very, very lucky, you will reach London in a month at the earliest."

I was depressed by this expected delay. Piotrowski consoled me that the Polish government in London would certainly put pressure on the British and that he himself had contacts with British intelligence in Stockholm.

This time my stay in the Swedish capital was somewhat like a prison sentence. I was put up in a hotel and was not allowed to show myself in the consulate, the legation, or the Polish Red Cross, where they still remembered Jan Kwiatkowski. At 5 P.M. each day I had to be in my hotel room next to the telephone, waiting for the signal for my departure. This would come at the very last moment, no doubt for reasons of security.

The boredom of waiting was interrupted by a comical adventure, which might have ended tragically, however. My meetings with Piotrowski and Mrs. Jozefa Leonhard must have been carefully guarded from the Swedish police. The Swedes certainly knew about the colonel's mission and kept an eye on him to see whom he was meeting. The greatest danger was that they would connect "Nowak" with Kwiatkowski. One evening Piotrowski and Mrs. Leonhard came to see me in my hotel room. We had ordered supper from the restaurant downstairs. Suddenly, without a knock, the door burst open. A slim, blond girl rushed in, ran up to Piotrowski, and a loud and violent quarrel in Swedish followed. I listened, astounded, with no idea what it was all about. Suddenly the Swedish girl pointed to me and

Piotrowski, and Mrs. Leonhard turned pale. I was even more astonished when Piotrowski asked the waiter to lay another place and the unknown woman sat down to dinner with us.

It appeared that Piotrowski was being watched by more than the Swedish police. He had a Swedish fiancée in Stockholm who was very jealous and irritated by his frequent disappearances. She had observed our meetings during my previous visit to Sweden, realized that here I was back again, and had come to have it out with Piotrowski. I was uneasy about the possibility of blackmail, but, at our next meeting, when we found ourselves alone, Piotrowski reassured me. "She knows that if we are blown, it will be both together," he said. "For me this would mean an order to leave Sweden and return to England, and she does not want to be separated from me. What she wants is not to be left alone too often." And so the girl was present at any subsequent meetings with Piotrowski and Mrs. Leonhard. She did not understand what the conversation was about, but seemed happy and contented just to be there. She and Piotrowski were married a few months later.

One evening, telling Piotrowski about my experiences at Gdynia, I mentioned casually that I had asked Jan Zgoda to tell me about German naval movements and that I had learned about the damaged pocket battleship *Admiral Hipper* being towed into the harbor. "For God's sake! Why didn't you tell me about this earlier? This is a plum for my Englishman!" he said.

The next day he took me to a private apartment where a tall, elegant gentleman of about forty was waiting for us. I repeated everything I heard from Zgoda. When I reached the story about the *Hipper*, the Englishman rose and started walking up and down the room, visibly excited, after which he began to cross-examine me. When was the ship brought into port? Who was the person who told me about her? How did he know about her? Did he recognize the ship? Was there any possibility that he could have made a mistake? How badly damaged was the ship? Had she gone into drydock? Had she been camouflaged against bombing, and if so, how, etc. I could answer all these questions almost automatically. After half an hour of this questioning, the Englishman turned to Piotrowski. "I am satisfied," he said. "It was the *Admiral Hipper*. I evaluate Nowak's information very highly and will cable London immediately."

I was astonished. I knew the news might be of interest to British intelligence, but had no notion that it could be as important as this. I knew that the British were a maritime nation, so perhaps my questioner was an admiral? The Englishman noticed how puzzled I was and explained: "The movement and location of German naval units, and especially battleships, is of primary importance for us in the light of the safety of our convoys in the Atlantic Ocean. We must know if and when they leave the Baltic area. Outside it, they are a threat. We lost sight of the pocket battleship *Admiral Hipper* in Riga in October, at just the time when your informer located her at Gdynia. She must have been well camouflaged because she was not identified from aerial photographs. I will have the photographs of the port at Gdynia checked again and compare them with what you have just told me."

Piotrowski now intervened: "If the news is accurate, we would like to receive a bonus in return. This officer" (he turned to me) "is the emissary of our underground military organization. He has an important and urgent mission to fulfill in London. He has been waiting for nearly a month for a place in an aircraft. Can you assure him of priority?" "I'll do what I can," the Englishman replied laconically. Piotrowski left very well satisifed. "The phrase 'I'll do what I can,' " he told me, "means much more than that in his case. You'll be in London next week." A couple of days later the telephone rang in the evening. An official of the British embassy told me to be at the airfield within forty-five minutes. "No questions. Goodbye."

In the waiting room at the airfield the English air crew, a pilot, co-pilot, and navigator, were waiting. Passport control was quick. My passport gave my profession as workman. The Swedish passport official looked ironically at my hands, then at my face. He must have known pretty well by then these "workmen" who kept leaving for Britain.

The Mosquito was a small bomber. The passenger seat was not in the cabin, but in the specially altered bomb bay: I was, quite literally, sitting where the bombs were supposed to be. One entered this compartment from beneath the fuselage, where the bomb bay doors opened. It was lit by a small lamp. There was enough room to sit or lie down. One could communicate with the pilot by intercom, but there was no other connection to the cabin.

As it happened, this was the first time I had ever been in an aircraft. Twenty minutes after takeoff I heard a voice in my earphones: "Are you all right?" "I'm fine," I replied, and asked where we were. "Still over Sweden," the navigator replied. "We are climbing now and flying north. In about half an hour we'll veer to the west." Several minutes later the voice in the earphones was heard again. It told me to put on my oxygen mask. "Don't light a cigarette under any circumstances," I was warned.

The navigator talked to me again after four hours' flying, saying that the aircraft was preparing to land. We were approaching the coast of Scotland. Only then did I learn that we were to land not near London but at the military airfield near St. Andrews, in eastern Scotland. The pressurizing of the bomb bay must have been faulty because when we landed my ears were terribly painful, but I was too preoccupied by the thought that I was nearing my goal to pay attention to such a detail.

And then, at that long-awaited moment when I would stand on British soil at last, with all my dangers behind me, I nearly lost my life in a most senseless, almost idiotic way. Right in front of my eyes was a warning sign: "Do not alight before the engines stop," but I did not understand the word "alight" and thought that this warning referred to the smoking of cigarettes while the engines were running. As the wheels of the aircraft touched down, the bomb-bay door opened automatically from both sides. After a moment the aircraft came to a standstill, although the engines were still running. By the light of a flashlight, I saw the asphalt of the landing strip through the open door, not more than four feet below the fuselage. I jumped down and began to extricate myself from my safety belt with the upper half of my body still inside the aircraft.

Suddenly I heard a furious shout next to me. An excited member of the ground crew was shaking me violently, cursing me at the top of his lungs. I could only understand three words of his many profanities: "You bloody fool!" I was at a loss to understand why I was being greeted with such a lack of courtesy by our British allies, but a few minutes later, in the guardroom at the airfield, I understood what I had done wrong. The ground crew man was about to send the Mosquito to its appointed parking area when, at the last moment, he saw somebody's legs underneath the fuselage. With a violent gesture he stopped the pilot. Had the aircraft moved on, I would have been broken in half like a match at the very moment when I had reached my destination.

Chapter 19

I had been expecting a Polish officer of Section Six to meet me on the airfield, in spite of the fact that we had landed in Scotland instead of London, but an unpleasant surprise was in store for me. Instead of a representative of Section Six, two British policemen and a black limousine awaited. I was greeted in a very courteous and friendly manner, and the two policemen assured me that they were extremely sorry, but that the regulations issued by His Majesty's Government concerning "foreigners landing in the British Isles" must be followed: one must endure a kind of political quarantine before being granted a "landing permit."

"I understand," I said, but tried to explain. "I am not an ordinary foreigner but the official representative of the authorities of an allied country. I am here on an important mission. Your authorities were informed about me. The Polish and British authorities know all about me. Please allow me to communicate with our government in London by telephone." Both the policemen were again extremely sorry: the regulations admitted of no exceptions of any kind.

Half an hour later, resigned but upset by still another delay, this time most unexpected, I found myself in a police station in the small town of Cupar. It was suggested that I take a nap on the sofa in the warm room. At ten the next morning I was awakened, and smelled the aroma of fried bacon in the air. On the table a Scots breakfast was waiting: porridge with milk, bacon and eggs, coffee, toast, and marmalade. Next to my plate were a Scottish newspaper and the *Polish Daily* from London. I could not complain about a lack of hospitality.

After I had finished my breakfast the Scots policeman on duty explained that Great Britain was in a state of war and must guard herself against Nazi spies, infiltrating in various disguises. In the afternoon I would be taken to London by train, and there, after "conversations" with the appropriate authorities, I would be free to move about at will. Meanwhile, he suggested that the two of us take a little stroll in the town. He warned me that I might see some Polish soldiers on the street. "It would be nice of you," he added, "if you would refrain from any conversation with them."

There were, indeed, many Poles stationed at Cupar. For the first time since September 1939 I saw Poles in military uniforms, not Polish prewar uniforms but English battle dress with berets. I felt happy seeing the badges with the inscription "Poland." The soldiers looked very fit and smart. There were also many soldiers on the London train on which, escorted by two civilians, I left that day. The Poles among them talked very loudly, and laughed even louder. On the other hand, the British passengers spoke to each other in undertones. The Poles seemed to feel more at home than the natives.

At dawn we arrived in the city, the very name of which was pronounced with great solemnity in Poland. My first destination was a school building on the south side of the Thames, nicknamed jokingly "Patriotic School" but whose official name was the London Reception Centre. I found numerous Poles there, mostly young, who had come to Great Britain by various, complicated routes of wartime wandering. There were Poles from France who had crossed the Pyrenees to Spain and thence to Portugal; escapees from the officers' prisoner-of-war camps and labor camps in Germany; people from the Middle East who had been deported to Russia; and volunteers for the Polish forces from every corner of the world. Every one of them had lived through a series of unbelievable events and experiences. Only God knows how many such fugitives had disappeared along the way, or gotten stuck in various quagmires—prisons or concentration camps—at a border. Those who reached their goal were indeed in seventh heaven—an atmosphere of euphoria pervaded the "Patriotic School."

My stay in this establishment lasted only a few days. Soon after arrival I was summoned by a British officer who spoke Polish like a native (or, rather, like a native of Lwow); it appeared that Captain Malcolm Scott had been brought up in Poland. Before he began the routine interrogation he asked me various questions about the situation in the country. I thought that this questioning was probing deeper than usual for a counterintelligence officer, even though the foreigner came from a country where he had spent a large part of his life. The conversation had an almost social character until Captain Scott asked me to tell him my real Christian name, surname, and date and place of birth. I refused: "For the safety of my people in Poland," I declared, "it is impossible for me to reveal personal data."

"In that case I won't be able to get you released from here," the captain said.

"Why cannot the Polish authorities take care of this? I have not come to England on private business and I am not a refugee."

Scott seemed upset. "Are you an officer on active service?"

"Yes, I am."

"Then you must obey orders."

"I shall obey only the orders of my Polish superiors."

"You mean of an officer of Section Six of the Polish staff?"

"Yes."

Scott's face cleared, and he sent me back to the main reception room. A few hours later, I was summoned again. This time Scott was in the company of a Polish officer of Section Six. "Please do not hesitate to give the captain all the true personal data," he said. "They will be regarded as top secret."

"My name is Zdzislaw Jezioranski."

"I knew exactly what your name is," Scott declared. "We have a Pole here who remembers you from before the war. You were together in a student's course in Bucharest. I only wanted to complete the formalities and check that you were telling the truth."

Of course I did not tell anybody at the Patriotic School my real name or that I was an emissary of the AK commander, so everybody in the building was surprised when I left soon afterwards, accompanied by another officer of Section Six, as the "quarantine" in the school usually lasted from two to three weeks.

In Upper Belgrave Street, where Section Six had its headquarters in a nineteenth-century house, the code name "Zych" was known to everyone in regular contact with Poland. I was taken to

210

dinner at a restaurant near Piccadilly Circus by Colonel Michal Prota-sewicz, the head of Section Six, and Halina Omiecinska, as I learned later, the *eminence grise* of the Hotel Rubens, Polish headquarters. We spoke about politics. All London was waiting for the outcome of the conference at Teheran, which had ended a fortnight before, and wor-rying about Churchill, who was now in the hospital at Marrakesh with pneumonia. "Pray God he survives," sighed Halina. So Churchill was not only an idol for Poles in Poland but also for Poles in London.

A few days later Colonel Protasewicz took me to meet the chief of staff, General Stanislaw Kopanski, and asked him to arrange an audience for me with the commander-in-chief as soon as possible. According to my Warsaw instructions, I was to repeat the report from General Bor which I had memorized only to General Sosnkowski himself. With General Kopanski and Colonel Protasewicz, I went to the office of General Sosnkowski's aide-de-camp at the Rubens Hotel. We were asked to wait. General Sosnkowski was taking a call from Scotland, where the Polish First Corps was stationed. "You are the first emissary from Poland to report to General Sosnkowski as commander-in-chief," General Kopanski whispered in my ear. "The last military emissary from our country reached London nearly a year ago."

What a piece of history this General Sosnkowski represents, I thought. He was a member of a secret fighting organization at the beginning of the century, as a student. Later he was a member of the secret Polish Socialist Party and took part in preparations for the fight for independence. When World War I broke out, he was Josef Pilsudski's chief of staff, the commander of the first Polish military unit fighting in Polish uniform in the Austrian Imperial Army. When Pilsudski decided to disobey the Germans and Austrians in 1917, Sosnkowski was imprisoned with him in the fortress of Magdeburg. After Poland became independent, he organized the army with Pilsudski, played an important part in the victorious war against Rus-sians in 1920 that saved Poland's independence for twenty years, and was a respected minister of war in the first years of independence.

If somebody had told me a year ago in Warsaw that I would be talking to the commander-in-chief in his study in the heart of Lon-don, only a few steps from Buckingham Palace, I would have thought he was mad. I was only an unknown second lieutenant of twenty-nine and a very insignificant person. But I was deeply conscious of

211

the importance of my mission as an emissary of underground Poland and of the AK commander. I was to explain the situation and the atmosphere inside Poland, answer important questions, and ask other questions myself. Meanwhile, the minutes dragged by. Kopanski was composed but began to show signs of impatience. The aide-de-camp, rather embarrassed, assured us that the general's conversation would soon be over. It must be something important, I thought, when Sosnkowski makes the chief of staff, the chief of Section Six, and an emissary from Poland wait.

Three-quarters of an hour passed; suddenly the door from the general's study opened and an officer rushed out and said to the aide-de-camp: "So the General finally decided to bring the band from Scotland." Filled with the importance of the moment and my own mission, I was taken aback both by the nature of the decision and by the fact that it had taken the commander-in-chief such a long time to reach.

When we were admitted to his presence, the general rose from behind his desk, stretched out his arms toward me, and, without a word, embraced me most cordially. The gesture was so spontaneous that I at once forgot my annoyance. I remembered his face from pre-war photographs. He looked about sixty. Face to face, his appearance was impressive. He was very tall, aristocratic, quite unlike General Bor, whose slight build and modest demeanor were strangely out of keeping with the legend surrounding him as leader of an organization encompassing almost the whole nation. Sosnkowski looked and acted like a military leader, with seriousness and authority allied to a most captivating manner.

After some brief exchanges concerning my journey from Warsaw, I began to enumerate the four points set out by Bor, Grzegorz, and the Chairman. The general listened attentively, nodded his head from time to time, not interrupting until I reached the matter of escalating our activity against the German troops as they made an orderly retreat through Polish territories before the pressure of the Soviet forces.

"This I don't understand," he broke in. "If the Russians invade Poland as a new occupying force—and everything points to this—what sense would there be in escalating the fight against the Germans? You would only provoke even harsher repressive measures against the population and incur increased losses. It would be justified if the Russians were to accept our frontiers, re-establish diplomatic relations with our government, and stop their propaganda campaign. In view of what is awaiting us, the logic of the moment dictates the avoidance of losses and the limitation of action against the Germans to necessary acts of self-defense. If the Russians enter Poland, the Home Army should remain underground or withdraw its detachments to the west or south of the country."

I was entirely unprepared for this polemic. My task was to repeat faithfully the thoughts and words of General Bor, but Sosnkowski's reaction seemed so far removed from the realities of the situation in Poland that I could not keep silent. "I believe, sir, that the very name 'Home Army' may be misleading. This is not a regular army, living in barracks under strict military discipline. One cannot command its soldiers to 'Halt! About Face!' One cannot move its formations at will from one end of the country to the other. It is a revolutionary or insurgent organization. The soldiers of the Home Army, with the exception of the career officers, are civilians who live in their native towns and villages. They are tied to their own territories and to their jobs. Headquarters can direct these revolutionary masses, can prevent spontaneous actions and provide a framework for a considered choice of place and time for an organized armed action, but only if its orders in some degree coincide with the prevailing mood in the country. I don't know," I continued, "if you, sir, realize the intensity of the longing for retaliation against them which the Germans have generated by their persecutions and atrocities! There is a revolutionary groundswell against the occupying power that will erupt when the first signs of German weakness appear. At the same time, the people hear constant accusations from Moscow that the command of the Home Army is trying to stop them from fighting the Germans. Instructions that would tend to confirm the Soviet accusations would bring results difficult to predict. At the moment of a German retreat, they might not be obeyed." My polemic did not seem to affect the cordial atmosphere of the meeting—on the contrary, I noticed that taking a stand on my own had made a good impression!

The meeting lasted a long time. As the most important task, the general ordered a detailed report to be prepared about the activities of Soviet partisans and communist formations, their relations with the Home Army and with the Germans. This was necessary in view of the Soviets' continuous tirade of accusations that the AK was

213

not fighting the Germans but the Soviet partisans and the Polish communists.

For my part, I explained that the second half of my mission was to gather information and material for the use of the Home Army command. I asked for free access to source material, to the correspondence between Sosnkowski and Bor, and other facilities. The general agreed to these requests without hesitation and issued instructions to Protasewicz to show me the more important current dispatches and those going back over the last few months. He advised me to report to the president (Wladyslaw Raczkiewicz), the prime minister (Stanislaw Mikolajczyk), the minister of foreign affairs (Tadeusz Romer), the minister of war (General Marian Kukiel), and the Polish ambassador (Edward Raczynski).

In conclusion, he asked, "What are you doing over the holidays? Have you got any family in London?" I replied that I had no plans. "In that case, perhaps you would like to join us at Swiss Cottage for supper on Christmas Eve.* We will then be able to talk further without interruption."

*Supper on Christmas Eve, not dinner on Christmas Day, is the traditional family feast in Poland.

Chapter 20

*I*n the first few days after leaving the Patriotic School, I felt somewhat lost in both Polish and British London. It was an unknown territory for me, and slightly dangerous. I lacked basic charts to the political and personal constellations here. In Warsaw the military defeat had swept away the prewar government, which was supported by the army and had had dictatorial powers since Pilsudski's military coup in 1926. Before the war, political parties could be active and publish papers (subject to censorship, but a liberal one). At present, the four largest political parties (the Nationalists, Christian Democrats, Social Democrats, and Peasant Party) had formed something like an underground parliament, which, joined by some smaller groups, adopted the name of Council of National Unity. The Council was a vast, democratic, anti-Nazi coalition which cooperated quite harmoniously with the military organization. The supporters of the prewar government had very little influence in Poland.

In London things were quite different. The ministers, a large proportion of the civil service, and part of the officer corps had escaped to Romania in 1939, thence to France, and, after the French debacle, to London. In Paris, General Wladyslaw Sikorski, Pilsudski's opponent, the standard-bearer of the prewar opposition, formed a new government composed of the four main opposition parties. Sikorski's many supporters inside Poland saw in him the symbol of their own aspirations, but he had many adversaries among the émigrés, who were closely affiliated with the prewar government. Because Sikorski combined the position of prime minister and commander-in-chief, he was able to keep a firm hold on the armed forces. When he was killed in the plane crash at Gibraltar, Kazimierz Sosnkowski became commander-in-chief in the usual way, on the basis of his seniority and rank. Around him gathered the former adherents of Pilsudski, while the post of the premier went to Stanislaw Mikolajczyk, the leader of the Peasant Party and an ardent opponent of the prewar dictatorship. There was great antagonism and mutual distrust between the two men—in fact, Polish London was divided into warring camps.

Under these circumstances, it was easy to make mistakes at the very beginning, and I got some friendly advice from the young officers of Section Six once they understood that I was not politically involved with any party and viewed my assignments as those of a soldier. They warned me, above all, not to allow myself to be labeled, which would make my task of gathering information much more difficult. These comrades advised me not to become involved in arguments on one side or the other regardless of what I personally believed. I was warned also that my assessments and information could be repeated in distorted form as part of internal political ploys.

Thus I went to the Christmas supper with General and Mrs. Sosnkowski already conscious of the fact that London and Warsaw were two distant and completely different worlds. For this important visit I donned the uniform with the insignia of my parent regiment, the Horse Artillery, for the first time. I cleaned shoes and belt as for a parade. Meanwhile the general, as if to underline the unofficial and family atmosphere of the meal, wore no military belt and was in an unpressed uniform.

After the meal, the general took me to his study and invited me to take a seat. He himself began to walk up and down, chain-smoking and forever adding more whiskey to his glass. He began by asking whether I realized what an enormously important part I had to play in the next few weeks. Communication with Poland was very limited. The radio operators inside the country were having increasing difficulties. There were greater and greater delays in sending and receiving the longer messages; sometimes only a few sentences came through each day. Then too, complicated problems could not be explained in telegraph-ese. The envoys to London had what were clearly technical or organizational assignments. Any newcomer whom one could introduce to the British and the Americans begins as a star, he said, the focus of general attention, but, with the passage of time, its brightness wanes. "You have before you a few weeks, perhaps a month, which you must use as best you can. I want to explain the situation to you so that you will know how to act."

He started by saying that in the last few days very important conversations had been held between Prime Minister Mikolajczyk and Anthony Eden, their first meeting since the conference at Teheran. Present were Raczynski and Romer. Unfortunately, Sosnkowski himself had the gist of the conversation only at second hand, but he understood that in Teheran Stalin had demanded that the Curzon Line be recognized as Poland's frontier in the east[*] and had offered territorial compensation in the west from Germany. Stalin had accused the Home Army of collaboration with the Germans and of murdering Soviet partisans and had demanded the removal of General Sosnkowski himself, as an enemy of the Soviet Union.[†] And "this was only the start," said the general. "Further conversations will take place when Churchill is better."

Sosnkowski regarded these future meetings with pessimism. He thought that Mikolajczyk was no match for people like Churchill and Eden. He assumed that both Mikolajczyk and our diplomats would make concessions and, under pressure, would accept all the conditions demanded by the British. They could be influenced not to do so only by the attitude of the armed forces, Polish public opinion, and the views from inside Poland. He took a negative view of the policy of the Anglo-American Allies. They claim not to favor the divi-

---

[*]The Curzon Line, running along the River Bug, was suggested in 1920 by Lord Curzon, the British undersecretary of state for foreign affairs, as the eastern frontier of Poland at a time when the Red Army was approaching Warsaw. After the defeat of the Soviet armies, the peace treaty of Riga drew the Polish-Soviet frontier two hundred miles east of the Curzon Line, a boundary recognized by the Western powers. In 1939, the line of partition of Poland between Nazi Germany and Soviet Russia more or less followed the Curzon Line but at that time was called the Ribbentrop-Molotov Line.

[†]The British did not acquaint their Polish allies with the full story of the Teheran Conference with regard to Poland. According to the British official history of World War II: "The Russians could regard the Teheran Conference as a success. . . . They had left themselves free in Europe to enforce upon the Poles territorial and political conditions which would ensure their subservience to the Soviet Union" (*History of the Second World War*, edited by Sir Llewellyn Woodward [London: Her Majesty's Stationery Office, 1971], vol. 3, p. 104).

sion of Europe into spheres of influence, he said, but everything points to the fact that such an unwritten division exists, the best proof of which is that in the fall of 1943 they stopped the drops of arms and ammunition for the Home Army. Of course the British always cover up by talk of technical obstacles, but it is obvious that they are guided by political considerations. The British, in Sosnkowski's opinion, in fact care little for the Home Army. They want to withdraw from their commitments to Poland without loss of face; they want the Poles themselves to relieve them of all their obligations as allies.

I asked myself whether Sosnkowski was not going too far in his distrust of the Allies. But the general had evidence to support his views. He cited to me the example of Yugoslavia. The previous May (1943) the British had recognized Tito, an established agent of the Comintern in the service of Moscow,* and his communist partisans, and they were now receiving British assistance on a large scale. Somehow in Tito's case the technical difficulties that hampered the supply flights to Poland were not present. On the other hand, assistance to Mihajlović and his Chetniks had been stopped a few months ago. Sosnkowski said that he had pointed out to a high-ranking British officer that, by helping Tito, Britain would push Yugoslavia into the arms of Russia and communism. The officer replied that military considerations were more important during the war than political ones. One must first defeat Germany; Tito is fighting the Germans; so Tito gets arms and ammunition. Mihajlović, on the other hand, according to that British officer, was limiting himself to defensive actions, and there were even indications that he was collaborating with the enemy against the communists. What point was there, then, in arming him, the British asked.

Of all I had heard so far from the general, this last story seemed to me the most incomprehensible. What sense did it make to the British to give the Soviets an opportunity to extend their influence to the Adriatic and assure them access to the Mediterranean? Could it be, I wondered, that the military aid to Tito was connected with plans for a landing in Yugoslavia and an offensive through the Balkans after the

---

*No one could guess that four years later Yugoslavia would break with Stalin and become the first communist country to become independent of Moscow. In 1943, Tito was generally considered (as I myself considered him at the time of this conversation) to be a Comintern agent.

occupation of Italy? Sosnkowski said no: the plans for an attack on the Balkans, if they had even existed, had been abandoned long ago under pressure from Stalin, who did not want anything to upset his plans to take over the whole of eastern Europe. He quoted in support of this belief his recent conversation with General de Gaulle, whom he had met during de Gaulle's recent journey to the Middle East. The final decision to open a second front in western Europe had already been made. The offers of capitulation on the part of Hungary and Romania had been rejected by the British and Americans. Although the Balkans were topographically not an easy area, politically they might well fall into the hands of the British and Americans like ripe apples. Poland's situation would be entirely different if British and American divisions eventually found themselves on the southern slopes of the Carpathian Mountains. But this would not happen.

I asked the general if he had any hope for Poland. He certainly had no illusions as to the Soviet plans. If Stalin succeeded in occupying Poland, she would be incorporated into the Soviet Union as its seventeenth republic—of course, after the usual plebiscite. But before the whole of Poland was occupied by the Soviets, a lot could happen. One could not preclude an earlier defeat of Germany, although nothing as yet pointed to that. The present position was the worst possible one from the Polish point of view. Since almost the whole burden of conducting the war lay upon Russia, the British and Americans had to have been in a very weak negotiating position at Teheran, unable to demand anything; they could, at most, only make requests. Moreover, they were afraid that Russia might conclude a separate peace and that the story of the Ribbentrop-Molotov Pact of September 1939 might be repeated.

"I don't exclude the possibility that, after reaching the line of the River Bug,[*] Stalin may halt his offensive and even suggest an armistice in order to help Hitler to turn the bulk of his resources against the British and Americans," the general continued. "However, the balance of power may change: Russia and Germany are being exhausted by the war, while the potential of the British and Americans is increasing fast. The alliance with the Russians will not be permanent. Toward the end of the war there will be no fear of a

[*]The partition line under the Ribbentrop-Molotov Pact.

separate peace, and there may even be a quarrel about the division of spoils which may turn into armed conflict if the Russians try to grab the whole of Germany for themselves. For the time being, one must make no concessions unless they will save something. The situation may change, but concessions made at the worst moment will be permanent and will have irreversible consequences. If the British support the Soviet territorial claims, our only answer is a firm 'No.'"

"Stalin demands that I should resign, accusing me of anti-Soviet views," continued Sosnkowski. "If, in return, he were to offer to respect our territorial integrity and our sovereignty, I would resign today, but he would then demand the resignation of five other men. Concessions would lead us on a downhill course, ending in the loss not only of half our country but of our independence as well."

At that point, the general began to speak about personal attacks on him. From a drawer of his desk, he produced books of press cuttings. In one book were pasted the monitored reports of Radio Moscow, the attacks in the Soviet press, and TASS communiqués. The second book contained attacks in the British press—the *Times*, the *Observer*, the *Daily Worker*, the *New Statesman*, and, given pride of place, an incredible article in the *Tribune* signed with a Polish pen name. The general read extracts to me; each one was worse than the preceding one. He maintained that at least half of the attacks in the British press were inspired by Poles. In this way, foreigners were drawn into internal Polish political intrigues. The blindness of some of our own people was so complete that they were prepared to support Soviet propaganda simply in order to get rid of him, Sosnkowski.

Listening to him, I had the impression after a while that he viewed himself as the focal point of the Polish cause. I could not but see his point: if one allowed Stalin to dictate which of the top Polish leaders should go and which should stay, which government would be "friendly" to Russia and which unfriendly, this would mean the end of independence.

It was long after midnight, the room was full of smoke, and, trying to keep the general company, I had drunk too much whiskey, but I tried to listen to each word with full attention. At last I felt an enormous weariness creeping over me and, despite the great respect that I felt for Sosnkowski, a slight impatience with him. In his monologue there was an unbearable egocentrism that jarred on me after my recent experiences in Poland.

The general ended the conversation at two o'clock in the morning. The Underground had stopped running long ago, and I was driven from Swiss Cottage to my hotel near Belgrave Square in the commander-in-chief's car.

It would be difficult to find two more dissimilar people than General Sosnkowski and Prime Minister Mikolajczyk. The contrast was apparent from the moment I entered the prime minister's office. They were total opposites in outward appearance, bearing, and ways of thinking. Sosnkowski, were he dressed in a nobleman's fur-lined coat and cloak, would look like a *hetman*[*] come alive from an old portrait. Mikolajczyk, small, squatty, bald, was a typical Polish peasant type whose good manners had been acquired through experience and acquaintances in life. Sosnkowski had a gift for expressing himself, speaking deliberately and slowly but fluently and precisely. Mikolajczyk thought and spoke logically but with some effort, and in the typical harsh accent of Poznan. The thin small mouth and determined expression bespoke a stubborn and strong-willed man.

The contrast was underlined for me after I had talked with both of them. Sosnkowski was one of the most prominent thinkers in the country. He had a great gift of analysis, but it was that of a scholar rather than of a leader of men. He could see clearly all alternatives and was for the most part accurate in predicting events at the front, but he often failed to draw any conclusion from his information that would point clearly to a course of action. Having outlined his principles and decided not to compromise, he cared little whether there was any practical way to implement them. He was therefore inclined to take an intransigent position rather than formulating a practical plan of action.

Mikolajczyk was not a match for Sosnkowski in intelligence and knowledge, but he compensated for this by his industry. He was self-educated; one must be impressed by the fact that within a short time after coming to England his English had become fluent enough,

[*]The traditional title of a military leader in old Poland.

though his accent was appalling. He certainly reached his political conclusions with difficulty, but once he reached them he stuck firmly to them. He was capable of making the most difficult decisions and was prepared to take full responsibility for them.

Those two men, Sosnkowski and Mikolajczyk, could have complemented one another very well, and the situation demanded close contact, a constant exchange of views, and common decision-making. Unfortunately, they disliked each other intensely and met only rarely, usually at meetings of the government or conferences with the president, never alone. I doubt whether they had met, even with other people present, more than five or six times during these first critical six months of 1944.

I met Mikolajczyk frequently and talked to him a great deal, especially during January and the first half of February, when the critical talks with Churchill and Eden were taking place and there was an exchange of important radio messages between Warsaw and London. He often invited me to his apartment in Bayswater late in the evening. On the floor in the drawing room lay stacks of Polish underground papers and all sorts of reports from Poland. Mikolajczyk devoted many hours to studying the situation at home. When I asked him how he found time to do so, he replied, "At night, when it is quiet."

My arrival in London was a time of momentous events. At the beginning of January 1944, the plans of the Home Army command were at last received, decoded, and passed on to the president, the commander-in-chief, and the prime minister. They concerned Operation TEMPEST, the contingency plan in the event that the front gradually moved across Poland and Soviet forces occupied the country. Almost simultaneously with the receipt of these plans, the Red Army crossed the 1939 frontiers of Poland. Churchill recovered from his illness, and, after a series of preliminary talks between Mikolajczyk and Eden, dramatic encounters followed between Mikolajczyk and the British prime minister. The re-establishment of diplomatic relations between Moscow and the Polish government and thus the recognition of Polish rights in the territories evacuated by the Germans, and the coordination of Home Army activities with the Russian forces, became the burning issues.

For the first time I learned from Mikolajczyk himself that the British had not only failed to defend the prewar Polish frontier with the USSR but, on the contrary, had actively supported Soviet territorial claims up to the River Bug: thus it appeared that the Curzon Line, which was not much different from the Ribbentrop-Molotov line, was to become the new Polish frontier. Mikolajczyk did not give me notes of these conversations (although I did read them just before returning to Poland) but told me of them in some detail. The rest I learned first from conversation with Foreign Minister Tadeusz Romer or Ambassador Edward Raczynski, Counsellor Wladyslaw Kulski, or Mikolajczyk's assistant, Jozef Zarański.

From conversations with Mikolajczyk and Sosnkowski I realized the differences in their thinking. When once, remembering what I had heard from the general, I asked Mikolajczyk whether one should not plan a delaying action until our position was more favorable, the prime minister said: "I know very well who put that idea into your head. Sosnkowski is convinced that it will pay us to play a waiting game because sooner or later there will be a conflict between the British and Americans and Russia, but I believe that Churchill is right and that there will not be a war against Russia. Time is working not for but against us. Stalin also favors delaying tactics; he avoids any understanding with the British about Poland because he expects to occupy the whole country within a year, create a *fait accompli*, and install his own puppet government in Warsaw."

Sosnkowski thought that British pressure on the Polish government should be resisted absolutely. Mikolajczyk believed that such a policy would play into Stalin's hands, that as a result of it the Polish government in London would be shunted up a blind alley by the British—deprived of the means of action, cut off from contact with the country, and restricted to empty gestures and protests. The British would cut off all aid to the Home Army, and the BBC would start broadcasting propaganda in support of Soviet territorial claims. At this point the British could influence the balance of power inside the country to the detriment of the non-Communist resistance movement, and its members would be even more vulnerable to extermination by the Russians.

Mikolajczyk held the view that Stalin was playing a crafty game, knowing very well that in the matter of the eastern frontier of Poland he had not only the support of Churchill but also of British and American public opinion, which was influenced by the knowledge that in our eastern territories Ukrainians and Byelorussians, not Poles, were a majority. Stalin also understood that when the question

223

of Poland's independence arose the situation would be reversed: both the British and the American governments would come to our assistance. This is why he now demanded recognition of the Curzon Line as a condition for any understanding: he assumed that the Poles would refuse to give up their eastern lands and in this way he could blame the Polish side for breaking down the negotiations.

In view of this Anglo-American position, the prime minister did not see how Poland could save herself alone or, rather, how she could recover the eastern territories without military action. At best, he thought, depending on the American attitude, we might be left with Lwow and the oil basin (because the Curzon Line did not reach that far south), but even that was doubtful. From the very beginning, he said, the British had given us no support in the matter of our eastern border, not even in 1941, when the Russians were suffering reverses. In contrast to Sosnkowski's belief, Mikolajczyk thought that Sikorski had obtained the maximum concessions possible at that time. In a conversation with Sikorski, Stalin had at first suggested a two-way compromise on frontiers, without the intermediary of the British and Americans: a "very small shift" to the west, he called it. Sikorski, however, according to Mikolajczyk, was so alarmed by the personal attacks on him by the London Poles that he at once broke off the conversation about frontiers. He was afraid to continue it, afraid even to ask Stalin what he meant by a "very small shift."

Mikolajczyk's own tactics consisted mostly in not breaking with the British, in not rejecting their demands outright, while showing goodwill and a readiness to compromise, to conduct talks in a way which would make the Russians and not the Poles responsible for the breakdown in negotiations. And most of all, he was determined not to let his government be pushed out of the Allied camp. To achieve his goals, according to Mikolajczyk and his nearest advisers, one had to move the center of gravity from the negative position of a dispute about frontiers to the positive one of a defense of Poland's independence. Mikolajczyk was under no illusion about the Russian determination to grab the whole of Poland, not only the eastern territories. He believed, however (erroneously, as it proved later), that if the Poles compromised in the matter of territories, the British and Americans would resist the USSR more firmly in the defense of Poland's independence.

Ambassador Raczynski, more cautious than Mikolajczyk in the

assessment of the Allies, once explained that the British and American mentality differed greatly from ours. They operate in politics, he told me, not with imagination—which they lack—but from empirical experience. They draw conclusions only when they have facts before them. Often, as was the case with Germany, they delay too long in drawing them. For example, with some foresight it would have been possible to prevent the growth of Nazi military power. If one explained to Anthony Eden that Stalin wanted to make Poland the seventeenth Soviet republic, and that it would be the turn of other countries after that, Eden would reply: "For the time being, there is no evidence that he wants to do so." The British believe that Stalin and the Russians are suspicious by nature, and so, according to them, Moscow must be persuaded that the capitalist countries have no evil intentions toward Russia, that they want agreement, compromise, and peace. In that situation the Polish side must give the British and the Americans tangible proof that this Soviet "suspicion" is merely a tactical move to disguise imperialistic and expansionist aspirations.

The prime minister favored the view that to agree to give up a large part of our territory was essential to preserving our independence as a country. Mikolajczyk, however, had had his freedom of maneuver severely limited by the balance of power in Polish London. He had against him not only all those who considered that to agree to cede almost half the Polish territory to the Soviets was treason, but also a considerable segment of the Army. The bulk of General Anders' troops in Italy were people from the eastern part of Poland, which was now claimed by the Soviet Union. They had been deported deep into Russia in 1939, after Stalin invaded the country in collusion with Hitler. The deportees had gone through hell in Soviet labor camps and jails; many of them starved or froze to death there. After Hitler's attack on the USSR, they were released on the basis of a Soviet agreement with the Polish government in London. Later they were evacuated from the Soviet Union and organized into what was now the Second Corps. What reaction could Mikolajczyk expect from these soldiers, fighting on the Italian front, should they learn that he was ready to cede their homelands to Russia? For them the war would have been lost and further sacrifice would be pointless.

Thus Mikolajczyk found himself in an impossible position. If he flatly rejected all territorial concessions, he would lose British support and be out of the game. If he attempted to retain Poland's independence at the price of losing the eastern part of the country, the London Poles and the army would certainly form a united front against him, in which case he would be forced to resign.

The British did not make Mikolajczyk's task any easier. Stalin was demanding the immediate acceptance of the Curzon Line as a condition for further talks. The loss of territory in the east was to be compensated for by territorial acquisitions in the west, from Germany. The British wanted agreement on the eastern frontier at once, but discussions on the establishment of the western borders were to be postponed until the end of the war. Ambassador Raczynski in a note asked the British what steps they intended to take to guarantee Polish independence in case of agreement to territorial changes. He also wanted to know whether, taking into account territorial compensation to Poland, the western border with Germany would be fixed and guaranteed simultaneously with the fixing of the eastern border, or at a later time. Eden, in an answer sent a week later, stated simply that the British government could not sign any definite undertakings before agreement was reached with the other interested Allied governments, especially with the Soviet Union.

Chapter 21

*B*y the middle of January I had behind me meetings with the commander-in-chief, the prime minister, the president, and almost every member of the government and the more important politicians, not excluding those from the opposition. On Protasewicz's advice I made a written report of these talks to safeguard myself against misinterpretations and misquotations. What mattered was that I summarized from my own appraisal and information brought from Poland rather than what I had heard from others. As all the talks revolved around the same problems, I wrote my report in the form of answers to questions most frequently asked of me.

With regard to the situation in Germany, I stated that, from my own observations of the activities of Action N, I believed that there was no serious organized resistance inside Germany, that a revolution was not likely, but that the crossing of the German borders by Soviet troops might cause panic and the end of the armed resistance to the western Allies. The Germans, faced with either Soviet or British and American occupation, would choose the latter. This view led to the optimistic assumption that an armistice might fix the front lines before the Russians occupied the whole of Poland. In this case a part of the country would be still free from Red occupation.

This most likely possibility, as I then thought, was eliminated by indiscretions in English political circles a few days after I filed it. I was told that at an afternoon tea at the house of Mrs. Elma Dangerfield, whose inviting drawing room served as a meeting place for Poles and English, a very excited British journalist, Frederick Voigt, came in with news which had the effect of a bombshell on those present. According to Voigt, who was coming directly from a meeting with the American correspondent James Reston, during the October talks in Moscow the division of Germany into Allied occupation zones had been decided. According to this agreement the line dividing the Soviet from the British and American zones of occupation was to run through the middle of Germany, leaving the whole of eastern Europe, including Poland, in Russian hands. This would put an end to any hope that the Polish government and armed forces, assisted by at least symbolic detachments of Allied troops, could return to those Polish territories not yet occupied by the Russians or that Poland would be occupied jointly by the three great powers. If the Russians were allowed to occupy the entire country, they would never leave voluntarily.

The next day I was invited to dine with the Raczynskis. Also invited was Edward R. Murrow, the well-known American commentator of the CBS radio network who had gained world recognition by his broadcasts in September 1939 from beleaguered Warsaw, where he stayed until its fall to the Germans. Asked about the rumor, Ambassador Raczynski said that he heard it at the end of the previous year from a British member of Parliament. The Polish government had asked at once for an explanation from Ambassador O'Malley, and O'Malley had offered solemn assurances that he did not know anything about it but promised to inquire at the Foreign Office. Two days later, O'Malley had reported a firm denial, the ambassador said. Murrow spoke up at this point, recalling that immediately after the Moscow meeting, the American secretary of state, Cordell Hull, had said at a press conference in Washington that Italy would be used as a model for the occupation of any other country. That meant that the Russians would have the right to set up their own military administration on territories occupied by them, just as the British and Americans had set up theirs in Italy. The Italian formula excluded mixed occupation. According to Hull, the military administration of each occupying power would decide how self-determination would be introduced in the liberated country. Murrow repeated this statement with visible disapproval. He concurred when Raczynski pointed out that Poland, an ally, could not be treated in the same way as Italy, only recently an enemy, and that the principle of self-determination meant something quite different to democratic countries than it meant to the Soviet Union.

Later, toward the end of March 1944, the London *Observer* published an article on the subject of the division of Germany into occupation zones, adding new details. East Germany was to be occupied by the Russians up to the Elbe line, south Germany would be the American occupation zone, and the north that of the British. Berlin was to be under the joint administration and occupation of the three powers. This time the news was not just a rumor. The lines of division, leaving Poland entirely under Soviet occupation, had been traced in advance, and would not be affected by the outcome of events on the battlefields.

Such was the international situation at the beginning of January 1944, when the Russians crossed the prewar frontier of Poland. The posture of the AK toward the Soviet troops had to be decided immediately. In view of the Soviet plans for grabbing the eastern territories and perhaps the whole country, was there any sense in supporting the Red Army through diversionary activities in the path of the retreating Germans, or should the Poles refrain from open fighting and remain underground? Adopting the second course would give Stalin a ready-made argument that the Poles would not fight the common enemy, that they had ceased to be an ally and did not deserve equipment, arms, or the support of the western Allies. To stay in the Allied camp meant to fight against the Germans to the bitter end. But how to cooperate with the Red Army when Russia had severed diplomatic relations with the Polish government in London, thereby cutting off all channels of communication?

In Warsaw I had been asked to remind London about the need for speedy instructions and decisions to settle this dilemma, but in London there was a divergence of views on this subject between the commander-in-chief and the prime minister. Only in October 1943, after long conferences and deliberations, were orders radioed from London setting out in detail what the AK should do in various situations. The most probable situation—Soviet forces advancing inside the country with diplomatic relations still broken—was passed over in a few short sentences: in such a case the Home Army was to come into the open, attack the retreating Germans from the rear, and, after the entry of the Russians, go underground again and await further orders from London.

This solution must have been assessed as impractical in Warsaw; at any rate, General Bor and his staff ignored it and issued their own order. It established that the Home Army would fight only against Germany, and forbade any attacks on the Red Army, the Soviet partisans, and the detachments of the People's Army. If there were any skirmishes against Soviet troops or communist organizations, we would be placed automatically in the position of fighting on the German side, even if no one involved had ever had any contact with the Nazis. The detachments that in the past had had clashes with the Soviet partisans were to be transferred to the west, away from the front line. The order also assumed either a general uprising in the whole country as a result of a complete collapse of Germany or an escalation of diversionary activities in the rear of the retreating Germans. Those "escalated diversionary activities," code-named TEMPEST, were to be mounted successively by the leadership of the Home Army and put in motion by agreed signals to be given by BBC radio from London upon a request signaled from Poland.

The orders further required that the population be discouraged from escaping to the West, and that the partisan detachments of the AK and the underground civilian authorities should stay put, ready to reveal themselves to the Russians as rightful hosts and representatives of the legal Polish authorities in London and to declare their readiness for further cooperation in the fight against the Germans under the military, tactical command of the Russians but under the political leadership of the Polish authorities in London. As the Polish partisan detachments had at their disposal short-wave radio sets with which they could contact London, it was hoped that military cooperation during the fighting would substitute for diplomatic relations and would allow the coordination of further joint operations by the two armies. The instructions did not make the plan conditional upon the previous re-establishment of diplomatic relations with Moscow or the recognition by Moscow of the prewar frontier. On this point General Bor's order, of course, was completely at variance with instructions from London and with the views of General Sosnkowski. Nor was there any mention in this order, which I was allowed to see, of continuing underground activities after the Russians entered the country.

When details of Operation TEMPEST reached London, a storm blew up in Polish circles. Sosnkowski decided, not without reason, that the leaders of the Home Army had shelved the government instruction and replaced it by their own. After reading Bor's message, I concluded that the center of gravity had indeed moved from London to Warsaw, as a result of what had been happening in London since Sikorski's death. The underground authorities had been constantly drawn into the disputes between the prime minister and the commander-in-chief. Several appeals had been made to the underground, as to an arbitrator, to resolve the conflicts in London at a distance. Under those conditions, official relations and the attitude in Warsaw toward superiors in London became lax. Polish underground leaders apparently recognized that they must make their decisions independently, and not look to London for orders. London's several-month delay in responding to Warsaw's request for detailed instructions for action in the event of a Russian entry before diplomatic relations were re-established had been the prime factor in that decision.

Soon after the dispatch about Operation TEMPEST was received, I was invited to lunch in the Rubens Hotel with General Sosnkowski. He was unable to understand the decision to come out into the open when the Russians appeared. To him it was obvious that the NKVD would arrest the leaders and probably execute them; the soldiers would be forced into Berling's Army;[*] and those resisting would be shot. What could the Home Army have had in mind in issuing such an order? "You have recently left Poland. Perhaps you can explain what sense there is in it."

I said that the decision to come out into the open seemed to me logical and sensible. In the underground there already was a Soviet outpost known as the Polish Workers Party, a communist organization. After the entry of the Russians, there would certainly be a number of opportunists in the ranks of the Home Army and in the political parties, even in the higher echelons, who would go over to the communist ranks. Keeping people in hiding with a native communist element within the organization would be impossible. The NKVD would have no difficulty in locating the underground. Therefore, having

---

[*]Berling's Army was a Polish military unit formed by the Russians in the USSR and politically and militarily subordinate to Moscow.

nothing to lose, the leadership preferred that the Home Army come into the open immediately after the fighting against Germany ended because it would then be protected by Western public opinion. If its members had to be tracked down and dragged out of hiding, they would sooner or later all be arrested and put on trial for conspiracy against the Soviet forces or for collaboration with the Germans. Leaders of the underground forces could be exterminated with impunity as long as they were anonymous and unknown, but once their names, ranks, and roles in the fight against the Germans were known, the liquidations of such persons as the Government Delegate or the commander-in-chief of the Home Army might have undesirable repercussions for the Soviets. Lastly, even if their exposure did not save our people, I said, they would have done our cause a final service: unmasking Soviet methods and objectives.

This reasoning did not seem to convince Sosnkowski. "If the intention to come into the open is dictated by such premises," he said, "then the decision is certainly heroic but it will lead to collective suicide. In that case my duty is to return to Poland to share the fate of the soldiers of the AK."

I drew the general's attention to the fact that his face was well known to too many people, and that hiding him from the Gestapo would present serious difficulties. He would be virtually a prisoner in Warsaw, unable even to go out into the street. But Sosnkowski laughed contemptuously. "Don't try to tell me such fairytales, Lieutenant. I was conspiring before you were even born. In case of necessity I can change my face so that even you wouldn't recognize me." The general, of course, as commander-in-chief could have amended the order for Operation TEMPEST but did not do so. He mentioned his intention to return to Poland several times after this talk, but eventually gave up the idea.

While Sosnkowski's reaction to Bor's order was skeptical, if not critical, Mikolajczyk greeted it with joy, as an important trump in the British and Russian political game. He could at last make a gesture of goodwill toward both: the Home Army, as part of the Polish armed forces subordinated to the legal government, was ready to cooperate with the Red Army in the fight against the common enemy without any preconditions. If such an offer were rejected by Stalin (the prime minister reasoned), the British would have to blame Moscow. This was at the same time the best refutation of Stalin's slanderous claims, repeated by all the Soviet propaganda channels in the world, that the Home Army was collaborating with the Germans or, at best, was doing nothing.

There was also another important issue at this time: in mid-September 1943 drops of personnel, ammunition, weapons, and other equipment to Poland were drastically curtailed. From the middle of October on, drops of parachutists carrying, in addition to "mail," money belts with funds for the Home Army and the Government Delegacy were discontinued altogether. In November Poland received no arms drops at all. In December 1943 and January 1944, the British allowed only a few flights. The master plan to supply the Home Army with arms and specialists by arranging about three hundred flights to prepare the Polish underground for large-scale action was frustrated at the outset.

The British side blamed everything on technical difficulties. The Poles were told that flights from Britain over Germany or by the circular route over southern Sweden would result in enormous losses. After the occupation of Italy, the British promised to establish a base on the toe of Italy, as flights over the Balkans seemed to be safer and shorter. Because things were developing fast on the Eastern Front the interruption of flights and the delays began to worry everybody concerned, particularly the military planners, as the morale of the Home Army was seriously affected. It was to be expected that Russia would start arming the communist detachments of the People's Army and would endeavor to saturate the country with its own partisans. It was also to be expected that people longing to fight the Germans would turn toward those who could give them the weapons.

Although the British continued to blame technical obstacles, the Poles began to feel that the ending of the drops of personnel and arms was dictated by political motives connected with the Soviet accusations that the Home Army was not fighting the Germans but was using its British-supplied arms against Soviet partisans. Bor's August order that action be taken against bands plundering the country was regularly quoted by Stalin at the conference table as evidence of this. The communist paper *Daily Worker* published Bor's order in full at the beginning of January. All anti-communist excesses of the Polish extreme-right organization NSZ (National Armed Forces), which acted independently, could from then on be ascribed to the Home Army. Mikolajczyk wished to send the British an emissary who had recently served in the ranks of the Home Army to testify to the falsehood of the charges. In his view, my principal task would be to convince the British and, in particular, members of the British war cabinet, but also public opinion in general, that the Polish underground movement was not some ephemeral group but a large, well-organized force that could play a considerable part in the Allied effort against the common enemy, that support for it would be valuable from the military point of view, and that politically it might facilitate an agreement with the Russians.

The way was opened for me by my predecessor in this role, Jan Karski. Endowed with great political acumen, very inventive, and commanding excellent English, Karski had done excellent political and propaganda work on both sides of the Atlantic. He had talked with Churchill, Roosevelt, and a whole range of influential politicians, members of Parliament, and British and American newspaper columnists. His book *The Story of a Secret State* was a best-seller in America. "I hope," said Mikolajczyk, "that you will turn out to be another Karski."

Chapter 22

*J*anuary and February were taken up with conversations and meetings with the British, organized either by Mikolajczyk himself or by our embassy in London. Mikolajczyk invited the members of the war cabinet to lunches, mostly held in a private room at the Savoy or, more often, at the Dorchester Hotel. There were meetings with Lord Selborne, a close personal friend of Churchill's and the minister of economic warfare (his department was responsible for helping underground movements); with Hugh Dalton, Selborne's predecessor, then minister of trade and a member of the Labour Party reputed to be friendly to Poland; and finally with Ernest Bevin, the labor minister. Wladyslaw Kulski, the counsellor at the Polish embassy, accompanied me on my visit to Anthony Eden and also when I talked with two high-ranking civil servants at the Foreign Office, Frank K. Roberts and Christopher Warner, and with the Roman Catholic bishop David Mathew, with Cardinal Bernard Griffin, archbishop of Westminster, and with William Temple, the archbishop of Canterbury. Lady Violet Bonham Carter of the Liberal Party introduced me to Sir Archibald Sinclair, the air minister, who invited me to his club near Piccadilly. The lunch with Sir Walter Citrine, the leader of the British trade unions, and other trade unionists from Transport House was organized by Jan Stanczyk, the socialist member of the Polish government. In meeting with His Majesty's ministers I was struck by their lack of guile and of self-importance. When the conversation turned to unwelcome subjects, some became careful and restrained, while others, like Dalton and Bevin, were brutally frank.

Officers of the Special Operations Executive also wanted to speak to me. This organization was most important to us since its job was to help underground organizations in occupied Europe. When I was in London, the chief of SOE was General Colin Gubbins, and the section dealing with Poland, Czechoslovakia, and Hungary was run by Colonel Harold B. Perkins. The officers of Section Six were rather wary of SOE. They suspected that that organization wanted to extract the greatest military advantage from the underground movements, pushing them to acts of sabotage and armed insurrection without regard to losses, having only British interests at heart. In conversations with the officers of SOE, especially Perkins, I learned that this view was totally unjust. The SOE, and especially its Polish section, was our most loyal and important ally. The SOE treated the underground organizations like its own children. Its personnel were deeply, even emotionally, involved with the affairs of occupied countries—and the achievements of the Polish Home Army, the French *maquis* or the Yugoslav partisans were a source of pride to them. The Polish section of SOE took the fortunes of our cause, and especially the AK's need for assistance, very much to heart.

Perkins, who at the beginning only asked questions, became quite talkative when I got to know him better. Before the war he had lived in Poland, had owned a small factory in Silesia, and spoke a little Polish, although he preferred to speak English. He expressed utter contempt for the Czechs, who were waiting timorously until the war was won for them. He considered the Polish underground movement to be the largest and best organized in Europe. Unfortunately, he said, the British public and also the military general staff did not realize this. He put the blame for this state of affairs on the Poles themselves: he considered the whole expensive Polish propaganda effort to be completely misguided. A large apparatus had been created consisting mostly of Polish officials or journalists who did not understand the British or the American mentality, who could interest neither the public nor the publishers, who had no contacts in Fleet Street, and whose arguments and polemical style were completely unconvincing. From this source a mass of pamphlets and books had appeared, first written in Polish and then translated into English, in translations ranging from mediocre to very bad, which no one wanted

236

to read. Perkins was of the opinion that the Polish information effort could be revivified only if Stratton House (the Polish Ministry of Information) were closed down and in its place a professional British publicity agency were engaged, employing a few capable English or American jounalists, with the role of the Poles limited to providing the raw material (Beneš had apparently used that method for the Czech propaganda, he said).

Meanwhile, the constant Soviet accusations, through diplomatic and propaganda channels, were bearing poisoned fruit. Perkins maintained that even at the very top, within the war cabinet and the general staff, there were differences of opinion about the role, strength, and importance of the Polish resistance movement. Polish reports were considered to be exaggerated and tainted with propaganda. SOE tried to counteract this, Perkins said, issuing its own assessments based not on Polish sources but on its own observations. It was stressed, for instance, that the picking up of air drops of supplies was organized better in Poland than anywhere else, which proved the existence of an efficient and widespread underground organization. Radio communication, contacts with Poland, courier liaisons, and above all the high opinion of the information provided by AK held by British intelligence were mentioned in SOE reports as evidence of the activity and strength of the underground movement in Poland.

From Perkins I heard how negative an effect the situation in Yugoslavia had had on the attitude toward the AK of the highest British authorities. He was only confirming, and amplifying, what I had already heard from General Sosnkowski. "As the Home Army finds itself in a similar situation to that of Mihajlović," he said, "and there is no British military mission on the spot in Poland, the British leadership is inclined, by analogy, to surmise that the Polish underground movement, under the growing threat from Russia, will also, to an ever greater degree, turn to fighting the communists and the Soviet partisans while limiting its activities against the Germans. The difference lies in the fact that the British have two military missions in Yugoslavia, one with Mihajlović and the other with Tito, but there are no British observers in Poland. If they do not want to believe the Poles, they have to rely on guesswork or false analogies with Yugoslavia."

From these conversations it became clear to me why the British had stopped arms drops and flights to Poland. It was also difficult to dismiss Perkins' criticisms of Polish propaganda. Poland got a very bad press in England, from the right end of the spectrum, the *Times* and the popular conservative press of the Beaverbrook group, to the left, such periodicals as the *New Statesman* and the *Tribune*. The *Times* articles, most dangerous because of the influence the paper had on the political elite, launched the concept of a division of Europe into zones of influence, steering Poland toward the Russian wing in advance. The *New Statesman* explained to its readers that Poland had no *raison d'être* as an independent state, having been created after World War I as a temporary phenomenon. In the *Evening Standard* each anti-Polish cartoon by the excellent cartoonist David Low did more damage than several editorials could have done.

Both in Parliament and in the press there was a Polish lobby. Writing in defense of Poland were the Catholic journals, with the weekly *Tablet* at their head, then the weekly *Time and Tide* and the monthly *Nineteenth Century and After*. There were many letters to the editors defending Poland in the *Daily Telegraph*. In the House of Commons a group of about twenty-five members, most of them conservatives, were actively engaged on our side. Not all our supporters were of equal importance. Allan Graham, the chairman of the Anglo-Polish Society, was the most devoted friend of ours but was not taken very seriously. Other conservative MP's, like Victor Raikes and Kenneth Pickthorn, a Cambridge professor, M. Petheric, and Professor Sir Douglas Savory, from Ulster, had more influence. In the Labour Party our ally was Ivor Thomas, with whom I became friends.

The motives of our defenders were not, however, always based on friendship for Poland, as became apparent during my lunch with the minister of trade, Hugh Dalton, an eminent economist whose name had been well known to me while I was a student at Poznan. Dalton, considered a friend of the Poles, was a man who had no taste for evasive language or diplomatic phraseology. I can't remember which of our diplomats was present at a dinner when one of the Polish guests began, as was the Polish habit, to talk about the expansionist intentions of Russia, which sooner or later would threaten Great Britain too. Dalton suddenly interrupted: "What are you trying to do? It is well known that the Polish question has already become a bone of contention in our relations with Russia. Is your policy to cause a split among their Allies? Only Hitler will benefit by that! If there is a breach with Russia or tension between Russia and ourselves because of the Polish question, Moscow might easily make a separate peace with Germany. Stalin is hinting as much to us in various ways."

Somebody pointed out to him that this particular coin had two sides: the British and Americans might also threaten Russia with a separate peace. "The country that would pay for any compromise with the Nazi Reich would be Poland," Dalton insisted. "Don't you realize that? Even if it were true that Stalin wanted to incorporate not only Poland and eastern Europe but the rest of the continent into the Soviet Union, one must not speak about it before Germany has been beaten." To end this polemic Dalton made another revealing remark: "I feel sick when I listen to your defenders in the House of Commons. With a few exceptions, they are the same people who supported appeasement of Germany and sided with Chamberlain at the time of Munich. Today, for fear of Russia and communism, they want to save not Poland but Germany, as a potential barrier against the Soviets."

After this outburst, there was a momentary silence. None of the Poles present could find a plausible rebuttal, because no one at that table wished to prevent the final defeat of Nazi Germany. The British and American fears of a separate peace between Russia and Germany were certainly exaggerated, but how could one convince the British of it? The British ambassador to Poland, Sir Owen O'Malley, must have guessed what the Polish guests were thinking, involved as they were in the contradictions of their tragic geographic situation between Germany and Russia. "You mustn't think," he said, "that we are like Pontius Pilate, washing our hands and turning away; it is not so. But you must understand that for the moment we have no means of putting pressure on Russia."

I timidly remarked that if our Allies could not for the moment do anything for us, they might at least not do anything against us. As a Pole recently arrived from my occupied country, I said, I was very depressed by articles in the British press which must be read in Moscow to indicate that Russia was to be given a free hand in Poland. In reply, Dalton repeated the old argument that I had encountered more than once: he, as a friend of Poland, deplored the attitude of some of the newspapers, but the minister of information could not give any guidance to the press that might be read in Moscow as anti-Soviet.

About a month later I had an opportunity to observe that Dalton was not completely wrong when he warned us against those who, pretending to be Poland's friends, were really concerned with Germany. A resolution had been moved in the House of Commons that the principles of the Atlantic Charter should apply to all countries, not excluding Germany. The resolution was aimed, of course, at the project of territorial compensation for Poland at Germany's expense, and it was supported by most of the members whom we considered to be among our most ardent friends.

Before every important conference I tried to prepare myself and was given all kinds of instructions and information. This was so before my meeting with the air minister, Sir Archibald Sinclair. On my agenda for that meeting, to which Sosnkowski attached a lot of importance, was the question of renewing drops for the Home Army and of allocating a suitable number of crews and aircraft for the purpose. Sosnkowski gave me detailed data concerning our air force: the number of squadrons, crews, machines, losses sustained, enemy planes shot down, etc.

Sir Archibald, a graying, thin Scotsman with an oval face, was considered to be friendly to the Poles. He was full of praise for the achievements and courage of our Polish airmen, and this allowed me to make my point at once. Under British command were six Polish fighter squadrons and three bomber squadrons. Was it not a paradox that Polish airmen flew over Germany or defended English towns during German air raids while flights over Poland with arms, ammunition, and personnel for the Home Army had been almost entirely stopped? If the Royal Air Force did not want to sacrifice its own crews, it might at least allow Polish airmen to help the Home Army.

The minister retorted that it was in the interest of Poland that the war should end as soon as possible with Germany's defeat. An early victory over the Germans did not depend on how many aircraft flew to Poland, he said, but on the best deployment against the enemy of limited equipment and personnel in accordance with priorities dictated by overall military strategy. For a speedy end to the war the bombing of Germany was more important than supplying the underground movements.

He denied categorically that flights over Poland had been stopped because of Soviet pressure. He explained, in some detail, that flights from English bases had become too dangerous when the Germans created a zone of powerful anti-aircraft defenses from the northernmost point of the Jutland peninsula to the center of the Reich. These defenses were built to protect Berlin from the mass raids of the RAF, and the crossing of that barrier was too dangerous for a few Liberators flying from England to central Poland: in one night in September the Germans had shot down six aircraft. An attempt had been made to avoid the barrier by circling it in a wide arc to the north, but the distance was too great even for the Liberators, and they returned with almost all their fuel used up. Sinclair maintained that the whole problem had been discussed with the Poles, but that they could not overcome their suspicions that the decision was political.

I cited the examples of Yugoslavia and Greece, not to mention France. Apparently the two Balkan countries, in spite of technical difficulties, were receiving many more air drops than Poland. The minister replied that in view of the proximity of the theater of operations in Italy the activities of partisans in the Balkans were more important than those in distant Poland. Poland should really be, in her own interests, armed by Russia. Unfortunately, the conflict between the two governments prevented this. He added that he was one of those politicians who fully appreciated Polish heroism and readiness for sacrifice. The Polish underground movement, he said, was most useful for the Allies in the sphere of intelligence, sabotage, and diversions. In such areas support was needed, but only in proportion to the importance of these activities. Sinclair assured me that flights to Poland would be resumed as soon as an Allied base in the south of Italy could be organized.

I tried to remind him that the importance of the Home Army was not limited to diversion, sabotage, and intelligence, that preparations were under way for an uprising that, at the appropriate moment, might play an important role. From files in Section Six I had learned of a plan, code-named "Barrier," that would consist of cutting all lines of communication across Poland to stop the Germans from transferring forces from the Eastern Front in the event of an Allied landing in the west. Such an operation could be strategically important from the point of view of the joint staffs, but it would need coordination and suitable equipment for the Polish detachments. Sinclair was doubtful about this. Tito, thanks to a mountainous terrain, could keep under arms a considerable force that could be put into action at once. The structure of the Polish underground movement was different: the strength of the partisan groups under arms which could immediately move against German transports was limited, and mobilization of the AK would take a long time and would come too late to cut off or hamper the mass movement of German troops.

This was one of the most instructive conversations that I had. Sinclair probably knew that I would return to Poland after the fulfillment of my mission, and that all that he had told me would be repeated a few weeks later in Warsaw. From what I heard, it was clear that the whole effort of Underground Poland, achieved with enormous sacrifice, had been completely out of proportion to the place and importance it occupied in British and American strategic planning. Not only were there political obstacles in our path but, most important, there was the problem of our distance from the future theater of operations of the British and American armies. The Home Army would be a political trump card if Poland had occupied France's place on the map, or if the principal offensive against the Germans were made through the Balkans. When it became an open secret that the second front would be opened in France and that the main assault on Germany would come from the west, the military role of the Polish underground became peripheral.

Against this tragic background, what was the position of the prime minister of the Polish government, Stanislaw Mikolajczyk? Of course his English was much less fluent than that of our diplomats, as he did not have their polish and education, but his bulky figure was itself striking proof that the Polish government did represent the entire nation and not, as the Soviet propaganda always maintained, just landowners and aristocrats. In the small circle around him it was known that he was under overwhelming political pressure in that period and had even been threatened in a series of talks he had with Churchill and Eden. His nerves must have been like iron because externally he was calm, he never showed any sense of inferiority, and he presented a facade of quiet dignity to the British, offering very apposite arguments for our position when the opportunity arose.

During luncheons with Mikolajczyk as host, differences of

opinion sometimes flared up, especially when the guests were the leaders of the Labour Party. During a lunch with Ernest Bevin, an English minister warned the Poles against any rash gestures and manifestations. He counseled the Poles to continue to cooperate fully with the Allies, cooperation to which the Polish government was committed. (He had in mind, of course, the participation of the Polish armed forces in the Allied war effort.) "We British," Bevin said, "believe in compromise. Without compromise there is no democracy. You Poles stick to the principle that it is better to lose everything than to give up one acre of Polish soil."

"I am in favor of keeping our country in the family of the United Nations to the end," Mikolajczyk promptly replied, "and I am prepared to agree to any reasonable compromise if somebody will convince me that territorial concessions will save our independence. However, do not create a situation in which we have nothing to lose, because we would have nothing left except a rash gesture." This answer must have impressed Bevin, for he nodded and ceased his polemic.

My part in these prime-ministerial luncheons was limited at first to conversation with my neighbor at table. As a rule, I was given a place next to the guest of honor. When dessert was served, Mikolajczyk would introduce me in a few words to those present, and in order to create sympathy he would mention, with some exaggeration, the dramatic circumstances of my journey from Warsaw to London. After this introduction, I would give a prepared summary of the situation in Poland, the activities of the Home Army, and the methods and mood of the Germans. As a rule I never mentioned the burning subject of Soviet policies and the activities of the communists in Poland, as I knew that the subject would be raised of its own accord. After the exchange of questions and answers a general discussion usually started, from which I would withdraw discreetly, leaving the field to Mikolajczyk, Ambassador Raczynski, or other diplomats at the table.

A clash arose during one dinner given by the Poles for trade union leaders. These were mostly people who, like Bevin, had been laborers before becoming potentates in the workers' movement. Their knowledge of Poland was derived mostly from left-wing weeklies. During the discussion, our British guests started to point out to their hosts their wicked political past: Pilsudski's dictatorship, Beck's politics, the occupation of the territories disputed between Poland and Czechoslovakia, and other trespasses. At the end Mikolajczyk was asked how he, the leader of a democratic party, could tolerate the presence in the government of General Sosnkowski and President Raczkiewicz, the representatives of the prewar military junta. I glanced uneasily at Mikolajczyk, as I knew that he was hostile toward Sosnkowski and at most extremely reserved toward Raczkiewicz. To the complete amazement of the Poles present, he replied: "You don't need to teach me democracy. All my life I have been in opposition to dictatorship. In London we cannot change the constitution because we have no authority to do so. It will be changed by the Polish parliament after liberation. Sosnkowski is a patriot, and he would undoubtedly resign if his person were a real obstacle to some agreement with Russia, but Stalin has demanded the resignation of both Sosnkowski and Raczkiewicz with nothing offered in exchange. The demand that the head of state should resign undermines our sovereignty. On the subject of the person of the president we will not have any discussion at all with anybody."

Not all these conversations are worth noting here, but, in aggregate, they give a certain general picture of the public attitude. A constant question was "what *can* we do for you?" It sounded like a rhetorical expression of helplessness. The archbishop of Westminster limited himself to listening to what I had to tell him and uttering a few conventional phrases, after which he concluded the audience by saying that he would pray for Poland. William Temple, the archbishop of Canterbury and the primate of the Anglican Church, who had the reputation of being a Labour Party sympathizer, tried to express his friendship for Poland in a more concrete fashion. When he asked "what can we do for you?" it was not rhetorical. He wanted to know whether he could be of any assistance in my efforts in London. After a moment's reflection, I asked him if he could help me get a letter from a British prisoner-of-war living in Warsaw printed in *The Times*.

As I mentioned before, Ronald Jeffery wrote this letter at my request before I left Warsaw. I don't remember whether I was introduced to him by Muir or somebody else. Following the advice of General Pelczynski, I brought his letter out on microfilm in my "mail" and handed it in to the Polish ministry of information. By this route it found its way to the editorial offices of the *Times*, which rejected it without explanation. Jeffery had given his rank, serial number, and military unit at the end of his letter so that its authenticity could not be doubted. It was well written and, as testimony of an Englishman living in Warsaw, would be more convincing to the English public than any article, even the best one imaginable, written by a Pole. In describing the atrocities against the population in Poland, Jeffery stressed in particular the extermination of the Jews and appealed to the Allies for some action that would stop further slaughter. This is from his letter:

> In 1939 the Jewish population of Poland numbered over three millions. Still living in a few small ghettos in various parts of this country, strongly guarded, under terrible conditions and awaiting their inevitable liquidation are about fifty thousand Jews. A second fifty thousand have probably escaped the German net and live in hiding. Many thousands left the country immediately after the outbreak of war. Of this army of three million souls, men, women and children from all walks of life, perhaps to make a more pleasant estimation, five hundred thousand will be found living after the war. The rest, two and a half millions, have been gassed, starved, poisoned, shot and tortured to death by the Germans.
>
> . . . . .
>
> Let it be made clear to the Germans that if there is no cessation of the repressions in Poland and other occupied countries the Allies will take counter-measures both now and after the war which will have very unpleasant effects on every member of the German nation.[*]

This testimony seemed to me to be particularly important for arousing public opinion in the West. The archbishop asked me to send him the letter at once. After a few days, he wrote to me. The editor of The Times "made it quite clear that it was concern for the security of British POWs in hiding in Poland which really decided him not to publish that British soldier's letter." The archbishop suggested that I might expect similar answers elsewhere, implying that it was military censorship which was preventing publication of the letter. If this were true, caution was reaching the realm of the absurd: The Times did not have to reveal the name of this Englishman. How could the publication of the letter help the Germans find a British prisoner-of-war hiding in a city of a million people? Thus one more

[*]For complete text, see Archives of the Polish underground movement in London.

cry to the world to stop the murder of several million human beings in the gas chambers was silenced.

The archbishop, however, did not limit his help to the futile attempt to have Jeffery's letter published. The Anglican Church had something like its own foreign office, a Council for Foreign Relations, and I was invited to give a lecture about Poland to this group. In those days the Poles were concentrating all their efforts on the British, as the Polish government was in London and its armed forces were under British command. Mikolajczyk, however, under pressure from Churchill to make one-sided concessions to Russia, was looking toward the United States for relief. To find out whether he could get any support from Roosevelt, he tried several times to see him, but each time the meeting was postponed. It looked as though the roles had been divided between the two powers, and Great Britain was left to deal with the Poles. Mikolajczyk was most worried by the resignation of the American ambassador to the Polish government, Anthony Drexel Biddle, who was said to be devoted to Poland. Biddle told the Poles that his resignation was a protest against the results of the conferences in Moscow and Teheran and Roosevelt's abandonment of Poland. His resignation was an ominous sign that the outcome of the Big Three meeting would be much worse for Poland than had appeared from what Churchill and Eden had told us.

Mikolajczyk advised me to call on the American official who, after Biddle's resignation, had taken on the function of chargé d'affaires to the governments-in-exile and committees of the occupied countries in Europe. His name was Rudolph Schoenfeld. He gave me the impression of a third-class civil servant who feared his own shadow. The fact that a man of such low caliber represented the United States to a country once referred to by President Roosevelt as "an inspiration to other nations" told its own tale. Schoenfeld was probably the only man to whom I talked in England who did not ask me a single question. He did not address a single significant word to me, and when I asked what I could say upon my return to Warsaw about the attitude of the United States to her Polish ally, I was treated to an empty, conventional phrase. Conversation with him was a complete waste of time.

My meeting with Anthony Eden was arranged for January 31, 1944. As usual, Kulski went with me. This time I was very nervous while we waited in an old-fashioned drawing room. On the walls were portraits of the foreign minister's predecessors, who had navigated British foreign policy over the last two centuries. I had brought with me a collection of photographs of the activities of the Home Army. Remembering my talks with Sir Archibald Sinclair, I had chosen shots of fighting and of the life of Polish partisans in the forest.

The clock on the mantlepiece began to strike four. Punctually to the second the door opened and the secretary announced: "The foreign secretary is ready to see you." A very elegant, smiling gentleman with the looks of a film star greeted us politely. Before I could speak, Eden began the conversation by announcing that he had heard about me from his associates and had read with interest the reports of the people whom I had already visited.

I began my presentation, which I knew from experience had to be short and concise, with something toward the end that would surprise the listener. Accordingly, I said that the Germans had been unsuccessful in their attempts to exploit Russia's effort to breach the solidarity of the Poles; that Poland had produced no collaborators with the enemy; that on the Eastern Front there were no Polish troops fighting with Germany against Russia; and that the activities of the Home Army against the Germans were increasingly effective. In spite of the Soviet diplomatic break with Poland, the Polish underground movement had given proof of its goodwill toward our eastern neighbor in the recent order by the Home Army commander to attack the German troops locked in battle with the advancing Red Army. In exchange, the Polish people, who in their darkest hour have remained loyal to their British allies, asked only that Polish independence and sovereignty be respected.

Eden replied that the news of the instructions issued to the Home Army by the Polish government and the Home Army commander was received by his government with great satisfaction. His government, he stressed, knew that the Polish underground movement had not suspended its fight against the Germans, that there was no collaboration with the enemy, and that it had ordered its members to avoid action against the communist partisans. The prime minister, Eden continued, was doing his utmost to bring about a Polish-Soviet understanding, but the Poles must realize that this goal could not be achieved without serious sacrifices.

At this point I interrupted: "If the Home Army is to play the part of a political trump card in the hand of the British government to

247

assist its efforts at mediation, it ought not to be weakened by halting the drops of personnel and arms." "That matter is the subject of deliberation by the competent authorities," said Eden. "The number of crews and aircraft destined for flights over Poland will probably be trebled, and the Polish government will be officially notified about this in due course." "This is the best news that I have heard in London," I told him.

Now came time for something new and unexpected. I asked Eden if he had ever seen authentic photographs of an underground army. He was puzzled, and extended his hand to my bundle of photographs. He quickly looked through the snapshots of partisans and of an underground printing press, stopping at one photo in particular. The Poniatowski Bridge and the Vistula were in the background; in the foreground, a low wall along the river. Painted on the wall in enormous letters was "Deutschland Kaputt, 1918-1943." Eden looked at this photograph for a long time in silence. At last he said softly, as if to himself, "Poor Warsaw."

Kulski looked at his watch and rose from his chair. The twenty minutes allotted for the conversation were just gone. When I was taking leave of him, Eden said one thing more: "I understand that the prime minister will see you next week." In the corridor, Kulski observed that that last remark, dropped so casually, had almost certainly been purposely kept until last—Eden was indicating that decisions on Polish matters were made by Churchill.

Chapter 23

On the day of my interview with Anthony Eden the Foreign Office spokesman issued a one-sentence communiqué that was published the next day throughout the country and broadcast by both the domestic and foreign services of the BBC: "The Foreign Secretary, Mr. Anthony Eden, received today an emissary of the Polish underground movement and discussed with him the situation in Poland." The popular paper *Daily Sketch* illustrated this news with a cartoon representing Eden greeting a mysterious figure in a huge black soft-brimmed hat, his face covered in the folds of a black cape.

That sentence became my key to many doors that had been shut to me until now, beginning with newspaper editorial offices. The next day I met Stefan Litauer in the corridor of Stratton House. He was a man whom the Polish community treated with distrust and suspicion, a friend of the TASS correspondent Andrew Rotstein, and suspected of having secret contacts with the Soviet embassy. However, this reputation did not prevent our Minister of Information, Professor Kot, from retaining him in the important post of correspondent of the Polish News Agency. In this capacity he had been sent to London a few years before the war. He had extensive contacts among British journalists, was very influential, and could be most helpful to his friends.

On hearing his name upon introduction, I told him that a few months before I had met his son in Warsaw and that I had been friendly with him at school, when we were both boy scouts. I did not then expect that I should soon meet his father, I remarked. Litauer turned pale and was visibly shaken. "I was sure that the Germans had murdered Kazimierz," he whispered. "I have had no news from him since 1940." As a Jew by origin, Litauer had good grounds to fear for his son's life. He took me to a pub and bombarded me with questions. I had to repeat several times that there was no possibility of a mistake: I had seen Litauer many times and had spoken to him frequently. I told his father that he had adopted the name of Litynski and, as he did not look Jewish, was moving freely about Warsaw. He was maintaining himself by trading in foreign currency, had a good income, and was in good health.

"How can I be of service to you? asked Litauer as we parted.

"You could organize a press interview for me."

"With which paper?"

"Preferably *The Times.*"

Two days later in Litauer's own apartment I met the diplomatic correspondent of *The Times,* Ivreach Macdonald. My host had told me that this twenty-nine-year-old journalist was a favorite of the publisher, Colonel Astor, and a rising star in British journalism. The conversation lasted two hours. Its fruit was a full column on the news page of *The Times.* It appeared under the headline: "Poland under the Terror—Well-Organized Resistance—Patriot Officer's Evidence." The article gave great pleasure to Poles, whose morale had suffered deeply when reading all the unfriendly comments in the British press, and especially *Times* editorials.

After the interview with Macdonald, the long-established and widely read weekly *The Illustrated London News* sent me one of their graphic artists, with whom I spent several hours. The outcome of that meeting was a four-page insert containing his sketches with the caption "Poland's militant underground fights on: scenes enacted in the very shadow of the Gestapo, drawn by our war artist, Captain Bryan de Grineau, under the direction of an officer of the Underground Army, who has arrived in this country after four years of work in Poland." The artist showed a great deal of imagination, representing a street search by a German patrol, an underground jury deliberating, the execution of the chief of the Arbeitsamt, Kurt Hoffman, and the execution of SS Oberscharführer Franz Bürckl, deputy commander of the Pawiak Prison in 1943.

Another illustrated paper, *Picture Post*, published an article by Ivor Thomas, "Is Europe a Volcano?" which the *Post* told its readers was based on "the evidence brought to London by an officer of the Polish Underground Forces." It was illustrated with the photographs I had shown to Eden. Thomas confided to me, however, that his original article was changed at the request of the editor, Edward Hulton, and that, in addition to the photographs from Poland, others of the French resistance had to be included. For further political balance, the same issue carried an illustrated report from the Eastern Front praising the heroic achievements of a Soviet armored train.

After the *Times* article was published, I received an invitation to the so-called editorial lunch, which was held in the paper's editorial offices every Thursday. Each week people in the news were invited to it. Before lunch I had to pay an official call on Colonel Astor. The luncheon was held with some ceremony. The atmosphere of the editorial rooms, with their Victorian furniture, matched the eminence and age of the paper.

A pleasant secretary showed me the seating plan for the affair, and I noticed with some embarrassment that I figured on it as "Captain" Jan Nowak.

"I am only a second lieutenant," I said. "We do know that," she whispered. I understood that I had been "promoted" in view of the eminence of the other invited guests.

The place on the right of the host was reserved for General Walter Bedell Smith. A few days before he had been named General Eisenhower's chief of staff, with the task of preparing plans for the invasion of the Continent. On the left was Air Marshal Sir Arthur Coningham. I was placed between Mr. Robert Barrington-Ward, the editor of *The Times*, and Sir Irving Albery, a conservative member of Parliament. On the opposite side of the table sat Rear Admiral Wilson, a naval attaché and chief of staff of the United States Navy. Our attention was drawn to Lieutenant General Bedell Smith. Stiff as a ramrod, with equally stiff manners, he was unlike any other American I had ever met.

Taking advantage of my proximity to the editor-in-chief of the most important English newspaper, I turned the conversation to a recent series of articles by Professor E. H. Carr and his concept of a division of Europe into zones of influence, which would place Poland under Soviet control. That prospect caused deep disquiet among my fellow countrymen. I asked if Professor Carr's views as put forward in *The Times* were a reflection of the position of the government or of the paper, or whether perhaps they reflected only the opinion of the author. Barrington-Ward denied that *The Times* had ever represented the view of the government or been inspired by the Foreign Office. In the past, he said, the reverse had frequently been the case. It occasionally happened that the opinions voiced in *Times* editorials later emerged as government policy, although this was by no means always the rule. As for a division of Europe into zones of influence, he pointed out that Anthony Eden had publicly denounced the notion. What mattered was a realistic understanding of the postwar possibilities for Great Britain. "Influence" was not the same as "control" or "domination." Soviet influence in eastern Europe after the war would be a logical outcome of geography and the balance of power. Carr did not mean that Poland would cease to be an independent country. At most, it would remain, like the other east European countries, a "junior partner" of Russia tied to its powerful neighbor by treaty. "Beneš and Czechoslovakia don't fear a partition of Europe into spheres of influence," he said.

I asked my neighbor to imagine the situation in Poland, with both a Soviet occupation and the fate that had befallen our Ukrainian neighbors and the other countries incorporated into Soviet Russia much in our minds. "You Poles," said Barrington-Ward with a smile, "remind us of the Irish. You possess too long a historical memory, too many prejudices and attitudes inherited from the past. Under the influence of war and the alliance with the western nations, Russia is undergoing a tremendous revolution. For the moment there is no reason to disbelieve Stalin when he assures us that he wants a strong and independent Poland. You will see, my friend, that your fears are groundless." "Everybody believes what he wants to believe," I said to myself; Poland is not alone in living on illusions." The difference was that in Poland our illusions resulted from lack of information, while the British government had a superb apparatus for collecting facts from all over the world.

I had proof of that when I was invited to deliver a talk to officials at the research department of the Foreign Office. I had an audience of about eighty, most of them experts on eastern European and Polish affairs. The chairman of the meeting was the director of the department, the world-famous historiographer Professor Arnold

Toynbee. His deputy, Sir Alfred Zimmern, to whom I owed the invitation to lecture, had told me that my audience would be interested in facts rather than opinions, so I had prepared a paper of an informative character without many details. I already knew that long, detailed lectures had this effect: after the first five minutes the British stop listening; after ten minutes they begin to yawn. This time, however, I was surprised. My short talk was greeted with an avalanche of questions whose character indicated that I had told my audience nothing new. The questioners had studied German newspapers, the Polish underground press, the material supplied by our ministries, and our reports. Every bit of printed paper had been minutely analyzed in this enormous laboratory. True, this information was exceedingly fundamental, detached from the mood, outlook, and conditions of everyday life. Later I frequently wondered how much of the assessment of Russia and her politics pronounced publicly by British politicians at that time represented real delusion or ignorance and how much was only a pretense.

Such factual knowledge was not limited to those specialists for whom studying our part of the world earned their daily bread. At various meetings during question periods population statistics were hurled at me to prove that Poles were a minority in the eastern territories and that when they fought for the maintenance of the prewar frontiers they were striving not for their own freedom but for the right to rule over minorities. When I was reprimanded for incorporating Wilno into Polish territory by force, persecuting minorities, and conflict with the Ukrainians, I longed to remind those British moralists of their relationship with Ireland (which would have been only fair, given British fondness for comparing the Poles with the Irish). What mattered, however, was that I persuade, not antagonize, my sometimes influential audience. The troublesome questioners continued, but in time I mastered some standard replies. I would remind the questioners that in the Sudetenland the Czechs were also in a minority and that the Munich agreement by which it was incorporated into Germany had opened the way for the annexation of Czechoslovakia. What was at stake was not a part of our country but the whole of Poland: we were facing a new Munich. The word "Munich" seemed to have a magical effect on the British: it stopped the polemics at once.

The most difficult meetings were those with the editors and

253

columnists of left-wing newspapers and weeklies who were unsympathetic to Poland. Before such hostile audiences a direct attack on Soviet propaganda claims would have produced an adverse effect. Only by moderation in speech could one hope to alter the image presented by the Soviets. At one such gathering Kingsley Martin, the editor of the *New Statesman and Nation,* asked me whether the people of Poland realized the strength of British sympathy, support, and admiration for Russia. "Yes," I replied, "and in Poland everybody realizes that an ally which has sustained the biggest losses at the front and carried the main burden of the war for nearly three years must arouse great sympathy in England." Martin was not satisfied by this answer. He went back to his question, accusing the Polish Section of the BBC of speaking too little about the pro-Soviet feeling in Great Britain. I asked him whether, in his view, this friendship for Russia should go so far as to sacrifice on its altar a small, weak, but loyal ally like Poland. Such a sacrifice is not expected by the Poles, I said, for they trust Britain absolutely. My answer was greeted by applause, and I was pleased when the great cartoonist David Low, who specialized in cruel anti-Polish cartoons, came up to me after the discussion, shook my hand, and gave me a pat on the back.

I had been invited by the Anglo-Polish Parliamentary Committee to make a ten-minute speech to the members of the House of Commons. Two weeks before the appointed date, I was lunching with General Sosnkowski and some of our people at the Rubens Hotel and mentioned this invitation. The general said, "Be very careful." You will have in the audience not only friendly MP's but enemies as well. They will ask you leading questions. I bet you they will ask you who murdered our officers at Katyn. They will try to make you out an agent of Goebbels sent here to England to sow discord among the Allies."

"What do you advise me to say if such a question is asked?"

"Recite the facts that are known to you. They can draw their own conclusions."

Two weeks later I found myself with Jan Karski in the House of Commons. Karski spoke about the structure of the Polish underground state and I about the actual situation in Poland, the military activities of the Home Army, the steady increase in the German terror, and the need for outside support for our struggle. Each of us was allowed no more than ten minutes. The chairman of the meeting was

Allan Graham. When someone in the room directed a question to me, Graham would quickly write his name on a piece of paper and slip it to me. The usual questions began. What is the attitude of the Poles to Soviet creations such as the Union of Polish Patriots in Moscow or General Berling's Army? How would that army be greeted on entering Poland? How can one prevent the drops of arms destined for Poles from falling into German hands?

Then came the first attack. The speaker was Lord Marley. He asked about the attitude of the Home Army to the Soviet Partisans, and, without waiting for my reply, he stated that the Home Army was killing them. As proof he quoted a Polish publication in English that had appeared in London. I denied this categorically and quoted Bor's order to the AK to avoid any clashes with the Soviet partisans.

Then Tom Driberg took the floor and asked: "How did the Polish community receive Goebbels' revelation about the discovery of the mass graves in Katyn and the communiqué of the Polish government in London? Who, in Polish public opinion, was guilty of the murder—the Germans or the Russians?" "Aha," I thought, "Sosnkowski was right." Allan Graham disallowed the question. A discussion of Katyn was not in the public interest at the present moment, he said. There was uproar in the hall. Driberg demanded an answer. "Let him answer," some cried, while others supported the chairman.

I had half a minute in which to collect my thoughts, then I asked Allan Graham to allow me to answer. I said that many Poles who found themselves in Soviet prisoner-of-war camps represented the best of the educated class. I mentioned the names of friends and acquaintances of mine who were sent to Katyn. I said that I knew for a fact that they had written letters to their families from Kozielsk and Starobielsk, letters stamped by the Soviet censor, and that they in turn had received letters from home. These exchanges had all stopped suddenly at the same moment, spring of 1940. I particularly stressed the date, as it was of vital importance in establishing the perpetrators of the crime. In the spring of 1940 the prisoner-of-war camps and the areas where mass executions took place were under Soviet authority. Only a year later were they occupied by the Germans. Since the spring of 1940, no one—not one person—had had a sign of life from these prisoners. In some cases letters to them were returned stamped "Addressee Unknown." I had several such enve-

lopes in my hand. I concluded, "This is all I know and all I can say."
The good Allan Graham breathed a sign of relief, but Driberg and a
few others seemed disappointed.

A subject often discussed in conversations with Sosnkowski
and Mikolajczyk was the idea of sending a British military mission to
Poland. Sometime early in 1944, I was invited to lunch at the Wel-
lington Club by an SOE officer, Andrej Kowerski,* who had adopted
the name Kennedy. He asked me what I thought of the proposal for a
mission similar to the one that was already in Yugoslavia. I answered
that it should be sent at once. To hide it from the Germans would not
be very difficult. The presence of the British on the spot would be
doubly welcome: they would be able to form their own opinion about
the scope of the underground activities and about the effects of the
German occupation, and, more important, direct contact between
British officers and the leadership of the Home Army and the Government Delegacy would enable the Polish side to assess the attitude
of the British toward Poland, which was most important.

Kowerski told me that this was his view, and that his superiors
in the SOE agreed with him and were trying to gain support for the
project, but were encountering opposition within the British government. Reportedly, General Sosnkowski also had some objections.
One could understand the opposition in British quarters, as they
were afraid of offending the Russians. But why should Sosnkowski
object?

I asked the general about it when I saw him in the second half
of February. "How can you be sure that the British observers would
report what they saw on the spot, and not what they had been
ordered to report?" said Sosnkowski. "The example of Yugoslavia
should be a warning to us. I personally do not believe in Mihajlović's
collaboration with the Germans." He still suspected that the British
were trying to find a formula to withdraw, without loss of face, from
their Polish commitments. If this really were so, the presence of a
British mission in Poland would neither help us nor harm us, I

*The English author Madeleine Masson mentions this meeting in her book *Christina*,
dedicated to Krystyna Skarbek, the Polish heroine of SOE (London: Hamish Hamilton,
1975).

256

thought. In order to wash their hands of us, the British did not need to send observers to Poland.

Sosnkowski had another argument, which he put forward, as he often did, in the form of a question: "Don't you think that the presence of a British representation in Poland would encourage the British to join forces with the underground authorities over the heads of the government and the commander-in-chief?"

"I am completely sure of the total loyalty of the commander-in-chief of the Home Army and of the Government Delegate," I replied.

"I am too," said Sosnkowski, "but in any community you can find disloyal people at the lower levels who, prompted by ambition, would be ready to conspire with the British on their own account." I left the commander-in-chief's study worried but unconvinced. The presence in Poland of British or American representatives, especially at a time when the Russians were occupying the country, seemed a matter of utmost importance.

As it later turned out, the British, apart from the SOE, had not the slightest intention of displeasing the Russians by sending their own mission to Poland. When Mikolajczyk wrote a letter demanding that a mission be sent, they delayed their reply for a long time. Eventually a refusal came from the British—and from the Americans as well. Meanwhile, Sosnkowski had changed his mind and had begun to demand a mission himself.

This matter arose also in a conversation with Mikolajczyk. The prime minister summoned me some time around the end of January. First he swore me to complete secrecy. "I have brought you here to act as a kind of litmus paper," he began. "I've sent a long and important dispatch to the Government Delegate. By the time it is coded, gets to Poland, and is decoded, a month or more will have elapsed. Meanwhile events may move fast and every day may count. I don't give a damn what my countrymen in London think of me, as I know that whatever I do I will be denounced as a traitor. I want to know your view of the reaction to this dispatch in Poland."

He then read me parts of a long dispatch, a précis of the latest conversations with Churchill and Eden containing their demand that Poland accept the Curzon Line as her eastern frontier in exchange for a guarantee of her sovereignty. The British warned that in the case of a Polish refusal the Russians would have a free hand to produce *faits accomplis* in Polish territories. In informing the Polish authorities about this, Mikolajczyk demanded that he be told whether he could negotiate on the basis of acceptance of the Curzon Line, pointing out all the negative effects of a complete rejection of British demands. New to me in the telegram was Stalin's extra condition—that communists be admitted to the postwar government.

I realized that this matter was of crucial importance, and, in accordance with Mikolajczyk's wish, limited myself to a direct reply to his question. It was my deep belief, I said, that the reply would be decidedly negative. Poland was completely unprepared for such a shock. After some weeks in London, I realized that not only the people in Warsaw but their leadership were completely ignorant of the desperation of our situation. Their perception of the Anglo-American relationship to Poland was based on pleasant fantasies, and totally wrong. The shifting of the onus of decision from London to Warsaw seemed to me to be a mistake, as important political decisions can only be made by people in possession of all the necessary facts, and that meant people in London.

Mikolajczyk looked glum: "The message presents the truth gently and provides all the important facts for the Government Delegate. If you feel that the recipients of it in Warsaw will not believe their head of government, why are you wasting your time collecting information and talking with the British? Do you think that they will believe you sooner than me?"

I said that he had a point and that, as I became more and more aware of our situation here in London, I became more and more anxious about the reception of my report on my return to Warsaw. I feared that people there would react to it with incredulity, perhaps even with suspicion. "What of it?" asked Mikolajczyk. "If the government begins to act independently without informing the country about its action, it exceeds its powers. But when I try to inform people and consult them, you say that one cannot shift responsibility onto the shoulders of people inside Poland. I am damned if I do and damned if I don't."

I then repeated my conversation with Kowerski in which we agreed that it was imperative that there be direct contact between our people in Poland and the staff of the British and American missions. Government envoys should be included in such a joint team. "The idea is not new," said Mikolajczk. "It has been discussed informally. The British, as usual, raise difficulties of a technical nature. They say that in Yugoslavia, in a different mountain terrain, one can ensure the safety and protection of such mission, but in Poland it would be endangered as soon as the Germans learned of its presence.''

"Since the fall of France,'' I said, ''a number of British prisoners-of-war have been in hiding in the middle of Warsaw. Most of these men can't speak one word of Polish. They live under the protection of the Home Army, move about in the streets, and are quite safe. If we can shelter a number of escaped prisoners for three years, why can't we hide a military mission; even in Warsaw itself?''

Mikolajczyk became interested and asked me to give him a note about the conditions under which these escaped prisoners lived. I promised to write such a note but said that there would be nothing new in it for the British authorities, as I was interrogated about this subject in detail, soon after I arrived in London, by a special section of the War Office in charge of escaped prisoners-of-war. Personally, I was convinced that if the British refused to send a military mission to Poland, their refusal would be dictated solely by political considerations.

Chapter 24

In my war diary of 1944, under the date February 10, I find a scribbled note: "11 A.M., 10 Downing Street, Major Morton. Meet Zarański at 10:30." As Mikolajczyk was personally interested in my meeting with Churchill, I was to be accompanied by Jozef Zarański, his political adviser. Two days earlier Zarański had telephoned me to say that the answer to the formal request for such a meeting had arrived from Downing Street. We were to go to see Churchill's special adviser, Major Desmond Morton, to settle the date and hour of the audience.

I was astonished when we stood in front of 10 Downing Street, that legendary building. It was an ordinary house of its period, with a brass knocker, no different from many other such houses in London. One policeman, armed only with a rubber truncheon, stood guard in front of it. The contrast with Hitler's bombastic, monumental chancellery in Berlin, surrounded by bunkers and barbed wire, was striking.

Major Morton had already heard that I learned to speak English in Warsaw from a Scot who had escaped from a POW camp. He also knew that I brought an "important message" from Warsaw for the prime minister, but first he wanted to hear how I had managed to get to London from Poland.

Telling about my own expedition, I profited from the occasion to mention the continuous activity of couriers and emissaries maintaining regular communication between Warsaw and London.

Morton then asked what message I had to transmit to Churchill. I mentioned three things: to convey to the prime minister the confidence and hope that the Polish nation placed in him; to give the reasons behind our requests concerning the drops of arms and equipment; and finally to hand to him personally an anti-German pamphlet which I brought from Warsaw and which was dedicated to him, and to explain its origin.

Morton said that unfortunately the prime minister was extremely busy and that he was not sure whether he would be able to receive me. As far as the supply of armaments was concerned, all requests should be directed through the proper channels, i.e., the Polish government. Here Zarański interrupted to point out that I was in London in an official capacity as an emissary of the Polish underground army, and that Prime Minister Mikolajczyk had asked for an audience with Mr. Churchill for me because he thought it important that the head of the British government should be personally acquainted with the situation inside Poland. I appealed to Morton personally to try to arrange for me to see the prime minister since I was to return to Warsaw in a few weeks time and wanted to be able to tell my superiors that I had complied with their request and personally handed Churchill this modest example of our efforts.

Morton replied noncommittally, after which a long discussion took place about the role of the Home Army. He asked about the AK's strength, the deployment of its forces in the country, its arms, the tactics it used against the enemy, and its military plans for the future. I replied as best I could from my own knowledge, remarking that precise statistical data and accurate full information could be obtained from Section Six of the Polish general staff in London.

At this point the major complained that while France, Yugoslavia, Greece, Czechoslovakia, and even Bulgaria(!)[*] had provided detailed information concerning the activities of their underground movements and their needs, the Polish government had supplied no such data. Both Zarański and I received this remark with astonishment and incredulity, but Morton insisted that it was so. Four days earlier, he said, a conference of chiefs of staff was held, presided over by Churchill himself and devoted, among other things, to the prob-

[*]There was no underground organization in Bulgaria.

261

lems of help to underground organizations in the occupied countries. Unfortunately, nothing could be decided about Poland because the Polish government had not supplied the necessary data.

I knew that this could not be true, but argument would have been useless. We both said that we would immediately report what he had said to our authorities and then left 10 Downing Street with uneasy feelings. We both knew that the office of General Gubbins, head of the SOE, received answers from Section Six to all its questions relating to our underground movement and that detailed reports were passed on by the SOE. Why would Churchill's adviser make accusations that were so easy to refute?

The following afternoon, the telephone rang in my apartment in Lowndes Street. Colonel Protasewicz, sounding rather excited, asked me to get a taxi and come to him at once. Feeling that something unpleasant must have occurred, I went at once to Upper Belgrave Street. Protasewicz was waiting for me with Colonel Perkins. They both seemed worried. "What have you done, Lieutenant?" Protasewicz asked me with irritation. I looked at him in astonishment. "I have no idea what you mean."

Perkins told me that Lord Selborne and General Gubbins had been telephoned by Major Morton to complain that the emissary of the Polish underground army had disavowed all the data supplied by the Polish staff. Apparently a map had been spread on Morton's table during our meeting, supplied to the SOE by Section Six, showing the disposition and numerical strengths of the units of the Home Army. Nowak, according to Morton, had declared that the map was sheer fantasy, and, pointing his finger at it, gave a few false figures as examples. Moreover, Nowak had maintained that in the present political situation the Polish underground movement must limit itself to self-defense.

Horrified by these falsehoods, I demanded that Jozef Zarański, the witness to the conversation, be summoned at once. He appeared very soon and, after listening to Perkins' account, threw up his hands in utter confusion. "In my whole career," he cried, "I have never heard anything like this."

Perkins was quite certain that Morton had already made a similar false report to Churchill and that an attempt must be made at once to repair the damage done. Zarański telephoned Mikolajczyk and Protasewicz telephoned the chief of staff, Kopanski. Both said that

Zarański should demand a minute of the conversation from Morton and send him his own version. The next steps would depend on Morton's answer. Everybody agreed that this was a very murky intrigue, although no one could understand its purpose or who was supposed to benefit from it.

Zarański took me straight from Upper Belgrave Street to Mikolajczyk's residence. The prime minister listened to our report and with a gloomy face said to Zarański, "If Morton's reply to the letter and minutes do not settle the matter, you must go to Ambassador O'Malley and ask for an explanation of what all this means." Then he muttered, as if to himself, "This was the worst possible moment."

As we left, I asked Zarański what Mikolajczyk meant by his last remark. "He was probably thinking about his last conversation with Churchill and Eden at Chequers a few days ago," he replied. "I was not present, but I read some of Romer's report. Churchill again insisted on our acceptance of the Curzon Line as a basis for negotiations and on the personnel changes in the Polish government in accordance with Stalin's wishes. Otherwise, he threatened, Britain herself, without Polish participation, would come to an understanding with Moscow. He was quite brutal at times. Mikolajczyk refused, but did not reject the possibility of a compromise. Polish-British relations are tense at present."

Zarański sent Morton a very detailed minute of our conversation. The answer came immediately and was only a few lines. Though he was pleased to meet Lieutenant Nowak, he said, "I hardly feel that what he had to say was of sufficient importance to warrant an agreed record."[*]

Zarański's report and the exchange of letters with Morton were at once forwarded to Lord Selborne, General Gubbins, and Ambassador O'Malley. The ambassador was visibly upset by the incident and just as worried as we were. He promised Zarański that he would try to clarify the matter. After a few days he told him that he could not learn anything about it at the Foreign Office.

I used to visit the O'Malleys informally in their house on Chelsea embankment overlooking the Thames. They had two daughters, the older of whom, Jane, worked in the Polish ministry of information

*See the Appendix for this note.

263

and had a Polish beau. The family had many Polish friends and was deeply concerned with our problems and the whole political situation. Ambassador O'Malley was a thoughtful man of rare intelligence. Under the name of Ann Bridge, his wife was a well-known novelist. As a diplomat O'Malley had to carry out the instructions of His Majesty's Government loyally, but from some of his remarks one could deduce that he was somewhat critical of British policy toward Poland. One day at the O'Malley's, when I was alone with the ambassador, I asked if he could explain to me in confidence what he thought the odd behavior of Major Morton meant. He said he did not understand it himself, and could only guess: in Churchill's entourage there were a few men, close friends from prewar days, whose attitude toward Poland was unfriendly, even hostile. He named three members of the Government: Lord Beaverbrook, the press lord; Brendan Bracken, the minister of information; and Lord Cherwell, the minister of communications, whose name was Frederic Lindemann and who was a professor at Oxford.[*] Morton belonged to this group, which, where Polish affairs were concerned, had had a negative influence on the prime minister. Before the war, he said, when Churchill was only an ordinary Member of Parliament, Morton had worked in intelligence at the War Office and had supplied Churchill with confidential information for use in his parliamentary attacks on Chamberlain's policy.[†]

Meanwhile, at the beginning of March, another incident occurred which proved that my experience with Morton was not unique. I was summoned to Section Six in order to verify the identity of an Englishman who had arrived from Poland claiming to know me. I was astounded to see Ronald Jeffery waiting for me in Colonel Protasewicz's office. The British officers escorting him wanted me to confirm that Corporal Jeffery, who had gotten out of Poland and reached Britain by his own devices, had contacts with the Home Army. I told them that Jeffery was extremely courageous and very intelligent, that

[*]Questioned later, Ambassador Raczynski confirmed this opinion in its entirety as it pertained to Beaverbrook; he denied, on the other hand, that Brendan Bracken, whom he knew well, had any anti-Polish prejudice.

[†]In Churchill's memoirs (*The Gathering Storm* [New York; Bantam Books, 1961], p. 72-73) his close ties with Major Morton, which date back to World War I, are described. In the book, Churchill views Morton as his closest adviser.

he had taken part in various armed activities against the Germans and had acted as a commando, that he had learned not only fluent Polish but also German, and that he had undertaken various missions to Germany. O'Malley was immediately informed about Jeffery's arrival by the SOE. He invited him to tea and was so impressed by his reports that he took immediate steps to arrange an audience for him with Churchill and Eden.

Jeffery, an impartial observer, confirmed all that the Poles had told the British about Poland's situation. His audience with Eden had already been scheduled when British counter-intelligence unexpectedly intervened and asked for a postponement. They then began to question Ronald about his escape from Poland. Until he provided a suitable explanation he was to refrain from any contacts with the press and from giving any public lectures. I was again summoned as an expert and, after studying Jeffery's report, I concluded that his adventures were extraordinary but within the limits of the possible. Interrogation of Jeffery lasted for a few months, after which he was given a military assignment outside London. The audience with Eden or Churchill never took place; perhaps Major Morton, through his intelligence contacts, was also responsible for that.

After the war O'Malley told me about a third such incident when I visited him in western Ireland, where he had settled with his family after his retirement. At about the time when I was pursuing my activities in London, an emissary from Mihajlović, his adjutant, had appeared on the scene. He spoke excellent English and quickly established good contacts. This did not please somebody in Churchill's entourage; some time earlier they had decided that support for Mihajlović and his Chetniks was a lost cause. One day, without much ado or excuse, they put the young emissary on a plane bound for Cairo. Thence on his own initiative he returned to his abandoned leader and probably perished along with him.

My own brush with Morton had a different epilogue. One of the characteristics of Mikolajczyk was a peasant doggedness; he would never take no for an answer. "With or without Morton," he told me, "Churchill must receive you. We will just wait a little while."

Meanwhile, less than a fortnight after my conversation with Morton, I had an opportunity to see and hear the British prime minister. It was a depressing experience. Churchill's report to Parliament on the conduct of the war and on foreign policy had been arranged for February 22. Thanks to Ivor Thomas, I got a ticket to the gallery, and he sat next to me in order to explain the proceedings. He said that it was awaited with great interest. The ritual and decorum, the procession of the Speaker in a white wig at the opening of the session, the archaic language and courtesy with which members referred to the Speaker and to each other—the continuity and strength of tradition of all this impressed me greatly.

Churchill's place on the government bench, the first to the right of the Speaker's chair, was empty. I knew that for several days our diplomats had been urging that the prime minister not touch upon the Polish question and not express support for Stalin's demands in public and thus still further weaken Poland's position in Moscow's eyes. I waited, tense and excited, for the arrival of one of the greatest statesmen of our century.

The session began in somewhat boring fashion: ministers were answering questions earlier presented in writing by deputies. They pertained neither to foreign policy nor to the war. After hearing the minister's reply, the deputy posing the question had the right to ask an additional question orally. Suddenly loud applause and cheers resounded in the House; Churchill was entering the chamber. He bowed his head in thanks and walked slowly to his seat. He seemed to be short; his stomach, covered by a waistcoat, was as round as a globe and across it hung an old-fashioned gold watch chain. On this smallish body sat a large head covered by sparse reddish hair. The whole figure would have been grotesque were it not for his lion's face.

The questions and answers continued before Churchill could catch the Speaker's eye. Then he began. In the first part of his speech he talked of the war. Germany, he stated, was still strong, nothing pointed yet to a speedy collapse, and the Allies were preparing to open a second front in the spring or summer. He gave no details except to say that it would be a combined sea, air, and land attack and would be a joint Allied operation. The Allies would throw all their forces into the offensive.

The first disquieting element in the speech was Churchill's statement that during the war all ideological differences between the Allies must be subordinated to the joint effort to combat the common enemy. This introduced a statement of the position taken in the face

266

of incidents in Yugoslavia. Churchill accused Mihajlović of making overtures to the enemy, preceded by the gradual limitation of partisan activity against the Germans. He showered praise on Tito, whom he referred to as "Marshal" Tito. It was Tito who had organized the resistance, and only his detachments were fighting the Germans, inflicting heavy losses on them. It was true that Tito's partisans were now also fighting Mihajlović's forces, but that was inevitable. Churchill ended the part of his speech devoted to Yugoslavia with an assurance that Great Britain would give Marshal Tito's forces all the support and help that she could spare. This is Mihajlović's political death sentence, I thought. Tonight Churchill's words, broadcast by the BBC, will circulate throughout Yugoslavia. Tomorrow everybody will leave Mihajlović except those prepared to die with him.

It seemed odd to me that Churchill's next statement was that Great Britain would not abandon or disown King Peter. A moment before he was handing the country to the communists, who could not be called, now or ever, monarchists. Poor Yugoslavia. In 1941, its resistance to the Germans postponed by at least a month Hitler's strike against Russia and in this way saved Moscow, which would certainly have had to surrender if the Germans had reached it before the onset of winter. How quickly the mighty of this world forget the contributions of small nations to the war!

Churchill spoke quite differently about Greece. The Greek communist partisans were not concentrating on defeating and driving the enemy out of Greece, but only on getting power after the defeat of the Germans. And what about Tito? I thought. Is he any different? Is it possible that the boundary line of the zone of influence runs between Greece and Yugoslavia?

I now nervously waited for the words about Poland and the Home Army. A few seats away, in the gallery reserved for diplomats, sat Zarański, a notebook in his hand. A troubled look was forming on his intent face. I asked Thomas in a whisper whether Ambassador Feodor Gusiev was present too. No, he was not there, but Thomas pointed out the Soviet press attaché and the TASS correspondent.

At last Churchill began to speak about Poland. Silence in the House; the members' faces showed great interest. The small, distant country in eastern Europe again found itself for a moment the center of the world's attention.

After a few meaningless phrases in praise of Polish bravery, and after reminding the House that Britain had entered the war in Poland's defense. Churchill took up the question of frontiers. He declared full support for the Russian annexation of the Polish territories up to the Curzon Line; Poland never had any right to them, she took Wilno by force, and Britain had never approved. In 1919 Great Britain was already standing by the Curzon Line, he said. (The fact that after World War I the Polish eastern frontier had been officially recognized by successive British governments was not mentioned.) Russia, he continued, had been attacked twice by Germany through Poland; she had the right to safeguard her western border. Russia would achieve this end, the prime minister announced to Parliament and to the whole world, not by sheer military strength but with the approval and sanction of the United Nations. The British government would help her to achieve this aim. Poland would be given territorial compensation in the west.

When I listened to these arguments I was filled with a rage I could hardly contain. When the British maintained that the war against Germany tied their hands and that in the current situation they could do nothing in our defense, it was at least understandable. But here was a public offer to agree in advance to Russian annexation of almost half of our country even before they had occupied the territory. And most shocking was the travesty of recent history, standing the events of four years ago on their heads to make it seem that Poland had provided Germany with an avenue to attack Russia.

Churchill repeated with approval Stalin's assurances at Teheran that he desired Poland's reinstitution as an independent state and one of the leading countries in Europe. "I am convinced," said Churchill gravely, "that this declaration presents the approved policy of the Soviet Union." Did Churchill really take Stalin's words at face value, or did he only pretend to believe them? I turned toward the two Russians in the gallery. Both were listening with smiling faces, and the embassy official was taking notes feverishly. In an hour's time messages would be sent to Moscow. The disastrous implications of Churchill's words were obvious: Stalin had been given the green light; the way to Poland was open. He would be able to do what he wanted with us with no risk of conflict with the Allies. He had in advance a public assurance that he had nothing to fear over the Polish issue.

If only Churchill, when expressing support for expansionist

Russian intentions, had at least warned that the British would defend that putative independent state, that Britain would not agree to a puppet government being imposed on it. This most important point was missing from the address. Mikolajczyk's entire tactics had been based on the assumption that with concessions in the matter of boundaries he could gain the strong support of the Anglo-Americans as protection from a Soviet blow at Polish independence. This strategy was now worthless.

Feeling very bitter, I turned to Thomas: "I cannot see the sense of this speech. By giving away everything in advance to the Russians, he weakens his own negotiating position vis-à-vis Stalin." Thomas shrugged his shoulders: "Perhaps he wanted to bring the Poles down to earth," he said, "and induce you to make concessions. Unfortunately, the pressure should have been put on the other party."

When I stepped into the corridor, Eden and his secretary appeared. "How are you, my friend?" he said with a smile in response to my bow. The next person I met was Zarański. "What do you think about it all?" I asked. "Well," he said, "Churchill has repeated all that he and Eden have been telling Mikolajczyk at every meeting they have had since Teheran. The difference—unfortunately a very important one—is that he has now said it all in public."

An air of gloom spread over the Polish community after this speech. Although everything that Mikolajczyk let fall at cabinet meetings about his conversations with the British usually spread throughout Polish London very quickly, Churchill's speech deeply shocked all Poles, soldiers and civilians alike.

Chapter 25

*B*esides our embassy and Section Six, which cooperated daily with SOE, the third area of contact for Poles and British was Polish Radio and the Polish Section of the BBC, which employed a number of our prewar journalists and broadcasters. The BBC's duty was to present the British point of view to listeners in Poland, while Polish Radio, a continuation of our prewar radio services, was an organ of the Polish government. Both these broadcasting services were subjected to wartime censorship. In Poland, most people did not know that they were quite different organizations; they were referred to jointly as "London." As all radios had been confiscated by the Germans, few people could listen to these radio bulletins directly, but almost everyone knew them at second hand through the monitoring reports in the underground press.

I met with war censorship at the BBC almost immediately after my arrival in London, and that in a drastic way. I was invited to record an interview for a current affairs program destined for the Home Service of the BBC. As my English was not good enough for me to be interviewed "live" on the air, first I was to have conversation with an Englishman who was to ask me questions, note down my answers, and prepare a transcript so that I could read from it into a recorder for later broadcast. He wanted a "human story" that would appeal to a wide English audience.

I decided to tell him about an incident I knew through my

travels for Action N. I arrived in Brodnica, in northwestern Poland, the day after a public execution. A workman, his wife, and his six-teen-year-old son had been hanged in the marketplace. Two younger children were taken away to an unknown destination by the Germans as soon as the parents had been executed, probably to the Reich. The family, although poor, had sheltered an escaped British prisoner-of-war. One of their neighbors, a Volksdeutscher, acciden-tally found out about the Englishman and told the Gestapo. The pris-oner was taken back to his camp, and the Poles who had sheltered him were hanged as an example.

The interviewer noted every word with great interest. This tragic event seemed to make a great impression on him. Suddenly, as if remembering something, he put his pen down and asked: "Can you tell me where Brodnica is? East or west of the Curzon Line?"[*]

I felt as if somebody had slapped me in the face. I shouted vio-lently and impulsively, "I don't want any interview," jumping up from my chair. "Those people who gave their lives for a British sol-dier did not ask *him* political questions when giving him shelter."

The journalist, visibly worried, followed me into the hallway and began to explain that he had not meant any harm: there had been so much talk about the Curzon Line that he had asked the question from sheer curiosity. "I am very sorry," he added. I was willing to bet, however, that as soon as the door had closed behind me, that Englishman ran to the library to locate Brodnica on the map.

All the same, the story about the Polish family hanged in Brod-nica did reach some millions of British listeners and perhaps awak-ened some sympathy for Poland.

On the whole, though, British censorship of Polish programs was kept within reasonable limits, perhaps because the Poles fought hard over every word deleted. We had heard of some plans for the Polish Section of the BBC to broadcast a series of talks justifying the Soviet claims to our eastern provinces, but the Poles were able to scotch these.

I had some observations, and some requests, about the pro-grams from London, both my own and those of professional listeners in the office of the Government Delegate and in the office responsible

[*]The British were avoiding any references to the territories east of the Curzon Line as part of Poland.

for circulating the news and comments of London radio in the underground press. As a result of a conversation with Gregory Macdonald, the chief of the Polish Section of the BBC, or perhaps at his initiative, a meeting was arranged in a club, the "Polish Hearth," with some editors and other staff members of the BBC. They were interested in the comments of someone who had heard the English broadcasts in Poland, as they were hampered in their work to some extent by the lack of response from listeners. The meeting room was full; even Mr. Noel Newsom, the director of foreign services of the BBC, came to listen. I was warned that Newsom was one of those Englishmen who imagined Poland to be a country of feudal landowners living by oppressing peasants and workers; in any event, he was not friendly to the Poles. I spoke about the enormous influence of "London" in shaping public opinion in Poland and on the mood of the Polish population, then pointed out some shortcomings of the broadcasts. I also spoke about the BBC's German listeners, as I had had occasion to observe them.

That meeting had an unexpected effect. Among those present was Professor Christopher Salmon, in charge of talks for the Home Service of the BBC. He asked me to dinner, and a friendship began which from the outset was very fruitful. One of the Home Service programs was the so-called Postscript after the Nine O'clock News. This program had at least ten million listeners in the winter months and was reserved for the most important broadcasts. Salmon told me that he would like to do something for Poland, and suggested that I prepare a talk about the Polish underground movement. He advised against any political slant: to achieve the greatest effect, to win the most sympathy for Poland and her fight with the invader, one must know how to capture the audience. He suggested that I present a human-interest story from my personal experience. In this account I wanted to present to the listeners a picture of the struggles of the entire nation, its solidarity, its readiness to make great sacrifices— even to give one's life to protect others.

I decided to write about Zbik, about our cooperation and friendship, his exploits, his arrest, and his escape. The title was to be "What Friendship Means in Poland." For security reasons I renamed Zbik ("wildcat," in Polish) "Rys" ("lynx"), made him into a miner's son, and added some other fictitious details. The talk was accepted. A professional broadcaster from the BBC Polish Service was to read it and I was to say only a few introductory words.

A few hours before the program, at my request, the BBC sent a telegram to Mr. and Mrs. Muir, the parents of Tom, my English teacher, the escapee from a German camp near Lodz. The Muirs had not had any news of Tom for a long time. Only from Stockholm in the spring of 1943, by a circuitous route and by courtesy of the legation staff, had I been able to send them news that Tom was alive and hiding with the Poles in Warsaw. The telegram to the Muirs was brief: "We invite you to listen to the Postscript after the Nine O'clock News. You will find information of importance to you."

I began the story with my recent arrival from Warsaw, where I had been taught English by a Scotsman, a soldier taken prisoner by the Germans in France who had escaped and joined the Polish underground movement. My teacher had done his best, I said, but it would be best for the audience if one of my countrymen, who spoke better English, read my account. The talk was said to be written by "an officer of the Polish underground movement" and my name was not given.

Only thirty-three years later, looking through the British war archives which had just been opened to the public, did I discover with amazement that this innocent and completely apolitical radio broadcast was the subject of a behind-the-scenes correspondence between a high official of the Home Service, H. R. Cunnings, and two departments of the Foreign Office. Should a script written by a Pole on the subject of the Polish underground movement be broadcast or not? Eventually it was decided that, after deleting one sentence concerning communication with London, the talk could go on the air. The marginal comment by Allan Douglas of the Central European Department was quite telling: "I think it would be carrying self-effacement and deference to the Russians unnecessarily far for us to object to this." At the center of the British leaders' consciousness, fear of Russia operated like an unseen censor.

The reading of these secret documents in the archives led me to other discoveries. I thought that I was small fry, and was amazed to see voluminous reports and notes from the various people I met and spoke to that had found their way to the Public Records Office. I was astonished that even Eden had sent Churchill a four-page report of my conversation with him. I also found reports from lower-grade officials, experts in Polish affairs who wanted to speak to me soon after my arrival in London. Among these were Frank Savery, the former British consul in Warsaw, and Moray McLaren and David Osborne from the Political Intelligence Department of the Foreign Office.

In all these meetings I myself introduced the subject of the extermination of the Polish Jews and the destruction of the Warsaw ghetto. The crime of genocide, the slaughter of hundreds of thousands of people, the scale and methods used, unprecedented in history, seemed matters of the highest importance. Everybody had listened with interest mixed with disbelief. Thirty-odd years later, looking through the notes and reports of those interlocutors, I found all the references to the Jews omitted. Jan Karski, my predecessor, arrived in London from Poland in 1942 with extensive eye-witness information about the fate of the Jews. Before he left Poland Karski, posing as an Estonian policeman, risked his life by getting into the concentration camp at Majdanek to see with his own eyes what was happening to the Jews sent there. Karski met with Anthony Eden on his return to London and told me that at his audience he described at length the systematic and progressive extermination of the Jewish population. The undersecretary of state considered the conversation so important that a report on it was circulated to all members of the war cabinet. I looked this up at the Public Records Office and was astonished to find everything Karski had said about the extermination of the Jews omitted from the document. Why?

One explanation occurred to me. Soon after I first came to London, when the microfilms I brought with me had been developed and sent to the people interested, I was invited to meet Ignacy Szwarcbart, a Zionist activist who sat on the Polish National Council in London as representative of the Jewish minority. I was the first emissary to arrive in the west after the annihilation of the Warsaw ghetto.* Although I was in Sweden during the ghetto rising, I could give Szwarcbart tragic information about the martyrdom of the Jews which had been collected by various witnesses and which I had seen myself. Szwarcbart listened intently. Whenever he covered his eyes with his hands, I wondered whether he still had family in Poland and

*Walter Laqueur refers to my role as an emissary who brought information and documents about the ghetto rising and the Holocaust to London; see The Terrible Secret: Suppression of the Truth about Hitler's ''Final Solution'' (Boston: Little, Brown, 1981), pp. 237-38.

whether presenting my report, monstrous in its bald facts and figures, was not an act of cruelty to this man. But Szwarcbart, as if guessing my thoughts, insisted that I tell him all I knew. He interruped me only when I said that when I left Poland only a few hundred thousand Jews out of three million survived. "I beg you," he cried, "when speaking with the British, do not use these numbers!"

"But why?" I asked, amazed. "I did not invent them."

"Because they won't believe it. They are more likely to believe you when you tell them about those three Jewish children who escaped from the ghetto and were shot by some German civilians because the little ones could run no more—they might believe that. If you tell them that the Germans have exterminated a million or two million Jews in gas chambers, no one will believe you, *no one*—listen—the Jews themselves don't believe it."

"Is it simply distrust of the Poles?" I asked. "We have the reputation of wanting to impose the most severe conditions on the Germans when they are defeated. Polish sources may be suspected of deliberately exaggerating German atrocities."

Szwarcbart denied this: "The Polish government and the underground movement in Poland are our principal sources of information, but not the only ones. Besides, the Poles pass on to us reports and documents that come from Jews themselves."

"Do you think that if, in place of myself, a Jew had just arrived from Warsaw with this news, they would disbelieve him too?" I asked.

"They would not believe him either. An emissary of the Jewish organization BUND, Szmul Zygielbojm, reached the West. His comrades in Poland kept sending him reports here through the Polish underground. One report said that seven hundred thousand Jews had already been exterminated. One of the leaders of the Polish Socialist Party, Adam Pragier, who is himself Jewish by origin, told Zygielbojm that this was propaganda which nobody would believe, that one zero must be erased and one must say that *seventy* thousand Jews have been killed. Then public opinion in the West would accept it as possible." Zygielbojm, he said, could not bear the fact that even world-wide Jewish organizations cared nothing for his warnings. In the end he committed suicide from despair.

In the rest of the conversation it transpired that Szwarcbart had been informed of these events even before my arrival in London.

By radio and courier the underground authorities had seen detailed documents, photographs, and figures about the course of the extermination plans. The Polish government passed these on to the British and to the world Jewish organizations.

I had several conversations with Szwarcbart and with other Jewish leaders to whom he introduced me. On one occasion I suggested that, in order to save what was left of the Jewish population, the British or Americans, via the BBC, should threaten reprisals against the Germans. German cities were being bombed anyway, so why not say that the raids were reprisals for the genocide? This would at least bring moral relief to that doomed people. Szwarcbart assured me that he and other Jews had made all sorts of like suggestions but always came up against a wall of disbelief.

I understood that this skepticism was itself another Jewish tragedy. The very victims of this horrible slaughter, up to the moment when they stood in front of them, would not believe that their lot was to be the gas chambers. The murder of three million people organized like a factory on a kind of conveyor-belt principle was beyond the ordinary human imagination. For a long time the Jewish population thought that perhaps, if it avoided desperate acts of violence and any kind of armed resistance, only a few thousand would die and the rest might be saved, but that if there were armed resistance all would perish. When at last the Jews in Poland understood that they had nothing to lose but their human dignity, and did take up arms, neither their brethren in the West, nor the Western leaders, nor the public could believe that the sentence of total extermination had been handed down and executed.

Time filled with work passed quickly. By the middle of March 1944 I had completed my mission, which consisted of taking out from mental storage all information, knowledge, claims to knowledge, opinions, and personal assessments, so that they could be put to use by those whose emissary I was.

After the period of lively diplomatic activity which followed the Teheran conference there was a hiatus. Mikolajczyk's tactics, which, as he himself put it, consisted in shifting the blame for the failure of British mediation from the Poles to Moscow, had achieved their aim—except that no benefit had thus far accrued to the Polish cause from this victory. When the Russians crossed the 1939 frontier in the middle of January, the Poles issued a declaration which, before being made public, was shown to Anthony Eden. The British had crossed out various words and changed others in the draft declaration, and in the end it was Eden rather than the Poles who actually wrote the final version. This seemed to me a clever tactic because it pulled the British into the maneuvers between the Poles and Moscow. The Soviets' rude answer was aimed at the Poles but of course was also offensive to the British, who had reworded and then endorsed the Polish declaration. There followed a whole series of notes, declarations, and counter-declarations. The more moderate and conciliatory the Polish notes, the sharper, more aggressive, and brutal the Soviet replies.

The Polish authorities also learned at this time that various offers by Churchill to give Stalin all kinds of concessions at the expense of Poland had been flatly rejected. As soon as a danger of serious conflict with Russia arose, Churchill abandoned further efforts to reach a compromise and left Stalin with what he wanted: time necessary to set up a puppet government on the first piece of the Polish territory the Red Army "liberated" from the Germans and to recognize it instantly as the only "true" representative of the Polish people.

My last function as informant was to fill out a long questionnaire about the activities of the Soviet partisans in Poland, sent me by British intelligence through Protasewicz. My last political meeting was with Lord Vansittart, whom I visited at his beautiful family country seat at Denham, near London. Vansittart was interesting because he differed from the majority of British politicians of his generation in mentality and outlook and in every way imaginable from all the other British people with whom I had talked. He was one of the few Englishmen who, before the war, had repeatedly warned of expansionism in Nazi Germany. His views made him unpopular after Neville Chamberlain's efforts at Munich, and he was eased out of his post as permanent undersecretary of state, in which he directly influenced international politics. He then began to write for the press, warned the British about the inevitable approach of the war, and spoke frequently in the House of Lords. At the time, like Churchill, he was a voice crying in the wilderness. During the war he constantly urged that, after the defeat of Germany, the peace treaty contain conditions that would once and for all preclude any further acts of German aggression. On these grounds, Vansittart was attracted to the Polish position.

At our talk Vansittart was most interested in what I had to say about the Germans. He wanted to know whether there had been any moral revulsion in Germany against the Nazi crimes in Poland—in particular, the extermination of the Jews and the concentration camps—especially on the part of the Catholic and Protestant churches; whether the old opposition parties had survived, and if so, in what form; whether there was any underground movement or at least passive resistance among the Germans; and whether there was any chance that the German community would rebel against the Nazi regime. I replied within the limits of my own observations. (The fruit of this conversation was a long article in the *Daily Mail* by Vansittart entitled "The Nation in the Dock," in which he quoted as his source an anonymous officer of the Polish underground movement.)

The conversation then passed to Russia. Vansittart was very critical of Churchill's policy toward Poland. It is true, he said, that we don't hold any high cards, but in poker you can win even with nothing in your hand provided your opponents do not see your cards. He claimed that Churchill had made an unforgivable mistake by dispelling all uncertainty that Stalin might have had about the British attitude toward his expansionist plans. Alas, as was explained to me later, this brilliant politician had little influence in England; he was considered an extremist.

In the middle of March I presented to Colonel Protasewicz my request that I be sent back to Poland by the quickest and shortest route, i.e., by parachute. He smiled: "General Bor has twice asked for you, but I did not want to tell you that until you had finished your work here." It was agreed that I would be sent to Ringway, near Manchester, to join the next training course for parachutists. I was to make five practice jumps; the sixth would be over Poland.

On my return from Protasewicz's office, I received a telephone message that Mikolajczyk wanted to see me. He began as usual with sacramental invocations on keeping secrets. This time, however, they sounded even more severe and solemn than usual. I had to vow silence on my word as an officer. He reverted to the Morton affair. He had learned that Churchill had refused to see me because of Morton's hostile report, but, after a telephone call from Mikolajczyk, had agreed to allow me to hand him the pamphlet which I had brought for him from Poland. He would meet only in a private capacity; the meeting was to be off the record, informal, without minutes taken. No one but Mikolajczyk and myself were to know of it. It was to take place in a private house and not in the prime minister's office. "Why this secrecy?" I asked. "Is Churchill afraid of upsetting the Russians? Surely I am too small a fish for that." "It is not yet that bad," replied Mikolajczyk. "My guess is that he just does not wish to offend the people from his entourage, who, for some reason, did not want to let you see him."*

On the appointed day Mikolajczyk drove me to the meeting. He was in a good mood and told me about his previous encounters with Churchill. One of the most difficult conversations had taken place at Chequers, the weekend residence of British prime ministers. In order to console his Polish guests, who were depressed by what they had just heard, Churchill told them as they left: "Don't beat this poor donkey, which is trying to carry you to safety on the other side of the river." Mikolajczyk was intrigued by the choice of place for our meeting. He assumed that we were going to a place used for secret encounters that were to escape the notice of journalists and politicians. The car stopped in front of a house in a residential square in London. We entered not an office but a private apartment filled with antique furniture. A few minutes later I was before Winston Churchill.

From the first moment I felt paralyzed with fright. Churchill at close quarters made a much greater impression than he had at a distance in the House of Commons. A wrinkled forehead, cut by a vertical line, a vast chin, a small, somewhat crooked mouth, the lower lip thrust forward. From this countenance, looking like the face of an old woman, shone a powerful, overwhelming personality. One could not lightly think of saying no to this man. He greeted me with a handshake which was surprisingly soft and flabby; he did not smile or say a word of greeting, not even the conventional ones. He was not discourteous but by his almost grudging behavior he let me feel that the

*When looking in the Public Records Office in London for the documents referring to the incident with Morton, I discovered that the Foreign Office was indeed not informed about my meeting with Churchill, as the director of the Central European Department in the Foreign Office, at the instigation of Ambassador O'Malley, had continued to try to arrange an audience with the prime minister at Downing Street for me up until the time of the arrival of our emissaries from Poland on Air Bridge I.

Poles in general, and I in particular, were wasting his time and that he had more important things to do than to converse with some emissary from Warsaw.

Mikolajczyk began the conversation. He handed the prime minister the pamphlet with the inscription "Der grösste Lügner der Welt," with its cover picture of Churchill handing out guarantees to Europe. Mikolajczyk apologized on behalf of the authors of the pamphlet for using a cartoon of the prime minister in order to mislead the enemy. He put an explanatory letter signed by himself with the pamphlet, and then said a few words about the diversionary activities of Action N, likening it to the "black propaganda" conducted with great success by Sefton Delmer. At the end he said a few words about me.

The brochure was born in a secret Warsaw print shop. There was a dedication to Churchill diligently inscribed by an unknown calligrapher, evidence of Polish daring, now in the hands of the British war leader. If it had fallen into the hands of the Gestapo along the way, I would have been *hanged*. But Churchill glanced at it with no particular interest. He took his cigar out of his mouth and, turning to Mikolajczyk, said: " Thank you. I shall pass on this interesting pamphlet to the Imperial War Museum." Then he was silent and turned his head toward me, as if waiting to hear what I had to say.

Put out by this indifference, which seemed to border on outright hostility, and depressed by the impression which Churchill had made on me, I completely lost my bearings. I had prepared and memorized a short statement covering several very important points. Delivery of the pamphlet was in fact only a pretext. What mattered was to make Churchill understand that the AK was a real military force which played a very important part in the general Allied effort, that it deserved maximal support, and that it could be a trump card in diplomatic negotiation. With some facts and examples I wanted to make the point that what was at stake here was not a bit of territory but the independence of Poland—that Stalin intended not just to annex the western lands but to seize the entire country. In closing, I had planned to ask for a word of encouragement to carry back to our leaders and comrades in the underground movement.

But suddenly my mind went blank, my English escaped me completely, and I began to falter. I realized that I was not making sense; perspiration covered my forehead. I did not have to look in Mikolajczyk's direction to know that he was staring at me with increasing alarm. Suddenly the mask of bored indifference fell from Churchill's face. A friendly glint appeared in his eye, something like sympathy. Perhaps he felt sorry for me.

"Nowak," he said, "could you write down all that you wanted to tell me on one page of typing paper?"

"I shall try," I mumbled.

"All right! But remember that it must be no longer than one page. If it is just one page, I promise to read it with attention. If it is longer, my secretary will put it straight into the wastebasket. Agreed?"

Then he turned to Mikolajczyk. "Could you please pass Nowak's memo on to me through the normal channels as a 'personal message'?" Then, with a polite formula, Churchill saw us to the door and patted me on the back in a friendly manner. The audience was to have lasted ten minutes; it took seven.

On the way back Mikolajczyk was not very talkative. I felt that for the first time I had let him down, but I was in no mood to explain myself.

This unsuccessful audience concluded my three months' work in London. A few days later I reported at Ringway airfield for parachute training.

Chapter 26

I recovered consciousness in a Nissen hut. Two rows of beds and the sight of forms with arms or legs bandaged or in plaster attached to pulleys made me realize that I was in a military hospital. I closed my eyes again and tried to understand how I came to be there.

I had probably broken my arm just after I jumped. One of the parachute lines must have got under it while I was turning a somersault in the air, for when I tried to pull down on the harness of the parachute, according to regulations, my right arm refused to function and hung helplessly at my side. *"Pull down!"* shouted somebody from the ground, sounding irritated.

The wind tugged at the lines and the chute did not open wide enough. I tried to make a half turn by making a scissors movement with my legs, as I had been taught, but there was not much time for it. The ground was approaching very fast, much too fast. I hit it with my whole body, and only then felt a piercing pain in my right shoulder.

"Hello, John, what's happened?" asked my British instructor, running toward me. Before I could reply, I lost consciousness.

What bad luck! For years I had survived all kinds of dangers, and now this landing right on my own back had interrupted me in mid-flight. A rapid chain of events had suddenly pulled me into center stage in the historical drama unfolding between London and Warsaw, but in a few seconds an ill fate had cast me into an out-of-the-way corner of a military hospital, a backwater, still and quiet, somewhere in northwestern England.

The doctor said that the fracture was complex because when I had rolled over the ground, the broken bone had damaged a muscle, that I would regain movement in my right hand but that I would never again have full strength in it. There was no question of my repeating the jump in less than four months. Four months seemed to me an infinitely long time, so long that the war would probably be over before the end of it. The second part of my mission, which, against the background of general political and military situation, could have been very important, would come to naught.

The next day I got a letter from the seventeen lucky men from my course who were returning by train to London after five training jumps, to be scattered like night birds in various parts of occupied Europe. They were of many nationalities, four Poles along with myself. I don't know their real names; we all had cover names because all the people in the course were future or present members of underground organizations and thus were bound by secrecy rules.

Reading, after thirty-three years, the yellowed letter that the group sent wishing me a swift return to the highroad of great adventure, I wondered who those people really were, what part they played later in the underground and in postwar Europe. A Frenchman, about fifty years of age, an envoy of General de Gaulle, had to be someone of considerable importance, as indicated by the attention devoted to him by a younger, inseparable companion. Following the exclamation "Vive l'Europe Nouvelle," the older man signed the letter "Robert." A Serbo-Croatian emissary wrote "Mnoho Was Pozdrawia," and signed the name of his commander-in-chief: "Tito." Under the greeting "A bientôt sur les grand chemins," I read the name of "Ginette." Who was she, and what kind of assignments did this beautiful twenty-year-old French parachutist, the only woman among us, have? She was very courageous—able to overcome her fear before a jump.

At Ringway I had learned that the feeling of fear does not bear any relation to objective danger. The breaking of arms and legs was a frequent, almost daily, occurrence, but the accidents that ended badly as a result of a parachute failing to open completely or a bad landing were rare. The risk connected with the illegal crossing of a frontier was much greater than that of jumping, and yet when the moment came to step into the wide opening, like a very large pail without a bottom, we all felt as if we were committing suicide. Never before nor since have I experienced such fear.

Today parachute jumping is a sport which many young people enjoy. Our group consisted of men who had little to do with any sport and were mostly over thirty. I myself had a marked lack of talent for any kind of athletics. In the bus taking us to the airfield, silence always reigned. Our faces were tense and our mood was funereal. On the way back, in contrast, we were in excellent spirits, singing bawdy songs, telling each other jokes, and laughing boisterously. The next day before a jump the funereal mood would reappear.

The worst was the first jump we made from a balloon. We were seated in a semicircle around the opening. The narrow rim of the basket was protected only by canvas. One could see the earth falling away, and as the basket swayed, I was not sure that I would not fall outward instead of through the opening in the middle. It was much better to jump from an aircraft, where the passengers couldn't see anything. Before jumping one had to put one's legs across the hole, propping both hands over the edge of it. And God forbid that one should look down at the ground! One must sit with eyes fixed on the dispatcher.

When one found oneself in the air, after a few seconds of turning somersaults, the great silk mushroom opened over one's head, and a moment of indescribable bliss and euphoria followed, although the earth was still far below. In order to slow the movement of the parachute one had to pull both lines down toward the body, holding the palms of the hands against the chest, legs together, knees bent. The non-observance of this instruction could lead to breaking an arm or leg on landing. The instructor repeatedly reminded us about it, shouting from the ground: "Pull down, feet together!"

There was a Pole among us who came straight from our forces in the Middle East and was, I suspected, destined for a jump over the Balkans. He did not understand any English at all. After jumping from the plane, he must have forgotten what he was supposed to do because he was floating down with arms and legs spread wide. Luckily I was standing next to the instructor, who gave me the megaphone and told me to shout "Pull down, feet together!" in Polish. There was no reaction. My fellow Pole continued to float down in that dangerous position. At the last moment the instructor grabbed the megaphone and screamed *"pull down,* you bloody fool!" This rude command in a foreign language must have done the trick because at the last moment the Pole pulled the lines down and bent his knees, landing according to the form. "You see?" the instructor said, turning to me, "basic English is not difficult."

In hospital I had a lot of time to think what to do next. It was the end of March. In the next month or so the Soviet offensive in the east and the invasion of the Continent in the west might start. If my mission were to succeed, I had to hurry. Since the quickest and the shortest way, the air route, was closed to me for months, only the land route remained, best of all the route through Sweden which I had twice traveled. I wrote urgently to Protasewicz.

Three days after receiving my letter, he informed General Bor by radiogram about my accident and told him I would return overland. Soon after my return to London with my arm in a sling, Protasewicz sent two messages: one to Stockholm asking about the possibilities of obtaining a Swedish visa and the chances of crossing the Baltic on the old route back to Poland, the second to Bor asking whether I could count on Filarska's help in Gdynia. A few days later a shattering piece of news arrived from Warsaw: Jarach had betrayed the Zaloga people to the Gestapo.

This was a terrible blow. The Gestapo had given him nine months in which to uncover the entire leadership and network of contacts with the outside. In that period—from the time that Jarach left Action N for Zaloga until March 9—there had been no arrests at all. Then the blows fell suddenly and all at once. On March 9, twenty-two Zaloga people and their families were arrested. Only two women escaped by a miracle, Marcysia and "Zo," but Zo's family perished. Seweryn was saved, but he lost his beloved fiancée.

There were no interrogations at Gestapo headquarters: they knew everything from Jarach. Those arrested were executed on the spot, perhaps for fear that the agent provocateur would be blown by a note sent from prison. Jarach, who was himself arrested at first, presumably for his own protection, disappeared into thin air. After having performed his shameful duty, he was probably allowed to return to Czechoslavakia, where he lived before the war.

Each dispatch from the country contained the names of more

people arrested and more tragic news. The arrested were not limited to the Zaloga headquarters but spread to all the "boxes" and points of contact on all the courier routes. I read with despair of the arrest of my people in Gdansk and Gdynia, and I was terribly upset about the loss of young Maria Filarska and Stodolski the stockbroker. Without the generosity and help of those two I would never have reached England. Now the overland route through Sweden and all other routes were closed for a long time. One of Jarach's victims was "Goral" (whose real name I don't know to this day), who had been the first to warn me against Jarach (then called "Redhead") in the summer of 1943. Alas, he did not act on his suspicions at the time.

Six weeks after Jarach's treachery, at the end of April, British intelligence passed on to Section Six the news that the Gestapo in Gdansk were looking for Jan Kwiatkowski, who had twice been a courier to Sweden, and that the local Gestapo chief, Jacob Loellen, knew my name. It was not clear whether the Gestapo knew my real or adopted name. I broke out into a sweat when I thought that with Jarach's help the Germans might have found my mother and brother. A request to the British to check brought no result. I begged Protase-wicz to send General Bor a dispatch, which I drafted. I reminded him that Redhead had known me, and asked for protection for my family. Throughout May I waited in fear that I might have lost them. At the end of the month, to my great relief, I received the reply: "Zych's family safe and well."

Meanwhile, my return to Poland seemed more and more doubtful. Surgical examination and X-rays showed that I would not be able to lift my right arm for at least a year, and one had to be able to pull the lines of a parachute with both hands when jumping. My hope for a return was reawakened by an unexpected event. On April 17 a British aircraft carrying arms, "mail," and two couriers landed safely in Poland and on his return flight brought a delegation from the Polish underground consisting of four people from the military and civilian leadership: General "Tabor" (Stanislaw Tatar, the deputy chief of staff of the commander of the Home Army and the chief of operations) and three others. Transfer of personnel, arms, and "mail" by air were quite frequent between Britain and France. The success of the first landing in Poland raised the possibility of future ones. I immediately applied to Section Six as a future passenger. The response I got, however, was that there was no assurance that the opportunity would arise again.

The Polish delegation reached London on April 21 and four days later was received by Churchill, this time on a British initiative. They were introduced by Ambassador Raczynski. The gist of the conversation was known all over Polish London the next day. On the Polish side the main speaker was Zygmunt Berezowski, a leader of the National Democratic Party. Ambassador Raczynski acted as translator. The meeting was important because it occurred almost immediately after the arrival of the delegation in London. Berezowski made a statement to the effect that Poland counted on British guarantees of her independence and territorial integrity. Churchill replied: "Independence—yes, we shall *help* you to preserve your independence. Territorial integrity—no! We stand behind the Curzon Line." It was significant that Churchill, in response to Berezowski's plea that Britain should assure Polish independence, used instead the word "help."

But Berezowski was not deterred by Churchill's words and went on to explain that the Polish nation would never reconcile itself to the loss of its great cities of Lwow and Wilno. If necessary, it would fight to defend them. Churchill replied that if somebody wants to commit suicide, nobody can deny him his right to make such a decision.

About a month before the establishment of the first air bridge, the envoy of the government, "Jur" (Jerzy Lerski), whom I had already met in Warsaw, returned from Poland. He had started his return journey in January 1944. The first air bridge passengers made the journey from Poland to London in a few hours, crammed into the plane like sardines in a tin. On that trip they had escaped the single mortal danger which threatened them: meeting an enemy fighter plane or an anti-aircraft barrage. Lerski's journey, however, had been long and wearisome. It took him two months, across Germany, France, and Spain, to reach London. He spoke English well and could begin immediately the most important work of an emissary: conversations with the British. Lerski became the third link in the chain which began with Karski.

We met in the Allies Club near Hyde Park. This time the roles were reversed: six months earlier in Warsaw Lerski told me about

Polish London; now I was telling him about the international situation and Polish affairs in Great Britain. Lerski was very enterprising. Immediately he suggested arranging a lunch with Arthur Greenwood, a Member of Parliament whom he had met before his expedition to Poland, and before I could comment he went to telephone about it. Greenwood was the leader of the Labour Party Parliamentary Club. He felt a bond with the Poles because of a particular episode, of which he was proud and which, as it became apparent in conversation, he considered a high point of his parliamentary career. On the first of September 1939 it was he who, speaking for his party, had replied to Prime Minister Chamberlain's speech after Hitler's attack on Poland, appealing to Britain to fulfill her obligations toward her ally without delay.

Greenwood accepted Lerski's invitation. During the lunch at Brown's Hotel Lerski treated the elderly and experienced politician with great familiarity, and Greenwood, although he was old enough to be our father, was equally relaxed. The British, whatever their political allegiance, did not take kindly to critical remarks by foreigners about Churchill. Greenwood, however, when we were discussing Russian policy and the Russian threat to Poland, offered several very candid assessments. Churchill, he said, was a typical war leader: no one else could have led a nation from defeat to victory mainly by talking! At the same time, in Greenwood's opinion, he was and always has been a mediocre politician. The defeat of the enemy was his one objective and occupied his mind entirely, to the exclusion of everything else. He did not seem to care what would happen later—what kind of Europe would emerge from the postwar chaos. Churchill would certainly win the war, but he might lose the peace if Soviet Russia were to replace the Nazi Reich in Europe.

One evening I returned to my top-floor room in Lowndes Street so tired that I immediately fell asleep. When the sirens went off toward dawn, I did not rouse myself. Air raids on London were by then becoming rarer and shorter, as the Germans exhausted their supplies of fuel and aircraft. I had just gone back to sleep when I was wakened again by some kind of noise of a nearby plane. I went to the window, from which I had a fine view, and saw, flying low, just over the rooftops, a small, noisy, rattling aircraft. In silhouette and size it differed from any other German machine that I knew. It could not be a fighter because it flew slowly on a dead straight course. It had almost disappeared from sight when the noise suddenly stopped. After a second or two of silence there was an explosion and, far above the roofs, a billow of smoke.

"They got the Krauts," I thought with satisfaction, and was about to return to bed when I heard a similar noise and saw a similar machine coming in from the south at a slightly higher altitude. The sequence of events was repeated: the clatter suddenly stopped, and after a few seconds there was another explosion, much closer than the first. After the second explosion my house shook and the windowpanes rattled. The raid did not stop until early morning. At seven I turned on the radio and heard that London was under attack by the new weapon long promised by Hitler.

At this point a new chapter began in the life of wartime London. Until then the raids had been more or less intense but only at night, lasting approximately an hour. Then they were over, and a certain relief followed. More fearful people spent the night sleeping on mattresses on the Underground platforms, which had been transformed into communal sleeping quarters, crowded but safe. Now the population of London found itself like soldiers in the trenches under permanent attack. The V-1 rockets were harder to bear than bombs. Danger was announced by the louder and louder noise of the engine. Nervous people were especially frightened by the few seconds of silence before the explosion. Only after the explosion came an un-Christian but pleasant sense of relief that it had hit somebody else.

I did not guess at the time that there was a close connection between my own fortunes in the war and Hitler's new weapon. After the V-1 it was the turn of the V-2 rocket. The Germans had been trying these out on practice ranges in southern Poland.

The Home Army intelligence lay in wait for the mysterious weapon until the fateful day when one fell like a meteor from the sky onto the village of Sarnaki and was captured intact. Detailed descriptions were sent to London by radiograms. The British asked that the principal parts of the rocket be sent with an expert by the only route possible, the air bridge.

This was to be the third successive landing of an aircraft in occupied Poland. About the second I learned too late, as with the first. It occurred at the end of May. It took only two passengers to

Poland, and it became clear to me that I must await the next opportunity not in London but in Italy, at the Brindisi air base.

The commander of the Home Army came to my assistance. Two days after the debut of the "flying bomb" in London, General Bor sent a dispatch which read: "Officers Zych and 'Dowmuntt' are to be sent back immediately."[*] This request was categorical, and I at once went to see Protasewicz and requested a passage to the base in southern Italy, but he could not help. He referred me to General Tabor. General Tabor, after coming to London, was nominated by Sosnkowski as assistant chief of staff for Polish home affairs and took over the work of Section Six. He accompanied Mikolajczyk on his journey to Washington, took part in his talks with President Roosevelt, and had returned to London that very day.

And then a new and most unexpected obstacle to my plans arose.

[*]"Dowmuntt" was an emissary of BIP who accompanied the delegation which had come from Poland on Air Bridge I.

Chapter 27

No one in London, not even General Sosnkowski, could understand why the commander of the Home Army had decided to send General Tatar to London. Only after the war was it learned that since the beginning of 1944, Tatar had represented at headquarters the view that the underground should "come to terms" with Russia without unduly worrying about the views of London. As Tatar was not averse to sharing his opinions with his subordinates, he was considered to be a dangerous man. Instead of transferring him laterally, the Home Army command decided to get rid of him altogether by sending him to London.

Soon after Tatar's return from Washington, I reported to him with General Bor's dispatch. I asked him to arrange a flight for me to the air force base at Brindisi as soon as possible. "And what's the hurry?" asked the general. "You are in too much of a hurry, my friend. If you want to go to the base, please yourself, but you will go by convoy, by sea."

Taken aback, I protested that the voyage by convoy could take a month, or even two. For a long time I had been collecting military and political information in London, and had been lucky enough to talk with many important people. The information I had might help the commander-in-chief of the Home Army and his staff make decisions in the next few months that were of vital importance for the future of the country. General Bor had clearly advised an immediate return.

The time for decisions was approaching; every day counted. A delay of up to two months might render my mission useless.

Tatar shook his head. "You, my friend, only imagine that you are very important," he said. "You are not a VIP and you will go by boat, like all the other parachute-jumpers."

Keeping my temper with difficulty, I once more stressed that the commander of AK had three times requested my return and that his latest order was clear.

Tatar looked at me with malicious satisfaction: "Don't waste your time, my friend, *here* it is *I* who decide!"

I left the room without another word. In the afternoon I went to the Rubens Hotel to see Halina Omiecinska, an *éminence grise* on the staff of the commander-in-chief. I asked her to repeat to General Sosnkowski, word for word, my conversation with Tatar. The next day I was summoned to the Rubens Hotel and stood before the commander-in-chief.

"I have heard about your difficulties," said Sosnkowski crisply. "In the next few weeks I intend to fly to Italy to inspect the Second Corps. You will fly in my plane. Prepare for departure at once. The formalities with the British will be dealt with by my office."

"What am I to report to General Tatar?"

"You will repeat to him the order of the commander-in-chief: "Here it is *I* who decide!"

When I told General Tatar of this decision, I had the satisfaction of seeing his fury. I did not foresee that he would make one more attempt to frustrate my mission. What could have been the motives of this man, with his glum, evil look? Since my arrival in London I had succeeded in maintaining friendly relations with both antagonists—General Sosnkowski and the prime minister—an achievement which was not insignificant. In my conversations with English people I had strictly obeyed the instructions of the head of government, but I also informed the commander-in-chief of everything of note; he sometimes gave me good advice but never hampered me. I came to the conclusion that these good relations with General Sosnkowski must have awakened Tatar's suspicions. For Mikolajczyk the military activities of the Home Army were an important element in the endeavors to regularize relations with Moscow with the help of the British, while Tatar approached the problem in a much more primitive way. If Nowak is Sosnkowski's man, he may have thought, he will try to thwart the prime minister's plans in Warsaw. It would be safer if no emissary appears in Warsaw at that critical moment. I found that this guess was correct only after I had reached Warsaw.

Now, however, I began to supplement my information and bring it up to date. I asked Ambassador Raczynski and Minister Romer, separately, for access to all the important documents and for their own opinions about the situation. I began with Raczynski. From the outset I had great respect for his intelligence and knowledge and for his unselfish patriotism. He was without a doubt our expert on British politics.

Raczynski took me for a walk in Regent's Park, not far from the embassy, on a fine warm June afternoon. We sat on a bench and talked. The ambassador understood that I was only a messenger and that what he told me was destined for those who would bear the great burden of decision-making, so he weighed each word carefully. It was obvious that he wanted to stick to facts but did not wish me to give up whatever hope was left. He doubted that the Moscow-London-Washington alliance would hold together after the war, but that did not mean, in his opinion, that there must be another war. He quoted Churchill, who foresaw that Britain would emerge from the present war much less powerful than she had entered it. The United States would have a much bigger part to play internationally, but its postwar policy was largely unknown. The British realized that their position was becoming weaker and wanted to arrange their relations with Russia on the "live and let live" principle.

It was on this basis that they wanted to settle the Polish question as well. As a matter of fact, they had devoted a disproportionate amount of time and attention to Poland when one considers that eastern Europe had traditionally been outside the area of their interest—an offshoot of either the Russian or the German problem. Raczynski had no doubt that both Churchill and Eden sincerely wanted to assure the independence of Poland. He repeated Churchill's warning to some Polish visitors, which Mikolajczyk had already repeated to me, not to beat the donkey which was about to carry them to safety. Unfortunately, the ambassador continued, when the British are not strong enough to impose a solution to a problem by pressure and threats, they resort to appeasement of their adversary and hope to contain him with concessions. They had supported Soviet territorial claims and, more recently, even demands regarding personnel,

293

imagining that in this way they would achieve a compromise that might save us. Their intentions may not have been evil, but such moves could only harm rather than help. Raczynski told me of his conversation with former Prime Minister Puricz of Yugoslavia, who at one time asked the English to stop concerning themselves with Yugoslavia if they were unable to help her, as their aid, intended to protect King Peter, was actually pushing Yugoslavia into the arms of communism and Russia.

Polish tactics in the face of British pressure had achieved some limited results. It was important that Churchill's mediation, were it to fail, should not do so through Polish obstinacy but only because of Stalin's intransigent attitude. A successful Allied invasion of the Continent would alter the military and political situation of the British in their favor, and so in our favor. The rest would depend on the behavior of Russia after the war: would she aim to exploit the postwar chaos in order to engulf Germany and western Europe, or would she concentrate on the restoration of her country and accept the help of the United States? In the first case there would be another armed conflict. Churchill, in conversation with the Poles, had disclosed his vision of the postwar world: the nations of the three continents would constitute three councils—a European, an American, and an Asian one. The European council would be formed without the participation of Russia and Great Britain. The United Nations council would consist of representatives from Continental councils. At the top of this pyramid would be the Big Three, as a supervisory and, he hoped, a dominant body.

With all his suppleness of mind, I felt that Raczynski was against any partitioning or subjugation of Poland receiving the stamp of Polish approval. Some of his associates thought differently. For instance, Minister Kulski thought that the most important question was the preservation of the Polish "biological substance" (that phrase appeared often in conversation among Poles) and that this aim justified concessions, even far-reaching ones. Soviet armies already hovered over Poland, poised for the next attack; under that shadow the number of people who shared Kulski's view was growing. The majority, who thought differently, saw treachery in this, but Kulski and others like him were not opportunists. Kulski told me that he would not return to a country under Soviet domination, though London did not lack for crafty people who already were quietly constructing catwalks to the other side—preparing themselves for positions under Communist administrations.

Both Raczynski and Romer did everything in their power to acquaint me with the whole truth before my flight to Warsaw. Now I was spending whole days on end in a large room of the embassy, studying piles of secret reports, telegrams, notes, and minutes of conversations. I attempted to commit all of this material to memory and to consolidate it in my mind as well as I knew how.

That was at the end of June and the beginning of July. V-1 rockets were falling on London without respite. The big window-panes in the embassy rattled restlessly. Whenever the ominous sounds could be heard approaching, the secretary in the adjoining room would crouch with fear over her typewriter. But I was so engrossed in my reading that nothing around me, not even bombs, penetrated my consciousness. The gist of the documents was familiar to me, but seeing with my own eyes the minutes of conversations with, for instance, Churchill was a shock. The naked truth was unfolding page by page: the government in London and the people in Poland were fighting a losing battle. One could draw no other inference from the long talks of Mikolajczyk and our diplomats with Churchill, Eden, and more recently also with Roosevelt.

In the dossier to which I had been given access, I found once again full confirmation that the division into occupation zones between the three major powers had been decided in 1943 in Moscow and Teheran. The Soviet armies were to occupy the whole of Poland and eastern Europe up to the River Elbe. The agreement anticipated in detail the joint occupation of a Berlin divided into three zones (the French participation was not yet being considered). The German capital would therefore find itself in a much better position than Warsaw. Both the British and the Americans had rejected Mikolajczyk's requests, made at the end of February, that military missions be sent to Poland. This decision made the Soviet influence rather exclusive.

The handing over of all Poland to a Soviet occupation prejudiced everything else, in my opinion, and created an irrevocable situation. The Russians would be able to do what they liked with Poland. They would not willingly withdraw. Getting rid of the new occupant, I thought, will not be possible without war.

I was convinced that when I arrived in Warsaw I must present these conclusions with brutal frankness, and as persuasively as I could, to the commander of the Home Army and the Government Delegate, though I at once doubted that they would believe me. In London the whole truth about our position was known only to some Polish leaders: a dozen people at most. The rest had some inkling, were guessing, were apprehensive. In Poland, people lived in an atmosphere of complete dissociation from reality, unaware of the helplessness of the situation, not even guessing anything.

This was not the fault of the London government. The very fact that all secret files had been opened to me proved that. A person who has for many years lived in isolation, fed exclusively and onesidedly on selective radio information, who believes deeply in something because this belief is dictated by his instinct for self-preservation, can understand how far the reality is from his imaginings only if he has direct contact with it: no intermediary will do. I asked myself what the reaction would be when I told them in Warsaw that we have been left entirely at the mercy of Russia. I would not have believed it myself if I had not seen the documents with my own eyes. I would have said that such an attitude on the part of the Allies was contrary to their own interests and safety, and therefore to logic and good sense.

And even if a few people at the top believed me, what conclusions would they draw? Their freedom of action was doubly limited, on the one hand, by the mood of the people, and, on the other, by the presence of a Communist diversionary group which might exploit popular feelings and turn them against the legitimate authorities. This was a weighty element that had not been taken into account in Polish London. A mood is an elusive thing for a person who is not experiencing it. This truism applies to politicians as well as to historians.

After the study of the documents it was time for conversations with representatives of the various parties. Before I left I also wanted to hear for myself the views of the British government. A private conversation with Ambassador O'Malley was not sufficient for this purpose, and I asked Ambassador Raczynski to set up an official meeting. He told O'Malley in confidence that I would be returning to Warsaw and would inform my superiors of the British government's view of the present situation.

O'Malley asked for questions in writing, no more than five. I compiled the following list.

1. Can Poland count on Great Britain's help in defense of her independence? What would this help consist of?
2. What is the attitude of His Majesty's Government toward the Soviet demands that there be personnel changes in the composition of the Polish state authorities?
3. To what extent is Great Britain interested in the military activities of the Home Army, and to what extent would Great Britain support them?
4. Can the soldiers of the Home Army count on being helped by Great Britain in the event of reprisals from the Soviet side after the conclusion of operations against the Germans?
5. What am I to report to my superiors on the subject of future Polish borders? Is there a "linkage" between the British support of the Curzon Line in the east and territorial compensation for Poland in the west?

I was assured at the embassy that those questions had been asked the British not once, or twice, but ten times over, but that it did not matter if they were asked once again.

O'Malley, in spite of the typical reserve of a well-bred Englishman, tried to be as cordial as possible. He arrived at the embassy driving his own car, and took us somewhere outside London. On the way he told me that he attached importance to every word and that before drafting his replies he had consulted his "colleagues" at the Foreign Office. I guessed that "colleagues" may have been meant as a cryptic reference to Eden.

Replying to the first question, O'Malley assured me that Poland's independence was in Great Britain's interest, as indicated by the amount of time and effort which the War Cabinet was devoting to the matter. How Great Britain intended to defend this independence was a subject that could be discussed only when the threat to it, a real one, became more concrete.

This answer was clearly evasive. To my additional question as to how Great Britain would respond if Soviet expansionism reached the Rhine, O'Malley replied that, if Russia attempted to take the whole of Germany by force, the result would be a military confrontation, if only because in all probability the Allied armies would soon find themselves on German territory. That eventuality was too remote to be taken seriously. The Russians were too weakened and their country too devastated for them to be able to attack the joint British and American forces. Without the help of the United States, and especially without its shipments of trucks, the Russians would not be where they are today. The Poles would gain more by good relations between Moscow and the Allies than by a conflict. Russia would be likely to plead for postwar economic help and might be ready to pay for it by political concessions.

As to changes in the Polish government, the ambassador understood the reluctance of the Poles to make concessions without any assurances and guarantees of their sovereignty's being respected. But one must face reality, such as it was. If the Poles wished their government to return to Warsaw, which most probably would be occupied by the Russians, it was in their own interests that it consist of people who could cooperate with the Russians in a friendly manner. "That means communists?" I asked. The ambassador winced. Even among the Union of Polish Patriots in Moscow, a completely Russian creation, the majority of the members had never been communists.

O'Malley declined to answer military questions, advising me to consult General Gubbins or Colonel Perkins. As to territorial compensation in the west, Great Britain supported this in principle. The ambassador knew, however, that Churchill and Eden believed that, for her own security, Poland should not bite off more than she could chew. "Linkage" between the borders in the east and the west exists, but not in time. The eastern frontier was a matter of great urgency because the Soviet offensive was in progress and the line between the Polish and Soviet administrations must be drawn immediately. The frontier with Germany could be fixed only after Hitler's defeat: one cannot divide the skin of a bear that has not yet been shot. The rest of the conversation was filled with pleasant platitudes.

Meanwhile the Soviet offensive, which had begun in the northern sector of the front on June 23, 1944, was gaining momentum daily. More and more often the question arose of whether the German retreat would degenerate into a rout. In every instance events at the front brought to the fore the activities of the Home Army and the matter of its eventual support by the Allies. When taking leave of Colonel Perkins, I asked him the question that O'Malley had refused to answer: were the Allies interested in the Polish Operation TEMPEST (a code name for guerrilla warfare behind the retreating German troops), and how could they help the Home Army apart from the normal drops of personnel and arms? Perkins advised me to read, before my journey, a letter that had just been sent to Colonel Protasewicz. The British side, he said, was not interested. In view of the distance between Poland and the western theater of war, there was no possibility of any coordination of the military operations of AK at the rear of the German armies in the east with those of General Eisenhower's staff. Only the Poles themselves, assessing the situation on the spot, could decide whether or where to take up open warfare. Perkins stressed that he could consider only the military aspect of the Polish plans: TEMPEST might have great importance for the normalization of Polish-Soviet relations, but such political considerations were outside his responsibility.

The letter Perkins mentioned was of course top secret, but I had no difficulty in seeing it at Section Six so that I could ascertain that Perkins had presented its contents accurately. I was struck by the similarity of the argument to what Sir Archibald Sinclair had told me six months before. Interest in the Home Army awakened shortly before the invasion and ceased after its success.

There still remained two important final conversations. During lunch with the commander-in-chief, Sosnkowski said he would tell me all that he wanted to say to the commander of the Home Army during the flight to Italy. I notified Mikolajczyk that my flight was fixed for July 11. Shortly after this, the telephone rang. A secretary announced that "the prime minister expects you in his apartment at 3 o'clock on the afternoon of July 10."

At the appointed hour I appeared at the prime minister's apartment in Bayswater. The floor of the sitting room was strewn, as usual, with telegrams, reports, dispatches, and newspapers. He told me that he would be very frank and swore me to secrecy as usual. During the conversation I understood that secrecy was especially important because some points discussed might not be generally known.

He began telling me about his recent trip to the United States and his conversations with Roosevelt, about which I already knew something from the notes of our ambassador there. He stressed the cordiality of his reception, which, our ambassador thought, was caused by the proximity of the presidential election. Mikolajczyk attached much importance to Roosevelt's statement that he hoped to save the city of Lwow and the petrol-producing area for Poland. He also disclosed Roosevelt's idea, which he spontaneously put forward during the talks, that he should send a cable to Stalin suggesting that he invite Mikolajczyk to Moscow for direct talks.

"The reply came soon after my departure," the prime minister continued, "and it resembled all the previous ones. Stalin's condition for my visit was that I should accept in advance all conditions that might be the subject of our talks, and in the end he even stated that the meeting would have no purpose. But, given the prospect of the Soviet offensive and of the moment when events would reach a climax, I decided to make an attempt to start direct talks with the Russians here in London [the initiative actually came from the Russian side—J.N.]. Beneš always told us that English mediation harms rather than helps in regularizing relations with Moscow, and Stalin does not want to have a client country of Britain close to him. Beneš thought that in direct contact, as per his example, one might achieve much more. All right; I decided to find out how much truth there was in these statements. The initial talks took place between Grabski and Ambassador Lebiediew before my departure for Washington. After my return I myself spoke to him in Grabski's presence. All talks took place in Grabski's apartment. I suggested to the Russians the immediate re-establishment of diplomatic relations, the supplementing of the July agreement of 1941 with a protocol about military cooperation on Polish territory, and an agreement on taking over the administration of those areas. I finally suggested that a demarcation line should be established until the final settlement of the borders question. Should the Russians accept these conditions, I was ready to form a government which, by its composition, would assure friendly cooperation with the Soviet Union. At first, Lebiediew was so friendly that for the first time I saw a ray of hope, but at the last meeting, our third, he came in a completely different mood. He declared at the start that there was nothing to talk about if the Polish government did not agree to the Curzon Line as the final demarcation; if the president and the commander-in-chief did not resign at once along with two other ministers; if the Polish government did not abandon the Polish Constitution and publicly disavow the "slanders" relating to Katyn. Lebiediew asked me whether I could accept these conditions; yes or no? I replied that I saw no point in common between these demands and the assurances of Marshal Stalin that he wanted a strong and independent Poland. At this point, the talks broke down."

"How do you explain this sudden change?" I asked.

"The last meeting with Lebiediew was on June 23. On the same day the Russians started their offensive, and our government was viciously attacked by the radio and press of the Union of Polish Patriots."

What do these two events have in common, I wondered? The Russians probably wanted to split the government before they reached the center of the country. They probably thought that Mikolajczyk was not going far enough in his concessions and that their plan would not succeed. If so, they had made a mistake in their own strategy: the change to a government more "friendly" in composition could not be achieved within the political structure of Polish London. Any such attempt would probably have ended in a crisis and Mikolajczyk's resignation, and also a possible split in Warsaw.

"I did not disclose these reflections to the prime minister, but instead asked: "Mr. Prime Minister, from what has happened, it would appear that there is again a deadlock. What shall I tell them in Poland? How do you envisage breaking this deadlock, and what will be the future course of events?"

"The initiative is again in Churchill's hands," Mikolajczyk replied, "and at any moment one can expect the resumption of talks with Moscow, or in Moscow."

He was silent for a moment, then continued, not looking at me, as if thinking aloud: "The Russians will occupy Poland, that is certain, and with the approval of the Allies they will annex the eastern territories up to the River Bug. We can protest against it, but what use are protests?" He waved his hand contemptuously. "If Russia decides to Sovietize the rest of the country by force and terror, we don't stand a chance. But this is not likely. In France and Germany after the war, strong Communist parties may come to the fore. The frightening example of Poland would jeopardize all their chances. The Sovietization of Poland by force cannot outstrip the victories of Communists in western Europe. If this thinking is correct, one cannot let a political vacuum occur in Poland, for in such a case the Communists would fill it themselves without resorting to force. So one must aim at a compromise and be on the spot. The Anglo-Americans

assume that the Russians are guided by their own security considerations. If this is so, Stalin, confronted with the choice between a Communist minority facing a hostile population and a government both
supported by the majority and prepared to consider an alliance with
the Soviets, might decide that the second solution is in his interest. In
the first eventuality, he would have to conduct a policy of brutal
oppression toward the Poles with all its negative effects on international communism. In the second eventuality, he might avoid this. So
I see a possibility that at the price of giving up our sovereignty and
subordinating ourselves to Russia in foreign policy, we might be able
to save our internal political freedom.''

"I don't ask you what your views are,'' he continued, "but
I want you to tell our people in Poland that Mikolajczyk does
not believe in a war between Russia and the West. Tell them"—he
stressed each word—"not to take this eventuality into account at all.
There won't be any war in the next twenty or thirty years. We must
have two objectives: to save the 'biological substance' of our nation,
and to prevent ourselves from being Sovietized. Our trump card is
the support of our people. I personally believe in our nation. We must
use this card to show that we are ready for honest cooperation with
Russia. The Home Army must fight against the Germans to the end
and support the Red Army whatever the difficulties. We cannot let
ourselves be pushed out from the family of allied nations at the last
moment.''

When seeing me to the door and saying goodbye in a most
friendly fashion, Mikolajczyk suddenly made a mysterious prophecy:
"Next time we shall meet in Warsaw . . . quite soon . . . in not very
pleasant circumstances.''

I was aghast, but before I could ask the prime minister what he
had in mind, the door shut behind me. As I walked away, I was
pondering what I had heard. What did he mean when he said that we
would soon meet again in Warsaw? Did he also plan to be parachuted
in, or to land in Poland at some dramatic moment? No, he was much
too down-to-earth for such meaningless gestures. There was only one
possibility left: he must hope to reach Warsaw by way of Moscow,
following liberation of the capital by the Red Army—in other words,
with the consent of the Russians. I was disturbed. The whole notion
which Mikolajczyk had unfolded could not have originated with him.
It was certainly an inspiration of one of his trusted advisers. Knowing

the prime minister, I had no doubt that once he had embraced an idea as his own, he would not easily part with it.

During this conversation neither of us knew that the attack on the left wing of the First Byelorussian Front was already being prepared. The tide which was to bring Warsaw its tragic fate was about to surge forward.

Chapter 28

*T*here was silence in the plane, although no one, not even Sosnkowski, was asleep. Over this flight hung the memory of that flight exactly a year ago which ended with the death of Prime Minister Sikorski at Gibraltar. Sikorski's pilot had been a Czech, a Captain Prchal. This time the choice of both pilots and the navigator had been personally approved by Sosnkowski. The pilot was a pleasant young Polish lieutenant. He appeared to be only about twenty years old but, judging from his Polish and British decorations, must have had much experience. The commander-in-chief had an entourage of six people. His aide-de-camp carried a heavy suitcase filled with military decorations made by the London firm of Spinks, as the general would personally decorate officers and soldiers outstanding in the Italian campaign.

The British had taken unusual security measures. From the military airfield near London the Dakota *Balmoral Castle* took off soon after 4 P.M.; two hours later we landed unexpectedly somewhere in Cornwall. It seems that apart from Sosnkowski, no one had been told about this stop. Both on takeoff from London and here, at St. Mawgan, the aircraft was surrounded by armed guards.

After midnight our flight to Gibraltar took off once more. Sosnkowski sat in the first row on the right, next to the window. Someone whispered to me that Sikorski used to sit in that same seat, and that he too had been accompanied by a courier from Poland going in the other direction, from Warsaw to London. I couldn't help noticing the similarity.

The nights in July are short. At daybreak the plane was flying quite low over the Portuguese coast. There, the continent of Europe is bordered by a chain of high mountains dropping straight down to the sea, an extremely beautiful sight. The rocky mountains, golden in the rays of the rising sun, were covered by a transparent haze of light blue mist. Although the message which I was carrying was unspeakably tragic, I had a moment of joyous elation. I remembered Ginette, the young woman from the French *maquis:* "A bientôt, sur les grands chemins!" And here I was again on my "great trail." The six months in London had been both sad and fascinating: sad, because I had to watch a Polish drama from close quarters. Others could see only one side of the moon, but I had had before me the scene viewed from both Warsaw and London.

Around 7 A.M. the aircraft made an enormous circle over Gibraltar. The Rock plunged into the sea like an outstretched human arm with powerful bulging muscles. At the foot of this barrier was the military port, full of toy ships, from long cigar-line submarines to large cruisers with armored turrets and big guns.

The landing was smooth. Through the door of the aircraft hot air puffed in, as though out of an overheated stove. A Polish liaison officer reported to the general that Governor MacFarlane was not in the fortress, as he was ill. Sosnkowski's face fell: a "diplomatic illness"? But the Polish officer was already introducing a very young British officer with a boyish face but with three pips on the epaulettes of his short-sleeved shirt. He saluted and, on behalf of his mother, invited the general and his party to the governor's palace for lunch. The governor's young son was public relations officer in the colony. He suggested that we should tour the fortress before lunch. Some of us gladly accepted, others preferred to rest in the cool rooms of the palace. Outdoors, under a parching sun, the heat was unbearable.

We drove away from the airfield in the governor's limousine, with its flag flying. Despite this official appearance, we were stopped by the guard at the entrance to the fortress. The British NCO on duty saluted, the governor's son produced a military pass. "Your hat off please, sir," the NCO requested. The young captain doffed his forage cap, the NCO carefully compared his face with the photograph, then returned the pass and once more saluted smartly. At that point the captain asked the guard, "Tell me, how is Ann?" We learned that Ann was well and expecting her baby any day. It was obvious that in such a small garrison everybody knew everybody else, and I asked young MacFarlane why these formalities were necessary. "Regulations," he replied.

The Rock was like an anthill, a labyrinth of tunnels and hidden gun emplacements. The car was now struggling up an incredibly steep and winding road which plunged now and then into dark tunnels and then emerged suddenly into the blinding noonday glare. I tried to imagine the scene if all the guns with which the Rock bristled were fired simultaneously. Only when we reached the top did I realize the range of the artillery in the fortress. To the south the African coast with the line of the Atlas Mountains could be seen clearly. To the north was the enormous bulk of southern Spain, an area friendly to the Germans. Straight below us, at the foot of the Rock, there was an old town, behind it the runway, and beyond that the Spanish frontier, marked by a double line of cement bunkers which, from that altitude and in comparison with the size of the Rock, looked like a child's building blocks. Young MacFarlane shrugged his shoulders with contempt: "One barrage and they're finished."

Straight ahead of us, in the Mediterranean facing the runway, perhaps 750 yards away, a lonely buoy was rocking on the waves. Young MacFarlane followed my glance and guessed my thoughts: "Yes, we moored the buoy in the place where General Sikorski's plane hit the sea." Again a long silence. No one asked any questions. We knew that every morning workmen came from pro-Nazi Spain to their jobs in Gibraltar, and that, among them, a Nazi or Soviet agent might well have crossed the border. I did not for a moment believe that the catastrophe was the work of the British. If Sikorski had proved troublesome, they could have gotten him out of the way by political means.

After the tour, we went to our luncheon. The interior of the governor's residence in the old palace was magnificent. The hostess, a distinguished lady, did her best to honor her Polish guests, but she was not at ease, and throughout the meal the atmosphere was rather strained, with long silences. At coffee, a Polish officer sitting next to me whispered that the British were terrified lest anything should happen to General Sosnkowski at Gibraltar and that they would heave a sigh of relief when he took off safely. The ghost of Sikorski was ever present. My luncheon companion recalled that the day before his death Sikorski was entertained at a meal in this same room and had occupied Sosnkowski's place on the hostess's right.

In the afternoon, in beautiful weather, we started for Algiers, flying over the north coast to Africa. South of the green belt along the coast the desert stretched out toward the horizon. While we were still over England the commander-in-chief had informed me that I was to fly with him to the Polish Second Corps at the Italian port near Ancona. "I want you to be a link between the two parts of Fighting Poland," he said, "and report back to our country about the mood and activities of the Second Corps." I received this order with mixed feelings. Of course I was overjoyed at the thought of encountering our front-line troops, which had become a fresh legend in the country, surrounded by the glory of the victory at Monte Cassino, but I was afraid of arriving late at "Jutrzenka," the base at Brindisi. Section Six had told me that Operation WILDHORN might begin any day. The general dispelled these fears: he had his own plane and could deliver me to the base within an hour. The necessary orders would be given to the commander of Jutrzenka. He added that he himself would brief me if he had time during this tour.

That opportunity arose on July 13, during a stop at Algiers. We were quartered in the beautiful villa of some French millionaire which, during the Allied invasion of Sicily, served as Eisenhower's headquarters. We talked in a beautiful oriental garden, filled with the scent of flowers. Sosnkowski showed me two radiograms he had sent to "Lawina." The first, rather short but most important, had been sent a week earlier, after talks with Mikolajczyk. In the second, much longer one, sent on the day of his flight from London, Sosnkowski made a *tour d'horizon*. He knew from experience that those long radiograms to stations in Poland were received in bits and pieces, a few sentences at a time, and were slow to reach Warsaw; they could take a month, sometimes two. He reckoned that I would reach the capital ahead of his second radiogram by at least a few weeks.

He began by reading the first dispatch, which was worded more in the manner of a chief of staff than that of a commander-in-

307

chief. In it he made various suggestions: he opposed a general uprising over the whole country which, under the present political and
military conditions, would not make sense, but he did not rule out
the possibility that the situation might change. One must therefore be
in readiness for such an uprising, while continuing Operation TEM-
PEST, that is, increased guerrilla activities behind retreating German
armies in accordance with the instructions of the commander of the
AK issued in November of last year. He warned against calling Operation TEMPEST, "UPRISING." The most important point in the dispatch
was that he foresaw yet a third variant: the possibility that the Home
Army might take over for a short time a large town or a clearly
defined area of the country just before the entry of the Russians. The
general strongly recommended that, if circumstances permitted, an
opportunity to do so should be seized. It was necessary for the world
to know that the sovereign Polish nation was fighting on its own soil
between the German and Russian armies. (I found just this situation
in Warsaw two weeks later, at the end of July.) Sosnkowski then
moved on to talk of international matters and the internal situation of
Poland, basing his remark on the text of the later radiogram, one sent
on the day of his departure.

As he spoke, I compared his ideas with what I had heard four
days before from the prime minister. Mikolajczyk thought one could
follow a foreign policy of alliance with Russia while "not succumbing
to communism" domestically. Sosnkowski rejected such a possibility
in advance. He foresaw the repetition of the Russian occupation policy of 1939 through 1941: mass deportations of the population, a false
referendum, incorporation of Poland into the USSR, and finally an
extermination of the national identity on the Ukrainian model.
Mikolajczk firmly rejected the possibility of a third world war.
Sosnkowski, if asked on what one could base one's hopes for the
future, would answer: on the assumption that there will be an
improvement in the international situation, as he did not believe in
the fixity of relationships among countries. Though he was not specific, his reasoning led one to think that he foresaw an outbreak of
war with Russia, although, as always, he was not quite sure.*
Because of the attitude of the Allies, neither Sosnkowski nor Miko-

*In an earlier conversation Sosnkowski predicted to me that a third world war would
break out within five years.

lajczyk believed that Polish independence could be preserved. Yet the prime minister, although he spoke only about the support of the Polish population, was obviously counting on the help of the western Allies in achieving a compromise which would save the "biological substance" of the nation and at least preserve internal freedom. Sosnkowski expected a mass exodus to the West of the most threatened elements and valuable people. It was clear that they could return only as part of an army entering Poland at the moment of a Russian defeat. He was against any kind of concessions: we must not forfeit any of our rights, he said. We must preserve for the future all the moral and formal rights of Poland as a wronged ally. For the immediate future, he was very pessimistic. He feared that, should Mikolajczyk indeed go to Moscow, the journey would end with capitulation to Stalin. The effects of this would be immeasurable. The armed forces would not tolerate it; there would be a revolt. The soldiers would prefer barbed wire to another partition and slavery.

The general then spoke of his own difficulties. I heard again everything that he had said during the Christmas supper at his home, but with the difference that now he was reading sizeable extracts from the dispatch in which he presented the general policy to the authorities in Poland. Its focus was Sosnkowski himself. Again everything revolved around his person. His treatment was to be the touchstone for all English conduct toward Poland. The attacks on the commander-in-chief and the Soviet demand that he resign were an attempt to destroy Poland's independence. Sosnkowski did not hesitate to accuse Mikolajczyk himself of engineering attacks on him in the British press.

I thought that such an assessment of the situation would be poorly received by those to whom it was addressed. In Poland events were seen in a different perspective. There would be a storm soon, in the most literal meaning of the word, and any week now the AK leaders might find themselves in the eye of it. They must foresee that they themselves would be swept away. Under such circumstances personal matters seem remote, and Sosnkowski was putting them at center stage. In short, in Sosnkowski's analysis there was too much about Sosnkowski.

I listened attentively to all this, of course, without betraying my own thoughts. I had every reason to be grateful to the general. From his hands I had received the highest Polish military distinction, and he had promoted me to the rank of lieutenant. He had always treated me with fatherly kindness and had never tried to make me a pawn in his game—he did not play games. And yet I could not help but feel that, behind this magnificent facade and great mind, the decisiveness needed to meet this crisis was lacking.

The conversation lasted almost four hours. Toward the end the general talked of the attitude of the British toward the Home Army. Only then, in this context, did I learn that the plane in which I was to fly would bring back to England parts of yet another of Hitler's weapons (the V-2). In Section Six, all intelligence matters were secret, and I had had no knowledge of such a plan.

The next morning we flew to Italy, and in the afternoon were in the wonderful Bourbon palace at Caserta, near Naples. Quite unexpectedly I was called to see Colonel Demel, the general's trusted aide, who told me that the commander-in-chief had changed his mind and decided it would be better if I flew straight from Naples to the base, rather than visiting the Second Corps with him. He did not explain the general's motives, and I did not inquire. I did ask to say goodbye to him personally, to thank him for taking me with him from London. But Demel said that he was resting and was not to be disturbed, so I went to Naples at dusk without seeing him, wondering what could have happened to change his mind.

Chapter 29

I wasted two days in Naples waiting for a military plane. On the morning of July 17, I finally reported to the Polish base "Daybreak" (Jutrzenka), near Brindisi. A short time later I attended a briefing which familiarized me with details of Operation WILDHORN. I was put in command of our small team of four.

"Please note this spot here very carefully," said the briefing officer, pointing to a place on the huge map that took up all of one wall on the operations room. Our eyes focused on the spot indicated, located in a triangle formed by the confluence of two rivers, with a railway line as its base. "I advise you to make a mental note of all distances, of the road to the nearest railway station, and of the names of nearby villages. It may well be that what you can remember of this map will be your only guide."

"The entire operation," continued the briefing officer, "from landing to takeoff, including unloading and reloading of men and material, must not take longer than six minutes. That was also the case with our last mission. As leader of the team, you, Lieutenant, together with the copilot, will be responsible for the order of loading for the return trip: first, the special supplies"*—this he particularly stressed—"then the accompanying expert, 'Rafal'; 'Brzoza' goes

---

*Parts of a V-2 rocket stolen by the Home Army from the Germans.

next, then 'Tomasz,' and last the two couriers. The order is important in case the total weight is too heavy for the aircraft. In that case, you will not take aboard everyone scheduled but will leave some behind, starting from the bottom of the list. However, the material and the expert must be taken aboard no matter what.''

''When may we expect to go?'' someone asked.

''Could be tomorrow, could be in a month. It all depends on the weather. The plane will have to cross three weather zones on its way to Poland. If it's sunny over the Balkans, it's likely to be cloudy or rainy beyond the Carpathians, or vice versa; if weather conditions in Italy are good, the landing place in Poland will probably be ankle-deep in mud after a day of rain. Eventually, a day will come when the weather is good all along the flight path, the landing field is dry, and the local air 'clean,' with no whiff of a German in the vicinity—then you take off.

''The whole thing's a piece of cake. At 10 A.M. we get our meteorological report from the British, advising that everything is OK. At noon the radio station at the landing site sends a signal that they are ready to receive the flight. If that signal is repeated at 5 P.M., you get ready to go. The plane will take off at 8 P.M., so as to cross enemy territory after dark and return to the base before daybreak. We'll send a message advising your departure, and the BBC will confirm your flight following the 7 P.M. news by a prearranged tune. You should arrive there shortly after midnight. Then it will be their turn to notify us of the plane's departure, and a few hours later we'll let them know the plane got back here safely. That's all there is to it.''

We were given passwords and addresses of hideouts in Warsaw. Unlike those who had parachuted into Poland before us, we were to fly not in a Liberator or a Halifax, but in a much slower Dakota, chosen for this mission because it could land and take off on a very short strip.

The following days of waiting were sheer torture. We were quartered in a ramshackle Italian village, miles from anywhere. If the morning weather forecast was good, we anxiously waited for the clock to strike noon. The sensible wireless operator in Poland assigned to Operation WILDHORN would seldom be provoked by calls from Daybreak, being unwilling to court danger for himself and others. Once in a while he would signal that he was there and listening; occasionally he would break off with the signal "danger," to indicate that there were Germans in the area.

By that time the Germans had the ability to track down our radio stations in a matter of minutes by taking goniometric readings from a truck or a plane, which forced our operators to move their shortwave sets out of town into the forests or other remote locations, and this seriously handicapped communications with London. Aware of this danger, I was worried about the signals we received and the frequent sudden interruptions in transmission. Our own operators on the base thought that their colleague in Poland must be a cool type who took no chances. As it happened, barely six months later, I ran into him in Poland and learned of the difficult circumstances under which Operation WILDHORN was prepared, and how close it came to being scrapped at the last moment or ending in disaster.

For the time being, our life at Daybreak was growing more monotonous and nerve-racking as the days passed. Each morning I would go over to the operations room and hear the same words: "Nothing today." I would then walk to a neighboring house to hear the news broadcast from London. Events rushed on at a crazy pace as if on a movie screen gone haywire. The broadcast brought a new sensation almost every day. The Russian juggernaut rolled steadily on toward Warsaw. I watched the meandering red thread of the front line on the map in the operations room with mounting anxiety. Since the day of my arrival at the base it had moved considerably closer to our scheduled landing place. When they crossed the River Bug and occupied Chelm, the first town west of the Curzon Line, the Russians announced the formation of the Polish Committee of National Liberation. This was yet another in a series of moves by which Stalin hoped to knock the free Polish government off the board and replace it with his own pawns. First, the Soviets created a supposed counterpart of the underground Home Army, called the "People's Army." Then General Berling's Army, supposed to be a duplicate of the Polish Armed Forces in the West, was organized in Russia. Next came time for a spurious copy of the underground parliament, called the Polish National Council; it operated under sham banners and counterfeit tags of our old political parties. And finally, the Polish Committee of National Liberation appeared—a quasi-government,

313

although Stalin prudently refrained for the time being from calling his creation a "government," so as to leave the door partly open. But once he had occupied most of Poland, or perhaps even the entire country, what sort of compromise could possibly be reached?

Plunged into enforced idleness, I gritted my teeth in helpless rage, less and less certain that I would ever get to Warsaw. The Russians were pressing on toward the capital, and the distance between the front line and our intended landing place had shrunk to less than a hundred miles and was therefore already in the zone near the frontier full of retreating German troops. The landing of a British plane there seemed nothing short of madness. The failure of the coup against Hitler and the advance of the Red Army on Warsaw further complicated the politico-military situation.

The news of the creation in Chelm of the Polish Committee of National Liberation did not reach us until the morning of July 24. On that same day the meteorologists reported the weather fine all over eastern Europe. At noon Poland signaled readiness for Operation WILDHORN. Surely this must be the day, we thought, but at 5 P.M. the operation was called off. Apparently some difficulty other than the weather had arisen, though drops of arms were to take place as scheduled. We were advised that our landing site might have to be changed.

The Polish commander of "Daybreak," Major Jazwinski, drove me to the airfield at Brindisi, the starting point for the Liberators and Halifaxes scheduled to fly over Poland. The sky over the airfield was swarming with planes. On a clear day like this, a hundred or more planes would take off, about two minutes apart, each carrying weapons, ammunition, and men for the partisan units in northern Italy, Yugoslavia, Greece, Albania, and Poland. An RAF officer ticked off each plane's destination as it left: "North Italy, North Italy" (this was repeated most often) "Yugoslavia, Greece." Out of one hundred aircraft leaving the field that day, only two were destined for Poland. The disproportion was glaring.

Major Jazwinski bemoaned the fact that he had only nine aircraft and six Polish crews. In addition, the Polish squadron's Liberators and Halifaxes were frequently assigned to flights not over Poland but other occupied countries. One arms drop was made in Poland for every three drops in Yugoslavia, Greece, or northern Italy. The British failed to make up for losses in men and matériel, nor did they replace the old crew, rotated after three tours of duty, with new personnel. The major added that flights over Poland had begun only last March. I recalled that in January I heard from Eden himself that the arms drops for the Home Army would be tripled in the near future. A demand for more arms from the West was the main topic of all my interviews with people at various levels in the British government. What I saw and heard at Brindisi confirmed my conviction that, despite all denials, the modest amount of military assistance given to the Home Army through air drops was dictated by purely political considerations.

We waited until the last plane took off. Then the British officers asked us to join them for dinner at the nearby officers' club. At the entrance to the club's dining room a stern warning was posted: "After 1800 hours, officers wearing shorts will not be served. Long trousers are obligatory." This was an embarrassing predicament. I was the only one in our group wearing shorts and a uniform shirt with short sleeves. The British officers clustered around me, hoping to smuggle me to a corner table which had a tablecloth reaching to the floor. We thought we had managed it when the maître d'hotel materialized at our table like a stern genie. "Gentlemen," he announced. "I am extremely sorry, but we shan't be able to serve you. That gentlemen over there is in shorts."

I thought I was about to forfeit a good dinner in pleasant company, but Colonel Morgan began negotiating with the maître d'hotel, and it all ended, as usual among the British, with a compromise. Colonel Morgan went off in search of a pair of trousers for me to wear, and the rest of us addressed ourselves to the hors d'oeuvres. I had managed to make my way almost through the whole meal by the time Colonel Morgan reappeared. "The city commander is prepared to loan you his own trousers," he proclaimed triumphantly. "Please follow me."

I broke off in mid-dessert and went along with the colonel to the British command a few blocks away. The commander, as it turned out, would have made Napoleon seem a giant. I barely managed to squeeze into his pants, and there was no way to button them up. Moving gingerly, I returned to the officers' club clad in "long" trousers that reached a bit below my knees. Visually the difference was not all that great, but formally my attire was proper and my hosts seemed greatly pleased.

Among the British officers at my table was the famous Colonel Hudson, a tall and friendly gentleman with a pleasant manner. He led the first British military mission ever sent to an underground army in an enemy-occupied country. He landed on the Yugoslav coast in the autumn of 1942 from a British submarine, and his mission was to operate alongside the General Mihailović. During dinner the colonel showed a great interest in Poland, in the Home Army, and especially in the partisan operations in the forests. I could have no idea that his last assignment in World War II was going to be a parachute jump into Poland at the head of the British mission sent after the Warsaw Uprising, just before the Red Army occupied the entire country. Colonel Hudson and members of his mission were captured by the Russians and carted off to jail, inconvenient witnesses that they were. They were not released until the game was over, after the Yalta Conference.

The following day our weatherman again promised good conditions along the entire route. I heard this without much excitement, steeling myself for another disappointment. The message about the possibility of a last-minute change in landing place did not fill us with optimism either. Talking to our fliers the night before, I had learned that a landing place must fulfill a number of quite specific requirements. A clover field is the best, they told me, especially if it has been under clover for three consecutive years. To find another field that would meet all these requirements would not be easy.

And yet the noon signal that day was clear: they were ready to receive us. This message was confirmed at 5 P.M. One hour later we were in our jeep, still wearing our uniforms, on the way to the airfield. Once there, we disappeared into one of the tents and shortly emerged as four mysterious civilians, our pockets bulging with guns and other paraphernalia.

Next we were subjected to a thorough and painstaking search by British experts. They made us empty our pockets, and examined every item in our suitcase. All this had nothing whatever to do with customs duties or politics. They were anxious to be certain that, once in Poland, we had nothing with us that could in any way identify us as birds of a British feather, alighted from the sky. It was very easy to forget to remove a label from a hat lining or from a suit. Never in my life have I been searched for so long or so thoroughly. Even so, a few days later my fiancée, Greta, much to her amazement, discovered an old copy of the *Daily Telegraph* lining the bottom of my suitcase and a small bottle of hair dye marked "made in Britain."

We took off precisely at 8 P.M. The Polish and British officers from the base waved farewell as our plane took off, and the Italian coast was bathed in the rays of the setting sun. Our aircraft made a wide circle over the town and the port and then headed northeast. Two Polish Liberators accompanied us for a while and then disappeared to their own destinations.

I was on the last lap of my course from Warsaw to Warsaw, a journey that began on a rainy autumn night at Warsaw Central Station. Then I had traveled north, to Stockholm; now I was returning from Brindisi, from the opposite edge of the continent.

By the time we were over Yugoslavia, it was getting dark. We could see probing searchlights and fires blinking from the mountains below: partisan outposts awaiting their drops. I had never imagined there would be so many of them. From the air, these signals seemed like mysterious voices calling out to us and made a profound and peculiar impression on me. The Balkan cauldron was bubbling that night with vitality and fight.

The cold in our cabin was biting, and we reached for our thermos bottles of hot tea. It was now pitch dark, and I could not tell whether we were over Yugoslavia or Hungary when we saw a bright line of tracers wending their way up toward our Dakota like glowing little sausages. We could see them coming at us until their flight stopped in midair in one final sudden flash of flame. Long searchlight beams wandered through the sky. Our Dakota swerved a few times, swayed slightly, but then flew on without taking much notice.

I silently pondered the matter of how relative a concept a feeling of security is. Our aircraft, a DC-3, was unarmed and its top speed was very slow. To lighten the weight because of our additional fuel, not only its guns but also its protective armor plating had been removed. The Dakota had been chosen for such missions solely because it required an exceptionally short runway, but against fighters it was as helpless as a baby. Any encounter in the air was bound to be fatal. To be sure, we had not been told that a week earlier three four-engine aircraft from Brindisi had been shot down over the Hungarian lowlands by German night fighters. (I learned about this some twenty-nine years later, from an account by our first pilot, a New Zealander named George Culliford.) Even so, we were fully aware that a night landing on a rough field in enemy-held territory was probably not much safer than parachuting from a bomb-bay. And yet for some reason I did not feel that indescribable fear that I had experienced before every parachute jump in training in England.

This train of thought was broken by our copilot, the only Pole in our crew. He entered the cabin and told us: "Get ready. We're flying over Poland now, north of the Carpathians. Move forward and sit on those fuel drums over there—that'll help to balance the aircraft during the landing." We glanced respectfully at the four huge drums of petrol. "Suppose they decide to explode," I muttered unenthusiastically. "My new trousers will be ruined."

Our plane swooped lower, and directly below us curled the narrow ribbon of the Dunajec River. A strong beam of light called to us from below. Was this the place? Not yet. We flew on. In the next few minutes we flew over two more outposts keeping watch on the ground. Finally we saw below us a large, irregular rectangle. A long lighted arrow at one side showed the wind direction. In the center of the rectangle a faint light signaled the letter "M" in Morse. Our Dakota blinked our prearranged letter, "K," with the running lights on the wings. This was our landing site. We made a big circle over the area and came in for landing. Two blinking beams of light exploded under the wings of our aircraft, flooding the landing area.

Perched obediently on our fuel drums, we held our breath and waited for contact with the ground. The plane seemed about to touch down when suddenly, at the very last moment, the pilot opened the throttle full and climbed steeply again. The Dakota lurched violently, first to the right, then to the left. For a moment we thought that we were about to crash. All the lights went out, the dark edge of the woods and the treetops flashed by, and we were in the air again, once more circling the landing strip. The people below were obviously agitated—their signal lights blinked faster and faster. Blinded by the beams of light, our pilot had probably overlooked the weak glow of the stable lanterns marking the strip. Realizing at the last moment that he was flying straight into a wall of trees, he had managed, with a great effort, to pull up again. We approached the landing strip a second time, and this time all worked out well. We felt one strong jolt, and then our Dakota was rolling swiftly along the field. The Pol-

318

ish copilot burst into our cabin and threw open the outside door.

From below many hands were stretched out for two long heavy sacks. In a matter of seconds we had tossed nineteen heavy cases of equipment out of the plane. Outside we could hear a hubbub of voices, brief commands, shouts of men calling to each other. Our aircraft was surrounded by a wildly excited crowd of peasants, some barefoot, all armed with guns and machine pistols. As I was about to jump to the ground, calloused peasant hands lifted me out. At that moment, a gust of Polish wind welcomed me by snatching away my London hat. I caught a glimpse of a white goatee on an elderly man in a black suit, and I remembered that I was responsible for the order of loading for the takeoff. I tried to shout, to argue, but my voice was lost in the clamor.

They finally put me down about a hundred yards from the plane. I turned around to look for the others—all here. We were told to run through the field into the woods, where two horse-drawn carts were waiting. I almost lost my boots—like my hat—when I fell into a ditch full of water in the dark and got stuck ankle-deep in the mud. At last we scrambled onto the peasant carts and I could collect my thoughts. We were to wait until the Dakota took off with its new load and passengers. I glanced anxiously at my watch. The six minutes allotted for landing, loading, and takeoff had gone by. The plane's engines were running all the while, and their drone seemed like thunder in the silence of the night—enough to waken the dead, let alone any live Germans within a few miles' radius.

Meanwhile our coachman, blessed with true peasant impassivity, explained the situation to us. "In that village over there," he pointed with his whip, "there are some Krauts. They came yesterday morning, so they'll probably push on at daybreak. There's a dozen or so tanks there and a lot of vehicles,[*] but they're worn out and all the fight's gone out of them. The Russkis whipped them good, and they wouldn't want to take any chances in the woods at night. Too bad our boys on the far side of the woods were told to stand by until an hour past midnight, and then hop it."

A breathless messenger arrived. The wheels of the Dakota were

---

[*]The driver's information turned out to be exaggerated. The village of Wal Ruda was indeed only 500 yards away, but there were only a hundred soldiers in the German unit; they had two small-caliber guns and no tanks.

319

bogged down in the field, which was soggy from rains. The crew and the peasants were trying to get boards under the wheels of the plane. Perhaps that would do it. Minute after minute ticked by. The noise of the engines died down, but the commotion and shouting could be heard far away. If the Germans were really so close why didn't they hear, why didn't they make a move? Our driver shrugged: "At night, they're scared stiff," he explained. "How would they know how many of us are here?" Just in case, I checked the safety catch on my pistol. By any sane reckoning, a clash with the Germans seemed imminent.

Meanwhile the Dakota tried again to take off, with an ear-splitting roar of its engines and two bright beams of light from under its wings casting a bright glow over the horizon. The pilot revved his engines, trying to get out of the bog. We listened tensely. Would he be able to take off, or would the other passengers and crew join us on our cart? Another few minutes and the engines stopped. The planks under the wheels did no good; the Dakota would not move.

Suddenly, angry voices arose from the crowd milling around the aircraft. There were shouts and yells, snatches of some heated arguments. Another quarter of an hour passed and then, suddenly, everybody stepped back. They were about to make another try. We heard the engines spring to life and the plane finally rose into the air.

"Happy landing," sighed Bilski.

"They'll have to fly over the Balkans in daylight because of the delay," I said.

Captain "Wlodek," the man responsible for all technical arrangements for the landing, ran panting to our carts. He went through some tough moments that day, but the important thing was that everything finally worked out all right. He and a Home Army officer from Tarnow, a stocky man in raincoat and hat, were the only ones who were not peasants among the armed crowd that so enthusiastically received their guests from the sky on that Polish meadow. It seemed to me that, apart from those two, Operation WILDHORN had been carried out entirely by the peasants.

Wlodek hopped onto our cart and, as we moved off, talked feverishly, obviously unwinding from the nervous tension of the past hours. He told us that when the plane failed to take off the second time, the British pilot decided that he would have to set it afire. "He told us about it through the Polish copilot, and I said: 'Well, that's too bad, but if we really can't do anything else, let's destroy it.' The peasants heard this and started yelling: 'We won't let you do this!' They fell to digging and scooping out the grass and the soil from under the wheels with their bare hands. We had thought of everything but bringing pickaxes and spades . . . can you imagine that? We had only one small spade among us. All's well that ends well, though."

Only when listening to Wlodek did we fully understand that steely determination it had taken to send that signal of readiness we had been awaiting so anxiously in Italy, and what a deadly risk was involved. Wlodek told us that on the preceding day two German Storch aircraft had landed on the site we were to use, and that on the very day we were to land some German units had arrived at the nearby village.

"We sent our signals of readiness—one after the other—with the Krauts breathing down our necks, expecting that at any moment some more Storchs might land on the site. But at the same time we knew that it had to be now or never: the front is very close."

What a wrench it was to move so quickly from one world to another: a few hours before I had been speeding along a sun-drenched Italian highway in a jeep, between rows of ramrod-stiff palm trees standing at attention on both sides of the road. Now, on a creaking peasant cart, we were creeping slowly along a sandy forest trail. The leaves were hustling, crickets were chirping, frogs on a distant pond croaked their tune, the cart wheels squeaked their sing-song in the sand, the branches of the trees by the track bowed lightly in welcome.

It was already dawn when we glimpsed the whitewashed walls of a farmhouse through the green of an orchard. Our hosts and their neighbors were waiting for us in the courtyard. It was quite a gathering. The farmer's wife opened her eyes wide at the sight of our barefoot escort armed with machine pistols.

"Soldiers," she whispered to herself. "*Our* soldiers . . . our *Polish* soldiers."

Chapter 30

Wednesday, July 26

The large room was crowded, and everyone was in a good mood. Along with our armed escort, Wlodek, and the passengers from Operation WILDHORN, there were many neighbors. Food was plentiful; no lunch at the best restaurant in Soho had been as tasty as these chunks of whole-grain bread thick with fresh butter, cream cheese with chives, hard-boiled eggs, and cold sliced pork—all this washed down with *bimber*.* Our energetic host, "Skory," had taken charge of everything from the moment the plane took off. From talking to him I learned that he was the commander of the local Peasant Battalions, with the rank of lieutenant. He did not allow us to stay very long. The Germans, who were afraid to show themselves at night, might begin a search of the area at any moment. I reckoned that the farmhouse in which we found ourselves was only a few miles away from the landing place.

Hosts, neighbors, and the peasant soldiers' fraternity bade us farewell with great cordiality. Skory directed everything in a military manner. He put two of us in each horse-drawn cart, along with peasant women with baskets full of butter, cheese, or chickens. This was to make it seem that we were off to the market, although our London

*An illicitly distilled home brew made with corn and potatoes, similar to American moonshine.

suits betrayed us as "townies." Skory decided that we were not to go to the nearest railway station because it might be watched; we would go farther on, to Slotwina-Brzesko. He urged us to hurry because the train to Cracow was due at six-thirty. We left to cries of "May God guide you!" "God speed you!" "God be with you all!"

It was a glorious sunny morning. Everything pleased me: the peasant huts, sheaves in the fields, even the honking of geese and the clucking of chickens. I was lost in the enjoyment of the comfortable setting. Barefoot girls, carrying rakes, hurried into the fields. Bilski nudged me with his elbow: "Pretty, huh?"

"Cast your eyes down!" I answered reproachfully. "Think of Audrey!" (Bilski had left a fiancée, an English girl, in London.)

Skory continued the story which Wlodek had begun last night. For two weeks the guard and staff of the air bridge—about one hundred armed men—had been waiting, hidden in barns near the landing place. Although they were allowed to go out only at night, such a crowd was difficult to hide. The whole neighborhood knew that something important was going to happen. Each day of delay increased the possibility of failure. Yet everything had gone all right; no one betrayed them. There, I thought, I had hardly set foot on Polish soil before witnessing the silent conspiracy of a whole nation.

Skory's organizational efficiency passed the test. On the way to the station at Slotwina he had posted scouts. On the way into the town a peasant standing by the roadside half-whispered that the coast was clear and we could proceed.

Skory bought our tickets but did not go onto the platform with us. With fervent handshakes we said goodbye to him and to the women who had served as our camouflage. We split up on the platform but kept an eye on each other. Each of us had to board a different coach. There was no timetable. The train for Cracow was running late and we had to wait a long time, first at Brzesko and then in Cracow for a train to Warsaw.

The compartment was full of people who talked to each other without restraint. I realized that during my eight months' absence the atmosphere had changed radically. People talked freely about the approaching front, the flight of German civilians, the German retreat. There was excitement in the air, and the view out the window confirmed what I heard from my fellow passengers. The train moved slowly, stopped frequently at the signals, always let military transports pass, and waited a long time at the stations. At the level crossings we saw long lines of German lorries loaded with civilians, furniture, and other chattels. People crowded to the windows to see the Krauts' exodus. One could sense not only the proximity of the front but also the expected and approaching crisis.

The train reached Radom toward dusk. A lady who had taken a seat in our compartment announced to us that the Russians had already crossed the Vistula. Until now I had been sitting quietly in a corner listening to this prattle in silence. Now I could stand it no longer, and asked the good-natured lady whether the person who told her that had personally seen those Russians. She swore on all that was sacred that with his own eyes he had seen Cossacks riding horses on this side of the river—she even described the spot! I knew, through and through, how rumors spread, so I received this assurance with disbelief as merely one more symptom of the mood that prevailed in Poland. Besides, who knows—one reconnaissance detachment, in the night, could have actually crossed the river on pontoons, but this would seem to indicate the lack of a continuous front line. Could it be that, so soon, the Germans lacked the forces to organize a line of defense at the Vistula?

I was struck by the fact that in all this talk I had heard not one word about what would happen when the Russians replaced the Germans. There was no anxiety, not a shadow of fear for that future which was literally at our doorstep. Everybody was completely and exclusively filled with the joyful thought that the nightmare of the occupation and the Nazi terror would soon be over. The hatred which the invader had shown day after day for five years had filled people's souls to the brim: they had no room for other thoughts. Nobody seemed to remember what happened three years before in Lwow, or Wilno, or other cities which found themselves under Soviet occupation for the first time.

My fellow passengers freely repeated the latest "novelty" from London, which they had heard in radio bulletins or read in underground papers. Everything they knew about events at the front and in the world at large came from London. No one quoted either Radio Moscow or another Soviet station, Kosciuszko. In spite of everything that had happened in recent months, nothing had changed in *that* respect since my departure. Everybody looked to and listened to the bulletins from London.

324

The train reached the Central Station in Warsaw at 9 P.M., after the curfew. We were furious, as we would have to stay in the station waiting room until dawn, which would probably mean another sleepless night. For my companions who had left Poland at the beginning of the war, the return was much more traumatic than it was for me. They stared around them. From the street we could hear the tanks rolling along Jerozolimskie Avenue.

Thursday, July 27

At 6 A.M. we went out into the city. It was too early to knock on the doors of people we didn't know, so in the first café that was open near the station we had coffee and Varsovian rolls. Soon after, at the address in Wspolna Street to which Bilski and I had been directed, a sleepy man opened the door. The appearance of these strange people did not cause him any anxiety. After we had given the password, he asked us to wait in a small sitting room. Somebody would call for us, but notifying the right party might take a long time. Around noon a girl appeared to take us to the Warsaw suburb of Zoliborz. (We had said goodbye at the station to our two companions of the flight.)

There, in a comfortable flat in Krasinski Street, two charming Warsaw "aunties" (women who sheltered "birds" or parachutists) greeted us pleasantly. They were a mother and her young daughter, about sixteen, with a slight limp. It was a strange situation: here I was, in my own city, with my own apartment only a short streetcar ride away and in it my mother and brother. I was impatient; I wanted to report as quickly as possible to the commander of the Home Army. From the girl who brought us to the flat I learned that Mikolajczyk had left London for Moscow the day before. So Churchill's mediation had worked at last! At the moment, I was not to leave the flat. Bilski and I were to wait patiently until someone called to pick us up, like parcels. There was no other way—keeping in contact in these circumstances was most important.

Our "aunties" were called Zgorzelski. I found the name easy to memorize because it was that of one of my great-grandmothers, whose daguerreotype portrait used to hang over my grandmother's bed. In the small sitting room there was a large portrait of a man in officer's uniform. The two ladies noticed me looking at it, and asked: "Did either of you meet Major Zgorzelski in England?" They were very disappointed when we both said that we had not met him. From

325

further conversation we gathered that both women lived only for the thought of Major Zgorzelski. From time to time they received parcels, from Switzerland or Turkey, but otherwise no sign of life. They had offered a shelter to parachutists in the hope that one of them might recognize the portrait and give them some news.

This was a fairly common story of family separation in wartime, but my meeting with the portrait of the major had an unusual epilogue six months later. After my return to London I was lunching with some officers at the Rubens Hotel when a major who had just come down from Scotland asked permission to join our table.

"Major," I said, "I'm sure we have met before."

He looked at me blankly; he could not remember. All through lunch, I tried to remember where I had seen this face. At last I asked: "Forgive me. Could you tell me your name? I did not catch it."

"Zgorzelski."

"Major!" I exclaimed. "I know your face from your portrait. I was given shelter by your wife and daughter in Warsaw before the Rising, after my return to Poland."

Zgorzelski went white and did not say a word. There was a lengthy silence at the table. All eyes were fixed on him. I was trying to guess whether this man still reciprocated the love and yearning of those two women. The major retained his stony expression and betrayed no feelings, nor did he ask questions. When I was about to leave the dining room, however, somebody touched my arm. Major Zgorzelski spoke to me in a broken whisper: "Thank you . . . thank you . . . you have given me the happiest moment I had had since the beginning of the war. Tell me something about them. My little girl was twelve when I said farewell to them."

From the windows of the flat in Krasinski Street the view was an unusual one. Although it was a side street, it was often filled with German columns marching from the direction of Praga on the other side of the Vistula. Apparently, after crossing the bridge, part of the movement was directed through side streets. The word "marching" did not describe what I saw before me. The soldiers dragged their feet and kept no order. Their uniforms were unbuttoned, their rifles and helmets hung limply, their faces were dirty and sweaty, and they were clearly dead tired and totally apathetic. Mixed in among the troops were lorries, carts, and German civilians. From across the Vistula came whole families, with suitcases, trunks, and sometimes even

326

furniture. It was not a retreat: it was almost a flight. A defeated army was shuffling by the window.

It was by then nearly 4 P.M., and I could not contain myself any longer. I debated whether to telephone home, but caution prevailed: God only knows what I might find and who might answer. I decided to go to Mokotow, to the apartment of Julia and Greta, as Greta had promised to keep in touch with my mother and brother. Bilski remained in the flat in case someone came to pick us up.

At No. 11 Grottger Street I pulled the bell, then knocked. There was no answer. The girls were out, I thought, but just then I heard a movement inside the apartment. Someone was there. Why didn't they call out or open the door? I went around and knocked on the kitchen window. The figure of an unknown man wearing a cap appeared in the window. Taken aback, I walked quickly away. I was filled with terrible anxiety; something awful must have happened.

Somewhere on Pulawska Street I saw a familiar figure, which I recognized as Major Jan Kamienski from the commander-in-chief's staff. I knew he was to have jumped into Poland in March or April. I stopped him and asked him urgently to tell the Chairman, Bor, or Grzegorz that I had returned, and gave him my address in Krasinski Street, but he had more important things on his mind. He worked at headquarters and was on his way back from an important briefing. The Home Army would attack any day now; perhaps even the next day. I explained that I had to pass on a report of great importance that was directly connected with the matter. At this the officer changed his tone and promised to notify the Chairman at once.

I knew what "at once" meant in the underground: a day or two, at least. I decided to telephone home from the nearest pharmacy. I felt an immense relief when I heard my brother's voice. My greeting was followed by a long silence, then an incredulous question: "Is it really you?"

"Yes, it's me. Let's not waste time. Wait for me at the corner of Warecka Street and Napoleon Square."

As I ran along the Warsaw streets I saw one of my former schoolmasters; like myself, he had a job in the Housing Administration. He stopped and looked at me with disbelief, as if he had seen a ghost. I saluted him and quickly walked away. After a minute, I looked round. He was standing looking in my direction with the same look of indescribable stupor. "What the hell," I thought.

327

"People disappear from Warsaw for long periods all the time and then return. Why this amazement?"

Shortly afterward Andrej and I fell into one another's arms. He, my mother, and our dog Robak were all well, as was Greta. "Don't show your face near the house," my brother warned me. "Two months after you left I had to invent something to explain your disappearance, so I told people that you had died a tragic death in unexplained circumstances. Your office had to be informed. For weeks on end Mama and I had to accept condolences from friends and neighbors, including the good janitor, with sad and composed faces." Now I understood the amazement of my old schoolmaster a moment ago!

Andrej said that Warsaw was like a volcano which might erupt at any moment. He was clearly anxious, and asked whether I knew of the latest order of Fischer, the German district governor, that the whole male population from young boys to old men must report the next day to dig ditches. The order had just been announced through loudspeakers. Everybody suspected a trap. They might make a mass deportation to the Reich, especially of the young men. Actually now that the Germans were retreating, people wouldn't allow themselves to be carted off like cattle, I felt. If the Germans used force, it would lead to an outbreak.

In the evening I returned to Zoliborz, and Bilski said that no one had called for us. That night we had hardly fallen asleep when explosions were heard. We rushed to the window. "Flares" were soaring over the city. Our hostesses didn't understand that word, imported from London. They corrected us—in Warsaw they are "Chinese lanterns."

It was a Soviet air raid. The sounds of the explosions came mostly from Praga, on the other side of the Vistula, but then from the western part of the city as well. Only later did the sirens sound. The Germans must have been taken by surprise. The sky became reddish; there must have been many fires.

Friday, July 28

We were awakened by the distant sound of artillery. The front was approaching Warsaw. At nine Marcysia appeared to collect Bilski, who had been sent as an emissary of Section Six to improve cooperation with Zaloga. Marcysia was astonished by my presence.

"We did not receive any notice from London that you would be coming. It's a complete surprise. I have no instructions as to what to do with you."

"Take me to General Bor as soon as possible," I replied.

"And do you know his address?" asked Marcysia ironically. "I don't. You must understand that it is not so simple and may take a few days to arrange."

I briefly explained the purpose of my mission. The thought passed through my mind that Tatar either had deliberately not sent a radiogram about my arrival or else had sent it so late that it would not arrive in time.* He could not stop my flight by air bridge, but he wanted at least to delay my report. Marcysia at once understood that the matter was urgent. She promised that, after taking care of Bilski, she would devote all her efforts to making contact with headquarters. I knew the untiring energy of that young woman and grew calmer. We learned from her that the order for the mobilization of the Home Army had been issued the previous day. People had been collecting at the rallying points ever since dawn. "W" hour was to be named at any moment.

In the afternoon I took a streetcar to the center of the city. On the corner of Jerozolimskie Avenue and Nowy Swiat I saw a German armored column going toward Praga. They were proceeding in exemplary order, fresh, clean, and rested—a complete contrast to the troops I had seen in Zoliborz. I now understood why those other troops were marching along the side streets. The traffic was two-way: some troops going back, others being sent to the front.

The order of which Marcysia spoke must have been heard by the whole city. The mobilization of many thousands was proceeding almost openly, under the eyes of the Germans, in an occupied city. There was no possibility that Gestapo informers had not got wind of it. German military intelligence must also have had its informers. Why were neither the military nor the police taking any preventive action? Apparently only a handful of people had reported to dig trenches that morning. There was only one possible answer: the Germans were too weak. They must have realized their danger, however, because German buildings were surrounded by barbed-wire

---

*The practice was to give notice about the arrival of an emissary at least ten days ahead, but Tatar, as I later learned, sent a radiogram announcing my arrival only on the day of my departure, that is, July 25. It reached Warsaw on the day before the Rising.

entanglements, and one could see the gun barrels protruding from the bunkers. Clearly, those were to be used for defense.

Chapter 31

Saturday, July 29

In the morning a liaison girl sent by Marcysia arrived. I was to report at the given address at 11 o'clock. At the appointed place I met "Teresa," a very serious, slim, tall lady of indeterminate age. General Bor decided to see me at once, and Teresa took me in a droshka to the meeting place in Sliska Street. On our way she told me that the halls and stairs of the apartment houses and the apartments themselves were full of armed and unarmed young people, waiting for the order to start fighting. That day some of them had gone back to their homes, but many had waited in hideouts in town. A general attack on the Germans was imminent.

She turned to me: "You have just come from there [London]. Our last hope lies with you. Perhaps you will tell them, persuade them, not to do this." I didn't answer. In the general atmosphere this appeal seemed a lonely cry: Warsaw, or at least the part of it that would be engaged in direct fighting, was feverishly and enthusiastically preparing for battle with the retreating Germans.

At the apartment at No. 6 Sliska Street, I sat at a round table. On my left sat Bor, next to him Grzegorz, then the Chairman and an officer unknown to me. On my right sat Colonel Janusz Bokszczanin ("Sek"), next to him Major Janina Karas, a woman officer known as "Haka." My entrance interrupted an important discussion. I had memorized a complete plan of what I had to say. I did not know how long they would let me speak, so every minute was precious and I wanted to be sure not to utter a single superfluous word.

During a few introductory remarks, Bor interrupted with a question: "Have you brought any instructions or orders from the commander-in-chief?" I began to summarize the three options suggested by Sosnkowski in Algiers. Bor again interrupted with a comtemptuous gesture. "Listen, we know all this from radiograms. When did you last talk with the general?"

"Two weeks ago, on July 13, in Algiers."

"But you just said that you flew to Italy with Sosnkowski?"

"Yes, but on July 14 the general told me to report direct to the base at Brindisi, while he himself went on to the Second Corps. After that I had no more contacts with him."

Bor exchanged a quick, meaningful look with Grzegorz, and asked me to continue my account. I repeated all that I had memorized, beginning with a reconstruction of the talks in Moscow and Teheran on the basis of Mikolajczyk's conversations with Eden, Churchill, and Roosevelt. I stressed very strongly the point that the occupation zones for the British, Americans, and Russians had been set without regard to the probable location of the front when the Third Reich collapsed, and that the presence of Allied troops on Polish soil was not foreseen. The British and Americans had refused to send even a mission of military observers to Poland.

I quoted only the statements and assessments of others, carefully refraining from offering my own opinions, so that those present would be aware that I was acting only as a reporter. I summarized the various points of view but also omitted everything relating to internal personal intrigues. I spoke quickly, trying to cover all my material. Those present at the table, most of them fed until now on a diet of laconic radiograms and optimistic broadcasts from London, listened to me silently, with great attention and growing gloom.

At about 1 P.M. there was a break for luncheon. The owner of the apartment served thick potato soup and bread. Burning my mouth with the hot soup, I continued to talk. At last somebody interrupted with a question about Mikolajczyk's journey to Moscow. How did it come about, and what did the prime minister expect to achieve by it? Everybody seemed to wake up. This was most relevant to what was happening in Warsaw and around the city. Here at last was some more hopeful topic. I repeated exactly the substance of the last conversations with Lebiediew and Mikolajczyk's views. The prime minister, I said, would try to conclude an agreement with Stalin that would allow military cooperation and operational coordination between the Home Army and the Red Army and the creation on the spot, after Warsaw's liberation, of a government primarily based on the four principal parties, with the participation of the communists as a fifth element. I stressed that the prime minister did not tell me this explicitly, but I believed that it was clear from what he had said and from what I had heard from other people. My own assessment of the outcome of the talks in Moscow I gave as pessimistic.

My report was interrupted more and more frequently by people coming in from town with news about the military situation. Some gave oral reports, others brought bits of paper with monitored reports from Moscow, the German radio stations, and London. The names of places near Warsaw, some only a few miles away, were mentioned. Somebody reported that German sappers had been seen "fiddling around" on the bridges, probably laying charges to blow them up. Every time such talk began, I felt that my report had been a purely academic lecture, and not a very timely one at that. Those present were pondering whether to start now, or to wait. It was clear that the die had been cast, the decision taken, and that events had already begun their course and acquired their own momentum.

Bor was mainly interested in whether or not Warsaw could count on massive drops of arms and the dispatch of our own parachute brigade from Britain. To these questions I replied firmly in the negative, insisting that I had personal knowledge of the matter. The chief of staff had told me about his conversations with the British, which had ended in placing the Polish parachute brigade under British command, where it would be used, in the near future, for operations on the Western Front. It was unthinkable that the British would spare it at this moment. As to drops, I told them about the shortage of crews and operational aircraft at Brindisi, quoting what I had been told before my departure by the commander of the base: at the time of my departure, he had only six Polish air crews and nine aircraft.

"All right," somebody interrupted, "but in England we have our own bomber squadrons which might be used in the battle for Warsaw." I explained that our squadrons were an integral part of the RAF and were dependent on their ground crews and on British supplies. Mikolajczyk told me before my departure that he intended to demand from Churchill himself a transfer of our crews and machines to the Polish air wing at Brindisi, but that the British attached major importance to the bombing of Germany.

At that moment somebody entered to report that a Soviet armored patrol had been seen on the outskirts of Praga. A discussion immediately began, and Bor asked everybody present for their recommendations. The words of "Sek" (Colonel Bokszczanin), who was sitting next to me, impressed themselves vividly on my mind: "Until the Russian artillery open fire on the town on the left bank of the Vistula, we have no right to move." I was struck by the calm assurance with which this was said, but saw signs of conflict among the others.

Having consulted with all those at the table, Bor turned once more to Bokszczanin: "What precisely did you want to say?"

"Soviet artillery fire," said Bokszczanin sharply, "is so far only intermittent and light. It does not seem to be an artillery preparation for a general forced crossing of the Vistula and an attack on the city. The armored reserves which the Germans are directing to the front near Warsaw are fully equipped and prove that they intend to fight at the bridgehead. Until the Soviet army shows clear intention of attacking the city, we should not start operations. The appearance of some Soviet detachments on the outskirts of Praga does not signify anything. They may simply be reconnaissance patrols."

Just before four o'clock somebody else entered the room. I learned later that he was "Monter," Colonel Antoni Chrusciel, the commander of the district of Warsaw. As he came in, General Pelczynski took me aside under the window and said: "You look at all this with the eyes of an outsider, but one well informed about the political situation. Do you see and understand the meaning of what we are doing here?"

"I don't know the details of the military situation," I replied, "but if you in Warsaw consider Operation TEMPEST to be a political and military demonstration, it will not influence the policy of the Allies in the least. As far as public opinion in the West is concerned, TEMPEST will be, literally, a tempest in a teacup. We must not confuse what are really two separate things: the Polish communiqués of the BBC and the reactions of the British and American press and public opinion. Those are two entirely different matters." However, I added, if the outbreak of fighting disclosed the strength of the Home Army and the support that it enjoyed from the community, that would undoubtedly facilitate Mikolajczyk's talks in Moscow and his political maneuvering with the British, especially if our own forces were able to hold Warsaw.

Pelczynski then said: "I have no illusions about what awaits us here after the Russians enter Warsaw and we come into the open, but even if the worst fate should befall me, I would prefer that to giving up without a fight. We must do our duty to the end."

Meanwhile, Bor had decided that he must interrupt my report, although he knew how important it was and that I had not had time to finish. He promised to call me back again later to ask many other questions. In the meantime, he ordered me to report to the Government Delegate as soon as possible and to repeat all I had said to him. Colonel Rzepecki arranged for me to go to his safe house the next morning at eleven, where I would be given a contact to the Government Delegate.

I left the apartment at Sliska Street with a heavy heart, feeling very sorry for these people. Pelczynski's words, "I have no illusions about what awaits us here after the Russians enter Warsaw," still resounded in my ears. Indeed, these men could have no illusions— they were live torpedos: the Soviets regarded them as enemies. Coming into the open could at best mean imprisonment, at worst death, unless Mikolajczyk succeeded in coming to terms with Stalin. After the Soviets established the Polish Committee of National Liberation at Chelm I had given up hope. It was a clear sign that Stalin wanted a puppet government and would reject any compromise. My mission was too late; it could at most deepen the inner conflict of these people at a time when every decision was the wrong one. From that one sentence uttered by Grzegorz it was clear that whatever the political situation, these leaders did not see any alternative to an attempt to take over Warsaw.

I was struck by the difference between my meeting with Bor-Komorowski, Pelczynski, and Rzepecki a year ago and this one. Then they referred to Sosnkowski as subordinates refer to a superior officer to whom they are sending a formal report through an emissary. Now I was talking to a group which had concluded that it must make decisions on the spot, without reference to London. I had found one more confirmation of what I had suspected In England: since General Sikorski's death, the center of gravity had shifted from the Thames to the Vistula.

Sunday, July 30

In the morning I took a streetcar from Zoliborz to go to mass at the Church of St. James. I was to meet Colonel Rzepecki near there after the service. I got to his apartment while all the department heads of BIP were being briefed. Kowalik was also present. They were all busy with preparations for the Rising, and there was no room for discussions, doubts, or vacillation. One person reported on the violent increase in Soviet propaganda. The Union of Patriots and the Kosciuszko stations had been broadcasting endless appeals for an immediate start of open fighting, the takeover of the capital, and support for the Red Army in the crossing of the Vistula. The agitation of the Polish Workers Party was exactly in tune with the radio propaganda from Moscow. The communists were spreading a rumor that the commander of the Home Army and his staff had fled from Warsaw, and that in the city only the leaders of the AL (Armia Ludowa, the People's Army) and the Polish Workers Party remained. Some posters to this effect had apparently appeared on the walls. The PWP agents were preparing to take the initiative from our people and then present themselves as true leaders both at home and abroad. All those present were certain that the communists, on Moscow's orders, were making their own preparations for the Rising.

After a general conference I had a moment's talk with the Chairman. He asked me what assignment I had been given for the moment of the Rising. I said that I had none as yet. Would I like to be attached to headquarters or to his people at BIP? After a moment's reflection I asked whether mobilization plans included transmission to London on news destined for the English radio and press—something like war correspondents' dispatches. It appeared that this had not yet been thought of. I then said that I would like to be with BIP because I could be useful in this area, and asked to be assigned to Kowalik, who was to be in charge of insurgents' propaganda. The Chairman then gave me the address at which I would meet the Government Delegate the next afternoon, July 30. Rzepecki had also arranged for me to meet officials of BIP and the representative of the department of foreign affairs at the office of the Government Delegate. I was to repeat to them in full my report of the previous day.

Kowalik then led me to his place, asking on the way about the international situation. He was animated, and very lively. The hour of "Roj" (the Hive) was about to strike; this department which he led had been making preparations for two years to mobilize a large propaganda apparatus at the time of the Rising.

At Kowalik's I met Greta. The appearance of a workman in the window of her apartment was now explained. He was a bricklayer, and the practical Kowalik had ordered him to build a hiding place for people in a large niche in the wall of the hall. The entrance to it was to be hidden by a wardrobe filled with books. In that niche a few people, supplied with food and water, could hide for a number of days. It was to be a refuge if the Russians started making arrests after entering the city. Kowalik and some of his close collaborators were additionally guilty in Soviet eyes because of Action R, an anti-communist and anti-Soviet propaganda effort which he had been conducting since December 1943.

I looked at my watch when getting off the tram in Theatre Square on my way to meet the Government Delegate and found that I was an hour early, so I went off to a nearby café. A few moments later, I heard shots. I ran out of the café to see what was happening. People were shouting and running in all directions, but Theatre Square, crowded a moment ago, was now completely deserted. Somebody went into the cafe, and I followed him and asked what was going on. "Our people attacked a German patrol. They disarmed the Krauts, killing two of them, but the third one has escaped. Nothing's happening except that one must arm oneself while there is still time."

The city was really like a barrel of dynamite. Strike a match in one place, and everything would blow up. I decided to push off before the police vans appeared and closed off the square, as was the rule. Now I saw with astonishment that the normal traffic in the street had resumed, with no trace of the German police!

The Government Delegate, Stanislaw Jankowski, opened the door for me himself. There was no one else in the apartment. He was a man of middle height, balding, wearing glasses, with a solemn look of deep concentration. The conversation was unlike my report of the day before. I had no need to hurry and I did not omit details. Jankowski interrupted quite frequently with his own observations

337

and questions. He impressed me as a strong personality, a determined individual, very resolute.

As on the day before, my audience was most interested in Mikolajczyk's journey to Moscow. I repeated verbatim a sentence from the prime minister's conversation with Lebiediew: within the framework of a general understanding with Moscow, he would be ready to "select a governing team which would assure friendly cooperation with the Soviet Union." This wording seemed so important to me that I had memorized it. I added that, as far as I knew, Mikolajczyk had in mind a government constituted in part on the spot, inside Poland, based on the four principal parties, and with the participation in it of communists.

Jankowski did not seem astonished or taken aback: "This is nothing new for us. We recently had an emissary from London whom Mikolajczyk recommended to us as a man enjoying the trust of the British. He sounded me out, along with a few political activists, about the possibility of forming here, in Warsaw, such a government as the one Mikolajczyk mentioned to you. I know that he also, on his own account, made contacts with the Polish Workers Party, but I never found out what the results were, as I did not support him in that attempt."

Jankowski did not mention any name, real or assumed, and in the underground one did not ask for names. Only later, from a prewar friend, a former director of the treasury in the office of the Government Delegacy, I learned that the man in question was "Salamander" or "Birch," alias Dr. Jozef Retinger. I recalled my conversation with him in January in London, and later the strict orders at Brindisi to give "Birch" priority over Tomasz Arciszewski (leader of the Socialist Party) when loading passengers on the Dakota. After the war I learned that immediately after that return flight Mikolajczyk and Retinger had a four-hour conversation in Cairo. Retinger had returned to London ill; from the airfield he was driven straight to hospital, where Eden himself visited him. The soundings which Jankowski mentioned must have been of immense value both for Mikolajczyk and for the British government.

The Government Delegate, as if thinking aloud, summed up our conversation. "It is a gloomy picture that you paint; in fact, it leaves almost no hope. But we have no choice. TEMPEST in Warsaw is not an isolated episode. It is a link in a long chain that began in September [1939]. Fighting in the city will take place, whether we like it or not. To use a vivid comparison, I ask you to imagine a man who had been gathering speed for five years in order to leap over a wall; he runs faster and faster, and then, one step before the obstacle, the command is given to stop! By then he is running so fast that he cannot stop: if he does not jump, he will hit the wall. Thus it is with us. In a day or two, Warsaw will be at the front. I don't know; perhaps the Germans will withdraw at once, or perhaps there will be street fighting as there was at Stalingrad. Do you imagine that our young people, who are longing for revenge, who have been training for years for this moment, who have been given arms, will passively stand by or let themselves be transported to the Reich without resisting? If we don't give them a signal for battle, the communists will forestall us. People will really believe then that we wanted to stand by and do nothing.

"Here our concern is not about ourselves and about discrediting the leadership," he went on. "We are facing a gigantic fraud, mounted to convince both other countries and our own people that Poland has, of her own free will, put a dog collar around her neck, and that the will of the people will henceforth be expressed by a ring of Soviet agents. We cannot stand by and watch this kind of game."

On the same day I was present at another meeting. In the evening I had a long conversation with two officials of the BIP, Alexander Gieysztor and Stefan Kieniewicz. Dr. Tadeusz Chromecki, whom I had already met, was present as a representative of the Government Delegate. Kieniewicz was carefully writing down every word said.[*] As in my conversation with Kowalik, I was more restrained than in my talks with Bor and Jankowski. The usual question was put to me: what did I know and what did I think about Mikolajczyk's journey to Moscow?

Monday, July 31
There were visible signs that the German domination of Poland was coming to an end. At the newspaper stand I was told that the "reptile paper" *New Warsaw Courier*, put out in Polish by the German

---

[*]Information from a note from "Relacja Janka Po Bytnosci w Centrali." The minutes of this meeting, taken by someone present, are now in the Polish underground movement archives in London. See Appendix for the complete text.

authorities, had ceased publication. In Three Crosses Square (Plac Trzech Krzyzy) I passed a cluster of people waiting in vain for the usual daily German news bulletin on the loudspeaker. The loud-speakers were silent. The crowd commented on this fact—indeed, people were completely relaxed, as if the Germans had already left Warsaw. Late in the evening I bid farewell to the Zgorzelski ladies in the Zoliborz apartment and moved to Grottger Street.

Tuesday, August 1

In the morning, "Wolf," who was the head of the action department in Action N, rushed in, wringing his hands in despair. What are they doing? he lamented. In this situation the Rising makes no sense. What a tragic paradox that we should help the Bolsheviks to occupy Warsaw. I recalled that two days before, a liaison girl, Teresa, had spoken in similar terms when taking me to my meeting with Bor. The discussions about the Rising had begun before the outbreak of any combat.

Greta was to bring me instructions for my future contacts and talks. The meeting of the liaison girls and the exchange of "mail" took place at different hours each day. Greta had found a place for me to stay somewhere in the suburbs. About 2 P.M. there was a knock at the door, and she rushed in like a hurricane. "Today," she called from the doorstep: "It starts today. 'W' hour is at five o'clock. Assembly at four!"

The point of assembly selected by the Chairman was in the center of Warsaw, in Jasna Street, so there was still time to go to Grottger Street to get the revolver and ammunition given me before my flight from Brindisi. From Grottger Street we rushed with Greta to the assembly point, partly on foot, partly by streetcar. The city had suddenly changed character. For the second time in four days a planned mobilization of the insurgent army was going on. The first time it was called off after one day. Thousands of young people were hurrying to their assembly points, from which the nearest German objectives would be stormed. At first sight one could tell those who would become soldiers in a few hours from the ordinary passerby. An atmosphere of excitement pervaded the air. The approaching outbreak felt like an oncoming storm.

There were many more German patrols and light armored cars in the streets. It was a miracle that the Germans had not yet made a

340

preventive strike. Every little while the sound of shooting from various sides of town came nearer. It would burst forth and suddenly stop. No one paid any attention. At a distance two familiar figures flitted by: Mrs. Zgorzelska and her daughter. I wanted to pause, to warn them. But, after all, half the town knew, and there was no time to lose. In the gateway of the house in Jasna Street armed civilians asked us for the password. For the first time I saw the soldiers of the Home Army openly carrying weapons. In the apartment upstairs we found Kowalik, the Chairman, and a crowd of people with whom, though we did not know it then, we were to live through the next sixty-three days. The apartment on the other side of the hall was occupied by the commander of the Warsaw district, Colonel Monter, and his staff. Greta's sister Jula was also there. She seemed strangely sad and serious. We had our personal armed guard in the persons of two twenty-year-old boys, in full insurgents' outfits, carrying rifles, with hand grenades on their belts. The company was not complete. The front doors were closed and guarded. Nobody was to be let out. Suddenly we heard shooting. I looked at my watch: it was 4:30—half an hour early. The windows of the apartment overlooked the court-yard, as though we were in a well, so we didn't know what was happening in the street. After a while the shooting stopped.

The time for conspiracy and secrets was over. Someone was loudly saying that I was the parachutist who had just arrived from London. Among the gathering, particularly in the midst of our armed escort, this news created a sensation. They looked at me as on a supernatural phenomenon. I was swamped with questions: When will the war end? When will the British or Americans come? Will there be a landing in Warsaw? I lied like a trooper. In this moment and mood, for all the money in the world I could not have brought myself to speak the truth.

We learned that the apartment on the first floor, with windows onto the street, was occupied by the family of a Volksdeutscher, an official in a Warsaw district office. With our armed escort we entered it. In the apartment suitcases and trunks lay about—everything prepared for an escape. They had not made it. Yesterday's representative of the Herrenvolk was now on his knees, pleading for his life: in his eyes animal fear and tears. In the corner of the room I noticed a radio receiver and confiscated it at once. Now we would have our own monitoring post for London and the other stations.

At that moment we heard the deafening, drawn-out sound of an exploding grenade, followed by a second, a third, and a fourth. Simultaneously machine guns and rifles began to fire. From the windows of the Volksdeutscher's apartment we could see pedestrians running into doorways and hear the banging of the shutters in the shops. Insurgents were pouring out of the courtyards, running along the walls toward some nearby target. Exactly five! Hour W! It began! We put on white-and-red armbands with the letters "WP," for "Wojsko Polskie," the Polish forces. Some had eagles on them.

Chapter 32

*I*n the next few minutes a short battle for the nearby Hotel Victoria was fought. It had been earmarked as headquarters for Colonel Monter and his staff. From there he would command the Rising all over the city. In the hotel ("Nur für Deutsche") five German policemen were trying to shoot it out, but after a few minutes their resistance was overcome.

It appeared, however, that it was impossible to cross the street to the Victoria. The fighting broke out while a German armored column was crossing Warsaw. The tanks turned into narrow side streets, and there the armored colossi were trapped. From the windows of the buildings, bottles filled with petrol and grenades were thrown down on them. They caught fire, and the crews trying to escape were mostly shot down within a few yards of their vehicles. But somewhere nearby an armored car had found a protected position and kept the whole of Jasna Street under fire.

The inhabitants of our house, soldiers mixed with civilians, knocked a hole in a cellar wall, and within a few minutes we had an underground passage to the courtyard of the next house. From there, through an opening in the wall, we got into the Hotel Victoria. The same thing was going on in the other houses. What a paradox! Almost at the very moment when the AK came out into the streets after five years in hiding, a labyrinth of underground passages emerged spontaneously and the pedestrian street traffic went underground.

We took up new quarters in the spacious hotel. I moved into a room on an upper floor with the idea of securing the best radio reception. I had carried the enormous radio set under my arm and set it up at once. The windows of the room opened onto the courtyard and a sizeable garden. I heard the sounds of heavy firing from the direction of Napoleon Square. At that moment somebody tugged at my sleeve and pointed to something high against the sky: on the top of the Prudential Building (the only skyscraper in Warsaw) a huge white-and-red flag waved proudly and gently. I experienced a moment of violent emotion. The flag must have been visible throughout the city and on the other side of the Vistula in Praga as well. An hour later we learned that the flag had been raised by a seriously ill tuberculosis patient, Ensign Garbaty from Section Kilinski, who had left the hospital only a few days earlier following the removal of a lung. When others were breaking into abandoned German offices, he put the flag under his jacket, took a long pole in his hand climbed to the sixteenth floor, got up on the roof under heavy fire from a German garrison in the Main Post Office, and put up the flag. He could not get back down on his own, and others carried him down.

I tuned the radio to London. News of the successful offensive in Normandy was being broadcast. A week before I would have been pleased, but now the action on other fronts seemed strangely remote. It was too early to hear about the outbreak of the Rising, but what was of interest to me was news from the front near Warsaw and any mention of Mikolajczyk's visit to Moscow. Only two days ago I had explained, with total conviction, that nothing good could come from that meeting in the Kremlin. Today I already had the mentality of a person looking for help and seeking hope. I heard the laconic statement that Mikolajczyk was received by Molotov in Moscow on July 31, the day before.

I began to search for one of the Soviet stations broadcasting in Polish. At last I got the Kosciuszko radio station, which repeated over and over again that Praga was being shaken by the roar of Soviet guns. I could hear them with my own ears. Above the noise of the firing in the streets, the distant heavy boom of artillery announced the approach of the front. Radio Kosciuszko said that any day now Polish forces would begin to fill the streets of Praga. It called Poles to action: "Attacks on the Germans are the duty of every Pole. Your sufferings will be over in a few days. Listen carefully and obediently to our authorities, the Polish National Council, and the Committee for National Liberation." Not a word about Mikolajczyk's presence in Moscow and about the Rising, although the Russians, if they were near Praga, must have been able to see the glare over Warsaw.

I got someone who knew German well and asked him to listen to what the Germans were saying. The daily communiqué of the German headquarters said that near Warsaw the enemy was maintaining heavy pressure. The use of a well-known formula, "the German forces are successfully performing movements aimed at breaking contact with the attacking enemy," indicated that they were in full retreat. Radio Paris, still in German hands, broadcast that Marshal Rokossowski was trying to take Warsaw by an encircling maneuver from the south and the north. There was heavy fighting in Soviet bridgeheads south of Warsaw. The battle for Praga had begun.

I made notes quickly and ran to see the Chairman. It looked as if it would not last long. Rzepecki took my notes to Monter. The radio confiscated from the Volksdeutscher was for the moment the only monitoring post at headquarters. It was easier to learn about events on the different fronts than about what was happening a few hundred yards from us. We knew, however, that attempts to storm the Main Post Office had not succeeded, that our boys had occupied a German building in Marszalkowska, and that the Germans were holding out in the telephone building in Zielna Street. There was no short-wave transmitter in the hotel, and contact by courier with other districts of Warsaw was impossible, but, strangely enough, the telephones were still working. At dusk, the sky over the city glowed red: there was a large fire somewhere near the Central Railroad Station.

Kowalik sent Jula and three liaison girls to the building of the Polish Savings Bank about seventy yards away from us. That building was earmarked as the headquarters of the Department of Propaganda. Minutes passed, and Jula and the three other women did not come back. We were beginning to worry when they suddenly reappeared, but not alone. We could not believe our eyes: Jula was leading four disarmed Germans. "Prisoners!" she called. "We have captured them!"

"How?" somebody asked with disbelief, "with your bare hands?"

Indeed they had. Four unarmed women and Jan Teska, a mousy old man who was a translator for Action N, had taken pri-

345

soner four heavily armed Germans. It appeared that the building of the Polish Savings Bank was not empty at all. The crew of a destroyed tank was hiding in the stairwell near the entrance. Everyone going inside fell into the trap one by one until somebody escaped back into the street and warned others. Meanwhile, Jula began to explain to the soldiers in her broken German that they were surrounded and had no chance. We were not bandits: if they gave up their arms, they would not be hurt. In a little while, those who had discovered the soldiers were joined by Teska, who continued the persuasion in his fluent German. He succeeded: the Germans handed the girls their arms and their grenades obediently, and with raised hands let themselves be led from the building.

August 2

I woke up after a few hours' sleep. The popping sound of artillery from beyond the Vistula was now much stronger, closer, and more constant. This must be, I thought, the fire storm about which Bokszczanin spoke, which was to precede the establishment of bridgeheads and the attack on the city. We had not much time left.

It was starting to rain. The German artillery was trying to shoot down the flag on the Prudential Building but did not succeed. The enormous white-and-red flag still fluttered victoriously over the city.

All morning I had been by the radio listening for London to broadcast the news about the outbreak of the Rising. I listened to the Polish, English, and French communiqués. Nothing, not a word. I got more anxious by the hour. The radio message from headquarters must have been sent yesterday, just after 5 P.M. Why the delay?

News of what was happening nearby continued to reach headquarters in Hotel Victoria. The day before, our people had taken over the Land Credit Society building, in which the German Arbeitsamt had been located. The Telephone Exchange and the Main Post Office were still in German hands in spite of several attempts to storm them. Someone said that there were quite a few German soldiers lying on the roof of the Main Post Office, shot by our people from the windows of the occupied Prudential Building. It was impossible to tell who controlled the city. Some buildings were occupied by us, others by the Germans. Many streets were under fire from both sides and were in "no man's land." There was no real front line.

In our part of the city the situation radically changed in the afternoon. The Main Post Office was taken at last. A few tanks and armored cars that had been trying to relieve the besieged Germans were destroyed; the rest withdrew. Nearby streets were no longer under fire, and all of a sudden an excited crowd filled them. I wanted to rush out with the others, but I knew that London would broadcast in Polish at 1715 hours, so I waited impatiently by the loudspeaker. I experienced a moment of wild joy when after the announcement "This is Polish Radio in London," I heard, "Yesterday at five o'clock in the afternoon the Home Army began open fighting in Warsaw." No details, only this one sentence, but the announcer read it in a voice that was full of emotion. I now waited for the BBC broadcast in Polish. The same message was repeated, with similar emotion.

Now I rushed out into the street. I wanted to go to Nowy Swiat to see my mother. On my way, I stopped to see my uncle and aunt in Swietokrzyska Street. They were out on their balcony. We were witnessing a scene that I shall not forget as long as I live. The people who lived in the neighborhood, without any orders from above, were building a tank barricade across the street. Some were digging a ditch, others were either throwing out the window or carrying anything that they could put their hands on. They had few spades or pickaxes. People broke up the flagstones with whatever they had or pulled up lumps of stone with their bare hands, but they did it with such incredible speed and enthusiasm that a deep trench was dug within minutes. A week before I had seen the same enthusiasm: the peasants with the same feverish eagerness scratching the earth and turf out from under the wheels of the British aircraft with their bare hands.

In that crowd on the street below all class differences had disappeared: there were workmen and shopkeepers and university professors; a soldier with a white-and-red armband stood next to a civilian; there were old people working next to boys and girls. They dragged out heavy flagstones, they lugged boxes and pieces of furniture. It seemed to me that in this ecstatic moment they were ready to throw their own bodies on the amorphous pile of the barricade as it grew minute by minute.

In the gateway of the building opposite a janitor appeared with a white-and-red flag on a pole. The flag was terribly crumpled. "I have kept it in my cellar for five years!" he yelled. Applause greeted him. He triumphantly raised the flag over the gateway. In some windows other, smaller flags began to appear. Moments before this, white-and-red flags hurriedly tacked together from sheets and bits of cloth had blossomed in some windows.

Suddenly a captured armored car appeared with the painted emblem "WP," "Polish Forces," covered with our soldiers. There was an outburst of enormous enthusiasm. People in the street stopped digging, put down their picks and shovels, and, as if by unseen command, began to sing the "Varsovienne." The whole street, from Napoleon Square to Marszalkowska, was now singing, those on the streets and sidewalks, on balconies and at the open windows. My old uncle raised a deep bass voice in the hymn of the 1831 Polish rising against the tsar:

> This is the day of blood and glory
> May it be the day of victory.

I was filled with a sense of exultation that I had never experienced before and am not likely to experience again. I would have given my life to witness this one moment. We felt free again in this small Warsaw neighborhood reconquered from the enemy with our own forces.

But one could not indulge in emotion for too long, and I resumed my journey to my mother's home. In the gatehouse I was greeted by the astonished janitor, who had been convinced that I had, as he put it, "got my ticket from the Krauts a year ago." The neighbors also greeted me as a man returned from the dead. In a moment I was in my mother's arms, in my own home, barked at by Robak, who was jealous and wanted to welcome me too. In Nowy Swiat, like Swietokrzyska Street, spontaneously built barricades were rising at the street corners.

On my return to the Hotel Victoria, I saw Germans who had been captured in the Main Post Office, the Arbeitsamt, and other pockets of resistance lined up in two rows against the wall. They stood with their hands on their heads, in their eyes the terrified glare of people expecting death. They were in the hands of the "bandits," who would undoubtedly torture them before putting a bullet in their heads. But to their surprise a tall, middle-aged man in high boots and breeches appeared before them and in fluent German told them that they were not in the hands of bandits but soldiers of the Polish forces and would be treated as prisoners of war in accordance with the rules of the Geneva Convention. The Germans now looked incredulous, then relieved, then inexpressibly happy.

August 3

By sheer chance a Gestapo officer had been discovered with a girl in a room on the top floor of the hotel. He had gone there to make love to her on Tuesday and had been trapped by the outbreak of fighting. He was lying low, hoping to slip out unobserved at the appropriate moment. He had a revolver but did not use it. As it transpired, he was a German from Silesia who spoke Polish and had worked as a translator at Gestapo headquarters helping to interrogate prisoners. It was known that people of his kind took an active part in beating and torturing those arrested. The day he was found, a trial was held in the hotel according to the rule of law, with counsel for the prosecution, counsel for the defense, and three judges present. After a short trial the judges retired. The accused was kept waiting in the hotel salon in underpants and undershirt, crouched on all fours. Towering over him were four armed soldiers who shouted insults at him, though no one molested him physically.

In a corner of the room stood the twenty-year-old girl, white as a sheet.

"What'll happen to her?" somebody asked one of the guards.

"What should happen? She is an ordinary whore who went with him for twenty zlotys. For that one cannot shoot her."

Some time later the same tall man who had spoken to the German prisoners the previous day entered the room. The Gestapo officer came to attention smartly on seeing an officer of the Home Army. He heard the verdict condemning him, as a Polish citizen, to death for treason and other crimes. The relevant paragraphs of the Polish penal code were read him and he was asked whether he wanted a priest. He did not answer, but instead turned to the girl and gave her some personal message in Polish. From those few words one could deduce that the two were bound by something more than a casual street acquaintance. His hands were tied, his SS cap put on his head, and he was taken down the steps to the little garden. A number of people crowded at the windows, curious to see an execution. In another minute, three shots resounded.

Hotel Victoria witnessed another more important sensation the same day. A slim, black-haired man of medium height in high boots was brought in by soldiers. He introduced himself as Captain Constantine Kalugin, an intelligence officer of the Red Army who had been dropped with a radio transmitter and wireless operator in the German rear a fortnight before. He was led along the corridor to Monter.

I continued to listen to the radio and passed on the news to my superiors. I found a young girl who, in return for an insurgent's armband, helped me to monitor German and Russian broadcasts. That day Moscow reported that at one more point, near Sandomierz, tanks had crossed the Vistula; that is to say, there had been an encircling maneuver from the south. The Germans admitted that the Russians had increased their attacks but at the same time claimed that their tanks had regained Radzymin. London repeated over and over that a rising had begun in Warsaw. They obviously had no more recent news. An information service was needed to broadcast to the Western press and radio. I knew that Kowalik had been getting ready an insurgents' broadcasting station, but somehow nothing had resulted from this.

Meanwhile the situation in Warsaw was becoming clearer. The city was like a chessboard, but the areas occupied by the insurgents and by the Germans were being delineated. The spontaneously erected barricades prevented the German tanks and armored cars from penetrating into the city and operating there. Inside the area held by the Home Army there were pockets of resistance from which the Germans shelled the nearby streets and the barricades. Hotel Victoria was by now acting not only as headquarters of the commander but also as a hospital.

August 4

I again turned on the radio and heard Kosciuszko repeat its broadcast of the previous day: the People's Army had emerged in the streets of Warsaw, the Germans had been caught between two fires, and there were clashes between the People's Army and SS units. The Germans had tried to set fire to some buildings at Krakowskie Przedmiescie, but their attempts had been frustrated by units of the People's Army, said the radio, supported by the Warsaw population and some units of the Home Army.

I reported this news first to Kowalik, then to the Chairman, and suggested that I should edit the news each day to produce something like a war communiqué destined for the Allied press and radio. The military radio messages were not enough. It was clear that Radio London did not know what was happening in Warsaw. If the Russians occupied the city in the next few days, they could maintain that there was no uprising of any kind and that only the People's Army had been fighting.

Rzepecki agreed at once and suggested that I should try to get to Wola (a western suburb), to the main headquarters of the commander of the Home Army, obtain the approval of Bor or Pelczynski, and on the spot draft a dispatch which would be sent to London immediately, I accepted the task eagerly and asked Rzepecki for his assessment of the situation, which was indispensable for drafting my radiogram. According to Rzepecki, Monter was pleased. We had had success, not complete, but partial. The Rising had achieved its goal: two-thirds of the city was in our hands. The Polish administration had begun functioning in the liberated areas and the main German communication lines had been cut. The rest depended on external events. The Russians must hurry if they wanted to exploit the military possibilities created by the Home Army. The visit of Kalugin was a propitious sign.

I started to make my way from the Hotel Victoria to the other end of the city. I ran across Marszalkowska, one of the city's main arteries. It was empty and dead, divided by barricades of overturned streetcars, automobiles, and uprooted lampposts. The impression was of total chaos. There were no people and no traffic. I would have to go round in a circle in order to avoid being shot at from the telephone exchange PASTA, from which the Germans continued to fire at anything within range that moved.

So I went through cellars, courtyards and gaps in the walls of houses. Every few yards there was a sentry checking papers and indicating the way ahead. After a while I lost my sense of direction, and when at last I emerged in a street, I could not tell where it was. In the course of the last three days the streets had completely changed their appearance.

As I approached Wola, I passed some burning houses. In regular waves, every forty-five minutes, the Stukas flew over, nine planes in formations of three. The airfield must have been nearby. They were flying very low and dropping incendiary bombs right on target. The streets were crowded with people flying from their burning houses with bundles on their backs and carrying suitcases. Some luckier ones had hand carts and baby carriages filled with possessions which they pushed along. The entire wave was flowing toward the center of the city. "The Germans want to burn us out without a fight," I said to myself, and at the same moment I realized that the artillery fire from beyond the Vistula had stopped and the Soviet fighters had disappeared from the skies.

Not far from Kammler's factory, an enormous German tank with Polish recognition signs painted on it in white was in the middle of the road. In the Polish crew I recognized Wacek, a friend from Poznan Univeristy. He was wearing a German flak jacket and a German field cap with a white and red band. He had become the commander of the First Insurgents' Armored Squadron, the detachment that had captured a German Panther tank. There was no time to talk; the treads of the tank had been damaged, and my friend and his men were completely engrossed in repairing them.

At Kammler's factory I reported to Grzegorz, as Bor was busy. From the window of the room where he sat there was a grim view of the ruined buildings of the ghetto reaching as far as the Powazki Cemetery. The general at once agreed to the proposal for daily communiqués for the Western press and radio, and himself drafted a radiogram announcing "Radiograms clearly marked with the word 'Zych' and the serial number are for use in propaganda." It was signed "Lawina."

Before I returned to our headquarters the general took me to "Basil" (Kazimierz Puzak), a leader of the Polish Socialist Party and the chairman of the Council of National Unity. All the representatives of underground Poland has gathered in Kammler's factory to disclose their identities to the entering Russians. They had all very nearly fallen into the hands of the enemy when, as luck would have it, the factory was attacked by the Germans half an hour before "W" hour. A legend of battles with tsarism surrounded the name of Kazimierz Puzak. A former convict who had served a sentence at hard labor in Schlisselburg, he was slightly stooped, with gray hair, and an oval and ruddy face. He appeared to be about sixty years old.

For the fourth time I made my report, repeating almost word for word what I had said at the staff meeting of the Home Army and later, when meeting the Government Delegate. When I began to speak about the ideas and views of Mikolajczyk, Puzak sadly shook his head. "Mikolajczyk," he said, "comes from western Poland and has never had anything to do with the Russians. He does not know them as I do. The prime minister is deluding himself if he thinks that he can defend the country from Sovietization with communists in the government and the Red Army and the NKVD at his back. He won't have anything more to say. Today Moscow wants him to get rid of Sosnkowski and Raczkiewicz; tomorrow they will demand his head, or get rid of him themselves."

Chapter 33

When I returned from Wola to the Hotel Victoria toward evening of August 4, I found it partly bombed out. Luckily we had been moved to the Polish Savings Bank building before the raid. It seemed that the bombing was not accidental. The Germans must have learned that the headquarters was there. The Polish girl caught in bed with the Gestapo man was suspected. Apparently we were wrong in assuming that he was a casual client. She had not been guarded properly, and, the day after his execution, she escaped during some sort of disturbance. The building was hit a few hours after she disappeared.

The Polish Savings Bank building was an enormous block of offices. Fortunately the director's offices were carpeted, so we slept in them in rows, like sardines arranged in a tin. In the morning I again set off for Wola with a dispatch to London. The systematic burning of the city had made horrifying progress in twenty-four hours. The nearer you got to the headquarters of the commander of the Home Army, the more difficult it was even to recognize the streets. The walk there and back took me twice as long as it had the day before. There was also a different atmosphere at headquarters. The Kammler factory was threatened with a direct German assault, and the staff was discussing the transfer of headquarters to another section of the city.

The next day I tried to get to Wola with my dispatch for the third time, but soldiers stopped me halfway. There was no point in continuing: Wola was occupied by the Germans, and Bor and his staff were elsewhere—where, no one could, or perhaps no one would, say. I handed the undelivered radio message to Rzepecki, who consoled me by saying that he would find another method of getting my messages to London. That same evening, listening to the radio, I recognized with pleasure and some satisfaction the main points of the first radiogram Grzegorz and I had drafted.

The last of my messages was handed in on August 7. That day the Chairman and Kowalik summoned me to a conference. In the room was a rather short, dark-haired man wearing a French beret. "You know the English language and the British people," said Rzepecki. "You know how to talk to them. Instead of composing dispatches for the press, from now on you will be an editor of English programs for our own radio." He introduced the stranger to me as "Pawlicz," the chief of Blyskawica (Lightning), our broadcasting station.

I was delighted not only by the new job but also by the idea that an insurgents' radio would be established. Since the Rising had begun, it was important to do everything to see that it did not remain a tempest in a teapot, unnoticed by the rest of the world. The story of Lightning is a good illustration of how things never work out as we expect. For the last two years Kowalik, with his usual energy and eye for detail, had been preparing for large-scale propaganda during the Rising. The plans included a film unit, photojournalists, a public address system, a newspaper, posters, songs, a theater, and a radio station which would broadcast on the powerful prewar antennas at Raszyn and in Fort Mokotow. The communication department was to provide short-wave transmitters and all other installations. Entire archives of radio scripts, poems, and phonograph records, as well as a team of reporters, public speakers, journalists, writers, and poets, had been gathered. Even the words and music to songs about the Uprising had been composed and recorded in some gymnasium. Everything was ready and planned, but when the Rising started neither Raszyn nor Fort Mokotow was taken. What was worse, we were not able to take the Polytechnic building, where the broadcasting equipment was housed.

Luckily, Kowalik had in reserve another short-wave station at Czestochowa, and two weeks before the Rising, Leszek achieved a considerable feat: he had the whole radio apparatus, taken to bits and hidden in suitcases, smuggled into Warsaw on the train. The transport of these suitcases from a cache near the Central Railway Station must have been even more difficult than bringing them from Czestochowa to Warsaw. They were taken from the station and hidden in an area of intense fighting. During the night, in the middle of the bombing, the men assigned to protect the propaganda team fearlessly dragged the radio equipment over the barricades and through the fiery streets.

Unfortunately, the apparatus had been damaged by humidity and would not work. A team of technicians worked day and night to dry everything out and get it going. All this took a week. On August 7, they announced that everything was in working order, and on the morning of August 8 I started to write my first script. I would not write it alone, as my English was not good enough, so a Pole born in London, Adam Truszkowski ("Adam"), was assigned to help me. He spoke English like a native (in fact, he spoke Polish with an English accent!). Our collaboration worked like this: on one side of the desk I would sit scribbling in Polish, then shove the completed pages to Adam on the other side. A cigarette dangling from his lips, he would sit at a typewriter tapping out my text in English.

A little after ten that morning, our station signal was heard on the air for the first time: the opening notes of the "Varsovienne," and then, in Polish, the announcement: "Hello. This is Blyskawica, the radio station of the Home Army in Warsaw, broadcasting on short-wavelength 32.8 and 52.1 meters, medium-wavelength 224 or 251 meters." The first English-language broadcast followed in the afternoon at 2:30. Like the Polish ones, it consisted of news and my opening commentary. This first text I read myself, after a few rehearsals so that Adam could correct my pronunciation. For the good of the enterprise, Adam read all the subsequent commentaries, combining the functions of translator and announcer. A radiogram announcing our first broadcast was sent to London.

By comparison with most radio stations, Lightning was a buzzing bee. Its power was only a hundred watts, but we hoped that the BBC's most powerful advance monitoring receivers would pick up our voices. We listened to London that night in vain, and on the following days the story was the same: there was no echo. We left our microphones with a feeling of deep disappointment. The military radiograms from London confirmed our belief that Lightning could not be heard.

In Warsaw, of course, our English-language broadcasts could not even attract a small number of listeners in the city and its suburbs who had access to an illegal radio set and were following Lightning's programs in Polish. Nonetheless, day after day Adam and I followed the same meaningless routine: writing, translating, and broadcasting our programs in full knowledge that we were speaking only to the walls before us because nobody who understood us could hear us.

But while Lightning was broadcasting into the void, a new channel unexpectedly opened to let out the news from insurgent Warsaw to the British radio and press. On about August 11, a young Britisher came to see me. In a fluent, although incorrect and heavily accented Polish, he introduced himself as Flying Officer John Ward of the RAF. He wore a Home Army armband and a Polish eagle on his cap. He had been shot down over Germany some two years before, interned in a German prisoner-of-war camp near Poznan, and escaped. He was one of several British prisoners-of-war hiding in the city and one of those who had joined the Polish underground.

During the first week of the Rising, in downtown Warsaw, Ward met a courageous couple, the Korbonskis, who had operated their own short-wave transmitter for many years and now were transmitting to London in Morse from their flat. Korbonski had an idea: Ward should give him dispatches in English which he would transmit to London in Morse code. Thus, on August 7, the first dispatch from a British war correspondent in Warsaw was sent to London. Ward had come to us to secure a better flow of information then he had access to. As a flier, he was most interested in news of air drops of arms and ammunition. He was brave, bustling, very sure of himself, and slightly arrogant. He quarreled with Monter, to whom I took him at once, but what was more important was the fact that he was very much caught up in his mission and in the fate of the Rising.

I advised him not to send his dispatches into the void but to address them to important British personalities by name. Ward did not know any names, so I suggested Sir Archibald Sinclair, Colonel Perkins, and the chief of the prisoners-of-war department in the War Office. Knowing how suspicious and distrustful of Polish sources the British were, I imagined that they would doubt whether the messages were really from an Englishman, so I advised Ward to give his full name, rank, and last posting so that London could identify him. As he still doubted that he could reach such important personalities in this way, I drafted a radiogram of introduction to Colonel Perkins and sent it through military channels.

One did not need to tell Ward anything twice, and on the spot we agreed to help one another and to exchange information. The next day I learned that during the night of August 13-14 an important British drop of arms was expected. Orders were given to prepare signal lights in squares and on rooftops, and personnel were assigned to receive the canisters. Wasting no time, I crossed Jerozolimskie Avenue (with no difficulty this time) to see the Korbonskis. They were a well-matched couple, with a lot of courage and a great deal of luck, which together had enabled them to emerge safe from incredible scrapes. They took me to Ward, and I returned with him to the part of the city where the drops were expected. It was important that he should observe them from a good spot and at once pass on his observations to London.

We were lying on the roof of a six-story building in Moniuszko Street which housed the most fashionable night club in the city before the war, the Adria, waiting for the drops. The night sky was lit by the glare of fires all over the city. Suddenly anti-aircraft artillery started firing and searchlights cut the sky. In a nearby square fires had been lit in the outline of triangles. The noise of several aircraft was heard. "Halifaxes!" exclaimed Ward. "I recognize the sound of their engines."

They flew low over the city. Against the background of the dark purple sky the bombers looked like enormous black birds. It was an amazing sight, like some kind of eerie air attack by many planes flying just above the ground, lit up by the searchlights tracking them. One of the enormous planes, with Polish insignia on the fuselage and wings, flew over our heads with a deafening roar. Dark oblong bundles spilled out of it on the roofs, streets, and nearby Napoleon Square. For a second it appeared that the plane would hit the Prudential building. I watched it go, praying for the safety of the people with whom I had been talking only a few weeks ago on the airstrip at Brindisi. The plane disappeared in the darkness, and then suddenly . . . I could not help crying out in anguish at the explosion, far away, beyond the city. In the flash when it was hit, for a split second we could see parts of the wings and the fuselage scattering in all directions. This same tragic spectacle was repeated two or perhaps three times.

Meanwhile, Ward made curt expert comments. He counted fifteen searchlights and a number of anti-aircraft batteries. According to him, there had been at least twenty aircraft. The Germans, he concluded, had been well prepared for the reception, but the pilots had chosen well in flying low: the anti-aircraft batteries were aimed too high. The losses over the city, given the strength of the anti-aircraft defenses, said Ward, were inconsiderable. The real question was how many German fighters they would encounter on their way back. "No support or cover from the Soviet airforce," he suddenly exclaimed angrily. "They certainly must have airfields within a quarter of an hour's flying time from the city!" "Include that in your dispatch," I suggested. "No need to," he replied, "each crew will be debriefed on its return and they will report it."

The next day the mood in Warsaw improved suddenly. Our photographers had taken pictures of our soldiers opening the canisters dropped. Some had fallen into German hands, but most were recovered by our people from roofs, courtyards, or squares. The boost to morale in the city was powerful.

Personally, I did not share this mood. I listened each evening to London and knew that Mikolajczyk had not succeeded in reaching any agreement in Moscow. After his return to London, Soviet propaganda suddenly shifted 180 degrees. Until now, even after the start of the Rising, they had been accusing the Home Army of inactivity, even of collaboration with the Germans. Now the Rising was being called a crime whose instigators should be brought to justice.

The war communiqués of both sides were analyzed by Monter's staff, and it was thought that perhaps the Russians had suffered a local reverse near Praga which would not hold them up for long. The fact that they had maintained a bridgehead on the left bank of the Vistula, south of Warsaw, was considered a good sign. From there an encircling attack should be launched any day. The staff was not impressed by propaganda. It believed that military considerations would prevail: Warsaw and Poland lay on the route to Germany and Berlin.

In the corridors of the PKO building and among Monter's staff, anxious voices were heard. It was difficult to understand why British bombers must make such a long flight over enemy territory at the cost of considerable losses when Soviet fighters could take off from the outskirts of Warsaw. Further, why didn't the Russians drive off the nine Stukas that were systematically and freely strafing the city each day? The Russians could also easily have shelled the German batteries that were reducing the city to ruins.

On August 15 a happy event occurred in our group which for a moment chased all these worrying thoughts away. In the evening London for the first time confirmed radio reception of Lightning and repeated the gist of the broadcast given that morning. Incredible excitement! After a fortnight's struggle in the face of great difficulties the technicians had their moment of glory, and the journalists, writers, and poets knew that they were not talking to themselves. From then on, all those involved in programs broadcast in the morning sat next to their sets at night to listen to their own words returning from far away.

Even before that glorious day, the whole Propaganda Section, numbering about three hundred people in all, had moved from the PKO to the Adria building. Lightning, however, continued to broadcast from the studio in the PKO building.

After the war, during my three years' work in the Polish Section of the BBC, I met the men who for one week had stuck to their listening posts for days at a time during the Rising, trying to pick up a signal from Lightning. The moment when they heard its signal for the first time was a great event. Soon after the war, the BBC, in a broadcast devoted to its own history, recalled this episode in the following words: "This was the first and only time during this war that a broadcasting station had beamed programs directly from the battlefield in an occupied country."

From then on, all the insurrectional broadcasts were monitored and recorded near London on wax discs. The recorded texts were transcribed and distributed widely, landing on the desks of the members of the war cabinet and the editors of newspapers. The officials of the monitoring services, most of them Poles, listened for hours to these recordings, playing them ten times over in order to catch or decipher a faint word or garbled sentence. How difficult this was I found out personally after the war, when I found a whole stack of these discs in the BBC archives. I listened to the voices of my friends from the time of the Rising with great emotion. Hearing our theme,

Chopin's "Revolutionary Etude," again and again on these recordings was a deeply emotional experience. Chopin could not have foreseen that his response to the outbreak of the 1831 uprising would serve as an outcry from Warsaw to the world over a hundred years later.

Adam and I now worked with great enthusiasm. Apart from news and reports from the city, I composed various appeals directed to people of influence whom I knew in England, choosing friends made during my recent stay: Lords Tyrell and Vansittart, Ambassador O'Malley, Ivor Thomas, Sir Douglas Savory, Allan Graham, Arthur Greenwood, Lord Selborne, and Minister Hugh Dalton. Unfortunately, as it later appeared, only a few of these names were clear enough to be deciphered. As the BBC was saying little, or nothing, about the Rising in its English program, I appealed to Gregory Macdonald, the chief of the Polish Section of the BBC. He composed a long, courageous memorandum (which he showed me after the war) and sent it to members of Parliament and politicians. He maintained that his appeal was effective, and that after it was received the fighting in Warsaw was no longer played down by the English service. It appears that the behavior of the Russians and the public reaction to that behavior also contributed in some degree.

Zygmunt Zaremba, an activist of the Polish Socialist Party, provided a very well-written open letter to his comrades in the Labour Party and British workers. Attempts to locate other British prisoners-of-war in Warsaw led to the discovery of an Australian, Walter Smith, a native of Manly, near Sydney, taken prisoner in Crete in June 1941. He was hiding in Warsaw after escaping from a camp. Brought to the Adria, a tall, lanky fellow, he spoke into the microphone—without preparation—a simple but sincere hymn of praise to his Polish hosts who had hidden him, to the soldiers of the AK, to the organization of the underground movement, and to life in Warsaw during the Rising. He closed by sending greetings to his mother and family in Australia. This was one of our best English programs and produced a strong response. Not only was it rebroadcast from London, but a few days later the BBC in turn sent greetings over the air from Walter's mother, who for three years had thought that her son had been killed. In this way an exchange of radio signals took place between the son in Warsaw in the middle of the Rising and the mother in Sydney.

On the other side of Jerozolimskie Avenue, John Ward was pursuing his activities with ever better results. He had received answers to his messages from Sir Archibald Sinclair, the air secretary, and from Colonel Perkins, and soon the London *Times* suggested that he serve as their war correspondent in Warsaw. From that moment on, brief and matter-of-fact but for this very reason convincing radio-grams from Ward in Warsaw did find their way into the news columns of *The Times*.

The great handicap in our work was that both Adam and I were desk-bound for most of the day, and there was little time to get about and collect information and first-hand impressions. Our source of news was the daily briefing, to which all the editors of the insurgent press, radio, and propaganda sections came. Reporters brought information from the front, mostly limited to what was happening in the center of the city, and Kowalik told us what he had heard at their briefing with Monter.

Chapter 34

The period of improvisation was over. Liaison between the various quarters of the city, at first confined to couriers operating under fire, was made more efficient by the use of short-wave radio sets. A dispatch from Krucza Street to Moniuszki Street, a mile apart, went in a very roundabout way, via London.* Sometimes two points only a thousand feet apart also communicated by that route.

In the middle of August we sustained a loss that greatly affected Greta, Kowalik, me, and all in our little group. We heard from the "other side" of Jerozolimskie Avenue that our colleague Ela (before my departure for Stockholm, she had handed me Rowecki's order hidden in a cigarette), who was ill with tuberculosis, was safe. After terrible experiences during the first days of the Rising, she was trying to come over to us but was too weak to cross the Avenue† on her own. On the 16th, late in the afternoon, Jula went to fetch her. From this point on, I will let Greta tell the story as she entered it in a diary which she began immediately after the Rising.

It is nearly 2 A.M. and there is no sign of Jula. I am more and more anxious but comfort myself with the thought that perhaps

---

*Two weak radio stations could exchange signals only via a powerful transmitting station. Such transmitters were located near London.

†Jerozolimskie Avenue, a major boulevard, divided the center of Warsaw occupied by the insurgents. It was under constant barrage from the Germans at the Central Railway Station and the Poniatowski Bridge.

Jerozolimskie Avenue is blocked or there is firing and nobody can get through. . . . At 5 A.M. I realize that Jula won't be back today.

The sun glistens between the houses. On tiptoe so as not to awaken anybody, I slip out of the room and walk toward Jerozolimskie Avenue. Outside there is a strange silence—all the firing has ceased. I reach one of the first cross streets leading to the Avenue. The front doors are closed. I knock at the front door of the house from which one can "jump" to the other side. After a while a little window opens in the door and someone asks: "Where?" "To the other side," I answer. From behind the gate I hear a whispered conversation, then somebody's irritated voice: "Why do these women wander about at all hours? We won't let anybody across; there were too many victims in the night."

It takes quite a long time to persuade them. In the end they let me in. Something is pushing me, and after a moment I am standing in a break in the wall facing the Avenue. The far side was several yards away. So this is how "the other side" looks, this mortally dangerous sector of the street, soaked in the blood of messengers, liaison girls, and couriers. One must cross these few yards under the fire of snipers on the upper stories of the Bank of National Economy. The street I crossed so many times before the Rising is now lifeless. Where are the streetcars, the horse carriages, the carts heaped with fruit and vegetables, the crowds of pedestrians, and, finally, the German motorcars? All is silent and empty. I decide to "jump." I lean down, ready to run, when somebody tugs at my hand violently and pushes me down "What are you doing?" he shouts. "Are you crazy? Not now."

Staring at the Avenue I did not see the soldier. He is no more than sixteen years old; in a helmet too large for him falling over his ears, he kneels with a rifle positioned in a little window between sandbags, watching the movement of the Germans at the crossing of Marszalkowska and the Avenue on one side and the Avenue and Nowy Swiat on the other.

"At first," he says, "they showed their faces often, but now the Krauts are more careful. Look there, quick, there he is running. Don't lean out, or they will hit us." I just glimpsed a German running through Marszalkowska.

"Why don't you fire?" I asked, astonished.

"We must save ammunition," he answers. "We must wait until more of them start crossing."

I again look at the Avenue. The road and the sidewalk are covered with bricks and plaster. Torn telephone and streetcar lines, whole trees and branches are scattered about. The pavement is full of holes made by German machine-gun fire. I decide to return to Adria. The streets are now becoming more animated; the daily "traffic" is beginning.

In the evening a very excited Elzbieta, Rzepecki's secretary, rushes into Kowalik's room. They talk together in whispers. Kowalik suddenly grows serious, turns toward me, and says: "Jula was badly wounded during the night on the corner of Lwowska and Koszykowa Street."

I start at once to run and hear Tadeusz' voice calling after me in the stairwell: "Sano Clinic, in Lwowska!"

I go back to Widok Street. I wait in despair for two hours in a long line. I run across the Avenue, leaning down, remembering that the path runs slightly askew, to the left. I cannot make a mistake because that would be the end! Right away I find the hole cut just above the sidewalk, screened by sandbags. I am in the cellar. I run along the underground passage, stumbling all the time against the pipes and the knees of people sitting against the walls. I come out into the street at the crossing of Nowogrodzka and Krucza. I keep running, now in the middle of Marszalkowska. I am stopped by patrols once, twice, and asked for the password. I start running again. I reach the Clinic. I am sickened by the horrible smell of blood, pus, and carbolic acid. I stop a nurse: "Nurse, please," I ask feverishly, "where is the liaison girl, wounded last night, at the barricade, not very far from here, on the corner of this street? Please tell me quickly."

The nurse thinks for a moment. "Ah yes," she says at last. "She is in the garage."

"Why in the garage?"

"She died yesterday at six in the evening," she answers calmly. "She was very brave. She was hit in the stomach by a German sniper. It was one of those dumdum bullets. The operations lasted a long time, but we could not save her. . . . A priest came. . . . Only afterward did her fiancé come."

I cross the street and look for the garage in which Jula is supposed to lie. I find it, but it is shut. I wait until dawn in the empty hall of the Architecture Faculty of the Polytechnic. I have time to think about my sister and our parents in Cracow. In September, 1939, they lost their only son, eighteen years old, in the battle of Kutno—and now she is gone. . . .

I say my last goodbye to her on August 18 at 3 in the afternoon, together with her fiancé, Jan Kostrzewski ("Zajac"). There is a priest, many flowers, many liaison girls, and the owners of safe houses and friends. They carry Jula to the little garden of the house in Mokotowska, where there are already other fresh graves. Handfuls of earth mixed with stones resound on the coffin. . . . the priest does not want the righthand side of the coffin to be covered because "others will come here." On the grave we put a cross made of two birch branches and on it nailed a board with an eagle and the inscription "'Jula,' Barbara Wolska, aged twenty-nine, decorated with the Cross of Valor, died a soldier's death on 17.8.44." On the other graves there are often crosses with only two letters, "NN"—unknown. Some distance away is the grave of "Rosomak," who parachuted in from England. He had taken part in the fighting at Narvik and in Africa. Now he had perished in the attack on a Warsaw apartment house. By the next grave a still young woman is kneeling, almost touching the ground with her lips. I hear her softly saying to herself: "Don't cry, don't cry, remember you are the mother of a hero. . . ." I look at the tablet on the cross: "Soldier of the Home Army, aged 17," and I too am trying not to cry.

The same evening I return to our people. Jasiek suggests that I lead his patrol to our side. "You know the way," he says, "let's go." After crossing the Avenue we part in Widok Street. It is very dark. I am not sure if I am going the right way, so I stop a patrol and ask for directions.

"Ah, Adria," they say. "It does not exist anymore. An enormous shell fell there, you know, one of the huge ones from the Sebastopol cannon. . . ."

I don't wait for further explanation and hurry on.

The news of Jula's death came immediately after Greta left. While her funeral was being held, I was at my desk preparing a program for the next day. Suddenly I heard the roar of a shell falling. The six-story house shook and swayed. Then I heard the sound of breaking glass, and everything was hidden in a white cloud. One could see nothing and could hardly breathe. From all around I could hear desperate cries: "Water, water!"

Some moments later the cloud of plaster began to settle, and everybody rushed from their rooms into the hallways. We looked like well-floured millers. Through the masks of white powder one could see only eyes, clown faces. Near the stairwell there was an enormous hole which went all the way from the roof down to the ballroom in the basement. A few days earlier the Germans had positioned the heaviest guns in the world outside Warsaw, the guns they had used during the siege of Sebastopol. Buildings hit by the 24-inch shells, which weighed a ton and a half, collapsed like a house of cards, burying all the inhabitants in the rubble. It was such a shell that hit our Adria, cutting through all six floors and killing one woman on the way; when it reached the dance floor it plunged into the parquet floor and . . . did not explode.

We all ran downstairs. On the part of the shell sticking out from the floor we could see a strip of brass with a gauge. "Time bomb!" somebody shouted, and put his ear against it: "It's ticking!" All of us ran to the door. "Stop!" somebody else ordered, in stentorian tones, and then put his head against the shell and listened for a long time. "Nothing is ticking," he said. One could almost hear the general sigh of relief.

The Adria building accommodated several hundred people, the whole Propaganda Department and many hangers-on. They all had to be evacuated before nightfall. True, the missile did not tick, but any further shock might set it off. Kowalik at once sent out a few patrols of two people each in search of housing. I went out with a friend. The task proved impossible: apartments, cellars, and shops were all crowded with refugees from Wola and other parts of the city occupied by the Germans or from bombed-out houses. After a long search it appeared that the only place which could hold everybody was the lobby of the Palladium Cinema. Unfortunately, it had a glass roof, which by a miracle was intact, but in a quarter perpetually exposed to shelling it was safer to sleep in the open than under a glass roof.

It was decided that my colleagues had a choice: to sleep in Adria in the company of the monster shell, which might explode at any minute, or to sleep under the glass at the Palladium. Most chose the Palladium. I remained in Adria with a few others, on the top floor, as far as possible from the creature in the cellar, although, to be realistic, if it decided to explode in the night, we would merely have had a slightly shorter trip to heaven.

In the evening Greta returned. I was happy to see her safe and well. She had flown to Moniuszko Street, certain that none of us would be alive. With the exception of Greta, we all slept very well that night, not thinking about the shell in the ballroom. Early in the morning some explosives experts woke us up. "Get going," they said. "We will empty it. It contains six hundred pounds of tritole, which will be useful for making hand grenades."

With great difficulty we found quarters in an enormous paper store nearby. Since the beginning of the Rising the one-person editorial office of the newspaper *Fighting Warsaw* had been there. The store was underground and quite spacious. We could stay there in relative safety. Other people took shelter in the nearby shop of Emil Wedel, famous for the best chocolate in Poland. Lightning broadcast its programs round the clock from the Polish Savings Bank.

Barely had we settled in at the paper store when the air was filled with the roar of another enormous shell. We waited for the end for a fraction of a second. Then there was a deafening crash, and the floor shook under our feet. Reams of paper began to fall off the shelves onto us. The monster of Sebastopol had hit the nearby Warsaw Philharmonic Concert Hall. Unfortunately, this time the shell exploded, burying a whole detachment quartered in the cellars. They were all very young people, boys and girls. I used to see them almost every day and knew them all by sight. The previous day I had seen them going to their position, jolly and carefree, singing the most popular song of the Rising, "My Heart's in a Knapsack." People began to dig them out of the rubble. Most of them were naked; the force of the blast had torn off their clothes. The corpses were placed in rows in a little square in front of the bank and covered with newspapers. In the afternoon they were buried in a common grave. I watched this ceremony as if it were my own funeral.

In those days such successes as the storming of the Central Telephone Exchange or the headquarters of the German police were considered major victories. Indeed they were, if one considers that the insurgents had neither artillery nor heavy machine guns—nothing but Sten guns, rifles, and home-made grenades.

Listening to the radio in the evening seemed a greater burden than listening to the bombs and mines exploding during the day. A torrent of accusations, invective, and abuse was now pouring out of the Soviet radio stations. The London *News Chronicle* disclosed that the Russians had refused permission for British aircraft to land with supplies for the Rising. I tried to compose our English programs so that, while avoiding polemics, they would refute the Soviet propaganda attacks. I knew who these words would reach in London, and I tried to phrase the communiqués in a way suited to the mentality of the British. In our English-language programs we presented the Rising as an act of goodwill which would have led to military cooperation with the Russians had their attitude toward the independence of Poland been different.

I wrote with full conviction. If the Russians, like the British and Americans who liberated France, had wanted to liberate and not subjugate us, the Warsaw tragedy would not have taken place. The events in Paris presented a dramatic analogy. There a rising began without communication and coordination with Eisenhower's staff. The French wanted to liberate Paris with their own hands in order to purge themselves of the ignominy of capitulation and collaboration. London radio explained in detail that Eisenhower did not want to take the capital at the moment but wanted to encircle it in a wide maneuver. However, on the first reports of fighting in the city he altered all his plans. An American corps, together with the French armored division under General Leclerc, was directed to the relief of Paris. On August 26, after only a few days of fighting, Radio London broadcast the news that Paris was free.

On the day of the liberation of Paris somebody told me that a Belgian was hiding in the cellar of a nearby house. We found him at once. It appeared that this was a young smuggler who had been slipping gold and diamonds from the *General Gouvernement* area to Belgium. He had been trapped in Warsaw by the Rising. Rather an unimpressive type, he had no wish to leave his hiding place but was "persuaded" to do so. We dragged him to the studio and used him as an announcer in a short radio appeal in French to the *maquis* in Paris. It was broadcast the same day, and ran as follows:

> The soldiers of the Polish Home Army salute the soldiers of the French Home Army. Comrades in arms! At the moment when Paris, the capital of freedom, the heart of civilized Europe, is bravely throwing off the chains in which the enemy's might has put her, we, the soldiers of the Polish Home Army, who have been fighting for three weeks in Warsaw, send you our warmest congratulations. We are fighting for the same ideals of equality, liberty, and brotherhood. We remember that we share with you common historical traditions, a common fight against persecution and tyranny. We believe that Germany's defeat—the defeat of the enemies of freedom—will lead to a realization of those ideals in whose name Poland first took up arms five years ago. Warsaw has become the first occupied capital to rise in open battle. We are proud that the soldiers of the Polish Armored Division and our airmen have taken part in the fighting which led to that magnificent victory, and that this will open the way for France to defeat the enemy.
>
> Honneur aux vaillant soldats de l'Armée de l'Intérieur de la France! Honneur aux héros de Paris! Vive le France! Vive la Pologne! Vive la Liberté!

The smuggler read this appeal with dramatic expression worthy of a professional actor. It was recorded by the BBC and went out on Radio London to Paris, that city so much luckier than Warsaw, fighting alone.

The Lightning studio was moved on August 23 from the Polish Savings Bank to the empty Adria. One could not dismiss Monter's argument that a broadcasting station should not be located in the same building as the general staff of our forces. It is to this day a mystery to me why the Germans who eventually began to jam the Lightning broadcasts did not pinpoint the station from the air and destroy it. We always had an observer on the roof of the building who, on seeing an approaching plane, at once warned the technicians below so that we could go off the air immediately.

In the last week of August the agony of the Old City began. The commander of the Home Army, his staff, and the Government Delegate were forced to move, this time through the sewers to the Polish Savings Bank in the center of town. On Wednesday, August 30, I was summoned to Monter. He told me that during the night the garrison of the Old City would be evacuated. All the most experienced forces would be withdrawn from the center and concentrated for an attack on the German corridor running from the Saski Gardens across Iron Gate Square and the Mirowskie market hall, which separated the Old City from the main part of town. The Germans were to be caught in a crossfire, and we were to support our units from the Old City trying to join us.

"This will be the biggest military operation yet undertaken in Warsaw," said Monter. "I want you with me as a reporter who will describe it all and broadcast it in Polish and in English." Monter was in an excellent mood, full of faith in the success of this important operation. Around 10 P.M. we started toward Grzybowska Street. The nearer we got the more difficult it was to get our bearings. I had been brought up in Warsaw and knew every corner of it, but we were walking in a forest of stone ruins, along a winding path among the rubble, climbing over mounds of bricks. I kept asking my guide where we were.

Somewhere not far from Grzybowski Square we stopped in a courtyard surrounded by burned-out buildings. There was a considerable concentration of forces there. The soldiers sat against the walls awaiting the order to go. Officers were constantly reporting to

Monter. At one point I recognized a familiar voice in the darkness. I groped my way toward it and saw Kazimierz Bilski. We had separated a month before at Zoliborz, and it seemed to both of us that years had passed since then. He had been in the front line from the beginning of the Rising: as an experienced career officer he was in command of a battalion. He had a key task to perform that night. When he learned that I broadcast in English, he asked me to send his greetings to Audrey, his fiancée, in London. I promised I would not forget to do so. I asked what were our chances of the night attack's succeeding. From his expression I could see that he did not share Monter's optimism. "I have had quite a lot of experience," he said, "and I fought in France, but I've never been in such a desperate situation before. We are not strong enough to bring this off."

An hour or more of waiting followed. Monter told his troops that I had flown to Warsaw shortly before the Rising. Again I was questioned—about London, about our air force squadrons, our parachute brigade, and our navy. In answering their questions I tried to fill the time for them and divert their thoughts from what lay ahead.

After midnight Monter ordered a green flare fired as the signal for those in the Old City to begin. We watched the sky for a long time, waiting for an answer that did not come. I asked the colonel how strong the German forces were. "Three battalions," he answered, "and probably seven or eight tanks." He went on to explain his plan of action. There would be a diversionary attack in the Saski Gardens, which we hoped would deflect the attention of the Germans. Meanwhile, our men would break through the walls of the houses overlooking Iron Gate Square and the food depots at Mirowskie market hall and make a sally toward the Old City to join our people there. To avoid mistaking our own for Germans, both groups were to keep yelling the password, "Pine Tree."

Around 1 A.M. firing was heard from the direction of the Saski Gardens: short bursts of machine pistol fire, rifle fire, and exploding grenades. An orange flare shot into the sky: the Germans were asking for help. Then we heard the roar of tanks coming from the south. The moment of our attack was approaching. I stayed close to Monter listening to the incoming reports and the orders given.

Half an hour later, the colonel was beginning to look anxious. Somehow our attack had not begun. He decided to go forward to see what was happening, and I followed him closely. On the way there were acrobatics for which I was not fit enough—climbing up partly burned staircases, jumping from one bit of wall to another. At last we reached a row of damaged houses in Krochmalna Street which overlooked the Mirowskie market hall. Here the attack was to have started. In front of the colonel the silhouette of a young officer emerged from the darkness. He reported as platoon commander: Lieutenant "Janusz."

"What are you doing here?" Monter asked sharply. "What are you waiting for?"

"Sir, we have tried. The women sappers have blown a hole in the wall, but there is no way of getting through it. German howitzer shells are falling on the hole and the courtyard."

Monter who had been calm until then, raised his voice. "Obey the order! You are to begin the sally at once. We can't leave them over there without help."

"Yes sir," replied Janusz without enthusiasm.

I again followed Monter up something that must have once been a staircase. We stopped at a burned-out window. Two stories below was the courtyard, to the left the food depot. The courtyard filled slowly with young people. I recognized a group of girls; this must be the sapper team who had blown the hole in the wall. Suddenly something horrible happened: among that crowd of young people one grenade, then another, then many more, exploded. Behind them, our own petrol bombs for use against the German tanks began to explode too. There were girls' voices crying in fear. Flames lit up the Dantean scene below us: a tangle of wounded and burning people.

We rushed downstairs. The ambulance unit appeared, and the stretchers carried away dead or badly burned soldiers, girls with missing feet, and last a deathly pale Lieutenant Janusz. Both his legs were almost severed. He stared at Monter, who was leaning over him, and said: "I have obeyed your order, sir." He died a few hours later from loss of blood.

This was only what happened at one point. We went along the whole sector with Monter. The carefully planned operation had gotten little beyond the starting point. Toward dawn, the colonel ordered all detachments to return. Nearly one hundred people died that night; one hundred and fifty were wounded, some critically.

When Lieutenant "Lech," the commander of the sector, reported to the colonel that he had to withdraw from the Mirowskie market hall for fear of being cut off, Monter interrupted him sharply: "And who gave you the order to withdraw? Were you in a hurry to get yourself a cup of coffee?" The officer, on whose ghastly pale face the experiences of last night were clearly written, winced. He said nothing, but one could see how hurt he was by those words. Monter then extended his hand to him, and said: "From now on you will report to me as a captain."

This massacre later proved to have been completely unnecessary. In the next few days all the survivors of Colonel Karol Ziemski's besieged detachment in the Old City retreated through the sewers to the center. Only one unit, by some miracle, was able to cut its way across the Saski Gardens the following night.

September 2

In our part of the city there was pandemonium, beginning in the morning. Incendiaries and high-explosive bombs rained down incessantly, and at seven-minute intervals one heard the howl of the Sebastopol monster, which we called the "flying coffin." Fires started all around, and the Adria was in flames. A team of technicians dragged the radio transmitter and all the other equipment out and away from the burning building. Our broadcasts would have to cease for the moment.

Kowalik decided to transfer the whole department to the south of Jerozolimskie Avenue, where things were relatively quiet. For the second time we had to cross the road with all our gear. The path, which had been so narrow that two men could not run along it side by side, was by then much improved. At last a trench had been dug, protected by sandbags. The Germans hit it all the time from the ground with grenades and from the air with bombs, but special teams repaired the damage as it occurred, and the traffic continued to flow. We found a spot for our people in the Ericsson building, at 52 Mokotowska Street. We moved there the next night, September 3.

When crossing one street that day I was nearly shot by a German sniper on the roof; his bullet hit the wall a few inches above my head. In Mokotowska Street it was much quieter, but on the first day disaster struck. The power station near the Vistula, which was taken

373

over by the workers at the beginning of the Rising and had been sup-plying power to the city, was bombed the day after we moved in. Lightning could not broadcast without a generator, but where was one to be found?

The radio station was in luck: somewhere in Pius XI Street there was a small grenade factory that had its own generator, run on diesel fuel. Lightning was moved nearby to the Soviet Embassy building on Poznanska Street, in the greatest secrecy. Only a few people knew about it. The number of programs was now limited: we could broad-cast in English only once a day between 10 and 11 in the morning.

Chapter 35

September 5

When I heard that someone was needed to carry an important message to the Chairman, whose headquarters were then in Foksal Street, I volunteered immediately, thinking that this was a good opportunity to find out what had happened to my mother and brother and whether they were still alive. In the inner courtyard of the apartment house at 37 Nowy Swiat, bodies were laid out in a long row; in most cases they were lying face up, their open eyes seeming to scan the sky. I was reluctant to look too closely for fear I would find my dear ones in that ghastly row. To my delight they were among the crowd hiding in the cellar. All the tenants were huddled into a small space, along with many neighbors, who had fled their own destroyed or burning houses. They were crouching in almost total darkness, their electric light gone and candles long since exhausted. Here and there some daylight seeped through the small windows just above the ground. The walls moved with each nearby explosion. It was like being in a huge grave, packed tight with a wretched mass of people waiting to be buried alive. I ached to leave, to run away immediately.

"I'll be on my way back in half an hour," I told my mother. "I want you to go with me. We'll cross over to the other side of the Avenue. If you stay here, you'll either be buried alive or the Germans will get you. They're coming from the direction of the Vistula."

"What's the use, my boy?" my mother said quietly. "In a day or two they'll get to the other side too. Why bother?"

"Let's be together at least," I insisted, and this turned out to be the winning argument.

I rushed out to deliver my report to the Chairman, but on the corner there was a new obstacle. The whole length of the street was under fire from mortars and snipers stationed in the Bank of National Economy building, some two hundred yards away. The steady stream of refugees and wounded, evacuated from the Powisle district, along the bank of the Vistula, had been negotiating the crossing by darting across the street, one by one, under the doubtful protection of a high barricade. Shortly before my arrival, the Germans had succeeded in breaching the barricade with mortar fire. A few bodies—those trying to cross at that moment—lay sprawled on the pavement. Everything came to a standstill.

An elderly gentleman stepped forward from the crowd. "Let's rebuild the barricade!" he called out. "Come on, let's not waste time! Everyone making the crossing will take one brick along and drop it into the breach in passing. I won't let anyone through without a brick!"

He stationed himself close to the breach, where another grenade might explode at any time, and began taking bricks from those who crawled by him and tossing them into the gap. I managed to crawl all the way to the other side on my belly without any mishap, handing over my brick on the way.

The Chairman was no longer at the Foksal Street address. He and his staff had already moved to a new location in the southern part of the city. On my way back, perhaps a quarter of an hour later, I saw that the breach in the barricade was already closed. The elderly gentleman, beaming with satisfaction, was still at his post. But I had barely made the crossing and reached the corner of Chmielna Street when there was a deafening explosion and a shower of bricks. Turning back, I could see the barricade in shambles again and the old man stretched out on the pavement.

My mother and brother awaited me at Nowy Swiat, ready to go. I stopped briefly at our abandoned apartment to get a few photographs and small mementos. The apartment was a ruin. The floor was strewn with broken glass and plaster, papers were scattered all over the place by the wind, and books, pictures, and all sorts of other objects were lying about. As I looked around in dismay, I heard the old grandfather clock strike the hour. It was so tall that it touched the ceiling. As a small boy I used to hide in the narrow space at the base, which once housed the chiming mechanism. The clock was probably three hundred years old. It had been brought to Warsaw from a country house at the turn of the century, and several generations of our family were raised to the sound of its chimes. Both my brother and I loved the old clock like a living relative. Even when my mother had to pawn her wedding ring, we would not let the old clock go. In my mind's eye I saw it in flames or bombed into a heap of debris, and it made me heartsick. For a brief moment I paused to listen to its quiet, dignified heart, ticking away, unmoved by the disaster around it.

But this was no time for sentimental musings. We had to abandon everything we owned, everything that linked us with our past. Only people counted from now on, and those hours, or perhaps days, that they still had to live.

By the time we joined the crowd waiting for a chance to make the perilous crossing of Jerozolimskie Avenue, it was already dark. The broad street, which divided the north and south parts of the city, was under constant enemy fire. There was only one way to cross: a narrow trench, protected by a wall of sandbags. The crowd was mixed, soldiers and civilians, old people and children. Home Army men from the Old Town were easily identified by the stench of their clothing, acquired in their trip through the sewers. A pall of fear hung over the silent crowd, a feeling of impending doom. A German flare rent the darkness of the night. Usually, this preceded a barrage of fire, but no one moved or said a word. A single grenade could trigger a panic and turn the place into a slaughterhouse. But it was still dark. The German planes would not come over until daybreak.

We crossed to "the other side" with the first light of day, and only with the help of a friend, an army doctor. It was a miracle that our old mother managed to make her way through that trench, over a maze of pipes and ducts of all kinds. Robak, left to fend for himself, followed close on our heels. It was almost five in the morning when we finally arrived at Pius XI Street.

When I returned to the Ericsson building everyone was asleep but Greta. "You know," I told her, "this has to be the end. Powisle fell today, and I don't think that the Germans can be held along the line of Nowy Swiat. Tomorrow, or perhaps the day after, those

pockets of resistance that are still miraculously holding out will probably all collapse." She listened in silence to my account of last night's
events.

"Let's get married now," I said finally. "Let's get married
while there are still some churches and some priests left in the city."

"Why now?" she asked.

When her sister Jula was killed some days before, we promised
each other that we would get married immediately after the Rising.
We had no rings, so we exchanged wristwatches. I gave her my
Omega, and she gave me the small watch that had belonged to Jula,
since she had none of her own.

"The end is drawing near," I said. "Let's face it as husband
and wife."

We were married on September 7, late in the afternoon, at a
chapel not far from the quarters occupied by the Home Army chap-
lains. They were busy with funerals and last rites, though there were
a few weddings. We talked to a skeptical young priest who took a dim
view of marriages contracted spontaneously in the stress of battle. It
helped when I told him that I was returned from London and showed
him the narrow strip of paper Greta had sewn into my hatband as I
was leaving for Great Britain, on which she had written that she
would be waiting.

Greta managed to trade a tin of meat for a pair of copper wedding rings. On a balcony of a house on Wilcza Street I spied a win-
dowbox of petunias in bloom. The apartment was locked, and its
tenant was hiding in the cellar with the other residents. When I found
him and asked whether I could have the flowers, he looked at me as if
I were out of my mind, but then shrugged and let me have the keys to
cut the flowers. Thanks to him, the bride had a bouquet.

The news of the wedding of a parachutist and a Home Army
liaison girl traveled fast, and the chapel was full. With the Germans
three hundred yards away, we crunched up to the altar on broken
glass—not one stained glass window in the chapel was unbroken.
Our young priest was in a hurry. He had a funeral service scheduled
next. The wedding ceremony took not more than seven minutes. Two
young soldiers offered Greta a bunch of gladioli which they had
picked in the garden of the school for deaf-mutes and the blind. Our
RAF friend John Ward was also there, with a wedding gift: a beautiful
picture of the Black Madonna. Directly after the ceremony, we went

to Jula's grave and Greta placed her flowers on it. A surprise party awaited us at our quarters. Wasyl, whose young wife was the daughter of the owners of Warsaw's most famous delicatessen and grocery store, beamed proudly as he miraculously produced a bottle of wine, a tin of meat, and two tins of sardines.

On the thirty-seventh day of the Rising, this was indeed a wedding feast to remember. It was also the last time we ate any meat, with the exception of two pigeons killed a few days later by the air draft from a bomb which brought down the building on our corner. So many hands reached out for the poor birds that I barely managed to get them away to Ericsson. Later, when we were even more hungry, word spread that there were large stores of barley at the Haberbusch Brewery. I went over with a convoy and returned with a seventy-pound bag of barley on my back.

There were rumors in the air about surrender when suddenly, after long weeks of silence, the powerful roar of artillery burst out. The battle for Praga, a suburb separated from the center of the city by the Vistula River, which is wide at that point, was fought out literally before our eyes. When that suburb was occupied by the Red Army and General Berling's Army, we could see, through field glasses, troops moving in the streets and the Soviet motorized columns and tanks not more than a mile and a half away as the crow flies. The Germans were now concentrating all their efforts on the destruction and conquest of the Czerniakow bridgehead, on our side of the Vistula, which we still held, as it could be used by Soviet troops as a crossing in a surprise raid. Czerniakow was soon separated from the rest of the city.

At that time Lightning was broadcasting without interruption. Adam and I made daily expeditions to the abandoned Soviet Embassy building. In the middle of September, in that small portion of the center city that had been spared, we led a very odd life. All distinctions between the front line and the people behind the lines were blurred. By the end of August there was not a single place in Warsaw more than 120 yards from the nearest German position. To avoid hitting their own detachments, the Germans concentrated all their artillery—the "moaning cows," the "flying trunks," and mortars and aircraft—on the rear. The closer to the German positions you were, the safer you were. The front was the safest place. Sometimes soldiers who had survived tank attacks and heavy machine-gun fire were killed by a bomb during their rest periods in cellars at the "rear."

The so-called front line had a very strange shape. It ran, in every direction, through streets, ruined houses, and courtyards. Sometimes the Germans held the cellars of a building and our people the ground floor and above, or the other way around. In some apartment houses there was bitter fighting for every floor and for the stairs. Then one tried to encircle the enemy and catch him by surprise by rushing in suddenly through a hole blown in the wall of the next house by a plastic bomb. The Germans attacked by day, and our counterattacks followed mostly at night. Then it was relatively calm; fighting was confined to the hunt for hidden snipers banging away at anyone in their line of sight.

The rear began thirty or forty yards away—sometimes in the next courtyard. Here were the hospitals and first-aid stations, the field kitchens, the printing presses, and the arms and ammunition factories. Almost directly behind the sandbags and the submachine gun posts, the day's Information Bulletin was being printed. As late as mid-August a film shot during the Rising was twice shown to a large audience in the Palladium Cinema—the height of folly, as the Germans were only a little over three hundred feet from the theater. The sound which accompanied the film was unusual: Beethoven's Fifth Symphony, taken from a record, mixed with gunfire from the area of the Central Railway Station nearby.

At the back of one of the houses in Pius XI Street was the generator providing power for the ammunition factory and our radio station. I went along the street several times a day to our studio in Poznanska during the Rising. Its appearance changed from day to day as apartment houses were bombed or burned out, but the generator never stopped. Its rhythmical, monotonous hum gave us some kind of encouragement. This sound was like the heartbeat of Warsaw, proving that, in spite of the ruins and the ashes, the city was still alive.

Every Warsaw apartment house was now a small world of its own. Before the war one could live in such buildings for years without knowing even the name of a neighbor on a higher floor, but during the Rising all inhabitants came together. These communities were characteristic of insurgent life. They were communities of the shelter in the cellar, of the cauldron of soup and the slice of bread, of danger, and very frequently of death and a common grave. Its external expression was an altar, standing in the hallway, the courtyard, or the cellar, before which all the inhabitants gathered for common prayers—both the pious and those who had not crossed the threshold of a church for years. Gazing at the figure of Christ or the Holy Virgin, they prayed aloud: "Save us, O Lord, from unexpected and sudden death." People prayed most fervently for the preservation of their homes: no one stopped to ask why the Lord should take special care of their particular apartment house while all those around were crumbling or burning.

As the days passed the number of "tenants" of the little garden in the courtyard increased. On these graves were tablets with such inscriptions as "housekeeper from the first floor." No one bothered to establish a name; everybody living there knew the person, just as everybody knew that in the grave with the inscription "Mister Joe" was the popular janitor of the building who had never been called by any other name.

An apartment house that had not been entirely ruined or burned out had to be ready to defend itself from fire or from enemy attack at any moment. In the attic and in the gateway, guards—tenants of that house—were posted in relays day and night. The entrance was usually barricaded from the inside with earth, sand, bricks, and all kinds of objects. Contact with the outside world was maintained through the cellars and holes made in the walls. At dusk, huddled figures could always be seen sitting in the hallways. Through the middle of a cellar there would be a constant procession of soldiers, boy scouts passing out mail, nurses with the wounded on stretchers, and girls distributing the insurgents' press. Hundreds of hands were stretched out to the girls for the papers. The hunger for news was almost as acute as the physical hunger, and communiqués from the city and the world told of great events. While the Eastern Front was frozen, first on the edge of the Wawer Forest, on our horizon, and later on the other side of the Vistula, the victorious Allied offensive had liberated almost all of France and Luxembourg and half of Belgium. In the east, the capitulations of Finland, Romania, and Bulgaria followed. Five European capitals fell while Warsaw waited in vain for relief by the Red Army, that army we could see plainly from any rooftop.

A few months before, each German defeat was greeted with

waves of optimism and outbursts of wild delight. Now these events turned pale in comparison with the reality before us each day. The destruction of a few tanks in Krolewska Street aroused far greater interest than the pulverization of whole German divisions in the battlefields of Normandy. While Marseilles or Rouen were being liberated in the West, we were preoccupied with heavy battles as well—battles for Simon's Passage, St. John's Cathedral in the Old City, the Hospital of St. John the Baptist, the Town Hall or the Bank of Poland.

Chapter 36

*I*n our quarter all hopes were extinguished when, on the night of September 23, Captain "Jerzy"(Ryszard Bialous), the commander of the last redoubt on the bridgehead, forced his way through the German lines from Czerniakow with a pitiful band of survivors. I was present the next day when he told us about the fall of Czerniakow.

That same day I was summoned by the Chairman: "I heard that you were married during the Rising," he began, "but service comes first. General Bor has decided that you are to take a collection of documents out of the city, and start once more for London. I won't say any more about it to you; you must see Teddy Bear."

"Teddy Bear," General Leopold Okulicki, had been named Bor's successor should the AK commander be killed or taken prisoner. In that event he would take over command while remaining in hiding. At the start of the war he was the first commander of the Lodz region and the immediate superior of Major Zygmunt Janke, who spoke of him in superlatives as an excellent commander, a man both fearless and endowed with exceptional energy.

Teddy Bear received me at the Central Telephone Exchange on Pius XI Street, to which Bor had moved his headquarters after the bombing of the PKO building. I had to smile when I met him. Most people adopted underground names designed to deceive the Gestapo: a dark-haired man became "Blondie" and vice versa. In this case, however, the name was very well suited to its owner, a broad-shouldered man of average height with a kindly expression on his triangular, wide, pock-marked face. This bear-like countenance was complemented by his insurgents' battle dress of thick bluish cloth; it looked as though it had been made in a hurry for a much taller man. The general seemed to be a naturally happy man who was in a particularly good mood that day. The imminent collapse of the Rising did not seem to have dampened his spirits because he began the conversation by saying cheerily, "In a few days Warsaw will fall!" pounding on his thigh as if to illustrate that assertion.

I was shocked by the carefree tone in which he referred to this horrible tragedy, but I had no time to brood over it. Orders and instructions were showered on me. I was to contact the woman in charge of the sewer patrols at once and give her the order from Monter which Teddy Bear handed to me. I would have priority in being taken through the sewers to Mokotow, at the southern edge of the city, where I was to report to Colonel "Karol" (Jozef Rokicki). He would help smuggle me out of the city through the German lines. Within the German lines I should pretend to be a wounded civilian if the need arose. Once outside Warsaw, a British plane would land somewhere to pick up me and some others, together with our "mail." His second order was for Marcysia from Zaloga. She was to prepare and pack the "mail." From Marcysia I was also to get the details of contacts and passwords outside Warsaw. The general said that he himself would be leaving Warsaw soon to take over the command of the Home Army outside the city and that he would look for me. He postponed any further talk until our next meeting.

I asked whether I could ask two questions, one of a political, the other of a personal nature. My first was this: "The Russians are accusing us of having started the Rising too soon. Won't we now, in turn, be accused of giving in too soon? Won't the Soviet attack begin two or three days after our surrender to the Germans?"

"The Russians," he replied, "will accuse us whatever we do. The accusation about starting the fighting prematurely would have made sense had the Rising collapsed after a few days or a week, but we gave the Russians nearly two months, more than enough advantage for them to renew the attack and liberate the city." He added: "But don't be afraid. Before we fly the white flag, Marshal Rokossowski will be forewarned, and if we get any sort of indication from him that the Russians are willing to renew their offensive, all talk of surrender will be suspended at once. From this very spot we could talk to Rokossowski," he said, pointing to a telephone, "if only he were willing to pick up the receiver." Seeing my puzzlement, he explained: "We are sitting in a telephone exchange. From here the cables run under the Vistula to a little well on the other side of the river. All the Russians have to do is connect a few wires to make telephone contact with us. The necessary instructions have already been transferred to them. But the swine don't want to talk to us at all."

My second question was the personal one. Two weeks before, I married a liaison girl of the Home Army. Would the general let us leave together? Teddy Bear's face lit up in a smile. "Of course! Take your wife with you. You will feel more comfortable together. I have nothing against it."

The next day I went to see the leader of the guides through the sewers to discuss the problems of getting to Mokotow. A repulsive sewer smell was all around the place. There was a constant movement of girls guiding people or carrying important reports through the sewers. Some of them looked seventeen years old at most. In those last weeks of Warsaw's agony, this was the most important and most heroic service of the insurgents. The sewers under the streets in German-occupied areas were the only channels of communication to other parts of the city and were the "highways" for the transport of ammunition, arms, and food, and for the evacuation of the wounded, of armed units, and even of civilians. The manholes to the sewers, always strongly guarded, were not far from our quarters. I saw people pulled out of them exhausted and covered from head to foot in black, stinking mud. Most could not drag themselves out without help.

I could not see the woman in charge of those operations. The girl to whom I spoke looked at the date of the order signed by Monter, September 25, the night before my meeting with Teddy Bear. "That's invalid," she said. "Everything has changed since yesterday. Colonel Karol is not in that area any more; he went to the center through the sewers. Today all the passages are blocked by refugees from the Mokotow sector. Both soldiers and civilians who are navigating through the sewers are panicky. Before, there was some order, but now no one can control them. Many will get lost and perish, mostly those who stray into the side sewers. I doubt if there is still a way out of the city from Mokotow." We agreed that Greta and I would apply again when we were both ready to leave. The girl promised that we would be given a guide, but I felt that she said this without conviction. The next day news came that Mokotow had fallen. That escape through the sewers was closed.

I received my "mail" from Marcysia only after the city has surrendered. Most of it I collected myself. There were photographs of the insurgents' newspapers, proclamations, orders, posters, even poems, photographs of the fighting—in a word, as much of the archives of the Rising as could be collected under existing conditions and within a short time. Earlier mail had been put on microfilm, which took up very little space, and was given to me already hidden and professionally packed. Now Marcysia gave us whole rolls of thirty-five-millimeter film, which we had to hide by our own cunning.

A cease-fire was announced on October 1, to ensure the evacuation of civilians from the city. A few thousand people took advantage of it. The rest preferred to hang on in the cellars of those houses which were still standing. We might have left in that evacuation had we not still been waiting for our "mail." The news about capitulation was made public on October 3. I was in the courtyard of the house on Pius XI Street when a civilian with an armband appeared and called all the residents together. He read a short communiqué which said that, according to the surrender terms, all inhabitants were to leave the city, taking as much luggage as each could carry. The agreement guaranteed that there would be no reprisals.

I looked closely at the people around me. They all looked extremely exhausted; their faces bore the traces of two months spent mostly in dirty, dark, damp cellars, pervaded by a terrible stench, without light or water and with little food, subjected to shelling, bombing, and bursting mines, all the time expecting the cellar to collapse, burying them alive in a common grave. All this misery and pain had been in vain. It was now to end in a stream of homeless people wandering out into the unknown.

How many times in history had the garrisons of beleaguered cities been forced to give in not by the enemy but by their hungry, demoralized inhabitants? I never heard anybody in Warsaw, where people were tried almost beyond the limits of endurance, demand capitulation. But what would happen now? Would there be an outburst of despair and fury? Would they start cursing their leaders? Everybody listened gravely to the proclamation. When it came to an end, there was a moment's silence. Then an elderly man with a gray beard began to sing the Polish national anthem, which begins, "Poland has not perished yet."

Now began the tragedy of the wounded, the sick, the weak, and the old, and also of all kinds of domestic pets which had been lovingly protected by their owners during the sixty-three days of siege. Along with the great tragedies, there were some small ones. Our dachshund, Robak, had faithfully endured the war with us for years. Whenever I returned home from a short or long expedition, his joyful bark behind the door was a signal that all was well. Now we had to get rid of him. We would not leave him behind, so my brother Andrzej asked a dentist friend for poison for Robak. She indignantly declined to provide it. There was nothing for it but to take the little dog to the guards in the next house and ask them to shoot him. Robak was the soul of gentleness. He never bared his teeth, and even his growling was a bluff. Now, however, as my brother tried to take him away, he escaped into a corner under a large sofa and began to struggle desperately. His instinct told him what was in store for him, and he had to be dragged out by force. Having given him to the soldiers, Andrzej turned away miserably to go back to our mother, but a soldier ran after him with the dog in his arms. "Listen," he cried, "I aimed at him three times and each time the pistol failed to fire. This dog is fated to survive. *I* won't shoot him, oh no!"

That day, when my mother walked toward the barricade with the others, Robak was trotting at her side. The Germans put her on a lorry so crowded that one could hardly get a foot on it. Later, people on it were moved into a railway car, where the crowd was still thicker. How the dog got into this car no one knows. At the end of their wanderings, Robak looked like the skeleton of a dog, a set of bones covered with skin, but he stuck to my mother to the end, did not get lost in the crush, and survived.

On the day of the surrender Adam and I prepared our last English program, to be broadcast the next day, October 4. Lightning had moved for the fourth time and had finally found shelter in a public library on Koszykowa Street. Lightning, like the Polish Radio, had been broadcasting throughout, with only one- or two-day interruptions. From August 9 to October 3, 57 English programs, not counting repeats, went on the air, and John Ward relayed 65 dispatches in English on the short-wave radio in Morse.

Greta and I conceived the idea of hiding our microfilms in plaster casts. They were put on in a Red Cross hospital by a well-known surgeon. The rolls of film were first wrapped in pieces of waterproof oilcloth, which went under my armpit, and the arm down to the elbow was then wrapped in special plaster-covered bandages and put in a sling. The plaster extended down the right half of my chest. As I had broken my arm so recently in the parachute jump, it was easy to pretend that I had been wounded. There were not enough plaster bandages left for Greta, so a mixture of plaster and potato flour was slapped right onto her forearm. The rest of the film and "mail" she concealed in her voluminous handbag.

Then we left the hospital with the other wounded. Some dragged themselves along by their own strength, but most were carried on stretchers. As we walked in the direction of a barricade, we passed two women bent under the weight of their bundles. They looked like typical Warsaw peddlers. "Now then, my girls" (we caught a fragment of their conversation, heavily larded with curses like *psiakrew* ["dog's blood"] and *cholera*), "who would have thought it? *Psiakrew!* After two months, back to those *cholera*-ridden Huns again!"

We walked through the barricade and the square in front of the Polytechnic, then turned to look back. From the balconies near the barricade white flags were hanging limply. I took leave of the city where I had spent my childhood, my school years, the years of the war, and the days of the Rising. Every alley, street corner, and apartment building suddenly became precious.

We had started on a difficult and very long road, uncertain whether we would ever see Warsaw again, but wherever fate should cast our bodies, our hearts would always remain in this city.

Chapter 37

*L*eaving Warsaw with the wounded from the Red Cross hospital was not as grim as the route through the sewers to Mokotow and then through the German lines would have been, though there was an awful moment in the hospital at Milanowek, near Warsaw, where we arrived with our transport.

We asked to be excused from the medical examination and to be allowed to leave. The doctor said that our plaster dressings were made from some unsuitable material which would flake. He was preparing to change them, but I stopped him. "Please don't waste your time," I urged. "There are people more severely wounded than we are. Please let us go on through." He looked at us thoughtfully for a moment, then understood. He signed the pass, and we were free.

Before leaving Warsaw, I spent quite a long time with Marcysia. The experience of last July had taught me that there was no certainty that our "air bridge" would actually materialize, and just in case it did not, I wanted to learn everything she could tell me about the land route. Some higher authority probably also realized this because even before the Chairman told me about my new mission, a radiogram was sent to London, signed by General Bor, announcing that Zych would be sent by land and asking that a route be organized for me from the Reich either through the frontier with Denmark toward Stockholm or else through Switzerland. The old route via France and Spain had long since been cut by the front line.

All the archives of Zaloga were burned during the Rising. Of the international liaison team, two women of incredible energy and courage remained: Marcysia and her assistant Zo. During the two months of the Rising all contacts with abroad were cut off, and the cell which provided false identity papers was destroyed. Without the help of this cell, crossing frontiers was impossible; even movements within the *General Gouvernement* had become dangerous. After leaving Warsaw we were told to go to Kielce and wait there for an air force man, "Sum," who would be in charge of the air bridge and the choice of a pick-up point.

Later the same day we boarded a train to Kielce, which was so crowded that it was easier to get on it through the carriage window than through the door. At Kielce we did not go straight to Marcysia's contact. It was an old one from before the Rising, and much might have changed. We went to a friend of Greta's who had hidden her sister Jula for a few months when she had to disappear from Warsaw for a time after being "blown."

As people wounded in the Rising, we were received with open arms and great cordiality. Neighbors also came to see us. In the earliest days after the Rising people were very excited about arrivals from Warsaw; it was necessary to tell them the whole story from beginning to end. The poor-quality plaster with which my arm was bandaged had begun to crumble, and I was afraid that the rolls of film might start to fall out. Greta's dressing was worrying her because it was stuck to her skin. We had to get rid of this nuisance, but it was difficult to do so in the presence of our hosts, so concerned about the "wounded" from Warsaw.

Kielce was a small town. I quickly found out that our contact, who had been a teacher in a secondary school before the war, was still there. After giving the passwords as usual, we told him frankly who we were, what we were carrying, and for whom. I asked him to accommodate us in the safest place he could find. "I am not worried about my own skin," I explained, "only about our important mission."

The man pondered, then suddenly smiled. "It's always calmest near the eye of the hurricane. I will put you two in a building facing Gestapo headquarters. It won't be comfortable, because the people are poor, but it will be safe."

We had to get rid of the plaster and dressings before moving to the safe house, so we went into a hallway for the operation. I was much relieved when Greta got my plaster cast off. The rolls of film were transferred to the secret pocket in her bag. It was worse for her. The cheap mixture, put directly on her skin, without any gauze, was stuck so tightly that once we got it off, very painfully for her, it left a flesh wound about four inches long.

By a piece of bad luck, just as we were going back onto the street to find our new hiding place, we met Greta's friend, the lady who a short time before had said farewell to the "wounded from Warsaw." Now here they were again, without plaster or bandages. Astounded, she looked at us with utter contempt, and as we passed her we heard her exclaim: "What frauds!"

The safe house where we were lodged was really miserable. It consisted of a kitchen and one small room, in the ceiling an enormous hole, under the hole, an equally enormous basin. When it rained water poured into the basin in a steady stream. The inhabitants consisted of a mother, two daughters of seventeen and eighteen, and a fourteen-year-old boy. They gave us the one room and all moved into the kitchen. We were to spend ten days here awaiting Sum, the organizer of the air bridge.

From the first we felt that the mother and her children lived in a strange sort of isolation. The woman, although a talkative person, did not speak to her neighbors. The little house had many tenants, but none of them ever called upon this family. The children spent all day at home, paying little attention to the other teenagers playing in the courtyard—an odd family, we thought.

The riddle was solved accidentally. In our room two photographs of a young married couple hung on the wall. In the bride I recognized our hostess. "Is this your husband?" I asked her, pointing to the photograph. "Yes it is," she answered and her expression changed. "Is he dead?" She nodded without a word. "The Germans—," I guessed aloud. She answered by bursting into tears. "No," she sobbed, "not the Germans. Our own people!"

I was stunned. So this is the safest place in Kielce. We were in the home of a widow of a traitor, executed on the verdict of an underground court. "But it was a mistake!" she cried. "A terrible mistake!" When I did not respond, she ran out to the kitchen, sobbing. We wasted no time in seeking out our protector from the Home Army. Hardly containing my indignation, I asked him for an explanation.

"Go back there and don't lose any sleep. I have accommodated people more important than you there. And before you go to bed, don't forget to apologize to that woman. She has been of the greatest service to us, although she has every right to hate us. I can't tell you what that woman has lived through."

He told us the story briefly. "Before the war, one 'Witek' (apparently a Volksdeutscher from Yugoslavia) lived with his wife in Kielce. After the Germans arrived, he cooperated with the Gestapo and persecuted people. Because he knew everyone in and around town, he was a real terror. Because of him, many people went to jail, to concentration camps, and to their deaths. Witek's wife was a teacher in a public school. The husband of the woman in whose house you are staying taught in the same school. Witek's wife was afraid to walk home alone—she knew that she was in danger—so she terrorized this colleague into walking home with her each day. In this way the rumor started that he was somehow linked with the Witeks and thus was also a traitor. He received an anonymous letter sentencing him to death. He came to me with the letter and asked what to do. I told him: you have no recourse; you must disappear from Kielce. I do not know who issued the verdict, maybe the communists or perhaps NSZ.* So he did as I advised, left his wife and children, and transferred to a school in Checiny. A week or two later, he was found in his apartment dead on the floor in a pool of blood, with a bullet in his head."

"Sir," he continued, "what that woman suffered! Everyone said that since our people shot him, he must have been a traitor. Nobody would touch his body until his wife and children arrived from Kielce. Even the priest did not want to bury him. And yet she has been helping us all the time since, hiding people for us, and weapons too. Her place is safe because no one goes there and no one suspects anything."

When we returned to the flat I kissed my hostess' hand, and Greta kissed her on both cheeks. She did not say anything, but her

---

*The NSZ was an extreme right-wing underground organization which was not subordinate to the AK commander-in-chief.

eyes filled with tears. Perhaps this time they were tears of pride. I had no opportunity to confirm this story or to find out more details, but the visit of Colonel "Garda," the commander for the Cracow area, brought confirmation of a kind. He had come to talk with me, but I noticed that he greeted our hostess with great friendliness and warmth.

At last this mysterious Sum, who was to organize the air bridge, emerged. I had hoped that it would be the same man who received us at Tarnow, but it appeared that the Tarnow group had been dispersed long ago. Sum informed us that the British had approved sending a Dakota but that the preparations would take some time. Passengers would be notified and brought to the pick-up point when everything was ready. The next day we started for Cracow.

We made the trip with heavy hearts. Greta was bringing her parents not only a son-in-law but also the terrible news about the death of her sister. She did not want me to witness such a tragic homecoming, so we parted at the station, she to her home and I to the flat of a prewar university friend. A few hours later Greta took me to her parents. In spite of the terrible news they had just heard, they greeted me on the threshold with bread and salt, as the old Polish custom dictated. "We lost a daughter," said my mother-in-law, in tears, "but we welcome a son."

Before I had time to establish contact with Marcysia, I received an order from Teddy Bear to go to him at Czestochowa. At an appointed time I was to walk up and down in a prearranged place until he arrived. From the distance I saw him coming. He greeted me with a broad smile. "Let's go into the church," he said. "It will be safest there."

The situation he outlined to me was tragic. In the part of the country still held by the Germans, there was complete chaos and a defeatist attitude among the people. The Home Army was like a wheel, with all its spokes pointed at its hub—in Warsaw. At the moment of the Rising, when the city was cut off from the rest of the country, that hub was shattered and the spokes were strewn in all directions. The central command had, in a practical sense, ceased to exist. In the provinces each commander of a district ruled his own area and made his own decisions. The Home Army had become a body without a head. "Just imagine the situation after the defeat," he said. "When I had left Warsaw and was trying to take it all in hand, to rebuild the whole organization, there comes an order from the chief of staff in London, General Kopanski. The Home Army is to be directly subordinated to General Tatar in London. He is to command it from that distance."

He was so agitated that he stopped talking for a moment. Then he went on: "Were it not for 'the Doctor' [the Government Delegate], I would be penniless because I have been cut off from organizational funds. My authority with the area commanders has been undermined, and everybody gets in touch with the headquarters in London direct, behind my back, and does what he likes. How can one rebuild our organization and morale in such circumstances?"

Okulicki ordered me, while waiting for the air bridge, to go back toward Warsaw, meet the Government Delegate and representatives of the parties, and report to him on my return from the meeting. "I am confident that the air bridge will soon be successful," said Teddy Bear, "and that in a few weeks you will be in London." He wanted me to persuade our leadership in London that either he should be put firmly in command of the Home Army or Tatar should be sent back to Poland to take over. No underground organization, he argued, can be run from a distance. He also gave me a mass of detailed instructions pertaining to my post. The chief of staff of the Cracow area was to supply me with reports and material for military intelligence. Teddy Bear was very anxious that the British know that, after the collapse of the Rising, Home Army intelligence was operating as before. The Cracow area caused him the least worry. I was to be given a detailed assessment of the Rising prepared by someone on his staff, his own report on the situation after the Rising, and guidelines for the future.

Chapter 38

The six weeks after my meeting with Okulicki in Czestochowa were spent in a continuous shuttling between Cracow, Czestochowa, and the outskirts of Warsaw. The railway line from Cracow to Pruszkow had replaced Warsaw's Nowy Swiat as our main street. The authorities of underground Poland, who had been in the capital, were now scattered along this route, and the Government Delegate and representatives of the parties were to be found in the suburban localities.

The need for meetings meant that all the leaders were continuously on the move, and this was neither safe nor practical. It was much easier to lose oneself in a city of over a million people like Warsaw than in Czestochowa, not to mention the residential suburbs. Luckily, all the underground brotherhood had been submerged in the great mass of refugees fleeing from the capital. The railway line from Pruszkow to Cracow was used by everybody: some were looking for their families and friends, others only for a roof to put over their heads. As before, of course, there were also people who lived by smuggling in these hordes.

In Cracow, even before the train reached the station platform, the crowds would rush up to it and try to get on, through the windows if they could. Fights would break out. Those who acted alone had no chance, so partnerships were formed on the spot, based on the principle: first I lift you up, and then you pull me up. The crowding in the compartments and corridors surpassed all imagination. One of our political leaders swore that he had made the whole four-hour trip from Pruszkow to Czestochowa without having once touched foot to the floor of the car. Getting to the W.C. at the end of the car was out of the question, even if three or four passengers had not been crowded in there. Since the train dragged along unmercifully for hours, this was a truly agonizing problem.

The greatest difficulty, however, was the continual "thinning out" of the population, particularly the inhabitants of Warsaw, by the Germans in their searches on station platforms, on streets, and in homes. This procedure was all the more effective because identity documents, when false, were usually poor forgeries.

In accordance with Okulicki's orders, I first reported to the Government Delegate. He was decisive and firm, as he had been during our first meeting two days before the Rising. "That is the way people are," he began; "after every catastrophe, they try to place responsibility upon someone else so as to absolve themselves of it. Thus," he continued, "I order you to facilitate matters for our people in London by telling them that I, Stanislaw Jankowski, accept full responsibility for all that has happened. I was the one who made the decision and authorized General Bor to start the Rising."

I did not have the impression that, despite all that had happened, he regretted his decision or considered it to have been the wrong one. He maintained, just as he had done before the Rising, that there was no alternative. To refrain from fighting the Germans at a moment when it was clear that they were in retreat would have been a departure from the line Poland had consistently followed since September 1939: the nation would not have allowed it. A massacre could have been avoided only by voluntarily giving way to Soviet puppets. If this had been done, in all probability the Red Army would not have stopped its advance at the edge of the city.

Jankowski thought that the Uprising disaster and all that happened after it broke out had forced a change in policy only on one point: it made no sense for the Polish underground authorities to reveal their identities to the Russians. It might be possible but only within the framework of a guarantee of immunity and unrestricted political activity to the Polish underground leaders from the three great powers. Jankowski believed that sooner or later it would be necessary to come to such an agreement. The Anglo-Americans were not suicidal, he mused, nor, in their own best interest, could they allow Russia to decide alone, without them, the fate of half of Europe.

Jankowski's most important demand was that London arrange for supplies of food and clothing for the seven hundred thousand people who had been expelled from Warsaw. This help should come by all routes possible, he said—via the International Red Cross, the neutral countries, the Vatican, or, if no other way were possible, parachute drops.

After the conversations with the Government Delegate I had to prepare as best I could for my mission to London. A political test awaited me both with the Poles and with the foreigners. The documents, testimony, information, and facts I had collected were to constitute my arsenal, but I knew that in such situations much depends on one's own initiative. This time I was not left entirely on my own. Teddy Bear was most helpful in providing what was necessary for London. While waiting for the air bridge I frequently had long conversations with him. Okulicki's way of life demanded great personal sacrifices. His office was in a small ground-floor apartment, formerly belonging to a Jewish family, consisting of one room without heat, with bare walls and primitive washing facilities, furnished only with a table and a few chairs. He lived in conditions bordering on misery.

My conversations with Teddy Bear were not limited to service matters. He very willingly reminisced. The son of peasants in the village of Okulice, he had frequently looked death in the face. He became a member of the underground at the very beginning, when it was being organized. He took on one of the most dangerous commands, which was the Lodz district, and when things got too dangerous there, in 1940, he was transferred to Lwow, which was then under Soviet occupation. He was arrested by the NKVD on an informer's tip, given a death sentence, and imprisoned in Russia.

Freed from prison when Hitler attacked Russia and Stalin proclaimed an amnesty for all Polish prisoners and prisoners-of-war, he found himself in the ranks of the Polish army formed in the USSR under General Anders. He left the country with this army. In Italy, when a second Soviet occupation threatened and he was about to be given command of a division, he declared his wish to return to Poland. Undertaking a new task—the creation of an underground organization at the moment when the Germans were about to be replaced by a Soviet occupation—he had no doubt that sooner or later he would be returned to a Soviet prison and that this time he would not emerge. He assumed the AK command when the organization was in disarray, had lost its headquarters, and was threatened by anarchy.

He told me that, before the outbreak of war between Germany and Russia, the NKVD dignitaries would invite various high-ranking Polish prisoners for talks, accompanied by brandy and tea. Rumors were rife that some of them were willing to collaborate. After the outbreak of the German-Soviet war, when all these Poles were released from Russian prisons, they eyed one another with suspicion. Soon after their release, as a way of making amends, Stalin gave a banquet in honor of these recent prisoners. "At one point," Okulicki told me, "Stalin saw me at this affair, came up to me with a glass, and clinked it against mine. Ten minutes later, the same thing happened again. I at once felt the eyes of all those present turned in my direction: Stalin was singling Okulicki out! I was feeling very uneasy, and when Stalin came up to me with his glass a third time, I said to him, with due respect, but so loudly that I could be heard by the others, "Marshal Stalin, I feel honored that you have been singling me out, but I would be happy to know why." "You see," said Stalin, "you have the same kind of mug as a guide who once, in tsarist times, smuggled me across the Austrian border. That other man was also pockmarked, your height, and broad-shouldered. Whenever I see you, I think I am looking at that man."

When telling me this story, Okulicki added that he kept wondering whether Stalin's gesture was a calculated one—whether he was already looking for another Berling (the Polish general in the Soviet service) and trying to win him over—or whether his interest was the normal, human gesture he had said it was.

Okulicki made his decisions quickly and without hesitation. For example, he received a report that the Germans were to form a Polish National Committee in Cracow and local committees in every district. The Germans were to nominate the members of the committees, without consulting the "candidates." On the central committee a bishop was to sit, in each district a priest. Okulicki decided in a flash that all the people nominated should be warned so that they could choose between a German and a Polish bullet. Luckily the Germans did not have enough time to carry out these plans.

When I went to Czestochowa to say farewell to Okulicki, I

found him for the first time in a somber mood. I asked him whether something unpleasant had happened. "Yes," he said, "but let's speak about it later." I then asked him to explain in detail the military situation in Warsaw at the moment of the outbreak of the Rising. I had with me a small map of Poland. The general marked in pencil the disposition of the forces, the Soviet front line, and the main directions of the Soviet attacks during the offensive. I later had time to make a microfilm of this map and add it to my London "mail."

Before leaving, I asked him once more whether something disastrous had happened. "Yes," he answered, "just before you arrived, I received confirmation that my only son, Zbigniew, was killed in action in Italy. He was twenty. Until today I have been trying to believe that the report was not true. I loved nobody in my life as I loved him."

Chapter 39

*T*hrough all of October, November, and into the middle of December preparations continued for the fourth air bridge. It was to transfer an entire delegation from the underground to London, as well as trace an overland route which Greta and I would follow in the event that the air operation failed. The decision to travel together was not made for purely personal reasons this time. After the destruction of the cell that issued false documents, getting papers for safe travel across the Reich presented serious difficulties. Marcysia warned us beforehand that she did not have sufficient technical equipment to forge satisfactory identity cards. In those circumstances we came to the conclusion that a young couple traveling together would look less suspicious than a man alone. (Later events fully confirmed this guess.)

In Cracow the whole work of Zaloga was continued by the indefatigable women Marcysia and Zo. It seemed to me that in that period all Zaloga's efforts were focused on the problem of getting us safely to London. There were two possibilities: through Denmark to Stockholm or through Switzerland to liberated France. The task of headquarters—that is, London—was to arrange to have a guide meet us on the German side and to get us across a border.

Efforts to find a Danish route failed. On the other hand, ''Wera'' (our base in Bern in Switzerland) had some contacts with Swiss intelligence or counterintelligence, which had its network of agents in Germany near Freiburg. I protested when someone at Zaloga warned us that the people involved were German communists, but London sent a denial—as it later appeared, wrongly.

On December 8, Colonel "Rudy" summoned us to appear at the hideout near Piotrkow. Everything was ready for the fourth air bridge. From my own experience, however, I knew that this message did not mean that the operation would definitely proceed. Weather conditions are worse in December than in July: it might begin to snow at any time. Then too, the aircraft might crash or be shot down. In conversation with Marcysia we decided that in case of an accident Greta would go to Switzerland alone, taking duplicates of the "mail." If the air bridge were delayed more than ten days, I would return to Cracow and we would go on together. Fortunately, our photographer in Cracow had made the microfilms in duplicate or even triplicate just in case of trouble.

I collected Teddy Bear's "mail" from his liaison girl, "Janka," in the chapel of the monastery of Jasna Gora, where the famous picture of the Black Madonna hangs, for centuries the object of pilgrimages and worship, like Lourdes in France. I had made an appointment with her for early morning. To the accompaniment of trumpets and bass drums, the curtain screening the picture slowly began to rise and the eyes of the devout crowd were fixed on the serene face of the Madonna. At that moment Janka slid a tiny parcel to me under the bench, then, after a few moments, left the chapel. For the last time, I prayed before that miraculous picture, beseeching Our Lady of Czestochowa to intercede to see my "mail" safe at its destination.

The mail this time was bulky. It included Teddy Bear's guidelines, an enormously elaborate document containing his assessment of the situation and a program for present and future action. He had worked on it night after night and had written it out in longhand. Photographs of the Rising, ninety-five of them, made up most of the bulk. I had selected them myself before leaving Warsaw. A typewritten caption was stuck to every one of them. Because they were intended for the press, I would not let the photographic emulsion be removed before they were microfilmed. There were photographs of underground newspapers, proclamations, posters, etc. The photographs of the Rising were concealed in three batteries of a pocket flashlight. All the other stuff was hidden in a lighter and two door keys. Some German marks for a rainy day were buried in a stick of shaving soap, American dollars in a large spool of thread.

In Piotrkow, which we reached the next day, I met Wladyslaw Jaworski of the National Party. We were taken in a peasant's cart to a small hut in a remote village. The hut had one small room and one narrow bed. Neither of us was fat and we managed to fit into the bed, but turning over in the night was a problem: the one on the outside fell on the floor at least once each night, while the one next to the wall was safe, so, to be fair, we changed places every night.

The rest of the company, the representatives of three other political parties, "Rudy," the officer in command of the whole operation, and the wireless operator, "Gapa," with his colleague and their short-wave radio, were allocated quarters in a manor house a few miles away. The concentration of so many people in one place seemed to me careless from the security point of view, especially as the radio transmitter could easily be traced through goniometric readings. In those days manor houses were visited almost every night by the forest detachments of the Home Army, by partisans of the People's Army, or by the German police or Wlasow's gangs[*] that operated in those areas. The hut was cold, uncomfortable, and damp, but it was at least safe.

The days of waiting for the airplane began, but how different from those at the Brindisi base! I did not want to visit the manor house—there were too many strangers there—so I spent whole days with Jaworski, who proved an interesting and good-humored companion.

Winter had not yet set in; only here and there did thin patches of snow dot the fields. We wandered across pastures, meadows, and dikes along the banks of the Pilica and through the nearby woods. The feel of a late Polish autumn was in the air—tender melancholy and gentle calm. I inhaled the smell of damp earth and woods, feasted my eyes on sunsets, and absorbed that indescribable mood that Chopin expressed so well in his music, trying to fix the image of this land in my memory forever, somehow certain that I would never see it again.

We spent the long December evenings inside the hut, mostly in

---

[*]Wlasow's gangs were units of Russians, prisoners of war recruited by Germany, used against Polish partisans and the general population.

darkness but sometimes around a small petrol lamp, in a tiny circle of light. There was no radio receiver, but sometimes our future companions would call on us, among them Gapa, who was the operator on the third air bridge. He told us what it had been like at Tarnow while we waited near Brindisi for his Morse signals. Now the story was repeated. In the morning, if we were told that there would be no message that day, we could go out for walks. Some time after our arrival, a signal came that weather conditions were good along the entire route, putting us on alert. We waited in suspense for the next bulletin. Somewhere between one and two o'clock in the afternoon we heard that the alert had been canceled. "Rudy" consoled us by saying that conditions for the air bridge had improved since July because the plane could stop for refueling at Ancona, making the direct flight to Poland much shorter; also, he said, the long nights made flight conditions much safer.

At last, on December 15, the long-awaited signal came to us from the manor house. A few hours later they heard that the aircraft had left Brindisi en route to Ancona. Darkness fell around 5 P.M., and Brindisi informed us that the Dakota was to start from Ancona at 4:30 P.M. and to land near us about 8 P.M. This time we were certain that the operation would be on that day. Just before 3 P.M. a new message reached us: Rudy had canceled the operation. Soon the dismal news came that the air bridge must be postponed indefinitely and that for the time being everybody was to disperse.

I later learned that a group of Wlasow's people had appeared at the manor house and made a search. The number of men staying there did not arouse suspicion because all these manor houses were filled with refugees from Warsaw. The search was limited to the checking of identity cards. However, one of the officers stumbled onto the accumulators for the short-wave transmitter. The owner of the house explained calmly that the accumulators provided current for the alarm siren on the roof, and even pretended to test it to convince them. The rest was accomplished with generous doses of vodka.

I at once went to meet Rudy. I had to make a vital decision quickly—whether to continue to wait for the air bridge or to start the overland journey to Switzerland. By the first route, I could be in London within two or three days; by the second, the journey might last a month, two months, or even longer. The risk connected with the flight, compared with the trip through Germany and the crossing into Switzerland, was minimal, but would it materialize at all?

The present landing place had a much stronger ground staff than that for the third air bridge in July, Rudy claimed. Near Tarnow they had had a team of about one hundred men; here there was a concentration of about two thousand partisans, which undoubtedly reflected the importance Teddy Bear attached to the operation. I asked Colonel Rudy straight out why, with such a force at his disposal, he did not risk a landing under battle conditions. Two thousand people with any sort or arms could surely hold off an attack by Wlasow's gang, I thought.

"And what would happen to the ones who remain here?" he asked.

"They would have time to escape!"

"It's easy for you to say that. You would be in Brindisi, but all hell would break loose here. This area is saturated with detachments of Wlasow's units. I cannot take the risk."

I thought that Rudy, who had impressed me as a very courageous officer, was showing less determination than our Captain Wlodek, who in July had given the signal for the Dakota to come in and had not canceled it even though there was a German detachment some eight hundred yards from the landing strip. I therefore decided not to wait any longer, and told Rudy that. If the air bridge did come later, others would be available in London. On the other hand, if I did not go by land and nothing came of the bridge, nobody would get there.

Immediately after my return to Cracow, I began to prepare for our departure. We could not lose even one day. Headquarters informed me that the guide would wait near the Swiss border only until Christmas. Luckily, Marcysia had not wasted the week we spent waiting for the air bridge. Freiburg was at the German border near the front line. In order to find out whether getting there and moving about in the area would be possible for us, Zo set off to test the route. She took the train and returned without any mishap.

I now met Zo for the first time, but I had heard a lot about her from officers of Section Six in London. Even in the underground, Zo was a legendary figure. At the beginning of 1941 she was brought from Silesia to serve in Warsaw, where she was posted to Zaloga. From the middle of 1941 she had shuttled between Warsaw and Berlin carrying mail which, via some Swedes and our base in Stockholm, was sent on to London, and bringing back incoming mail from London. Later she was made assistant to Marcysia and in that capacity was sent to London in 1942 to improve the courier and mail service in collaboration with Section Six. Her route was long, across God knows how many frontiers. She was feared by all of Section Six. She would berate everybody, including the chief, for not giving Zaloga enough help. She returned to Poland by parachute; she was the only woman parachutist in the Home Army. Jarach's betrayal cost her an entire family. She had the reputation of being tough and unbending; but she did not spare herself either. Her devotion to duty was almost fanatical.

My impression at our first meeting upheld her reputation. She was of middle height, blond and blue-eyed, slightly masculine. She was serious, rather stern, tough, and very matter-of-fact. During our conversation she did not smile once, did not utter a single word of a personal nature, and stuck exclusively to business. She had no time to waste. But when we parted she did shake my hand firmly, sigh, and say, "Pray God that you get there!"

She gave me many valuable practical tips, described the route minutely, and gave me descriptions of the safe houses and the passwords. We were to go to Kappel, a village three miles to the southeast of Freiburg, pass through the village, and find a large lonely farm outside it. The farmer's wife was a tall, stocky woman of about seventy; the password was "Grüsse für Brunhilde" ("Greetings for Brunhilde").

In the Czestochowa Arbeitsamt (labor office) was an official who belonged to the organization. We applied through him for work in the Reich and obtained official, entirely authentic documents, directing us to work in a sawmill in Freiburg. Their drawback was that, like our train tickets, they were good only in one direction. If anything went wrong on arrival, there would be no return. The only safeguard was Zo's promise that after a time she would come to Kappel to see that all had gone well.

The false Kennkarten that Greta and I got from Marcysia were made out in two different surnames, so that the arrest of one of us did not automatically mean the arrest of the other. However, they were such bad forgeries that they might awaken suspicion even on a cursory inspection. We went to the market in Cracow where stalls sold second-hand clothes. I still remembered the ironic look of the Swedish customs officer as he read "workman" in my passport while looking at my clothes. This time there must be no mistakes: the Gestapo were not Swedes. I bought a much-used and slightly shabby, but warm, peasant's sheepskin, an old cap, a worn suit, and heavy scuffed work boots. Greta bought a pair of high laced boots.

We left Greta's parents house in the evening of December 19, 1944. The people who bade us farewell had been robbed by the war of two children, and now the third and last was leaving. They realized the danger to which we would be exposed, but they uttered not a single word to stop us or to appeal to their daughter's feelings, as they parted with the only treasure they had left.

On the hall landing we turned to look at them for the last time, and then they did not try to hide their tears.

They awaited our return, always hopeful, for twenty-four years of a lonely, frighteningly sad old age. They died in 1968, almost at the same time, and are resting in the cemetery of Cracow, far from the graves of the two other children who were killed in action.

Chapter 40

*O*ut of habit we lined up in front of the ticket window at the railway station; then I remembered that volunteers for labor in the Reich were entitled to free railway tickets to their destinations. Such a ticket could be an additional safeguard in case the Gestapo checked our documents, so we moved over to a special ticket window, quite unaware that this act was to save our lives later.

A minor disaster occurred when we were on the platform. Greta dropped the huge thermos flask filled with hot coffee that was to sustain us on the long trip, and it smashed to bits. "One for the road!" I laughed. "That's for good luck."

We decided to separate and board different carriages for safety, as our counterfeit papers were crudely forged. Just outside Cracow, we crossed the border of the *General Gouvernement*. The document control passed without a hitch. I kept looking out the window to make sure that Greta was not being hauled off along the platform; she was probably looking out of another window to see whether I was being taken away by the border police. When the train moved on at last, I groaned with relief.

Passenger rail traffic had been completely disrupted by the nightly bombings of large cities and the mass movements of evacuation trains. Our train crawled along, stopping at signals, waiting hours at small wayside stations. We had been warned that, even with the best of luck, our journey across the Reich would take at least two days and two nights.

Bleary-eyed and weary, I was standing in the train corridor when we finally reached Gliwice well past midnight. Suddenly the car was almost empty. I entered a compartment, sat down in a corner, and immediately fell asleep. I was wakened by a shout: "Raus!" A civilian with a suitcase was leaning over me. "Sitzende Plätze sind nur für Deutsche!" ("Seats are only for Germans!"), he shouted, adding a burst of German epithets. I got up without a word and went back to standing in the corridor. The new passenger sprawled across the empty bench with an air of triumph. Greta joined me toward morning, tired of this self-imposed separation. From then on we traveled together, trying to snatch some sleep while leaning against the wall.

By nightfall the train reached its destination, Nuremberg. At the station we found that we would have to wait till morning for a train to Stuttgart. We spent our second night in the station waiting room, thick with smoke and jammed with civilians fleeing from their bombarded cities. All the seats were taken, and it was hard to find even a spot on the floor for a few moments of sleep. Among this crowd I noticed a soldier in a worn and wrinkled uniform searching for cigarette stubs on the floor. "A deserter," I guessed, and then realized that there were no military police anywhere in sight and that there had been no examination of documents since we crossed the border. A year earlier there would have been at least three controls by then.

Some time around midnight the air-raid sirens screamed. The crowd in the waiting room jumped up and milled around in search of a shelter. The waiting room emptied in one second flat. At last we could stretch out more comfortably. As it turned out, there was no bombing that night—the Allied planes must have flown over to another target.

Early in the morning the train for Stuttgart finally pulled in. Standing in the corridor, Greta, whose German was much more fluent than mine, strained to catch snatches of the passengers' conversation, but the talk was only of the war and the bombings. Our German fellow travelers consoled each other with propaganda slogans gleaned from newspapers: "The war is not yet lost," "Many things can still happen." Was it only because of fear of the Gestapo that nobody was complaining?

Suddenly there was a movement at the far end of the car.

"Ausweise bitte." Two Gestapo men in plainclothes entered the car to check documents. They worked their way down the corridor from the opposite ends. Our faces set in masks of indifference, we awaited our turn.

The control was quick: a glance at the document, a short "Danke," and on to the next passenger. When it came to our turn, the Gestapo man glanced at our identity cards and hesitated for a moment. Then he carefully studied our documents from the Czestochowa Arbeitsamt and turned back again to have another look at our patently counterfeit Kennkarten. Finally, he raised his eyes from the papers and looked at us keenly.

"We're in for it," I thought. I tried to keep my face from twitching and was afraid to look at Greta. We had to endure that look without turning pale, with no sign of tension. With resignation I awaited the words I knew must be coming. But before the German had a chance to open his mouth, our train roared into a tunnel. There were no lights in the cars, and we stood there in total darkness. Even today I have no idea of the length of that tunnel on the Nuremberg-Stuttgart line, but when the three of us were standing there in the dark, it seemed the longest tunnel in the world. I knew the German suspected the authenticity of our identity cards, and a thousand wild thoughts ran through my head. My heart was pounding.

And then we were out in bright daylight again. The Gestapo man made up his mind. "Ihre Fahrkarten?" He examined our tickets, on which the station cashier in Cracow had jotted down the numbers from our documents issued by the Arbeitsamt in Czestochowa, thanked us briefly, and went on. I propped myself against the wall to assist my trembling legs.

Just two nights before our arrival, Stuttgart had suffered its heaviest bombardment of the war. The city was in ruins, the railroad station completely destroyed. Everywhere we looked was a vista of rubble. No one could tell us when, if ever, the next train to Donaueschingen would be leaving. All we could tell was that it certainly would not be before late that afternoon.

We went into town and there saw scenes all too familiar from Poland: people loaded with bundles, lugging suitcases, dragging trunks, scurrying in every direction like ants on a smashed anthill. The walls of the bombed and burning houses blossomed with small bits of paper—people everywhere were looking for a word from their loved ones or leaving messages to tell where they could be found. I had seen the same thing in the Warsaw Rising, when small knots of people, hour after weary hour, patiently scanned such notices amid the rubble.

In our wanderings we came upon the debris of a magnificent rococo palace. We picked our way through the litter of broken pieces of statuary, little angels' heads, remnants of once splendid ornaments and stuccowork, bits and pieces of intricate golden frames and woodwork. Much to my own surprise, instead of taking a vengeful satisfaction in all this, I felt a growing despondency. I could not feel about this devastation as I had when I saw the ruins of the Royal Castle in Warsaw or the ancient houses and buildings I had known and loved from my childhood. Still, the destruction of anything so beautiful was a sad sight, even in an enemy city I had never seen before. I felt keenly the dreadful pointlessness of this annihilation, of all those angels' heads, so painstakingly fashioned by the artist's hand two centuries ago, smashed in the rubbish.

By dawn we were on our way. Despite three sleepless nights and two full days standing on a train, the tension and the excitement as we approached Freiburg at last, made us forget our weariness. We got off at the small station of Kappelertal. Up to this point we had been traveling as volunteers on the way to work at a Freiburg sawmill. We had left our route to that city, and our travel documents were no longer of use. I looked around surreptitiously for a control at the exit, but there was no one posted there, not even to collect tickets.

From bits and pieces of conversations overheard on the train, we had learned that Freiburg had been bombed that very night, and the small country road to Kappel was jammed with homeless people seeking shelter in the countryside. That was all to the good, as far as we were concerned: two foreign laborers in this crowd were not likely to attract attention. After walking for a few miles we reached our destination.

In accordance with our instructions we went on through the village and looked for a farm some distance beyond, but on the edge of the woods there were two farmhouses, one on each side of the road. Which door should be knock at? Which house was the right one? What should we do if in answer to our password "Grüsse für

410

Brunhilde," they asked which "Brunhilde" we were talking about? How to stammer our way out of such a predicament in our halting German?

We made a quick sign of the cross and walked to the house on the left, trusting our luck. We knocked and entered a large room filled with people. No one paid any attention to us. An elderly woman wearing spectacles, her ample bosom covered with an apron, was busy near the stove drying dishes. I guessed she must be the lady of the house and approached her. My heart beating wildly, I whispered to her, "Grüsse für Brunhilde."

She stared, and dropped her dish towel. I could have hugged her. In the midst of enemy country she seemed someone near and dear. Without saying a word she motioned us to follow her. We climbed a winding stair to the attic, where a small, windowless space had been partitioned off with a few boards. The only light came from a little pane of glass in the roof.

"Herr General," the woman began, in a whisper. Because of her dialect, from the few words she spoke, Greta could understand only that the house was full of strangers, but that we were quite safe here. We were to keep quiet and not to open the door to anyone unless there was a special knock, which she demonstrated: knock— pause—knock, knock. She promised she would soon bring us something to eat and drink and told us that "Max" would come for us tomorrow.

I was somewhat startled by my sudden elevation to general's rank but guessed that those who had made the arrangements in Switzerland had decided that a promotion would enhance our standing with these people. Later, while we were eating the meal she provided and thinking of taking a nap, the special knock came at the door. Greta drew back the bolt and in the doorway we saw a German officer, elegant in a major's uniform complete with Iron Cross. He saluted smartly, as befitted one of higher rank, and addressed me as "Herr General."

After a few words he realized that I could not follow what he was saying and asked whether I spoke French. When I said that I did, he asked me in impeccable French whether I would be meeting "Joshua Two" "on the other side." "Of course," I assured him promptly, "I'll see Joshua Two." I had no idea what he was talking about. From radio messages between London and Cracow I had gath-

411

ered that he would be in the hands of a German espionage network which worked for the Swiss. I guessed that the major was a Swiss agent, convinced that we were but two more cogs in the same big wheel.

The major asked me to notify "Joshua Two" that his leave would end soon, on such and such a date, that he would be returning to his unit, and that he would then be able to carry out his assignment. I promised to pass this message on. I noticed that my reticence evoked a growing respect: the major asked whether he could help us in any way. "As a matter of fact, you could," I answered. "We have no Swiss money whatsoever. A few small coins might come in handy."

The major promised he would do what he could. He seemed tempted to sit down and have a good chat with us, but generals do not encourage such behavior. I gave him my hand and wished him good day. He bade us farewell, clicked his heels, and left. When his footsteps had gone, we looked at each other and burst out laughing.

Our hostess also came to see us a few times, trying to strike up a conversation. We managed to make out that both she and her husband were working for the Swiss not just for money but also because they hated Hitler. "Der Krieg ist verloren! Gott sei dank! ['The war is lost! Thank God!'] Any day now the Americans will liberate us from that devil!" She hoped we would not forget them and would come back to visit her, driving a big American car.

We spent two nights at the farmhouse. On the morning of Christmas Eve, our guide, Max, a puny little fellow with large ears sticking out under a floppy cap, came to pick us up. In saying goodbye our hostess gave us a Swiss half-franc piece left for us by the major. Talking constantly, Max led us up a steep path. We gathered that he worked in a nearby copper mine; he was one of a dozen or so communists there. They had made friends with some Russians, forced labor brought from the Soviet hinterlands. They all hated the fascists and could not wait for their downfall. After midnight, Christmas Day, we were to start for Switzerland so as to take advantage of the holidays. While in his house, up on the mountainside, we would do well to stay clear of his downstairs neighbors, he warned us. His wife, Kunegunde, could be trusted, but we had to be careful in front of his son because one never knew what a boy his age might repeat at school.

About a mile up the hill, walking through snow-covered woods, we came to a small clearing and a lonely log cabin muffled in snow. Spruce branches weighed down with pillows of snow brushed against the windows. The peaceful silence was occasionally broken by the sound of distant artillery. The front was only some eight miles west of us on the Rhine. Suddenly there was a deafening roar of engines, and six light bombers passed in formation just above the treetops. It was good to see the American markings on the wings.

Upstairs in the cabin where Max lived, there was a large kitchen and one other smaller room. Max's wife, a plump little *Hausfrau*, was clearly unenthusiastic about our arrival and worried about her husband. She moped in the corner, tears in her eyes. This was the strangest Christmas Eve ever. The coming of darkness brought with it memories of what in Poland was traditionally the most hallowed family occasion of the year. We thought about our parents, who would be sitting down to the traditional Polish dinner, wracked with anxiety about our fate. We thought of my mother and my brother, who had left Warsaw for some unknown destination.

Out hosts did not celebrate Christmas Eve. Only the radio, playing "Stille Nacht" over and over again, reminded us of the day. At one point the speaker announced, in solemn tones, an address by Dr. Goebbels. The minister of propaganda was to deliver his last Christmas message to the nation. He began with dramatic greetings to the besieged and surrounded German units in the French ports on the Atlantic seaboard: "Wir rufen Dunkirchen! Wir rufen Lorient!" ("We are calling Dunkirk! We are calling Lorient!").

I could not stand the sound of his voice. I walked over to the radio and turned it off. Immediately eight-year-old Fritz ran into the kitchen to complain to his father. "Vatti," we heard through the half-open door, "that man does not want to listen to Dr. Goebbels!" Max entered the room and, without a word, turned the radio back on. Later, when the boy was out of the room, he growled: "Don't play with fire! It's dangerous! He could say something about this at school."

We still had hours of waiting ahead of us. It was completely dark when our second guide, "Hans," came in. He brought with him two young Russians deported from the Orel region to the Reich two years before. They worked in the same copper mine and were allowed to move freely within a specified radius around their place of work. They had "UdSSR" painted in white on the back of their clothing, followed by some numbers. They looked no older than eighteen.

For lack of something better to do, we began talking with the Russians in a weird mixture of German, Polish, and Russian. When political subjects were mentioned, I was amazed to hear them repeat old slogans from *Pravda* and *Izvestia*. Was it possible, I wondered, that after two years in Germany they still feared the NKVD? But soon I had to conclude that they were speaking with conviction. Like an old record, they repeated mechanically everything that had been impressed on their minds at school and by newspapers, books, and radio. We had before us typical products of an indoctrination carried out under conditions of total isolation from the outside world. With a pang I thought that after twenty years or so of communist education our own children in Poland might be turned into automatons like those two. How wrong I was!

Around 2 A.M. we began to get ready. The Germans brought out three guns, two for themselves and one for us. It was pretty obvious that Max had had little military experience, for as soon as he had loaded his gun, he accidentally pulled the trigger. The noise of the shot reverberated like thunder in the room as the bullet went into the floor. We all grew pale and listened for a few minutes for some reaction from the neighbors downstairs. Everything was quiet down there, and so we started on our way.

It was a beautiful night, but very cold. Frozen snow crunched under our boots and the sky was so full of stars it was almost as bright as day. We walked in single file up a steep path, first Max and Hans, then the two of us, with the two Russians bringing up the rear. "What a world!" I whispered to Greta. "Here we are, sandwiched between the Germans and the Russians, just like Poland. German and Russian communists escorting the Polish underground!"

After some time we reached the copper mine and entered. It was deserted at this hour. We moved along the narrow winding corridors hewn out of rock, walking on slippery pathways and duckboards. Down in the mine it seemed even colder than outdoors. Finally we left the underground labyrinth and continued our climb on a steep trail in the woods. After two hours the woods ended and we reached the top of the mountain. Flickering flashes of light crisscrossed the horizon to the west. We could hear the rumble of artillery from that direction, muted by distance but still loud. The view from the summit made me realize how close we were to the front line on the Rhine. Von Rundstedt's offensive in the north must have revived the fighting along the entire front if the firing kept up even at night.

Almost at the same moment we both looked toward the northeast, where the mountains gradually dissolved into a vast plain, stretching beyond the horizon. In answer to our unspoken thoughts, Hans waved his hand in that direction and said: "Ihre Heimat ist da"—"your homeland's over there." We soon began the descent into the valley, and another life.

Chapter 41

In this part of the country, the border between Switzerland and Germany ran along the Rhine. To swim across, in plain view of Swiss and German border guards, was not a good strategy, but there were two spots along the frontier where Switzerland held small enclaves on the northern bank of the river: the larger one was near Schaffhausen; the other, much smaller, was around Basel, which sprawled on both sides of the Rhine. At this point the Rhine curves at a right angle, and its northward course becomes the Franco-German border.

Before leaving Cracow we had been told that our guides would take us from Kappel to the vicinity of Schaffhausen and then pass us on to "John," an agent sent for us from Switzerland. But when we came down to the tiny village at the foot of the mountain, Todtnau, a difficulty developed. Throughout our arduous hike, our four companions had dragged four bicycles along. In Todtnau we found out that the two Russians were now supposed to go back, while we went on our way by bike.

There was one thing wrong with this scheme: all my life I had always been hopeless at sports and had never learned to ride a bicycle either. Hans therefore tried to carry me on the bar of his bicycle, but I was too heavy and his bike was too light; he quickly had to give that up. What could we do? We were still some forty-five miles from the border. After a brief consultation, Max and Hans decided to change plans and board a small commuting train running from Todtnau to Lörrach. From Lörrach we could cut through the woods on foot and cross the border near Basel. I did not like that idea. We were in a front-line area, I argued, and our documents had been invalid since we left Freiburg, our supposed destination; any control on the train was bound to end in disaster. Our guides reassured us that the Todtnau-Lörrach train was for local workers only and there were no controls. When we reached Todtnau station, however, we found that the train did not run on holidays. As it was Christmas, we had only our feet to count on.

The distance from Todtnau to Basel is no shorter than Schaffhausen to Basel but is far easier to walk than the winding Black Forest trails. Accordingly, we took the road running south parallel to the Rhine, leading to the border town of Lörrach. Agent John would wait in vain near Schaffhausen for our arrival. If all went well, we should make it to Switzerland on our own (with half a Swiss franc in our pockets).

Our guides proposed that they walk ahead about a quarter of a mile so that if they were stopped by a police patrol or border guards, we would have time to dash to the side, hide ourselves, and wait it out. Should we be stopped by a patrol from behind, our guides proposed to start shooting, creating a diversion that would permit us to escape. As a last resort, I had my own gun. The plan was not very practical because the road was crowded with churchgoers, but the fact that this was Christmas turned out to be a blessing for us. Some off-duty border guards returning home glanced warily at the two foreign laborers walking along with their hands in their pockets talking animatedly to each other, but they were in too much of a hurry to get home to their families for Christmas dinner to waste their time on a couple of strangers strolling toward the border. Had I been walking alone, at least one of them would have stopped me to check my documents, but a couple on a holiday did not arouse suspicion.

Our feet began to swell on the long walk on the asphalt, we were exhausted from lack of sleep and the hike in the mountains, but excitement prodded us on. We walked fast because our guides feared that they would be late in returning to work, although, of course, on their way back, they would ride their bicycles. Only twice did we stop to rest and catch our breath. Toward evening we followed our guides into an inn in some small village. It was packed with a festive crowd.

Greta pulled out a slab of bacon (still provisions from Cracow), and Max gave us each a slice of bread. This was our first meal since midnight and would be the last before crossing the border.

When we turned into a small side road leading into the woods, we could see the lights of the town of Lörrach. A military detachment passed by without paying any attention to us. It was almost dark. After walking for what seemed like an eternity, we realized that our guides were not familiar with this area at all. We were wandering aimlessly, with no map or compass. Just as we came out upon a hard-surfaced road cutting through the woods, we had to fling ourselves into a roadside ditch to avoid approaching headlights. A military car shot by above our heads. We were very near the border, and any encounter could end in disaster.

Another hour of stumbling, and Hans discovered that we were back where we had started from. Our exhaustion now made itself felt. I glanced at my watch: 9 P.M. The night was clear and bright, walking was easy in the moonlight, but the cold began to torment us. The thermometer at the inn showed 17 degrees Fahrenheit, but it was probably even colder now. At one point our guides stopped and consulted quietly. They told us that we were no more than half a mile from the border. Hans remained behind, while we followed Max with the utmost caution.

We entered a path running alongside a deep ditch. Max told us to wait. He would go ahead, get his bearings, and then return for us. We went off the path and hid among the trees. Minute after minute ticked by, but there was no sign of Max. Finally we heard feet on the path and saw the outline of a human figure. But was it Max? I could not tell in the uncertain moonlight. As it passed, I called out in a low voice: "Max?" Fortunately, it was Max. He told us that in a hundred feet we would be in Switzerland. We followed him to the top of the hill and saw the glow of the lights of a big city. Basel! A city without a blackout, a city in a neutral country! You are in Switzerland, said Max. All we had to do to reach our goal was to cut across a bit of woods.

We thanked Max effusively and he rushed off without wasting a minute. We hid our Kannkarten under a patch of moss; we would not need them any more. Forgetting our exhaustion, we charged into the woods in the direction of the lights. We had gone no more than a hundred yards when a double row of tangled barbed wire, over six feet high, rose before us. The border! We were furious. Either Max had got cold feet at the last moment or had decided that he and Hans had to start back immediately if they were to get to work in time.

A well-trodden path ran the length of the fence. A delay here was dangerous. We decided to try to get through the barbed wire. Greta crawled along the ground, flattened out like a squirrel, and managed to make it to the other side. I tried to go over the top and ended spread-eagled on the barbed wire. Greta helped me to get free, and I finally landed on the other side, though with my sheepskin jacket badly torn.

To the right there was a lighted building and a guard post with someone moving about, but we were afraid that if we ran into a Swiss guard right on the border we might be tossed back across the line to the German side, so we decided to walk toward Basel. We left the woods and walked across a meadow which gently rolled down toward the Rhine. We could see the empty sentry boxes of the border guard in the distance. Everybody was celebrating that day, either at home or at the inn. The lights of Basel seemed to grow nearer as we walked. Another half an hour, and we reached a sharp ridge. Below us we saw the river and a cluster of houses.

"Look," said Greta. "There's not one light in that village. It's blacked out." "In a tiny village like this everybody would be asleep at this hour," I said. "Let's go down." And so we did. The streets of the village were deserted. Not a soul around. In the small market-place I saw a sign on a building and turned on my flashlight: "Grenzach. NSDAP. Hilfe für Mutter und Kind" ("National Socialist Party of Germany. Assistance for Mother and Child"). We were back again in Germany! (Much later we learned that the Swiss border at this point ran into Germany in a thin triangular wedge. We had entered the narrow triangle on one side, crossed it, and gone out again on the other side. The tangled barbed-wire fences were erected on one side only, in the woods.)

We felt a surge of despair. It was close to midnight and we were at the end of our strength. Greta was a strong young woman in top physical condition, but she moaned that she could go no farther. With the utmost effort we dragged ourselves back into the woods overlooking the Rhine. In Basel, on the other side of the river, the church clocks chimed midnight. Salvation was very near.

I argued that by walking west along the Rhine we must come

on the border again. It had to be very close, perhaps only a matter of a few steps. But Greta could not even stand. I decided to go alone to reconnoiter. Trying to remember the exact spot where I left her, I started off. The frost was getting even more bitter. If we fell asleep out there, it was likely that we would never wake up, if we were not awakened by the Germans. I walked for two hundred feet or so, and there I found the same tangle of barbed wire that had so depressed and infuriated us two hours before!

I dashed back the way I had come, but could not find the spot where I left Greta. I was terrified at the thought of what would happen if I failed to find her. She would think that I had abandoned her. I ran from one tree to the other, my feet sinking to the knees in snow, pulling apart branches, peering under bushes. "O Lord, please help us, do not forsake us!" I prayed feverishly. I wanted to shout but knew that my cries would surely bring the German border guards down on us. It was only by a Christmas miracle that we had not run into anyone so far.

At last, I could think of no other way but to call her name. I heard a small voice answering me from a distance. "Listen," I cried. "We have no time to lose, not a second. The frontier is only two hundred feet away. Your life and mine depend on whether you get up and walk those feet." "I'll go with you—anywhere," I heard her answer. She dragged herself up and slowly staggered over to me. On we went together.

We kept hearing the church clocks of Basel striking the quarter hours. At the edge of the woods there was a field, about a hundred feet across and, farther on, the long line of a tall hedge around some park or garden. Beyond the hedge we saw lights in buildings and shining street lamps. To the right there was a break in the hedge, a gate of some sort, and a barrier with a strong floodlight. It was guarded by a man in uniform, but we could not tell whether he was German or Swiss.

From our hiding place in the woods we surveyed the scene for a long time. We saw another guard ride his bicycle along the hedge, a police dog following close on his heels. We waited till he disappeared and then ran across the field. Squatting down near the hedge we looked right and left, but saw nothing suspicious. It seemed that no one had noticed us. The excitement seemed to give us new strength. We got to the other side of the hedge and through a small gate and discovered that this was not a park or a garden, as we had thought, but an old cemetery. There was a large sign. Trembling, I took out my flashlight to read it. It was posted by the cemetery board of Basel. We were in Switzerland again!

We hurried through the cemetery, trying to find a gate that would open on the broad, brightly lit street beyond, totally deserted at this hour. No success. With one final effort we clambered over the hedge and jumped down to the street. At the bus stop we found a telephone booth and decided to use the only Swiss coin we had. Half a franc was not enough to reach our legation in Bern, we knew, but it was enough to reach someone, anyone we could find with a Polish name in the Basel telephone directory, to ask for help. We looked around—no one. We crept into the booth—and suddenly, out of nowhere, there was a Swiss guard, gun at the ready.

He took us to the police station. A yawning officer asked us exactly where we crossed the Swiss border. "This is our military zone," he explained. "For reasons of security we do not accept any foreigners here." "But we are political refugees," I argued. "If you return us to the Germans, we'll both be shot." "We're not returning *anyone* to the Germans!" The officer was offended. "We merely take you back to the border. They did not see you crossing this way; it's up to you to see that they don't catch you when you go back."

From broken German we switched to French. I explained that we were surrendering to the Swiss authorities with utmost confidence, that we were seeking asylum in Switzerland—the land of the Red Cross—that we were a young couple, just married. The Swiss officer shrugged. "It's not up to me, anyway. It's up to the sector commander. He will make the decision." He picked up the phone and dialed a number.

We waited in silent suspense. We were so exhausted that we could not even think about being sent back to Germany. My last coherent thought was to wonder how to get rid of our "mail."

After a few minutes of rapid conversation in a Swiss-German dialect (of which not even Greta could catch one word), the officer put down the receiver. "All right," he said. "You're lucky. The commander has agreed to let you in. Last week we had to take a dozen people back to the border."

The news revived Greta, but it did not help me much. The joints of my knees were aching agonizingly, and I could barely get down the stairs of the station. It was almost 3 A.M., but the Swiss had their procedures to follow. More dead than alive, we were first taken to a doctor to ensure that we were bringing no contagious disease into the country. Then we were taken to the city police station, where our personal data were recorded and fingerprints and photographs taken. It was dawn when they at last took us to jail.

We were each locked up in a cell with a slop bucket, an iron bed, and a metal chair. Before locking me up, the guards stripped me and took away everything in my pockets, including the "mail." Greta had to surrender only her handbag, in which she was carrying her share of the contraband. However, after two hours everything was returned to me, neatly placed in paper bags. I checked the contents, but nothing was missing. In the morning I was given a mug of black coffee and a plain slice of bread. Switzerland is perhaps equally famous for her Samaritan spirit and for her frugality. I sadly compared the reception I had been given in Sweden when I had twice landed there as a refugee.

That day Greta was transferred to the Zuchthaus, where most of her cellmates turned out to be streetwalkers. There were four Polish women among them—one can never tell where one may run into a compatriot! Some of the ladies were to be released shortly, so Greta wrote a brief and innocuous note to our legation in Bern, including in one sentence a prearranged code word. The Pole took the letter with her but, as we found out later, immediately handed it over to the matron. A few days later, on December 30, both of us were transferred to a schoolhouse on Elisabethstrasse, which served the entire canton as a collection point for refugees. In fact, it was a closed internment camp. The period of our stay there was not defined; the gate leading to the street was closed and guarded by armed soldiers. There was also an armed guard on duty round the clock inside the building. The only bright spot, for those who had some Swiss currency, was the well-stocked canteen.

The dormitories were truly scandalous. What had been schoolrooms were packed with men, women, and children, sleeping anywhere on the floor, on mattresses stuffed with straw. In one and the same room one could find there Volksdeutsche from Mulhouse fleeing before the advancing Allied troops, French collaborators running away from home in fear of retribution, escapees from German concentration camps; victims of Nazi terror, Jews snatched from the camp crematoria, and Italian partisans. Most of the Italians were communists who had been driven across the Swiss frontier by the harassment of the Germans or Italian police. The neutral Swiss packed them all in together, without partiality or favoritism. In our room was a Jewish couple who had escaped from Hungary. Before the war the man had been a university professor. They had lost all their relatives, including their own children, under macabre circumstances. The couple behaved with great dignity, but every night the woman would sob wretchedly, despite the tender whisperings of her husband. Not a word of complaint was heard in the room, though none of us could sleep at all. Those who had escaped the Nazi terror themselves knew this kind of despair all too well, and the Nazis among us who were in flight before the advancing Allies were afraid to open their mouths.

The interned refugees were assigned to various functions by the commanding officer, a captain whose looks and manner reminded us vividly of a Prussian officer. During the day all men were sent out to work unloading transports of military matériel at the railway station or stuffing army mattresses with straw. On Sundays and holidays we were taken to the local zoo—as visitors, of course.

On our first day at Elisabethstrasse I made an official request to be permitted to write to the Polish legation in Bern, and the Swiss made no difficulties about the letter. In it we asked for clothing and money. Not only was walking around in my threadbare work clothes, sweat-stained cap, and tattered sheepskin coat not particularly pleasant, but my outfit thwarted any plans for escape, which was more important. In this respect Greta was more fortunate; her coat and general appearance did not attract attention.

Within a few days through the camp office we received one hundred Swiss francs each and a huge package containing an elegant overcoat, a hat, shoes, and some underwear. Obviously, the recipients of our letter already knew who we were. It seemed strange that there was no reply enclosed with the package. Had it been confiscated by the Swiss? We had hoped to receive hidden instructions about what to expect and how to proceed. Looking for such a message, we opened everything that could be opened in that package and ripped every seam that could be ripped. Nothing! Instead, I was called into the office where Herr Hauptmann himself warned me in a loud voice that "leaving the place of internment and communicating with the Polish authorities and the Polish legation in Switzerland is forbidden."

I could see no solution to our predicament other than escape, since we had received no instructions or information of any kind from Bern. Because of the importance of our mission, every extra day of delay caused us great concern. The front gate on Elisabethstrasse was locked and guarded around the clock. It was impossible to break away in the course of our weekly forays to the zoo or work parties at the station without being noticed. The school courtyard was separated from the adjoining property by a six-foot wall. A garden at the back, also belonging to the school, was blocked on one side by a large apartment house and on the other by another high brick wall, running along a street parallel to Elisabethstrasse.

On Sunday night (January 7, 1945) we bought a bottle of cognac at the canteen and invited to our table a guard who was coming on duty that night. He joined us happily, leaning his gun against the wall. Luckily for us, at this level there were no problems whatsoever with fraternizing. Engrossed in our pleasant conversation, the young guard drained one glass of cognac after another, oblivious of the fact that his hosts were merely pretending to keep up with him. Toward the end of our little party, the guard's mood did not promise alertness that night. After lights out, we lay on our mattresses fully clothed, listening to the chiming of those clocks from the church towers that had marked each quarter hour of our flight across the border on Christmas night.

At 5 A.M. it was still quite dark. I left the room a few minutes after Greta; this was not likely to attract attention since toilets were located in the corridor. Downstairs our guard was snoring loudly. From a shed in the garden we pulled out a ladder that we had noticed there the previous day. In a minute we were over the wall and in the backyard of the adjoining property. Pulling the ladder over, we used it to climb the still higher wall separating us from the street. The ladder reached only halfway up, and the top of the wall was secured with a triple strand of barbed wire. Greta managed the obstacle first and jumped down to the street. I followed, after a lengthy struggle with the barbed wire, finally sliding down the wall minus one of my woolen gloves (from Cracow), which was left impaled on the wire like a calling card for Herr Hauptmann.

At that hour the street was still empty, but no sooner were we standing on the sidewalk than a newspaper boy pedaled his bike round the corner. Had he come upon us a minute earlier, he would have thought we were burglars and would have raised the alarm. Because of the work parties, I knew the way to the station and even the timetable of the trains for Bern. After a few hours on a comfortable electric train, we were there. We reached our legation without any difficulties, probably at about the time when our absence was discovered and the alarm sounded at Elisabethstrasse.

Since I did not know the real names of the officers in charge of our Bern liaison outpost, Wera, I told the janitor at the legation that my name was Zych and demanded to see the minister. "His Excellency never comes in before ten o'clock," I was told. There was not much we could do, so we sat down in the waiting room. After an hour or so, we were joined by three gentlemen in high spirits. They introduced themselves as Major Bronislaw de Ville, Major Choynacki, and Captain Wincenty Slawinski. We gave them our identification, a Polish five-groszy coin with a hole drilled in it, and with great elation surrendered everything we had brought out of Poland: flashlight batteries containing the microfilms of the archives of the Warsaw Rising, the contents of Greta's handbag, and the two keys with letters from General Okulicki, the new commander-in-chief of the Home Army. From then on, all these items would go on their way through safe diplomatic channels. We thought joyfully that the worst was over. And yet, though our hosts were very cordial, we sensed that their welcome was somewhat mixed.

"Why did you have to escape from that place in Basel?" De Ville finally asked. "Sooner or later we would have got you out of it anyway."

"Sooner or later!" I exclaimed indignantly. "We had no sign of life from you for ten days, not a sign of any instructions! What were we to do? We could not delay any longer."

"We'll have trouble with the Swiss," said De Ville. "But I expect we shall manage."

Captain Slawinski then took us to his own apartment. Leaving the legation, I felt some anxiety. Its extraterritoriality gave us a sense of security, but once out of it? Surely the police must suspect we had gone to Bern. I refrained from sharing my misgivings with Captain Slawinski, who was going out of his way to be friendly. "After all," I reasoned, "they must know what they are doing. We are nothing but a parcel in their hands, to be handled with care." The captain and his wife took us to a large department store, and a short while later we emerged looking elegant indeed, Greta in a handsome new coat and a brown velour hat with a broad brim. Everything we had on was now brand new and marked "made in Switzerland."

During the two days we spent in Bern, we had a chance to learn the organization of our mission from the other side of the fence, so to speak. We also heard that both our guides had returned home safely and that each had been paid five thousand Swiss francs per head. This last item did wonders for our morale. We knew that we were worth that much!

Two days after we slipped out of the camp, a countrywide search for us was instituted by the Swiss police. Soon they were making inquiries about us at the legation and were bound to arrive at Slawinski's apartment. That very afternoon, therefore, January 11, we left Bern for Geneva in "Consul" Choynacki's official car, sporting diplomatic plates "CC." The plan was that Major Stanislaw Mlodzianowski, our contact in Geneva, would pass us on to France. We were going by ourselves, in a car driven by a member of our liaison outpost, who was also the legation janitor and chauffeur.

As he said farewell, Slawinski thrust into my hand a handwritten note with Mlodzianowski's name, address, and the password. Without thinking, I slipped the note into my wallet, though I really did not need it at all.

On our way to Geneva we were delighted to see some of Switzerland. We drove along the shores of Lake Geneva and for the first time in our lives saw the snowy peaks of the Alps and majestic Mont Blanc, etched against the clear sky. Major Mlodzianowski's residence was in the elegant part of Vesenaz, near Geneva. He and his daughter and grandson occupied a handsome villa set in beautiful grounds. I recognized him as soon as I saw him. I had met this dashing cavalry officer before the war, as a young student on a visit to the estate of some relatives near Leczyca. A handsome ladies' man, he could dance mazurkas and other Polish national dances to perfection, and he excelled at bridge, an accomplishment which was to prove unfortunate for us.

Immediately on our arrival, the major reached for the telephone and reported happily to Major de Ville in Bern that "the passengers have arrived safely and are with us." I was taken aback by this boldness. "Don't the police tap phones in Switzerland?" I asked. "When I was in Sweden, I was not allowed to use the phone at all." "Don't worry about anything," said the major. "You leave it to me to make sure you are safe."

Major Mlodzianowski then apologized profusely for the fact that we would be alone that evening. He and his daughter had been invited some time ago to a bridge party, and it would be extremely awkward for them to beg off at the last moment. We of course assured them we would be perfectly all right by ourselves. When we sat down to dinner, however, we were not by ourselves but were joined by the Swiss governess of the major's grandson. Taken somewhat aback, I introduced myself as an employee of the Polish legation in Bern, here for a short visit. I could think of nothing else on the spur of the moment. A banal conversation followed. The Swiss woman asked how long we had been in Switzerland, whether we liked Bern, whether we had been on any sightseeing trips in the mountains. It was not easy to answer her questions, our knowledge of Switzerland being limited to a train ride from Basel to Bern and a drive from Bern to Geneva.

Soon I saw a flicker of surprise on the woman's face. Gradually, she transformed our small talk into a skillful interrogation. We changed the subject abruptly, but realized that she was suspicious. I wondered how the constant presence of a foreigner could be tolerated in a house that served as an important link in our clandestine network, and why we had been put in such a difficult and awkward position without warning.

The following day we were strictly among ourselves at table: Major Mlodzianowski and his daughter, Captain Kazimierz Jasnoch, an artist connected with the liaison outpost, and the two of us. We were on the last course when the maid announced: "Les autorités de l'arrondissement!" They said that they wanted to speak with the major's daughter. We fidgeted, instantly on guard, but the host reassured us: some formality, no doubt; they'll go away in a minute. Meanwhile the two civilian officials were talking with the major's daughter in the adjoining drawing room, separated from the dining room by a glass door. We could see that they were watching us closely all the while.

Now even the major began to be anxious. He told us to go out through the kitchen into the garden, go for a walk, and come back after an hour or so. Obediently, we went out into the garden and caught the coats the major tossed down to us from the balcony of our room.

We had barely put them on and started toward the gate when two other civilians emerged from behind a bush, whence they had a first-rate view of the entire operation. They doffed their hats politely and asked for our documents. "We have none." In that case, they said, would we be good enough to take our places in a car parked nearby?

We could see that the villa was surrounded by men in civilian clothes. There could be no doubt that their request to speak with the major's daughter was intended to create the impression that our presence had been discovered accidentally, in order to shield an informer.

The "car" in which we were placed turned out to be a standard prison van, but painted yellow outside and sporting the advertising slogan of a chocolate manufacturer. Inside it was completely dark. All of a sudden I remembered that I had Slawinski's note in my wallet. As ill luck would have it, Greta's cigarette lighter would not work. We were determined to chew up and swallow whatever we could find in my wallet, hoping to destroy Slawinski's note in the process. One piece of paper was particularly troublesome, and it was only after some time that I realized I was busily chewing on a ten-dollar bill.*

At that point, the door of the van was flung open and we were transferred to a different vehicle. During the brief ride we agreed hurriedly that we would give our names as Jan and Jadwiga Nowak, so that our friends could trace us more easily. At some point on our ride, we stopped and one of our escorts left the car, taking Greta away with him. The car drove on until we stopped before a tall building which smacked of prison, even from the outside.

There I was told to empty my pockets and undress. The officials noticed that everything I had on was new, and jotted down the name of the department store where we had been outfitted from head to toe just a few days before. From my wallet, which our efforts had only partly emptied, a piece of paper fluttered to the table: "Major

---

*Couriers were given a supply of American money before leaving the country. In Bern we had taken out some of this supply from our hiding places.

Mlodzianowski, code name 'Dabrowa,' villa La Vierzonne, Vesenaz, password _____ . We are from Cracow." We had gobbled up so many indigestible pieces of paper, we had destroyed a *ten-dollar bill*—and all for nothing! That one piece of paper remained, and was added to a small pile of items written in Polish which were set aside.

Greta was undergoing a similar search. She was taken from the van to a small upstairs room in a house that appeared unoccupied and told to empty her handbag. Methodically all her belongings were searched, mechanical pencils unscrewed, the mirror in her powder case removed, and so forth. She watched these proceedings with satisfaction, happy that we had managed to pass on the "mail" before this latest misadventure. The only dubious item she had left was another American dollar bill hidden in a spool of thread, but they failed to find this anyway.

After a long search, I was read an arrest warrant and locked up in a cell. I had a sense of *déjà vu*. I felt as I had in the forest near the border town of Lörrach, when our guide told us, after hours of wandering, that we were right back where we started from.

Chapter 42

My interrogation—in an office in a Geneva house where they took foreigners suspected of espionage or illegal political activities that might endanger Swiss neutrality—lasted many hours and was not without its comical side. Indeed, my answers did provoke the policemen to laughter, though my mood at the time was certainly not lighthearted. In spite of my fears, the police inspector and his assistant were not at all interested in the bit of paper with Mlodzianowski's name on it, although it lay on the table in French translation. The reason was simple: they already knew everything about him, which I understood as soon as they asked their first questions. The safe house on Lake Geneva was ''blown,'' and we had been arrested on the basis of the information provided by the governess, who was a paid police informer. They did not need to post an outside watch, for she reported everything that took place inside. The major's lovely villa, which was to have been a haven for couriers crossing into France, was a trap.

My interrogators knew exactly when we came to Geneva and what Mlodzianowski's functions were. What they wanted to know was where we came from, what transport we had had, where we had entered Switzerland, and who had supplied us with the the new clothes and money. They asked us whether I was one of the officers interned in Switzerland whom Mlodzianowski was to smuggle to France through the green frontier. (His governess could not supply all this information, of course.)

In my answers I tried not to reveal the existence of a base in Bern, and especially not to involve Adam Slawinski, who, as he was an officer, might have been put in an internment camp for the duration of the war as a result. The interrogation went more or less like this:

"You came to Geneva from where?"

"From Zurich."

"Not from Bern?"

"No."

"Why does everything you have on come from shops in Bern?"

"I cannot say."

"Where did you stay in Zurich?"

"I cannot answer that."

"By what route did you come to Geneva?"

"By train."

"Have you been in the railroad station?"

"Yes, I have."

"Can you describe what you saw as you left the station in Geneva?"

I had never in my life been in Geneva, and all I knew about it was that the city was on a lake. "One can see the lake from the station," I answered.

They burst into laughter. When they then told me that Greta had given a different answer to the same question,[*] I decided that further games would make no sense. "I am a Polish officer on active service," I declared. "I am bound by a code of honor that forbids an officer, a prisoner of war, to give any information to foreign authorities or to answer any questions. Please don't waste your time questioning me because you won't get any answers."

Unlike the thick-skinned captain in Basel, the police inspector in Geneva was a gentleman. The interrogation was at once broken off without pressure or threats.

Two days later I was summoned to him again. He told me that they now knew everything about us. They had gone to the shop at Bern where we bought our clothes with Mr. and Mrs. Slawinski, who were known there. The Slawinskis had been traced and interrogated.

---

[*]I found out later that Greta from the beginning of her interrogation had refused to answer any questions at all.

The inspector then produced a "Wanted: Escaped Prisoners" poster from the Basel police, describing us as fugitives from an internment camp; it had our photographs on it. "We learned from Slawinski," he said, "that you are emissaries of the Polish underground movement coming from the Warsaw Rising who are trying to get to France via Switzerland. From our point of view, however, you are people who have twice infringed our laws. You have falsely presented yourselves as refugees, you have infringed Swiss neutrality, and you have escaped from quarantine at Basel. You are in danger of deportation."

"In that case," I said, "I request that you deport us immediately to France. We are near the French border."

"It is not as simple as you think," said the inspector. "Basel demands your extradition, and, according to law, you must be sent to the canton in which you committed an offense. The cantonal authorities at Basel will return you to Germany."

"If the first participants in and eyewitness to the Warsaw Rising who have escaped to freedom are deported by the Swiss to Germany and executed there, the whole thing will make headlines in the world press and you will be condemned by international public opinion."

"That has nothing to do with it," the inspector said indignantly. "Even if no one ever learned about you two and no one claimed you, for purely humanitarian reasons I would fight against sending you to Basel. The matter will be settled by the federal authorities in Bern. You must be patient now."

"Will Slawinski have to suffer any unpleasant consequences?"

"He will receive a verbal warning that if he continues his illegal activities, he will be sent to an internment camp for the duration of the war. He made an excellent impression on us. You Poles do know the meaning of honor." I returned to my cell, resigned, although every day's delay further endangered our important mission.

But it was difficult to be bored in these surroundings. During the day, the door to my cell was left open and I passed the time chatting with my companions in distress. Most of them were French supporters of Laval who had fled liberated France and were trying to get through to some secret center in Germany. I learned with astonishment that they had formed their own underground organization in France, built around mutual aid; it devoted most of its efforts to organizing escapes to Switzerland. I asked one of them what he thought

432

his future would be after the fall of Germany. "We shall remain abroad for a year or two until the excitement dies down," he said, "and then we'll return to France." "And what will you do if the communists come to power in France?" I asked. "We shall paint ourselves red," the Frenchman said without hesitation, "and join the Party."

Two days later the same Frenchman demonstrated a simple but very ingenious escape plan. He began to complain of toothache and asked to be taken to a dentist in town. He was escorted on his way by a Swiss prison guard with fixed bayonet. When they were passing the railway station, the Frenchman said that he must go the lavatory. Like it or not, the guard had to accompany him, and when there, decided to follow his example. The prisoner had been waiting for just this (his own urgent need had been simulated). He ran out of the toilet into the waiting room and lost himself in the crowd. It was all done too fast for the Swiss escort to pursue. The Frenchman had disappeared without a trace, and the embarrassed Swiss guard returned alone to the prison, to be greeted by laughter from his charges.

Meanwhile, a young man arrested that day was put into my cell. He proved to be a Russian Jew, a diplomatic official in the Soviet embassy in Paris who was actually a spy. He had been caught when contacting some Soviet agents in Switzerland. Out of boredom, I decided to have a game with him. I pretended that I was a Trotskyite, enraged that the Soviet Union was betraying communism by concluding alliances with the capitalists. This intelligent young man tried to persuade me to leave this false path. For hours on end he quoted Lenin to me to support the thesis that a tactical alliance with one lot of capitalists against another was entirely justified if it served the ultimate goal of a communist victory. While this indoctrination was going on, I noticed that he was secretly maintaining contact with somebody on the outside and receiving notes through the intermediary of one of the wardens. As he considered me to be a communist heretic, he did not attempt to hide this from me.

The inspector called me to his office frequently, not for interrogation but for conversation. He was interested in what was happening in Poland, and asked me many questions about the Rising and about Russian behavior. He made no secret of his friendly attitude toward us. At one point, he produced a photograph album and asked whether I recognized any of the people in it. I recognized only Mlodzianowski and his daughter, but from his questions I guessed that the Swiss had uncovered the network that had been smuggling officers interned in Switzerland out to France to join the Polish forces. The police looked on this activity with indulgence but wanted to know more about it. Perhaps, I thought, he is showing me this album with the idea that after my release I can warn the people involved that they are known to the police.

Another question he asked, which was quite unexpected, was about my cellmate. "He is a dangerous Soviet intelligence agent," the inspector said. "We suspect him of maintaining contact in prison with a Soviet intelligence unit in Switzerland. Have you noticed anything suspicious?" I said no, instinctively.

Returning to my cell, I asked myself why I had not told him the truth. The Soviet agent was a political enemy, and I could contribute to the exposure of Soviet espionage by reporting on him, so what made me cover up? Should I go back and tell the inspector about the notes? After some thought I decided that under prison conditions an unwritten code requires solidarity; one cannot inform even on an enemy. The inspector knew what he was doing when he put an anticommunist Pole and a Soviet spy in the same cell. Wouldn't he lose his respect for the Polish sense of honor if I had betrayed my unsuspecting cellmate? I decided that I could not have acted otherwise.

At last, on January 20, the inspector informed me with visible pleasure that he had received a decision from Bern. We were to be deported to France at once. He wished me success in London, gave me his private address, and asked that I let him know how we got on. In the end, a small formality: he asked me to sign a note of thanks to the Swiss authorities for their good treatment of us in Geneva and Basel, which he had prepared and ready, and a declaration that we were leaving Switzerland without any complaint against the authorities.

We were taken by car to the office of the Polish Red Cross, where Prince Stanislaw Radziwill gave me back our suitcase of clothes and a safe-conduct document signed by the American authorities. I was also given a letter from Major Mlodzianowski to say that he was extremely sorry about what had happened, "but, alas, nothing can be done about it." A second letter was from Major de Ville, who expressed astonishment that "a note with the password and Mlodzianowski's name had fallen into the hands of the police." I

434

tore up the second letter in some indignation. "Could you kindly tell Major de Ville," I said to Radziwill, "that we are deeply grateful to him, and most of all to Major Choynacki, for organizing our passage across the frontier. Without their help, we could not have got out of Germany. About what happened to us in Switzerland, we might expect an apology, not reproaches."

From Prince Radziwill I learned that our legation had done everything it could for us but that we owed our speedy release from prison to energetic British intervention.

When we reached the frontier, Greta was already waiting. Saluted by the Swiss customs officials, we crossed the barrier to the French side together. How could we now explain ourselves to the French? I asked myself with some anxiety, What kind of reception awaited us? On the other side a civilian was waiting for us. "Mr. and Mrs. Nowak?" he asked in French. "A Polish officer with a car is waiting for you."

In a moment Cadet Officer Olechowski introduced himself to us in Polish. After roughly an hour's drive, we arrived at Annemasse, the house of Mr. and Mrs. Appenzeller. I recognized my host's face immediately from the album of photographs shown to me by the inspector, and took the opportunity to warn him that both Mlodzianowski's house and his own activities were known to the Swiss.

The next morning we began a breakneck journey to Lyon. We traveled by jeep across the mountains on narrow, icy roads, covered by snow. The jeep skidded on every bend. Olechowski drove like a madman, and we were sure that the expedition from Warsaw would end at the bottom of a French cliff. However, in the evening, we arrived in Lyon, safe though frozen to the bone.

I remembered the long wait for an aircraft in Stockholm, so I was astonished when a British officer called at our hotel the next morning. "My name is Major Vick," he said, "and I have been instructed to take you both to the airfield, where a military aircraft is waiting."

"But we have no papers."

"Don't worry. We know all about you."

He led us through the customs area to the aircraft. The Dakota was empty, and we were to be the only passengers. As soon as we were settled the door was shut and the engines started. It seemed as if the plane had been sent specially for us. The Dakota landed, how-

435

ever, not in London but in Paris. We left the aircraft with some anxiety, but the French police did not ask us for documents. "We know all about you. Come to the waiting room please."

It was nearly dark when we were taken back to the aircraft. This time the Dakota was filled with French and British officers and some civilians. "We shall be on the ground in an hour," I told Greta, "but you must expect them to take us from the airport to the Patriotic School, where we will spend a few days. Why didn't our people send my military identity card, my uniform, and travel orders over to France? Nobody thought about it, I suppose."

The flight to London took an unusually long time. We were in the air for at least two hours and our fellow passengers were beginning to complain when the pilot announced that all the airfields in southern England were fogbound and had refused us permission to land. We had to go back to Paris.

We were really angry. Up to the last moment of our journey there were to be obstacles and delays. But after a short time the pilot announced that we were flying to England after all—that the military airfield at Ford, in southern England, was ready to allow us to land. We sighed with relief, but I was still worried about the British in this small airport. How would they treat two foreign civilians without any documents apart from a strange American safe conduct?

At the entrance to the barracks, however, next to the military policemen checking the officers' papers stood a British officer. "Lieutenant Nowak?" he asked. "Welcome to Britain. The train to London leaves in an hour. Here are your tickets and a room reservation at a boarding house in Kensington."

On January 23, 1945, at 9:30 A.M., we arrived in Upper Belgrave Square to report to Colonel Marian Utnik, the new chief of Section Six, who had replaced Colonel Protasewicz.

Chapter 43

I beg you,'' Zygmunt Litynski, an official of the Polish Ministry of Information, whispered in my ear, ''don't botch this opportunity. You will be talking, quite literally, to the whole world. This won't happen again, ever. If you can't find an English word, I'll prompt you.''

''The whole world'' was situated within the four walls of the Ministry of Information conference room in Stratton House, Piccadilly. The room was packed with journalists. There were representatives of Reuter's, United Press International, the Associated Press, a French agency, and all the British national and provincial press from *The Times* to the tabloids. Ivreach Macdonald of *The Times* smiled at me from the audience. Next to him sat Sydney Gruson of the *New York Times*, Emlyn Williams of the *Christian Science Monitor*, whom I had also met, James Sloan of the *Washington Post*, Wilson of the Canadian radio, a representative of the Columbia Broadcasting System, and the correspondents of the *Journal de Genève, Neue Zürcher Zeitung*, and French and Scandinavian papers.

Sensations in the press are like soap bubbles which shine in the sun but burst very quickly. What everybody is talking about today is stale news tomorrow. At the same time, we had made this difficult journey to give a testimony of truth to the whole world. This was the climax of my entire wartime activity.

They had been drawn to this room by a double sensation: the

437

arrival in the West of the first participants in and eyewitnesses to the Warsaw Rising and a human interest story—about a couple of insurgents who were married during the Rising and who had made the difficult trip from Warsaw to London together.

Greta was sitting on my right, Litynski on my left, next to a stenographer from the Ministry of Information who was taking careful notes. On the table before us was a pile of ninety-five photographs of the Rising, now enlarged on glossy paper. The conference was opened by Litynski. Approaching his task from a professional journalist's point of view, he spoke more about us and our adventures than about the Rising. That subject he left to me.

At first, out of nervousness, I found speaking rather difficult. A few times my voice failed me; I had to pause to collect myself. Later I spoke more fluently. I began by quoting the words of Mikolajczyk. In our last conversation before I returned to Poland, he had urged that the Home Army endure to the end in the struggle against the Germans, supporting the Soviet forces and thereby giving testimony of good faith to the Allies. I then told of the calls of the Soviet radio stations upon Warsaw to attack the withdrawing Germans, of the ominous silence that fell on the other bank of the Vistula on the fourth day of the Rising, of the disappearance of Soviet aircraft from the sky over the capital as soon as the Germans had begun to destroy it systematically street by street; of the Russian refusal to allow parachute drops from their own airfields, only ten minutes' flying time from Warsaw, and of their refusal to allow Allied aircraft—the aircraft that was to bring help from distant Italy—to land. I spoke about the vain attempts to establish liaison with Rokossowski's staff, first through Kalugin and the western Allies, later directly by radio, and in the end even by the telephone cable still connecting Warsaw with the suburb of Praga, already in Soviet hands.

I spoke about the hell that the population of Warsaw lived through before seven hundred thousand survivors were expelled from their city to become wanderers. I spoke about the last appeal by General Bor-Komorowski to Rokossowski, warning him that the AK would have to surrender to the Germans if relief were not forthcoming in the next twenty-four hours, an appeal answered only by silence. I spoke about the commanders and soldiers of the Home Army at Lwow, Wilno, and elsewhere who had supported the Soviet forces on orders from London and Warsaw and who were imprisoned and sent away to the depths of Russia as a result. I spoke much longer than is usual in press conferences, but the hall was silent.

The questions began, some to the point, others petty and ridiculous. Gruson of the *New York Times* asked whether we would have accepted help from Soviet-sponsored Lublin Poles (Poles of the Lublin Committee of Liberation). I answered that in Warsaw then we would have accepted help from the devil himself, but that the Lublin Poles' only action had been to shower insults on the Home Army commanders while exhorting the insurgents to hold out. "Do the Poles continue to recognize the government in London, although power is now in the hands of the Lublin Committee?" "Freedom," I replied, "means the right to choose one's own government. Until the nation is deprived of this right, we shall recognize only the free and independent government in London."

"What are you expecting? What options are left to you?" This most important question was asked by a reporter from a small provincial paper in Scotland.

"Free elections," I replied, "guaranteed by the three powers and held under the supervision of British and American observers on the spot. They are the only way to save our future and the independence of Poland."

The rest of that day was filled with interviews for American, Canadian, French, and British radio stations. At one interview in London, Edward R. Murrow at the CBS radio network in New York joined in via cable.

The next day Litynski laid a pile of press cuttings on the table in front of me—for the moment only from the British newspapers. Our greatest satisfaction was a long and angry communiqué from TASS, which dismissed my statements as "a pack of lies," and an even longer declaration made in Paris by Stefan Jedrychowski, representative of the Lublin Committee in France. Both proved that I had hit my target.

On the morning of January 28 Colonel Stefan Zamoyski, who had been General Sikorski's aide-de-camp, telephoned to say that his friend Major Desmond Morton, Churchill's adviser, would very much like to see me and had asked Zamoyski to take me to Downing Street as soon as possible. To Zamoyski's regret, I refused categorically. "I have no intention." I said, "of exposing myself a second time to an intrigue by this dishonest and unfriendly man." Five minutes later, the telephone rang again. Josef Lipski, who was the Polish ambassador in Berlin before the war, was on the line. "Lieutenant," the ambassador pleaded, "I hear that you have declined an invitation from Churchill's adviser and friend. You can't do this! After all that you have achieved and this great press coverage, he is probably ashamed of what he did and wants somehow to repair the damage."

"Mr. Ambassador," I said, "a man who acted as Morton did for no reason is untrustworthy. I don't wish to talk with him."

"Listen to an old, experienced diplomat. I hope that you trust me?"

In the end of course I gave in, but I did insist that Colonel Zamoyski accompany me. Major Morton received me with exaggerated cordiality. "Last time we had a small misunderstanding because of language difficulties, didn't we?" he started. I reminded him that at our last conversation Josef Zarański, the Polish embassy counselor and a man whose English was most fluent, had been present and understood perfectly everything I had said and everything that Major Morton had said.

Morton disregarded this remark and at once went to the point of our meeting. He asked that I tell him exactly how we got to England. I remembered that the conversation a year before began with the same question.

Having satisfied his curiosity on this point, Morton passed on to questions about the Rising. He had read in the papers my account of calls to insurrection broadcast by Kosciuszko radio, by the Union of Patriots, and by Moscow. Did I hear them with my own ears, and was I sure that the broadcasts originated in stations controlled by the Russians? Mightn't the Germans have made them, masquerading as Russian broadcasters? I pointed out that the Germans had no interest in calling on the Poles to rise up against them behind their own front line. "I did not hear the summons with my own ears," I said, "but I know that the BBC monitors all programs around the world and identifies their sources. If the major would like to check the truth of what I am saying, he can easily check the daily bulletins of the BBC monitoring service for the end of July."

This answer seemed to put Major Morton's doubts to rest. He

then asked about my plans for the future. Very injudiciously, I said that the Polish government wanted to send me to the United States as soon as possible for some conferences and a lecture tour.

The day after my conversation with Morton, Zygmunt Litynski rang me up. "Lieutenant!" he cried, very excited, "what have you done now?"

"What do you mean?"

"I have just talked to the chief of the *New York Times* office in London, Mr. Daniel. During a lunch with Mr. Churchill's adviser, the conversation turned to Polish affairs and to you. Morton said, among other things, "So you see that one cannot trust the Poles. They produced for the press, with great hullabaloo, this Nowak fellow, who apparently has only just come from Warsaw. The prime minister was interested in what the *Times* wrote about the Russian calls for a rising. He instructed me to question Nowak about it personally. I asked Nowak how he knew that the radio stations were Russian. And he— imagine—gave me the frequencies of these stations, with precision, to the last digit, and maintained that only Moscow was broadcasting on these wavelengths. In Nowak's presence, I rang the BBC monitoring service and was told that only Beirut broadcasts on the frequency given! I repeated this to Nowak, and he with great impudence answered, perhaps Radio Beirut is under Moscow's control!"

I asked Litynski to be good enough to repeat Morton's statement word for word, to Zamoyski and to Lipski, and at the same time to be sure to pass on to Ambassador Lipski my thanks for his excellent advice. Putting down the receiver, I asked myself what could the Poles have done to Morton, that he was so obstinate in his attempts to harm me? I had no doubt that he had told the same story to Mr. Churchill.

I met Morton again three years later. As representative of the Polish Section of the BBC, I was recording the unveiling of a monument at Norholt, near London, to Polish airmen killed in action. A few steps from me stood Morton, probably representing Mr. Churchill. He recognized me at once and made a gesture of greeting. I ostentatiously turned my back on him.

Perhaps owing to Morton's intrigues, when our Ministry of Foreign Affairs applied for an American visa for me, it was refused.

No intervention could help. The reason for the decision was even disclosed: "In view of the emotionally anti-Soviet attitude of Lieutenant Nowak, his public appearances in the United States would not help the cause of Allied unity at this time."*

Shortly after our arrival in London, General Tatar passed on to me an invitation from Mikolajczyk to call on him. The matter was urgent, he said, as Mikolajczyk wanted to take me to see Eden. Mikolajczyk was now out of the government. In October of 1944, during his second journey to Moscow, in the presence of Churchill and Eden and under pressure from them, he agreed that the eastern areas of Poland should be ceded to Russia and expressed his readiness to return to Poland and lead a government to be composed partly of communists and their puppets and partly of the representatives of Polish political parties. As might have been foreseen, this agreement was rejected by the Poles in London. The conditions that Mikolajczyk accepted were considered not compromise but capitulation: with the Soviet forces and the NKVD present in the country, and agents of Moscow inside the government, the prime minister would have no chance to conduct an independent policy nor to stay in office should Stalin decide to get rid of him. The members of the government in London saw no reason to sign their own death sentences as handed down by Stalin and the western Allies. If one could not avoid political death, one could at least leave the scene with dignity. Mikolajczyk was forced to resign. The British government then suspended all talks

*The motives of Major Desmond Morton have remained the greatest unsolved mystery to me of all my experiences in the war. I learned after these incidents that Ronald Jeffery and I were not his only victims. Sir John Colville, principal private secretary to Winston Churchill during the war, wrote in his memoirs (*The Churchillians* [London: Weidenfeld and Nicolson, 1981], pp. 198-99) that Morton denounced the French admiral Muselier to Churchill as a traitor and an undercover agent of the Vichy government. On the basis of documents produced by Morton, Churchill ordered Muselier arrested on the spot. One week later, the admiral was released from jail with apologies, as the "proofs" presented by Morton had been shown to be the forgeries of French officers. Colville does not explain why M-15 (British counterintelligence) did not check their authenticity before Morton gave them to Churchill.

I was more fortunate than Admiral Muselier. When writing this book, I discovered in H.M. Public Record Office a Morton memo to John Miller Martin, dated January 17, 1944 (see Appendix for text), suggesting that I might be a member of the organization "The Sword and Plough," which, as Morton explained in his memo, was "thoroughly penetrated by the Germans." Since I had impeccable credentials as an emissary of the commander-in-chief of the Home Army, Morton's "suggestion" was promptly rejected by the Foreign Office, and I was saved the unpleasantness experienced by Admiral Muselier.

with his successor, Tomasz Arciszewski, a veteran of the revolution of 1905 and the leader of the Polish Socialist Party. Mikolajczyk now, on his own account, discussed with the British his return to Poland and participation in a government set up under Soviet patronage. The division of London into two hostile camps deepened. The majority of Poles supported the new prime minister, Arciszewski; the minority sided with Mikolajczyk.

I went to see the former prime minister with Arciszewski's knowledge and agreement. "Perhaps you will succeed in persuading him to abandon a course which will lead to high treason," said Arciszewski.

Mikolajczyk began our talk by saying that he would like me to see Anthony Eden, who wanted to hear from me directly the fate of the civilian leaders of underground Poland and, most of all, of the activists in the political parties: which of them had survived and how could one find them? "Why does Eden need this information?" I asked, astonished.

Mikolajczyk hesitated for a second before replying: "The British want to ensure their safety from the Soviet occupation authorities."

I realized that, since his resignation from the government, Mikolajczyk had had no radio contact with Poland. But the moment of hesitation before he answered my question made me think that the reasons for Eden's interest might be different: he wanted to establish contact with the political leadership in Poland over the heads of the London government, I thought.

"I will willingly give Eden any information he wants," I said, "but I must first have our government's approval."

"In that case," said Mikolajczyk, "you must decide whether you want to find yourself in a blind alley or to continue to be useful; Arciszewski's government has no future. The British and the Americans have stopped talking to him. The government can only indulge in protests 'taking a position,' and make propaganda gestures that won't change a thing. Poland cannot be saved in this way."

"And how do you propose to save it?"

"One might have saved a lot while there was still time, but I was not allowed to do so by our countrymen in London. Today there is no question that I could become head of a government in Poland. One could fight to obtain the largest participation in that government. But it is not important how many communists would participate.

443

What is important is to obtain guarantees from the British and the Americans that a free election will be held in Poland under international supervision and that the people who are now hiding in the forests and in the cellars can participate in it."

"Mr. Prime Minister," I said, "I remember our last conversation before the Rising. When I was leaving, you told me at the door that we should meet soon in Warsaw, perhaps under unpleasant circumstances. Only later did I understand what you had in mind. You were expecting that you would go straight from Moscow to a Warsaw that had been liberated by the Russians and that you would form a government which would be acceptable to Stalin. We in Warsaw have seen with our own eyes how Stalin has answered you. After what has happened, can one still have any illusions?"

At that point Mikolajczyk began to repeat exactly what I had heard on July 10, 1944. He believed in the support of the Polish people and would have the British and the Americans on his side. With those forces something could be saved in Poland, but not in London.

"It seems to me," I said, "that you would either be forced to compromise in Poland, which would rob you of the support and trust of the nation, or else, sooner or later, you would be liquidated. The Russians hate you, and the Allies won't go to war to protect you." I reminded Mikolajczyk of the fate of Colonel Wladyslaw Filipkowski ("Janka"), the commander of the Lwow District. After Operation TEMPEST he came out into the open with his soldiers, established a headquarters in Lwow, and awaited events. Three days later a Soviet general appeared and declared that the Soviet command could not tolerate the presence of a separate military organization. He suggested that Filipkowski's detachment form a unit in Berling's Army, Filipkowski agreed to everything and went to the army command with the Soviet general to discuss details. He was deported to Zytomierz, thence to Moscow, and was never heard from again. A few days after his disappearance, the Soviet command in the city called all his officers to a briefing. Those who duly appeared were arrested and deported to camps in Russia.

"Yes, it's all true," Mikolajczyk said, "but now I shall ask you what you expect to achieve here, in the West."

"I don't know. I repeated loyally in Warsaw your statement, sir, that you did not believe in a third world war. I myself am not so sure. I believe that, just in case, the Polish nation must also have a presence in the Western camp, that it must have a numerous representation here in the West. I believe that you, as former prime minister, should not acquiesce in the annexation of the eastern lands of Poland and the enslavement of the country."

"And I believe the opposite to be true," said Mikolajczyk. "Just because of the authority vested in me as former head of the Polish government in London, I might rally the nation around me and pull out the people from the underground to the surface. No one else could possibly do so in the country."

"Provided that Stalin will allow you to benefit from this possibility," I answered.

"Do you too see in me a traitor and a renegade?"

"No," I said, "but I wish to be frank. History and the nation will judge you in accordance with the concessions you are still prepared to make to the Russians."

"In that case," concluded Mikolajczyk, with a distinct note of bitter irony in his voice, "don't worry about that verdict of history."

"And what about our visit to Eden?" I asked.

"In view of your attitude, it won't serve much purpose."

This conversation took place on January 24. The conference at Yalta began ten days later. When I read in the papers the Yalta communiqué, with a formula announcing the creation of a provisional Polish Government composed of representative democratic leaders in Poland and in the emigration, I knew why Eden wanted to know the names of those leaders who had survived the Rising and the means of approaching them. I also now understood why, so quickly and without formalities, Greta and I had been able to leave Geneva for London. Perhaps Churchill and Eden wanted to have the names ready during the Yalta conference. At any rate, they got them from the Arciszewski cabinet, to whom I myself passed everything I knew.

In Mikolajczyk's mind this Yalta formula already existed in a crystallized form during our conversation. I saw him for the last time before his departure for Warsaw, some six months later.* On the eve

---

*He returned from Poland two years later, fleeing for his life, hidden in the trunk of the limousine of the United States ambassador. The latter not only swore him to secrecy but invented and had him spread a false story to cover the circumstances of that escape. Some years later the same ambassador unscrupulously disclosed the true story in his own memoirs, exposing the former prime minister of the country which President Roosevelt had called "the inspiration of the world" to some ridicule.

of his departure, on June 15, 1945, Moscow announced that the trial of the Polish leaders would begin soon.* But neither the deceitful arrest of the leaders of the underground nor other similar events in Poland could shake Mikolajczyk. Once he had accepted a point of view as his own, he clung tightly to it.

Perhaps history will judge Mikolajczyk's intentions more indulgently than did his contemporaries. He was certainly wrong in his assessment of the help that he could expect to obtain from the British and Americans, but he was willing to fight to the end to salvage whatever could be salvaged from the wreck left after Teheran and Yalta.

On January 30, 1945, the Polish cabinet, under Arciszewski, heard the last report of this emissary of the Home Army. By that time, General Okulicki's order dissolving the Home Army and instructing its soldiers to continue their work toward Poland's full independence had been decoded and deciphered.

---

*In March, 1945, the Soviets invited the leaders of the Polish political parties, including General Okulicki and the Government Delegate, Jankowski, to a meeting to begin negotiations to implement the Yalta agreement. All the guests were arrested, flown to Moscow, and put on trial.

Epilogue

*F*rom the perspective of more than thirty years, the dramatic events of 1944 appear different now, even to one who was directly involved in them. The Warsaw Rising, which ended in rivers of spilled blood and the almost total destruction of the nation's capital, seemed at the time to be a wasted sacrifice; for after Teheran, Poland's independence was irretrievably lost.

The first link in the chain of events which led to the Rising, I believed then and now, was the death of General Wladyslaw Sikorski in an air crash in 1943. The consequences of this tragedy went beyond the loss of an outstanding leader, painful though it was. As prime minister and commander-in-chief of the armed forces, General Sikorski held both political and military power. After his death that power was split between two personal and political enemies: Stanislaw Mikolajczyk, as prime minister, and Kazimierz Sosnkowski, as commander-in-chief.

Sosnkowski, as is evident in the transcripts of his communications to the underground commands in Poland, produced a stream of recommendations, warnings, and advice. What he failed to provide, however, was a clear-cut, unambiguous strategic plan for the Home Army. He proved unable to make firm decisions and or to command obedience. Even worse, he dragged his subordinates in Warsaw into

London's political squabbles by openly criticizing Mikolajczyk to them, thus undermining his own authority as well as that of the government. The prime minister, for his part, was trying to shift to Warsaw decisions on such vital matters as Poland's postwar borders, participation of communists in the government, and the issue of the general uprising. Since Mikolajczyk's policies were opposed by most Poles in London, he went to the homeland for support.

Under such circumstances, the underground leadership in Poland had no choice but to take matters into its own hands. Unfortunately, neither its leaders nor the Polish public realized that the fate of their country had been decided when the future occupation zones were agreed upon by the western Allies and the Soviet Union. At that time Poland was placed under the exclusive military and, by the same token, political control of the Soviet Union.

Occupied Poland had only one source of information, London radio. Both the BBC and the Polish Radio in London concentrated their coverage on Polish developments, which were of primary interest to their audience inside occupied Poland. The very fact that information originating in Poland, as well as information about Poland, was coming from outside—notably from London, the center of the Allied war effort—created a geographic egocentrism of sorts among the Poles: they suffered from the illusion that the attention of the entire world was focused on their country and that Poland, because she had fought so bravely, and at such a high price, against the Nazis, had become the object of general admiration among her powerful allies. Every Polish child knew Roosevelt's words: Poland was an inspiration to all nations (the president himself probably never realized what a misleading effect his lofty praise had on millions of people). The news of Polish exploits in partisan warfare—acts of sabotage or attacks on German personnel and military facilities—was beamed back to Poland by the BBC and the Polish Radio in London. In this way underground fighters tended to see their actions as a political statement addressed to the world outside.

The decision-making centers in Poland had at least two other sources of information: the intercepted Reuter's news service and radio messages from Polish headquarters in London. Of necessity, the information transmitted in this manner had to be condensed, laconic, and detached from background and political context. Such news as, for instance, Churchill's speech of February 22, 1944, even though it did reach Poland and was accurately reported by the underground press, tended to be interpreted in a much more optimistic vein by Poles in Warsaw than by those in London. Nothing could shake the Poles' deep-rooted faith that the western Allies would resist any open onslaught on the independence of Poland.

Soviet propaganda messages beamed directly from Moscow or spread through underground communist organizations in Poland strongly urged insurgency. Their allegations that the Home Army was avoiding confrontations with the Nazis, even that it was collaborating with Germany, had little effect on the public, as few Poles listened to Radio Moscow or read the communist press. It was a different matter with the underground leadership, however, where Soviet broadcasts constituted an important part of the daily information diet and Soviet accusations were not taken lightly. They were reiterated by Stalin at all his summit meetings with Roosevelt and Churchill and by all the pro-Soviet media in the West. During his first meeting with Eden after the Teheran Conference, Mikolajczyk was told that Stalin, on two occasions, had accused the Polish Home Army of fighting and killing Soviet and communist partisans. Not only did Eden not reject these allegations outright; he demanded that the Poles prove them untrue.

The Polish leadership was thus led to believe that, in order to counter Soviet lies, it had to escalate military attacks against the Germans and to refrain from clashes with Soviet and communist partisans active in Poland. A display of loyalty to the Allies was considered an essential precondition for obtaining their help in defense of Polish independence. When the hour of decision struck in Warsaw, the Home Army leadership was convinced that, if it remained passive, the Soviets, acting through their communist stooges, could easily create a "spontaneous" outbreak of fighting and take the lead in mass resistance, as a demonstration that the tiny communist minority spoke for the whole nation. Such considerations, which were in fact fully justified, as the official documents opened after the war make clear, played an important part in the decision to start an uprising in Warsaw.

Unfortunately, expectations that the Warsaw Rising might influence public opinion and policy among the western Allies were based on illusions and lack of information. Without solidarity between Churchill and Roosevelt, there was little chance that Great Britain alone could do anything to frustrate Stalin's plans. Indeed, Churchill and Eden were constantly pushing the Poles to make territorial concessons to the Soviets and to step up their partisan warfare against the Germans in order to demonstrate their goodwill toward the Russians. Churchill hoped that, in this way, Moscow could be brought to take a more conciliatory attitude. However, the British had neither the will nor the means to press effectively for Polish-Soviet compromise. Churchill subordinated everything to a single goal, the unconditional surrender of Nazi Germany. For the time being, nothing else mattered. A conflict with the Soviet Union over the Polish issue could have jeopardized this goal. Despite this consideration, however, Poland's allies did not have to become Stalin's accomplices in the subjugation of that country, and the rest of eastern Europe, to the Soviet Union at Teheran, Yalta, and Potsdam.

As George F. Kennan, then a U.S. embassy counsellor in Moscow, said of the Soviet betrayal of the Rising, the Allies should have told the Russians: "We can't stop you from doing this [subjugating Poland], but we also will not take responsibility for it. You will have to do it on your own responsibility. And you will have to take the blame before the world opinion. We will not help you. . . . We're not going to make war on you. . . . But we also are not going to support you in those policies."[*] The fact remains that under the conditions and mood prevailing at that time, neither the Soviet betrayal of the Warsaw Rising or all that followed, including the arrest of a group of Polish leaders by the NKVD in 1945 and the rigged elections in 1947, would change by one iota the policy of the western Allies.

Such were my conclusions at the end of the war. However, as time gave distance to these events, I began to see that my analysis

---

[*]Interview of May 30, 1972, quoted in J. K. Zawodny, *Nothing But Honour* (London: Macmillan, 1978), pp. 223-24.

was one-sided, incomplete, and, therefore, quite wrong. It was wrong to see the Warsaw Rising solely as a demonstration to the outside world inspired by false hopes. The underground leaders were also deeply concerned for the morale of the population, which had to be maintained to confront whatever the future had in store. For years millions of people who were active in daily clandestine operations had been longing for the moment when they would come out into the open and strike at the enemy. Regardless of the immediate premises and calculations of the Polish leadership, the real effects of the Warsaw Rising only became apparent in the years after the war, when Stalin succeeded in making Poland his satellite.

The forcible imposition on Poland of Stalin's political system and puppet government signaled the beginning of still another attempted conquest: the subjugation of the minds of the Polish people. Though Poland had no means to defend her independence, she successfully resisted all attempts at Sovietization. After a third of a century, Poland remains an island in the Soviet sea.

Twice in recent years the attention of the world has been focused on this small, remote country on the periphery of the Soviet empire: first, in 1978, when Karol Wojtyla was elected Pope, and then two years later, when the Polish workers won their bloodless victory. These seemingly unrelated events have common roots in the continued spirit of resistance which sprang from the experiences of the last war. Karol Wojtyla could only have been elected against the background of the Polish Church's successful struggle against the continuous incursions of communism. Like a fortress under siege, it withstood all onslaughts and remained united, powerful, and independent. But the Church could not have survived without popular support: the faithful repelled communist attempts at indoctrination and retained their independence of mind. To put it another way, the resistance to totalitarian rule of intellectuals, workers, and farmers, whether believers or not, would have been unthinkable without the presence of the Church.

For a long time the Soviet Union has reluctantly tolerated Poland's deviation from the orthodox pattern. The Kremlin, mindful of the lesson of the Warsaw Rising, is well aware that it is dealing with a nation which would make supreme sacrifices if it believed certain imponderable national treasures were at stake, while the Polish people have also learned, from their cruel experiences of the last war, to avoid violent confrontations. Because memories of the recent past are still very much alive, when the military crackdown came in December 1981, it met with almost no violent opposition. Yet Moscow and its junta in Warsaw may discover the limits of power based solely on repressive measures. The Solidarity movement has been crushed as an organized force, but it may continue to serve as a common front for people determined to use passive resistance as their ultimate weapon.

A nation which emerged from the last war broken and defeatist could not have repelled with such determination the continued assaults on its spiritual identity. Poland's postwar history is therefore rooted in the Warsaw Rising and that struggle for freedom to the bitter end. Though the Polish leadership in London and occupied Warsaw could not preserve the independence of the Polish state and make the defeat less costly, it saved *l'union sacré* of the nation. That union, forged in the resistance movement, remains intact to this day. The Soviet betrayal of the Warsaw Rising left an invisible barrier between the Polish people and their communist rulers, an estrangement which subsequent communist governments never managed to overcome. Poland's ''will to be'' may have led to a disaster at Warsaw in 1944, but it also led to that amazing moment when, in the heart of a Warsaw raised from the ashes, before a huge cross erected in Victory Square, a Polish pope celebrated mass for millions of his compatriots in full view of the entire world. When Poland was crushed by the German and Russian armies, Winston Churchill said: ''Poland has again been overrun by two of the great powers which held her in bondage for 120 years but were unable to quench the spirit of the Polish nation. The heroic defense of Warsaw shows that the soul of Poland is indestructible and that she will rise again like a rock which may, for a time, be submerged by a tidal wave but which remains a rock.''

I remember V-E Day in London, the end of the war against Germany. We stood in Piccadilly Circus among dancing and singing crowds, drunk with happiness and glory. There were no Polish soldiers or Polish flags in the great parade of the victorious troops of many nations in those streets, and another great parade was passing in our thoughts. We saw the faces of friends who gave their lives so that this day could come. Writing these closing words, I remember them again:

Railroad worker "Klimek"
    shot by the German Grentzschutz on the Polish border;
Courier "Wos"
    tortured to death in the Mauthausen concentration camp;
"Anatol" (Jan Lipsz),
    murdered in jail by the Gestapo;
"Hilda" (Halina Bigocka),
    killed after refusing to betray me, so that I might live;
"Robak" (Adam Plucinski),
    executed in the Grossrosen concentration camp;
Franciszek Trepczynski,
    shot in the Stuttgart concentration camp;
"Jula" (Barbara Wolska),
    killed by a sniper during the Warsaw Rising.

Their sacrifice was not in vain. Our day of victory will also come. One day the sun will shine on crowds of singing and dancing people drunk with joy in the streets of Warsaw. The free soul of Poland will survive until that day.

Personalities

General Wladyslaw Sikorski, commander-in-chief of the Polish armed forces and prime minister of the Polish government in London; perished in plane crash off Gibraltar, July 4, 1943

Stanislaw Mikolajczyk, Sikorski's successor as prime minister, July, 1943-December, 1944

General Kazimierz Sosnkowski, Sikorski's successor as commander-in-chief, July, 1943-September, 1944

General Stefan Rowecki ("Grot," "Kalina"), commander-in-chief of the Home Army, Armia Krajowa; arrested by Gestapo on June 30, 1943; executed in Oranienburg concentration camp in August, 1944

General Tadeusz Komorowski ("Bor," "Lawina"), Rowecki's successor; died in exile in 1968

General Tadeusz Pelczynski ("Grzegorz") chief of staff of the AK, 1940-1944

General Leopold Okulicki ("Teddy Bear"), commander-in-chief of the AK after the Warsaw Rising; arrested by the Soviets with fifteen other Polish leaders; died in unknown circumstances in jail in the USSR

Colonel Jan Rzepecki ("the Chairman"), chief of the Bureau of Information and Propaganda of the AK

Stanislaw Witkowski ("Zbik"), Action N courier, close associate of the author, co-organizer of the network of Action N agents in the Reich; arrested in May, 1943; escaped from German jail

Wojciech Sobieszczyk ("Wos"), Action N courier; arrested by Gestapo in May, 1943; executed in Mauthausen concentration camp

Tadeusz Zenczykowski ("Kowalik," "Kania"), chief of Action N and of Roj, the section for propaganda at the time of the Rising

Major Zygmunt Janke ("Gertruda," "Walter"), AK commander in the district of Lodz, later commander of Silesia

Elzbieta Zawacka ("Zo"), emissary and parachutist and one of the organizers of Zaloga, the AK unit in charge of communication with London

Tadeusz Niedbalski ("Seweryn"), Zaloga member who briefed the author before his first secret trip to Stockholm

Maria Pyttel ("Maria"), Zaloga member who provided the author with a safe house and help in the port of Gdynia; arrested by Gestapo in August, 1944; survived Stutthof concentration camp

Franciszek Trepczynski ("Franek"), a crane operator in the port of Gdynia who hid the author in a ship's coalbin; arrested in August, 1943; executed in Stutthof concentration camp only hours before prisoners there were freed

Appendix of Documents

I

Frank K. Roberts, Head of the Central Department of the Foreign Office, to Anthony Eden, Secretary of State for Foreign Affairs

The Counsellor of the Polish Embassy brought to see me this morning the latest member of the Polish Underground movement to reach this country, Lieut. Nowak, who left Poland early in November.

Lieut. Nowak, who made a very good impression, had been mainly occupied in spreading leaflets among Germans in Germany proper and in those parts of Poland to the West of the General Government. These leaflets were ostensibly propaganda by German underground movements and as such had been effective. Lieut. Nowak however said that the Poles had been forced to the conclusion that there were no effective German Underground organisations, with the exception of the Communists, who were however lying low.

Lieut. Nowak said that although German civilians were now trying to curry favour with the Polish population, the German authorities, Gestapo and soldiers, were proving more tyrannical than ever. Polish feeling was unanimously anti-German and not a single Pole was prepared to distinguish between good and bad Germans. They had rejected feelers put out some time ago that they should adopt an anti-Russian attitude and in return receive arms from the Germans to defend themselves against the Russians. Lieut. Nowak pointed out that the only country in Europe which had not at this moment got a National detachment fighting with the Germans on the Eastern front was Poland. This would continue to be the case.

There was no feeling against the Russians as such, and all the Poles wanted good relations with Russia. There was, however, deep distrust of the Soviet Government, based on the growing fear that the Soviet Government were determined not to allow a really independent Poland to exist after the war.

The strongest parties in Poland at the present time were the Socialists and the peasants, both of whom wanted good relations with Russia, but on a basis of genuine Polish independence. The only Party prepared to act on the instructions of Moscow was the small Communist Party P.P.R., but the leaders of this Party were now mostly Russians dropped by parachute, and a great majority of Poles regarded it in the same light as Quislings are regarded throughout occupied Europe. P.P.R. was now receiving arms from Russia, and Russian organisers were being dropped not only in the Eastern province, but in the woods around Warsaw. The Poles were not, however, frightened of the P.P.R. as they realised that it represented nothing, even if it were set up as a Government when the Russians came in.

Source: H. M. Public Record Office, Document FO 371-39422-02931, C1282.

Lieut. Nowak said that despite present difficulties there was a feeling of tremendous optimism in Poland regarding the future. This was based upon their conviction that Germany would soon be defeated and also upon their confidence that, since Poland's policy since the outbreak of war had been the honest and straightforward one of fighting the Germans, without any reservations or subterfuges, so the Allies, and in particular England and America, would see that Poland emerged as a really independent power from the war. To Poles at home the frontier issue seemed a false one, as they knew Russia did not need further territory. The real issue was whether Russia would let Poland run her own affairs in her own way.

Lieut. Nowak said there was great bitterness at home at our failure to supply more arms to the resistance movement. The Germans were making propaganda use of this, in view of our boasts regarding the present Allied aircraft production. What they really wanted were tommy-guns and explosives which could be used either in Poland or by Poles working in factories in Germany. I did my best to convince Lieut. Nowak that our difficulties were purely practical, and that if Poland were geographically more accessible she would receive more explosives and small arms.

Lieut. Nowak spoke about the way in which the resistance movement was organized. It had proved most effective, despite losses, and had never been broken up. Losses were, however, heavy. In his particular section of some three hundred people, thirty-nine, and among them the very best, had been killed.

Lieut. Nowak is, I understand, being received by the Prime Minister, to whom he has brought a special message from the Polish underground movement. The Counsellor of the Polish Embassy asked whether the Secretary of State would be willing to see him for a few moments.* I understand that Lieut. Nowak is going back to Poland (this is secret), so such an interview would appear worthwhile. Lieut. Nowak spoke enthusiastically of the prestige and influence of Great Britain in Poland.

*A definite recommendation on this point could perhaps await the views of Sir O. O'Malley, who is meeting Nowak to-morrow. Meanwhile I submit the paper for the light it casts on recent conditions in Poland.   FKR

Northern Department   OG Sargent[1] Jan. 21
N. Bentinck
Interesting. Prime Minister might like to see note of essential points in F. Roberts's minute. I should like to see Lt. Nowak, if Private Secretaries can fit in.

We are, I think, increasing aircraft available for Poles?

AE[2] Jan 22

Provisionally fixed for Monday Jan 31st.

[1]Sir Ormy Sargent, Deputy Undersecretary of State.   [2]Anthony Eden.

II

47, Portland Place,
London, W.1.

26th January, 1944.

Dear Brigadier Watt,

I should be most grateful if you could find a few minutes to receive me in the company of Mons. Nowak, an officer of the Polish Underground Army, who has recently reached this country and has brought the latest news from Poland.

I wish to add that Mons. Nowak will have the honour to be received by Mr. Churchill, who during his talk with our Prime Minister last Wednesday very kindly promised to see him. I, therefore, venture to suggest that perhaps it would be desirable for Mons. Nowak to see you first.

Yours sincerely,
(J. Zarański[1])

Brigadier G. S. Harvie Watt, T.D., M.P.,
Parliamentary Private Secretary to
the Prime Minister,
10, Downing Street,
S.W.1.

Source: H. M. Public Record Office, Document PREM 3-352/14A-06984, 932.

[1]Josef Zarański, Prime Minister Mikolajczyk's political adviser.

III

MR. MARTIN.

The Foreign Office tell me that Mr. Eden has sent the Prime Minister the attached note, understanding that the Polish Government had already made private arrangements for the Prime Minister to see Lieutenant Nowak.

If this is not yet the case, I assume you will be getting a letter from the Poles in due course.

I recommend taking with a grain of salt some part of what Lieutenant Nowak says about himself. He is not employed by S.O.E. or any other British Government Department, but directly by the Poles. His personal reputation, however, is that of a fine brave fellow.

On the other hand the Polish Resistance Movement is not the simple-minded united body which he seems to represent it, and only a small part of it is enthusiastic about the Polish Government in London. Naturally the Polish Government would like us to think otherwise.

S.O.E. tell me that there are a great many resistance movements in Poland. The big one, known as the Military Movement, is an organised disciplined body under a secret General officer at Warsaw. It was founded before war broke out by the VI Bureau of the Polish General Staff to meet the very need that has arisen. The Polish Government in London is afraid of this organisation, which directs the Polish Government much more than the Polish Government directs it.

In addition there are a number of resistance movements with a political foundation, each of them representing one of the many pre-war Polish political parties. The Polish Government in London only represents about six of the many pre-war Polish parties. Consequently the other political resistance movements are opposed to the Polish Government in London as well as to one another. There is strong reason to suspect that some of these movements are thoroughly penetrated by the Germans, in particular one known as the Sword and Plough, understood to be of a left wing but not communist nature. To which of all these does Nowak belong? Presumably the Military Movement.[1]   D. M.[2]

January 27, 1944.

Source: H. M. Public Record Office, Document PREM 3-352/14A-06984, 929-30. The author discovered this document in H.M.P.R.O. at the time when he was writing this book. He never claimed to be an employee of SOE or the British government and had no knowledge of "Sword and Plough." It was little known even in Poland that this small and obscure organization was indeed penetrated by both Nazi and Soviet agents. Major Morton could have learned about these connections only from M-15 (British counter-intelligence).

[1]Last two sentences added in pen and initialed "D.M." A handwritten note below says "F.O. confirm that this is so. F. D. W. B. [Brown]."
[2]Desmond Morton.

IV

SECRET

FOREIGN OFFICE, S.W. 1.,
31st January 1944.

Dear Brown,

As arranged I enclose a list of suggested questions for the Prime Minister to ask Lt. Nowak when he receives him.

Yours ever
V. G. Lawford[1]

F. D. W. Brown Esq.[2]

Questions for Lt. Nowak

1. How did Nowak get out of Poland?
2. How is the underground movement organized?
3. How far does it include all sections of the Polish People?
4. What are the sentiments of Poles in Poland towards:
   (a) the Polish Government in London.
   (b) Britain.
   (c) Russians as a race and the Soviet régime.
5. How does the underground movement treat communists sent into Poland from Russia?
6. How will it treat Russian troops when they get into Poland?
7. How far is the B.B.C. listened to?
8. Is there any danger of German spies penetrating the underground movement?

Source: H. M. Public Record Office, Document PREM 3-352/14A-06984, 927-28.

[1]Assistant Private Secretary to the Prime Minister.
[2]Assistant Private Secretary to the Secretary of State.

V

Interoffice Memorandum

Mr. Martin[1]

    I saw Lieutenant Nowak to-day. His only mission, in so far as the British Government is concerned, is that of presenting personally to Mr. Churchill a little paper booklet of Polish anti-German propaganda printed in Poland. He showed this to me, but said he could not hand it to anyone but the Prime Minister in person.

    Lieutenant Nowak was accompanied by M. Zarański as keeper on the excuse of interpreting. However, when I discovered that Lieutenant Nowak understood French perfectly, we conversed in that language to the visible horror of M. Zarański.[2] In English Lieutenant Nowak is desperately dull, being one of those rare cases which speak English much better than it understands the language. In French, however, Lieutenant Nowak painted the Polish Secret Army in such futile colours that I have at once got into touch with Lord Selborne to clear the matter up. The picture I got was so very depressing, and so very different from that which the Polish General Staff in London has given us, that I hesitate to report it to the Prime Minister without checking up against Lord Selborne's information.

D. M.[3]

February 10, 1944.

Source: H. M. Public Record Office, Document PREM 3-352/14A-06984, 933.

[1]John Miller Martin, Principal Private Secretary to Winston Churchill.
[2]Untrue; the conversation was in English. [J. N.]
[3]Major Desmond J. F. Morton.

VI

SECRET
(Copy)

Polish Prime Minister's Office.

18, Kensington Palace Gardens,
London, W. 8.

14th February, 1944.

Dear Major Morton,

Referring to the conversation which Lt. Jan Nowak and myself had with you on February 10th, I hasten to inform you that as stated in our conversation, we have both approached our superiors in order to elucidate the misunderstanding which appears to have arisen on the question of furnishing precise data concerning the Polish underground movement.

I am pleased to inform you that, according to information received, a special Section of the Polish G.H.Q. is in close collaboration with a British organisation headed by General Gubbins. This organisation is fully and regularly being informed as to the activities of the Polish underground Army, and I am certain that they could supply you with details and figures regarding the Polish underground movement. Furthermore, the Polish G.H.Q. provided the above mentioned British organisation with a map showing the O. de B. of the Polish underground Army, as well as with figures regarding its strength.

In view of the importance of the subject discussed between us, I have prepared a draft of the minutes of our conversation, which I enclose herewith, and venture to suggest that an agreed version might be useful. I would, accordingly, welcome any of the observations which you would care to make. I have left out deliberately any reference to the means by which Lt. Nowak reached this country and I am sure you will agree with me that it is not necessary to include it in the minutes.

Yours sincerely,
(J. Zarański)

1 encl.
Major D. J. F. Morton,
C.B., C.M.G., M.C.

Source: Instyut Polski i Museum im. gen. Sikorskiego, London [Archives of the Polish government in London], Year 1944. Zarański writes in English. [J. N.]

VII

SECRET
(Draft)

London, Feb. 10th, 1944.

Minutes of the Interview of Major D. Morton with 2-nd Lt. Jan Nowak, in the Presence of Mr. J. Zarański, on February 10th, 1944.

2nd-Lt. Nowak, who left Poland in November, 1943 as delegate of the Commander of the Polish Home Army, arrived to Britain in January 1944.[1]

After greeting him, Major Morton observed that he had heard about Lt. Nowak from Brigadier Harvie Watt, who told him that he had been taking English lessons from a Scotsman hiding in Poland after escaping from a German camp for prisoners of war. This British soldier was collaborating with Polish Underground Movement. Major Morton had also heard that Lt. Nowak brought a message from the Polish Underground Movement to Mr. Churchill. Major Morton then asked Lt. Nowak how he had managed to leave Poland.

After emphasising the need for strict secrecy, Lt. Nowak told Major Morton about his two expeditions outside the boundaries of Poland.

Major Morton then asked Lt. Nowak whether he had received any communications for Mr. Churchill and added that he was authorised to transmit any such communications to the Prime Minister. Lt. Nowak replied that he had been requested by the Polish Underground to transmit to Mr. Churchill three communications: 1) Express the Polish nation's admiration for Mr. Churchill and their unreserved confidence in him; 2) Hand to the Prime Minister the written message addressed to him; 3) Ask for increased supplies of weapons and explosives for the Polish Home Army. Lt. Nowak added that he had been requested by his comrades in Poland to hand the message personally to Mr. Churchill and that he was anxious to be able to inform them that he had carried out his mission. He asked Major Morton to help him to obtain an interview with Mr. Churchill, and told him about the immense popularity of the British Prime Minister in Poland. "After the death of General Sikorski, which was a serious blow for Poland" — he said — "people used to say: "We have lost Sikorski, but we still have got Churchill."

Source: Instyut Polski i Muzeum im. gen. Sikorskiego, London [Archives of the Polish government in London], Year 1944, Document 264/XIVA/44. Written in English. [J. N.]

[1]Wrong date; should be December, 1943. [J. N.]

Major Morton replied that, although he realised Lt. Nowak's anxiety to present the message personally to Mr. Churchill, he could not make any promise of an interview, owing to Mr. Churchill's numerous engagements. As to the supplies of arms, he pointed out that the normal channel for such a request would have been the Polish Government in London.

After explaining the official character of Lt. Nowak's mission and observing that he had been introduced to Major Morton by a member of the Polish Embassy in London, Lt. Nowak outlined the situation in Poland. He stressed that the attitude of the Poles in this war has been clear and unequivocal throughout: the Polish nation was fighting the Germans uncompromisingly and evidence of their policy was provided by the fact that Poland was almost the only European nation which never sent any military units against Russia on the Eastern Front. The attitude of the Soviet Union towards Poland caused serious misgivings among the Poles, but they did not take from the Germans arms which they could have received in unlimited quantities if they had been prepared to use them against the Russians. "Our position is clear" — said Lt. Nowak — "we have won a certain moral standing in Europe, which we want to keep. We need for that purpose weapons to be used in our action against the Germans."

Major Morton enquired about the Polish Underground Movement, its numerical strength, methods of organisation, equipment, territorial location, tactical possibilities (especially concerning the possibility of keeping in hiding for long periods, as in Jugoslavia). He observed that, unlike other countries (he mentioned France, Jugoslavia, Greece, Czechoslovakia and Bulgaria as examples) the Polish Government had not provided His Majesty's Government with information concerning the requirements of the Polish Underground Movement, its methods of action and plan of battle, so that the British Government did not have a clear view of the position in that respect. Major Morton added that four days earlier, at a conference of the British Chiefs of Staff, under the chairmanship of Mr. Churchill, the problem of help for the underground movements of Europe was discussed, but Poland's needs could not be dealt with, owing to lack of data. Britain, unfortunately, does not possess technical means for satisfying all requirements and the help to various European countries must, therefore, be apportioned according to accurate and objective data.

Lt. Nowak and Mr. Zarański undertook to pass on this information to their superiors, while Lt. Nowak added that agents abroad from Poland are not informed about the entire military situation of the country, for fear that they might be captured and tortured to force such secrets out. He admitted that his own knowledge of the military situation in Poland was not comprehensive.

Mr. Zarański asked whether the attitude communicated by Major Morton was not due to some shadow of a doubt concerning possible complications which might result from supplying the Polish Home Army with weapons. Major Morton replied, stating emphatically that the British Government makes its supplies of arms to the underground movements of Europe dependent on purely military and not political considerations.

As to the methods of action, Lt. Nowak explained them within the scope of his personal knowledge. He stated that the conditions in Poland are different from those prevailing in Jugoslavia, owing to the geographical position of the country and to its different configuration. He pointed out that the Polish Home Army has at its disposal considerable opportunities of action against the Germans, thanks to two facts: 1) The presence in Germany of two million Polish workmen, as well as the existence of numerous Poles who became German citizens under duress (Volksdeutsche), but are anxious to prove to their Polish countrymen that they remained Poles at heart. This permits considerable penetration into the ranks of the Germans. 2) The fact that all the main supply lines for the Eastern Front pass through Poland, while the Polish railway personnel is patriotic and well disciplined. "We know" — said Lt. Nowak — "that every act of sabotage of German transports calls forth mass reprisals against the civilian population. That is why we need adequate armament, not only for carrying out our attacks on the German transports but also for protecting to some extent the victims of reprisals". Lt. Nowak had met on his way to Britain Danes, who were well equipped with weapons of sabotage and other arms. He stated that if the Poles both in Poland and throughout Germany and Europe, had such assistance in arms, the results would be prompt and impressive.

Asked by Major Morton about the strength of the Germans in Poland, Lt. Nowak said that there are in Poland about 500.000 Germans capable of carrying arms. He added that, besides the military garrisons, there are numerous police formations. In Warsaw itself there are 14.000 German police of various kinds. Besides the ordinary Schutzpolizei, there are special formations: Bahnschutz, Werkschutz, Grenzschutz, Sicherhetsdienst, as well as Gestapo and S.S. formations.

As an illustration of the efficiency of the Polish Underground Movement, Lt. Nowak mentioned the fact that the poster sent to Poland by the British authorities was reproduced in numbers and distributed throughout the General Gouvernment. The news about its appearance was brought by the German radio which complained about this "subversive act."

Asked by Major Morton, whether the German terror in Poland had lately increased or relaxed, Lt. Nowak said that in the spring of 1943 Hitler had tried to exploit the political situation between Poland and Russia, by introducing a temporary appeasement of the Poles. After the failure of this attempt, there was a new wave of terror in June and July, 1943, and later new mass reprisals, notably public shootings since October, 1943. Mr. Zarański referred also to the sentence of death passed by the Polish Underground on General Kutschera, Head of the Gestapo in Warsaw, which was carried out a few days ago. As a reprisal for this execution, the Germans shot 100 hostages in the streets of Warsaw and imposed on the city of Warsaw a contribution of 100 million zlotys.

Describing conditions of life in Germany, Lt. Nowak (who had been in Berlin a year ago) stressed the contrast between the standard of living in

Britain and on the continent. He said that the effectiveness of the blockade and of air bombardment was even greater than was commonly realised in this country. He mentioned in this connection a conversation of a German officer returning from the Eastern Front, which he had overheard. The German officer had said to his colleague that owing to shortage of munitions the German soldiers could shoot only just enough "um den Mut aufrechtzuerhalten." The German civilian morale is poor and the population is dejected, but owing to the impossibility of any organised action against the Nazi Party, no revolution is to be expected in Germany. Lt. Nowak observed that the German people seem to alternate between political extremes: National-Socialism or Communism.

The interview, which had lasted from 11.20 A.M. to 12.10 P.M., was then concluded.

VIII

PRIME MINISTER
[Official Seal]

SECRET

10, Downing Street
Whitehall

14th February, 1944

Dear Monsieur Zarański,

In reply to your letter of 14th February I may tell you that, on behalf of the Prime Minister I am in close touch with Major-General Gubbins.

Although I was very pleased to meet Lieutenant Nowak, I hardly feel that what he had to say was of sufficient importance to warrant an agreed record. I would remind you that I twice asked him and he twice replied that the only mission with which he was officially charged was to deliver to the Prime Minister a certain special copy of a propaganda leaflet which had been prepared in Poland.

Yours sincerely,
(D. Morton)

Mons. J. Zarański
18, Kensington Palace Gardens
W. 8.

Copies:
1) Colonel Protasewicz
2) Ambassador O'Malley
        (JZ)
        15. 2.

Source: Instyut Polski i Museum im. gen Sikorskiego, London [Archives of the Polish government in London], Document PRM L.dz. 264/SIVa/44.

IX

Report by Jan Nowak after His Arrival in Warsaw before the Warsaw Rising

The Soviet-Polish Conflict

(1) Until the middle of 1943, Polish policy toward Russia was based on the assumption that Russia would be defeated and that the Soviet troops would not enter Poland. During Sikorski's visit to Moscow the possibility existed of concluding a lasting understanding at the price of insignificant territorial concessions with Poland keeping Vilno and Lwow. Sikorski at that time avoided any discussion.[*]

In October 1943, before the Moscow conference, Mikolajczyk took the initiative and asked Eden to mediate for the re-establishment of diplomatic relations between Poland and Russia. Eden pointed out then that the Russians would probably demand acceptance of the Curzon Line and stated that the only Polish trump card was a readiness to cooperate with the Russians in the military field. The Moscow conference took place in an atmosphere of coolness between the British and the Russians. Stalin, in conversations about Poland, stressed the unfriendly attitude of the Polish government toward Russia. He rejected at once, and most decisively, Cordell Hull's offer that the allies should co-operate on the eastern front. After his return, Eden limited himself to reporting to us on Russia's attitude.

(2) Teheran occurred in an atmosphere very unfavorable for the British and the Americans, at the moment of rapid Soviet advances and the halt of the Allies in Italy. Soviet propaganda spread a wave of rumors about a separate peace with Germany; Churchill and Roosevelt went to the conference almost prepared to plead with Stalin for continuation of the war. In addition, during talks Stalin kept isolating Churchill, manifesting his solidarity with Roosevelt. Churchill's position was extremely difficult, and in fact he paid for the trip by falling grievously ill. Stalin unexpectedly put forward a project that Germany should be totally destroyed (mass deportations for forced labor). He had two kinds of policy up his sleeve: either extermination from which Germany would never rise, or, if the Anglo-Americans opposed such a solution, a complete *volte face* toward policy of Rapallo. Meanwhile, the British aim was only to weaken Germany so as to prevent her from being

Source: Report of the meeting of Stefan Kieniewicz, Alexander Gieysztor, and Tadeusz Chromecki with Jan Nowak, prepared by Alexander Gieysztor (translation by the author), Studinun Polski Podzemnej [Archives of the Polish underground movement], London. The report was not authorized by me. [J. N.]

[*]That view was quoted by the author as Mikolajczyk's opinion. [J. N.]

a threat to them, but not to eliminate Germany as a factor in European politics. Stalin demanded that Austria be excluded from the German deal and treated as a separate state within Russia's sphere of influence. He wanted, furthermore, to take Bessarabia back from Romania in exchange for Transylvania, and to draw Turkey into the war (this did not succeed in spite of Eden's endeavors). It seems almost certain, in spite of official denials, that at Teheran it was established that Germany be divided into occupation zones: Russian up to the Elbe, British in the North-West, American in the South, and joint zones in Berlin and Austria. As regards Poland, Stalin reiterated his already known demands to Churchill: the Curzon Line and changes in the Polish government. He argues that the Home Army was collaborating with the Germans (Bor's order to fight against bandit gangs, the battle of Janow). One of the results was a curtailment in English drops of arms for Poland.

(3) Our political game with the Soviets in January/February 1944 had, as its main objective, the goal of winning the support of the British public opinion. We were trying to avoid being the side that would first say "no." From this point of view, our note of January 5 last was very skillful (it might have been drafted by Eden); the worst idea was that of a demarcation line which neither Russia, nor Britain, thought acceptable. Britain thought we were right in refusing governmental changes, but did not support our position as on frontiers, and therefore the question of our sovereignty had to be pushed to the fore. British pressure on us was very strong, on Churchill's part even brutal (Eden was biding his time). Churchill's main concern was winning the war, although he had a lot of good will toward us and wanted to drag us out of our predicament (He said: "Don't beat the donkey that wants to carry you across the river"). Eden, however, admitted, "I would advise you to have a change of government if it were to follow the already reached agreement; it would be different if this concession were only a preliminary condition to further negotiations.

(4) British pressure ceased after Stalin's reply to Churchill's telegram, for the reply had damaged Russia's reputation among the British public. In the long run, Stalin would have served his own interests better had he agreed at the time on a compromise with Poland, and then only later gradually engineered a legal liquidation of our independence.

Acting on a Hitlerite model, he gave us certain trump cards.

The Polish question seriously deteriorated British-Soviet relations. Churchill ceased mediating, not wishing to damage co-operation with Russia in the conduct of the war, and so the conflict remained unresolved. The fate of Poland still weighed heavily on Churchill and all Britain, like a reproach. They would be much relieved if the Poles voluntarily made a deal with the Russians, whatever the conditions.

(5) British policy is based on short term planning. What matters today is winning the war. Churchill would like to arrange the world as follows: at the top, the Big Three—the Council of the United Nations as a representation

without importance—and Continental Councils: European, American, and Asian. The European Council (without the participation of England or Russia) would be in its entirety Britain's partner on the European continent. Britain's future attitude toward Russia will depend on the latter. If Russian policies were affected by Russia's weakness after the present war (15 million killed, utter exhaustion of the population) then Britain would undoubtedly agree to a policy of assistance and co-operation with Russia. If, however, Russia decided to adopt expansionist policies and, in spite of her internal weakness, tried to benefit from post-war anarchy in Europe to spread communism in Germany, Italy, France, or Spain, then the conflict with Great Britain would quickly intensify. Today such thoughts do not enter any Englishman's mind, but the situation was similar in the years 1937-38 concerning war against Germany. Should this happen, the Polish question would again change its character.

(6) The touchstone of Stalin's intentions will be Mikolajczyk's visit to Moscow. It has not been prepared diplomatically; on the contrary, it took place at a time when the Russians have rejected far-reaching Polish concessions. Everything indicates that Stalin is confronting Mikolajczyk with very tough conditions, perhaps ones that are unacceptable. Stalin is insisting on creating an illegal government dependent entirely on himself. He would not tolerate in Poland a team of people with ties to the Anglo-Americans as close as those of our present London government. Perhaps Stalin would make an exception of Mikolajczyk, in light of his repeated assertions that he has nothing against Mikolajczyk personally. And whether the agreement is reached or not, we will still be faced with Soviet occupation, or actual loss of independence. Even with Mikoljczyk present in Warsaw, the Russians would rule here as they wished. Under these conditions, according to emigré circles, it would be more useful to our cause if a compromise were not reached and if there remained two governments: one in Warsaw, a passive tool of Russia, the other in London, a continuous thorn in the flesh. An agreement between Mikolajczyk and Stalin would perhaps partly save the "biological substance" of the nation, but in practice it would bring to a close the period of our co-operation with the British and Americans.

Index

Code names are indexed below, with cross-references to real names when known.

"Adam." *See* Czarnowski, Eugeniusz
"Adam." *See* Truszkowski, Adam
Adam (shipbroker), 199, 200
Albery, Sir Irving, 35, 251
Alphonse, W., 183, 184
"Anatol." *See* Lipsz, Jan
Anders, Wladyslaw, 225, 397
Appenzeler, Mr. and Mrs., 435
Arciszewski, Tomasz, 312, 338, 443, 445, 446
Astor, John Jacob, 35, 250, 251

Banks, Marjorie, Lady Bangor, 12, 157
Barrington-Ward, Robert, 251, 252
Bartecki, 72
"Basil." *See* Puzak Kazimierz
Beaverbrook, W. A. Aitken, Lord, 238, 264
Beck, Jozef, 243
Bedell Smith, Walter, 251
Beneš, Eduard, 192, 237, 252, 300
Bentinck, N., 460
Berezowski, Zygmunt, 287
Berling, Zygmunt, 131, 231, 255, 313, 379, 398, 444
Bevin, Ernest, 7, 235, 236, 243
Bialous, Ryszard, 383
Biddle, Anthony Drexel, 246
Bigocka, Halina, 111, 112, 116, 140, 148, 149, 156, 157, 159, 163, 176, 191, 453
Bilski, Kazimierz, 320, 323, 325, 327-29, 371
"Black Janka." *See* Halpern, Alicja
Blaskowitz, Johannes, 60
Bokszczanin, Janusz, 331, 334, 346
Bonham Carter, Lady Violet, 235
"Bor." *See* Komorowski, Tadeusz
Bracken, Brendan, 264
Brown, F. D. W., 462, 463
"Brzoza." *See* Retinger, Jozef
Bürckl, Franz, 31, 250

Carr, E. H., 251, 252
Celmer, Regina, 75, 77
Cepek, Henryk, 133
Chamberlain, Neville, 239, 264, 277, 288

"Chairman, the." *See* Rzepecki, Jan
Cherwell, Frederic Lindemann, Lord, 264
Chojecki, Miroslaw, 14
Choynacki, Major, 425, 426, 435
"Christina." *See* Skarbek, Krystyna
Chromecki, Tadeusz, 339, 471
Chrusciel, Antoni, 334, 341, 343, 345, 350, 351, 357, 359, 362, 370-72, 384, 385
Churchill, Winston, 13, 37, 104, 166, 197, 202, 211, 217, 222, 223, 234, 242, 246, 248, 257, 260-69, 273, 277-81, 287, 288, 293-95, 298, 325, 332, 334, 439, 440-42, 445, 449, 450, 452, 461, 464, 466, 467, 471, 472
Chwala, Lieut. Pawel, 322, 323
Citrine, Sir Walter, 235
Collville, Sir John, 442
Coningham, Sir Arthur, 35, 251
"Consul." *See* Choynacki, Major
Culliford, George, 318
Cunnings, H. R., 273
Curzon, Lord George, 217, 223, 224, 226, 257, 258, 263, 268, 271, 287, 297, 300, 313, 471, 472
Cyrankiewicz, Jozef, 52-55
"Czarna Janka." *See* Halpern, Alicja
Czarnowski, Eugeniusz, 65-69

D'Abernon, Edgar Vincent, Lord, 23
"Dabrowa." *See* Mlodzianowski, Stanislaw
Dalton, Hugh, 235, 236, 238-40, 361
de Gaulle, Charles, 219, 283
Delmer, Sefton 280
Daniel, Raymond, 441
Demel, Colonel, 310
Domanski, Eugeniusz, 133
Douglas, Allan, 273
"Dowmuntt." *See* Pomian, Andrzej
Driberg, Tom, 255, 256

Eden, Anthony, 13, 33, 35, 104, 217, 222, 225, 226, 235,
242, 246-49, 251, 252, 257, 263, 265, 269, 273, 274, 277, 293, 295, 297, 298, 315, 332, 338, 442, 443, 445, 449, 450, 459-60, 462, 471, 472
Eisenhower, Dwight D., 299, 307, 369
"Ela." *See* Rzepecka, Irena

Fetzer, Amtmann, 75, 181
Filarska, Maria, 196, 199, 200, 201, 285, 286
Filipkowski, Wladyslaw, 444
Filipski, Jan, 184

"Gapa." *See* Hauptman, Stanislaw W.
Garbaty, Ensign, 344
"Garda." *See* Godlewski, Edward
Gedymin, Wlodzimierz, 320-23, 404
George (author's liaison man), 180
"Gertruda." *See* Janke, Zygmunt
Gieysztor, Alexander, 339, 471
"Ginette," 283, 305
Glowacki, Jozef, 66
Godlewski, Edward, 393
Goebbels, Joseph, 254, 255, 413
"Goral," 192-94, 286
Gorzkowski, Kazimierz, 340
Grabski, Stanislaw, 300
Graham, Allan, 238, 255, 256, 361
Greenwood, Arthur, 288, 361
"Greta." *See* Wolska, Jadwiga
Griffin, Bernard, 235
Grineau, Bryan de, 250
"Grot." *See* Rowecki, Stefan
Gruson, Sydney, 437, 439
"Grzegorz." *See* Pelczynski, Tadeusz
Gubbins, Sir Colin, 236, 262, 263, 298, 465, 470

Halpern, Alicja, 70
"Hans" (author's German guide), 413-16, 418, 419
Hauptman, Stanislaw W., 402, 403
Herdegen, Witold, 46-48, 119
Hess, Rudolf, 78, 86
"Hilda." *See* Bigocka, Halina
Hitler, Adolf, 37, 52, 60, 78, 79, 89, 99, 101, 104, 107,

131, 132, 219, 225, 239, 260, 267, 274, 288, 289, 298, 310, 397, 468, 472
Hoffman, Kurt, 30, 250
Hudson, D. T., 316
Hull, Cordell, 228, 471
Hulton, Edward, 251

"Irena" (liaison girl), 195

"Janek." See Nowak, Jan
"Janka." See Filipkowski, Wladyslaw
"Janka." See Pronaszkowa, Janina
Janke, Zygmunt, 94-96, 383, 457
Jankowski, Leopold, 73
Jankowski, Stanislaw, 337-39, 394, 396, 397, 446
"Janusz," Lieutenant, 372
"Jarach." See Zazdel, Rudolf
Jasnoch, Kazimierz, 427
Jaworski, Wladyslaw, 402
Jazwinski, Jan, 314
Jedrychowski, Stefan, 439
Jeffery, Ronald, 190, 244-46, 264, 265, 442
"Jerzy." See Bialous, Ryszard
Jezioranska, Aniela, 25, 58, 59
Jezioranska, Elzbieta, 23, 24, 44, 59, 103, 113, 145, 168, 198, 328, 347, 348, 375-77, 387, 413
Jezioranski, Andrzej, 24, 44, 59, 61, 62, 103, 113, 145, 155, 198, 327, 328, 376, 387, 413
Jezioranski, Jan, 25
Jezioranski, Waclaw, 22, 24, 50, 121, 168
Jezioranski, Zdzislaw. See Nowak, Jan
Johanson (Swedish sailor), 144-49
"John" (author's Swiss guide), 416, 417
"Jula." See Wolska, Barbara
"Jur." See Lerski, Jerzy

"Kalina." See Rowecki, Stefan
Kalugin, Konstantin, 350, 351, 438
Kamienski, Jan, 327
"Karol." See Rokicki, Jozef
Karpik, Celina, 155, 156, 180, 184
Karski, Jan, 173, 234, 254, 274, 287
Kawczynska, Ewa, 177
Kawczynski, Antoni, 176-78
Kennan, George F., 450
"Kennedy." See Kowerski, Andrzej

Kieniewicz, Stefan, 339, 471
Klapp, Franciszek, 137-39, 141-43, 148, 196, 198
"Klimek." See Szewczyk, Klemens
Knoll, Roman, 175
Kolodziejczyk, Tadeusz, 80, 153, 154
Komorowski, Tadeusz, 165, 166, 186-88, 204, 212-14, 230-33, 255, 278, 285, 286, 290, 291, 327, 329, 331, 332, 334, 335, 339, 340, 351, 352, 355, 383, 389, 396, 438, 456, 462, 472
Kopanski, Stanislaw, 211, 212, 262, 394
Korbonska, Zofia, 357, 358
Korbonski, Stefan, 357, 358
Kostrzewski, Jan, 365, 366
Kot, Stanislaw, 249
"Kotwicz." See Smulikowski, Adam
"Kowalik." See Zenczy-kowski, Tadeusz
Kowerski, Andrzej, 256, 258
Kozlowski, Adalbert, 85, 103
Kukiel, Marian, 214
Kulski, Wladyslaw, 233, 235, 246, 248, 294
Kwiatkowski, Jan. See Nowak, Jan

Laqueur, Walter, 274
Lawford, Valentine G., 463
"Lawina." See Komorowski, Tadeusz
Lebiediew, Anatol, 300, 301, 333, 338
"Lech." See Zagorski, Waclaw
Leonhard, Jozefa, 139, 203
Lerski, Jerzy, 173, 287, 288
Leszczynski, 87, 92, 94, 156, 179, 181
"Leszek." See Szadkowski, Antoni
Lipski, Jozef, 440, 441
Lipsz, Jan, 95-97, 453
Litauer, Stefan, 249, 250
Litynski, Zygmunt, 437-39, 441
Low, David, 238, 254
Lulinski, Czeslaw, 182

Macdonald, Gregory, 272, 361
Macdonald, Ivreach, 250, 437
MacFarlane, Captain, 305, 306
MacFarlane, Noel Mason, 305
McLaren, Moray, 274
"Magdalena." See Straszewska, Zofia
Makiela, Roman, 74, 91
Makowiecki, Jerzy, 172
Malessa, Emilia, 157, 285, 328,

329, 331, 384, 386, 389, 390, 393, 400, 401, 404, 405
Malinowski, Mr. and Mrs., 168, 169
"Marcysia." See Malessa, Emilia
Marley, Lord, 255
Martin, John Miller, 442, 462, 464
Martin, Kingsley, 254
Masson, Madeleine, 256
Mathew, David, 235
"Max" (author's German guide), 411-14, 416, 418, 419
"Mazur." See Jankowski, Leopold
Mihajlović, Draža, 218, 237, 256, 265, 267, 316
Micuta, Waclaw, 352
Mikolaj, 179, 181
Mikolajczyk, Stanislaw, 214, 216, 217, 221-26, 232-35, 242-44, 246, 256-63, 265, 269, 276, 278, 279-81, 290, 292, 293, 295, 299-302, 307-9, 325, 332, 333, 335, 338, 339, 344, 345, 352, 353, 359, 438, 442-49, 455, 461, 471, 473
Mlodzianowski, Stanislaw, 426, 427, 429, 430, 434, 435
Molotow, Wiaczeslaw, 217, 219, 223, 344
"Monter." See Chrusciel, Antoni
Morawski, Eugeniusz, 133
Morgan, Colonel, 315
Morton, Desmond J. F., 260-65, 278, 279, 439-41, 464-68, 470
Muir, Mr. and Mrs. (Thomas Muir's parents), 273
Muir, Thomas, 104, 244
Murrow, Edward R., 228, 439
Muselier, Emile Henry, 442

Newsom, Noel, 272
Niedbalski, Tadeusz, 110-12, 126, 148, 156, 158, 190, 191, 193, 195, 197, 458
Nowak, Jadwiga. See Wolska, Jadwiga
Nowak, Jan, 13, 14, 29, 32, 33, 35, 42, 66, 74, 75, 102, 103, 112-14, 126, 128, 134, 140, 148, 149, 151, 152, 155-58, 160, 161, 169, 191, 195, 196, 203-5, 210, 251, 262, 263, 281, 286, 290, 292, 339, 352, 389, 425, 428, 436, 441, 442, 459-71

Okulicki, Leopold, 383-85, 393-98, 401, 404, 425, 446, 456

Okulicki, Zbigniew, 399
Olandson, Karl, 137-45, 152, 196, 198
Olechowski, Cadet Officer, 435
Olejniczak, Jan, 77
O'Malley, Sir Owen, 228, 229, 263-65, 279, 296-98, 361, 460, 470
Omiecinska, Halina, 211, 292
Onodera, Makoto, 136
Orientel, Kazimierz, 87, 88
Osborne, David, 274

"Pawlicz." See Zadrozny, Stanislaw
Pelczynski, Tadeusz, 164, 187-90, 212, 244, 327, 331, 332, 334, 335, 351, 352, 355, 456
Perkins, Harold B., 236-38, 262, 298, 299, 357, 358, 362
Petheric, M., 238
Pickthorn, Kenneth, 238
Pilch, Tadeusz, 128, 131, 132
Pilsudski, Jozef, 23, 211, 215, 216, 243
Piotrowska, Eugenia (author's grandmother), 24, 44, 59, 61
Piotrowski, Edmund, 128-30, 134, 135, 137-40, 143, 145, 148, 196, 202-6
Plucinski, Adam, 72, 75, 77, 79, 80, 82, 116, 153, 154, 163, 453
Pomian, Andrzej, 290
Postek, Jerzy, 133
Pragier, Adam, 275
Prchal, Edward, 304
Pronaszkowa, Janina, 401
Protasewicz, Michal, 211, 214, 227, 262, 264, 277, 278, 285, 286, 290, 299, 436, 470
Pszenny, Jozef, 133
Puchalski, Zygmunt, 133
Puricz, Bozidar, 294
Pyttel, Maria, 111, 116, 118, 152, 156, 190, 191, 458
Puzak, Kazimierz, 352

Raczkiewicz, Wladyslaw, 128, 214, 244, 353
Raczynski, Edward, 214, 217, 223, 224, 226, 228, 243, 287, 293, 294-96
Radziwill, Prince Stanislaw, 434, 435
"Rafal." See Retinger, Jozef
Raikes, Victor, 238
"Redhead." See Zazdel, Rudolf
Reichenau, Walter von, 78
Rek, Tadeusz, 91
Reston, James, 228

Retinger, Jozef, 311, 338
Ribbentrop, Joachim von, 44, 217, 219, 223
"Robak." See Plucinski, Adam
Roberts, Frank K., 235, 459-60
Rokicki, Jozef, 384, 385
Rokossowski, Konstanty, 345, 384, 385, 438
Romer, Tadeusz, 214, 217, 223, 263, 293, 295
Roosevelt, Franklin D., 104, 166, 234, 246, 290, 295, 299, 300, 332, 445, 448-50, 471
"Rosomak," 366
Rotstein, Andrew, 249
Rowecki, Stefan, 65, 67, 90, 91, 110, 112, 114, 115, 134, 139, 140, 163-65, 186, 188, 191, 192, 363, 455
Rudkowski, Roman, 401
"Rudy." See Rudkowski, Roman
Rundstedt, Gerd von, 415
Rybikowski, Michal, 135-36
Rydz-Smigly, Edward, 44
Rzepecka, Irena, 114, 134, 168, 186, 187, 363
Rzepecki, Jan, 114, 164, 165, 166, 172, 174, 186-88, 194, 212, 327, 331, 335, 336, 340, 341, 345, 350, 351, 355, 365, 375, 376, 383, 389, 456

Sadowski, Leszek, 379
Salmon, Christopher, 272
Sargent, Sir Ormy, 460
Savery, Frank, 274
Savory, Sir Douglas, 238, 361
Schoenfeld, Rudolph, 246
Scott, Malcom, 210
"Sek." See Bokszczanin, Janusz
Selborne, Lord, 235, 262, 263, 361, 464
"Seweryn." See Niedbalski, Tadeusz
Sikorski, Wladyslaw, 61, 64, 65, 104, 105, 128, 133, 164, 188, 189, 191, 215, 216, 224, 231, 304, 306, 307, 336, 439, 447, 455, 466, 471
Sinclair, Sir Archibald, 235, 240-42, 247, 299, 357, 362
Skarbek, Krystyna, 256
"Skory." See Chwala, Pawel
Slawinski, Wincenty, 425, 426, 428, 431, 432
Slawinski, Mr. and Mrs., 431
Sledz, Jan, 118, 152
Sloan, James, 437
Smith, Walter, 361
Smulikowski, Adam, 158, 161
"Sobieslaw." See Bartecki

Sobieszczyk, Wojciech, 92-94, 156, 176, 179, 453, 457
Sosnkowski, Kazimierz, 32, 33, 188, 189, 211-14, 216, 218-24, 230-32, 237, 240, 244, 254-57, 290-92, 304, 305, 307-9, 332, 335, 353, 447, 455
Stalin, Joseph, 131, 217-20, 223-26, 232, 233, 239, 244, 252, 258, 263, 266, 268, 269, 277, 278, 280, 294, 300-302, 309, 313, 314, 333, 335, 397, 398, 442, 444, 445, 449, 450, 454, 471-73
Stanczyk, Jan, 235
Stodolski, Jakub, 199, 201, 286
Straszewska, Zofia, 196
"Sum." See Wojcieszek, W.
Szadkowski, Antoni, 69, 70, 72, 88, 99, 100, 108-10, 112, 113, 167, 191, 193, 355
Szewczyk, Klemens, 91, 453
Sztajerowskis, (Miroslav and father), 91
Szwarc, Franciszek, 116-18, 120, 145, 151, 152, 156, 190, 191
Szwarc, Mrs., 116, 118, 120, 152
Szwarcbart, Ignacy, 274-76

"Tabor." See Tatar, Stanislaw
"Tadeusz." See Wesolowski, Tadeusz
Tatar, Stanislaw, 286, 290-92, 329, 394, 442
Taylor, Edward, 26, 27
"Teddy Bear." See Okulicki, Leopold
Temple, William, 235, 244
Teodorczyk, Roman, 182
"Teresa" ("Bor"'s liaison girl), 331, 340
Teska, Jan, 345, 346
"Thomas." See Makowiecki, Jerzy
Thomas, Ivor, 238, 251, 266, 267, 269, 361
Tito, Josip Broz, 218, 237, 242, 267, 283
Tokarzewski, Michal, 60
"Tomasz." See Arciszewski, Tomasz
Toynbee, Arnold, 253
Trepczynski, Franciszek, 117, 118, 120, 191, 453, 458
Truszkowski, Adam, 356, 357, 361, 362, 387
Tucholski, Ignacy, 89
Tyrell, Lord, 361

Utnik, Marian, 436

476

Vansittart, Lord Robert, 277,
278, 361
Vick, Major, 435
Ville, Bronislaw, 425, 426,
434, 435
Voigt, Frederick, 228

"Wacek." See Micuta, Waclaw
"Waclaw." See Wolinski,
Henryk
Wandelt, Kazimierz, 72, 75
Ward, John, 357-59, 361, 362,
378, 388
Warner, Christopher, 235
"Wasyl." See Sadowski,
Leszek
Watt, G. S. Harvie, 461, 466
Wesolowski, Tadeusz, 148,
149, 156-63, 176, 191
Widerszal, Ludwik, 174
"Wildcat." See Witkowski,
Stanislaw
Wilk, Jozef, 133
Williams, Emlyn, 437
Witek, Mr. and Mrs., 392
Witkowska, Jaga, 184
Witkowski, Stanislaw, 74-77,
80-82, 84, 85, 87, 91-93, 102,
108, 109, 113, 145, 146, 150,
151, 155, 156, 163, 176, 179,
180-84, 272, 457
Witkowska, Zofia, 74, 91, 103,
114, 145
Witold, S., 191
"Wlodek." See Gedymin,
Wlodzimierz
Wojcieszek, W., 390, 391, 393
Wojcik, Karol, 196
Wojtyla, Karol (Pope John
Paul II), 451
Wolinski, Henryk, 173
"Wolf." See Gorzkowski,
Kazimierz
Wolska, Barbara, 176, 327,
341, 345, 346, 363, 365, 366,
378, 379, 453
Wolska, Jadwiga, 34, 167, 168,
175-77, 198, 202, 317, 327,
328, 337, 340, 341, 363, 366,
367, 377-79, 386, 388,
390-93, 400, 401, 406-9, 411,
414, 418-26, 428, 429, 431,
435, 436, 438, 445
Wolskis (Jadwiga Wolska's
parents), 392, 406, 413
Woodward, Sir Llewellyn, 217
"Wos." See Sobieszczyk,
Wojciech

Zadrozny, Stanislaw, 355
Zagorski, Waclaw, 373
"Zajac." See Kostrzewski, Jan
Zamoyski, Stefan, 439-41
Zaranski, Jozef, 223, 260-63,
267, 269, 440, 461, 464-68,
470
Zaremba, Zygmunt, 361
Zawacka, Elzbieta, 285, 390,
400, 404, 405, 458
Zawodny, J. K., 450
Zazdel, Rudolf, 191-94, 197,
198, 285, 286, 405
"Zbik." See Witkowski,
Stanislaw
Zenczykowski, Tadeusz, 90,
112, 166-68, 336, 337, 339,
341, 350, 355, 362, 363, 365,
367, 373, 457
Zgoda, Jan, 108, 109, 111, 191,
196, 198-200, 205
Zgorzelski, Major, 325, 326;
family, 340, 341
Ziemski, Karol, 373
Zimmern, Sir Alfred, 253
Znamierowski, Czeslaw, 65
"Zo." See Zawacka, Elzbieta
"Zych." See Nowak, Jan
Zygielbojm, Szmul, 275

Jan Nowak served as director of the Polish Section of Radio Free Europe from its inception to 1976. He is now a national director of the Polish American Congress and a consultant to the National Security Council.

The manuscript was edited by Jean Owen, with translation assistance from Helen Suchara. The book was designed by Richard Kinney. The typeface for the text and display is Mergenthaler VIP Palatino, based on a design by Hermann Zapf in 1950. The text is printed on 55-lb. International Paper Company's Bookmark text paper. The book is bound in Holliston Mills' Kingston Natural finish cloth over binder's boards.

Manufactured in the United States of America.

Emory & Henry College   Kelly Library

3 1836 0006 9689 6